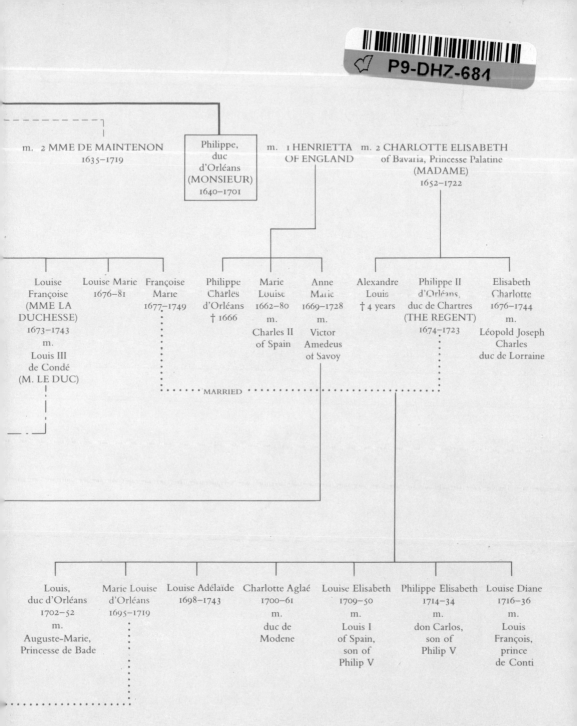

m.   2 MME DE MAINTENON
1635–1719

Philippe,
duc
d'Orléans
(MONSIEUR)
1640–1701

m.   1 HENRIETTA
OF ENGLAND

m.   2 CHARLOTTE ELISABETH
of Bavaria, Princesse Palatine
(MADAME)
1652–1722

Louise
Françoise
(MME LA
DUCHESSE)
1673–1743
m.
Louis III
de Condé
(M. LE DUC)

Louise Marie
1676–81

Françoise
Marie
1677–1749

Philippe
Charles
d'Orléans
† 1666

Marie
Louise
1662–80
m.
Charles II
of Spain

Anne
Marie
1669–1728
m.
Victor
Amedeus
of Savoy

Alexandre
Louis
† 4 years

Philippe II
d'Orléans,
duc de Chartres
(THE REGENT)
1674–1723

Elisabeth
Charlotte
1676–1744
m.
Léopold Joseph
Charles
duc de Lorraine

· · · · · · · MARRIED · · · · · · ·

Louis,
duc d'Orléans
1702–52
m.
Auguste-Marie,
Princesse de Bade

Marie Louise
d'Orléans
1695–1719

Louise Adélaïde
1698–1743

Charlotte Aglaé
1700–61
m.
duc de
Modene

Louise Elisabeth
1709–50
m.
Louis I
of Spain,
son of
Philip V

Philippe Elisabeth
1714–34
m.
don Carlos,
son of
Philip V

Louise Diane
1716–36
m.
Louis
François,
prince
de Conti

THE FAMILY TREE OF LOUIS XIV

Louis XIV

Louis XIV
A ROYAL LIFE

OLIVIER BERNIER

Doubleday
NEW YORK
1987

Book Design by Beverley Vawter Gallegos

Library of Congress Cataloging-in-Publication Data
Bernier, Olivier.
  Louis XIV: a royal life.

  Bibliography: p. 355.
  Includes index.
  1. Louis XIV, King of France, 1638–1715. 2. France
—History—Louis XIV, 1643–1715. 3. France—Kings and
rulers—Biography. 4. France—Court and courtiers—
History—17th century. I. Title. II. Title: Louis Quatorze.
DC129.B375 1987   944'.033'0924[B]   87–5445
ISBN 0-385-19785-3

Contents

Louis XIV

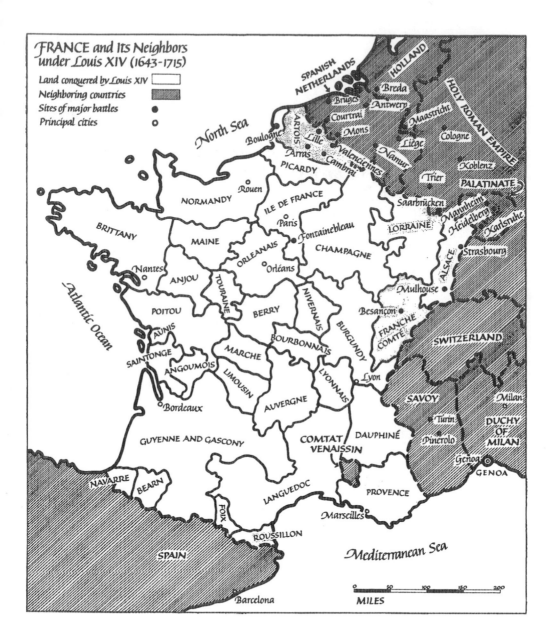

FRANCE and Its Neighbors
under Louis XIV (1643-1715)

Land conquered by Louis XIV
Neighboring countries
Sites of major battles
Principal cities

SPANISH
NETHERLANDS
HOLLAND
HOLY ROMAN EMPIRE
Breda
Bruges
Antwerp
Courtrai
Maastricht
Mons
Liège
Cologne
North Sea
Boulogne
ARTOIS
Lille
Namur
Koblenz
Arras
Valenciennes
Cambrai
Trier
PALATINATE
PICARDY
Saarbrücken
Mannheim
Heidelberg
Rouen
NORMANDY
ILE DE FRANCE
LORRAINE
Karlsruhe
Paris
ALSACE
BRITTANY
MAINE
Fontainebleau
CHAMPAGNE
Strasbourg
ORLEANAIS
Nantes
Orléans
Mulhouse
ANJOU
TOURAINE
BERRY
NIVERNAIS
Besançon
FRANCHE
COMTE
Atlantic Ocean
POITOU
BOURBONNAIS
BURGUNDY
SWITZERLAND
AUNIS
SAINTONGE
MARCHE
Lyon
ANGOUMOIS
LIMOUSIN
LYONNAIS
SAVOY
Milan
Turin
DUCHY
OF
MILAN
Bordeaux
AUVERGNE
Pinerolo
GUYENNE AND GASCONY
COMTAT
VENAISSIN
DAUPHINÉ
Genoa
GENOA
NAVARRE
BEARN
LANGUEDOC
PROVENCE
FOIX
Marseilles
ROUSSILLON
SPAIN
Mediterranean Sea
Barcelona

0   50   100   150   200
MILES

Many who are subjects would be very poor rulers; it is far easier to obey a superior than to command one's own self; and when we can do anything we want, it is difficult to want only what is right.

Louis XIV

I
A Gift from God

LOUIS XIII never meant to go, Queen Anne did not expect him: it took the prayers of a nun, the bad temper of an attendant, and a violent, freezing rainstorm to bring them together; but when he came, she set herself to please. They shared the same bed because there was no other; and nine months later to the day, France celebrated the birth of a baby boy whom his contemporaries and posterity alike have called the Sun King.

It was, many people said, a miracle, an act of God: after twenty-three years of unfruitful and increasingly bitter union, the King despised the Queen and avoided her whenever possible. It was not only that Louis XIII vastly preferred the company of handsome young men, or that in the early days of their marriage Anne of Austria* had miscarried three times: since then, she had joined the group at Court who fought the Prime Minister, the Cardinal de Richelieu, on every issue; worse still, she had actually engaged in a traitorous correspondence with her brother, King Philip IV of Spain, in the midst of a raging war.

Still, in spite of their hatred for each other, the King and Queen both wanted an heir: as things stood, Louis XIII's brother Gaston would inherit the throne and destroy all he had accomplished; and the Queen dreaded being sent away in disgrace. Unfortunately, the birth of a Dauphin (girls, in France, could not inherit the throne) was hardly possible as long as Louis and Anne abstained from all physical

* Anne of Austria, in spite of her name, was a Spanish Habsburg, the daughter of King Philip III.

contact. And given the situation, the King was most unlikely ever to sleep with the Queen again.

*W*HEN, on the afternoon of December 5, 1637, Louis XIII stopped in at the convent of the Visitandines in Paris, to see Louise de La Fayette, now a nun, and formerly his (chaste) love, he was on his way from Versailles, where he had a small hunting lodge, to Saint Maur, where he planned to spend the night, while the Queen was settled at the Louvre for the winter. And since, in the 1630s, royal residences were largely empty shells furnished only when the King lived there, Louis XIII's bed, linens, and other necessities preceded him to Saint Maur.

As it was, the King found his conversation with Louise de La Fayette so absorbing that by the time he decided to leave, night had fallen, while a torrential rainstorm was in progress. In spite of this, he persisted in his earlier plan, but M. de Guitaut, the Captain of the Guard, suggested that he go to the Louvre instead. Of course, Louis XIII immediately pointed out that his apartment there was unfurnished, only to have M. de Guitaut suggest that he spend the night with the Queen, adding that it would be inhuman on the King's part to expect his escort to ride out to Saint Maur in a rainstorm.

Instead, Louis decided to wait for a break in the weather. After a few moments, Guitaut repeated his suggestion. This time, the King answered that Anne of Austria, who had retained her Spanish habits, ate her supper at an impossibly late hour. Daringly, Guitaut answered that the Queen would, no doubt, change that to please him. This time, his master gave in. "He was forced to share the Queen's bed," Mme de Motteville, her faithful lady in waiting noted, ". . . so that it has been said that the encounter gave us our present King [Louis XIV]. When the Queen received this grace from Heaven, she badly needed it to save her from all the sufferings which seemed to await her [as the result of the correspondence]."[1]

There can hardly be any doubt that the birth of the Dauphin was the direct result of that unexpected encounter. Exactly nine months later to the day, the Queen was delivered of the long-awaited heir to the throne; and because neither parent had any doubt that this was the work of Providence, the baby was named Louis-Dieudonné, Louis, the Gift of God.

The Queen's unexpected pregnancy naturally caused a great stir. Already on January 14, 1638, Bouvard, the King's First Physician, officially informed Richelieu of the event, thus causing the usually pessimistic Cardinal immense pleasure. Still, there was much to worry about: Anne of Austria, after all, had a history of miscarriages; but by late April, it seemed, the worst was over; and for the first time in some twenty years, Louis XIII actually paid attention to his wife. "The King, at the beginning of [the Queen's] pregnancy, showed her how pleased he was, and was even tender with her,"[2] Mme de Motteville reported; indeed, a new harmony now united old enemies: Richelieu, well aware that, as the Dauphin's mother, the Queen would become a power in her own right, suddenly became obliging and amiable; while Anne, who was anxious not to be separated from her child, immediately started propitiating both the Cardinal and the King. As for the latter, he gave up following his army to Picardy, where the front still was, to stay near his pregnant wife; and, of course, he was present at the birth itself. More, according to Alvise Contarini, the Venetian ambassador, he held Anne in his arms as she was giving birth.

Of course, the baby might have turned out to be a girl after all, a fact about which no one seemed to worry; and medical complications were not unlikely since the Queen was about to give birth for the first time at the age of thirty-eight; but all went well. "The joy His Majesty feels in being a father is extraordinary," Contarini reported. "His Majesty went today four or five times to Monseigneur the Dauphin's room to see him breastfeeding† . . . Monsieur‡ was stunned when Mme Péronne [the midwife] showed him that the Queen had given birth to a son";[3] as for the King, he insisted on taking the Ambassador to the crib, there saying: "Here is a miraculous effect of the grace of our Lord, for that is how one must describe so beautiful a child born after my twenty-two years of marriage and my wife's four unhappy miscarriages."[4]

The King had good reason to rejoice: the birth of an heir must, everyone agreed, put an end to the long series of conspiracies based on the status of Gaston, duc d'Orléans; that should have become

---

† Well-to-do women, in the seventeenth century, never breastfed their own babies; they hired nurses to take on that duty. When the King visited his son, therefore, he did not see the Queen.

‡ Monsieur, with no name, was the title always borne by the King's brother.

3

truer still when, in 1640, the Queen was delivered of a second boy, Philippe; but old habits die hard. The last and perhaps most spectacular anti-Richelieu plot of the reign ran its course in 1641–42, and ended, but only just, with the Cardinal's reaffirmed supremacy.

It seemed fairly sure, however, that, as the Dauphin grew up, the duc d'Orléans, that linchpin of every plot, would become increasingly less important; on the other hand, France, like England, had a solid tradition of conflict between the sovereign and his heir, something the ever suspicious Louis XIII knew very well. "Monseigneur the little Dauphin was not even three before he apparently worried and annoyed [the King]," Mme de Motteville wrote. "One day, coming back from some hunting trip, the little prince saw [his father] wearing a nightcap; he began to cry because he was frightened as he was not used to seeing him like that. The King was as angry as if it had been a thing of much consequence; he complained to the Queen, accused her of teaching his son to feel aversion for him and threatened her very roughly with the removal of both children from her care."[5] This incident took place in 1641; with the Cinq-Mars conspiracy the following year, the King's suspicion grew, and it took very fast footwork and many a humble protest of devotion to both King and Cardinal before Anne could be sure of keeping her children. What that may have cost the proud Habsburg is not hard to imagine; still, she maintained her status: keeping the two boys not only satisfied her very real maternal feelings, it also ensured that, should something happen to the King, she would be in a position of power.

Those who banked on the King's death had been disappointed often before; as for Richelieu, who also suffered from a variety of excruciatingly painful diseases, his contemporaries seem to have thought him immortal. Thus, when on December 17, 1642, he succumbed to a final illness, his death took everyone by surprise. It was followed by a moment of intense suspense: would the King, now that he was free of the Cardinal's forceful personality, change his policies and the rest of his ministers? Would he be ruled by a new favorite favorable to the anti-Richelieu party? It is in fact a measure of Louis XIII's steadfastness that he did no such thing. Richelieu was succeeded by the very man he had chosen for his place, a brilliantly intelligent Italian of rather humble origin, Giulio Mazarini.

This gifted diplomat had started his career in the Pope's service, and shown himself from the first to be a friend of France. As a result,

4

Richelieu had requested his appointment as legate to the French court, then decided to train him as his successor. In 1639 Mazarini, upon being given his naturalization as a Frenchman, became Mazarin; soon after that, again at Richelieu's urging, the Pope made him a cardinal; but even if the new minister was now a prince of the Church, he never forgot his earlier diplomatic training: no one was more accommodating, more willing to fawn and flatter, than the new Eminence; and while the court deplored his appointment as prime minister, it was thought he was so easily influenced as to offer no great threat to those who were determined on a change of policy and personnel.

Unfortunately for them, however, there still was the King and to everyone's surprise, he went right on with the same political goals, the same methods of government. Taxes remained high, immediate obedience was still expected, the great nobles were still kept out of the Council, and, most important, the war with Spain continued. In the last year, the French army had won at least one great victory in its conquest of the Roussillon, that province on the French side of the Pyrenees which had heretofore belonged to Spain. Although the perennially gloomy Louis XIII was not given to underestimating his foes, the future looked promising: Portugal was seceding from Spain, Catalonia was in revolt and the Spanish Government nearly bankrupt. The war with both branches of the House of Habsburg, Spain and Austria, had been the fundamental choice of Louis XIII's reign: now, although the chief defender of that policy was dead, the King had decided to carry on all the same, and the amiable Cardinal Mazarin, different though he might be from the imperious and awe-inspiring Richelieu, fortified him in his resolve. Indeed, it was in that foreigner that, aside from the sovereign, the interest of France seemed most truly incarnate.

As for Anne of Austria, her position immediately improved. "The Queen, after this death which caused her no great sorrow, began to expect her future power because of the crowd which surrounded her. It was not that the King thought any more of her . . . but the Queen began to be regarded as the mother of the two little princes and the wife of an ailing king. She was coming close to a regency which was bound to be long-lasting so that she was considered as a rising sun from which everyone hoped to receive a favorable influence."[6]

What would happen if Louis XIII died was now becoming a burning question. As December, 1642, passed into January, then February, 1643, it became clear that the King was growing weaker and weaker. If he died, leaving the throne to a five-year-old heir, a regency would have to take over; but then, who was the Regent to be?

Precedent, that chain of the Ancien Régime, argued for the young King's uncle—as had been the case under Charles VI—or his mother: everyone remembered that when, in 1610, the nine-year-old Louis XIII had succeeded his murdered father, it was his mother, Queen Marie de' Medici, who had become Regent; the disasters of that particular regency, however, were also fresh in every mind, first and foremost Louis XIII's. On the other hand, Gaston d'Orléans, the other candidate, had betrayed his brother time and again and now stood ready to reverse the very policies the King wanted to see continued. It was hardly a happy choice, especially since Louis XIII distrusted his brother and his wife almost equally.

In January, 1643, the King was unwell, but then, he always was. Two months later, it became clear that this time the illness was even more serious than usual and Mazarin began to press for a solution. Finally, on April 19, having realized that it was now only a question of days, Louis XIII ordered that the Queen, his two sons, his brother, the princes of the blood royal, the dukes and the principal officials gather in his bedroom the next day. There, one of the servants wrote, "the King, after having ordered that the curtains of his bed be opened, and having spoken to the Queen, Monsieur, his brother, and Monsieur le Prince,* raised his voice and made a very beautiful speech to all who were present, then he ordered M. de la Vrillière [a secretary of state] to read aloud the act proclaiming the Queen's regency . . . The Queen was at the foot of the King's bed, seated in a chair . . . She kept weeping . . . All the others also cried . . . The King who, that day, had a pink complexion and looked pleased and unworried, showed that he had no fear of death. Everyone could see the greatest king on earth, after so many victories and conquests, leaving his scepter and his crown with as little regret as if it had been a bundle of rotten straw."[7]

That Louis XIII, a devout Catholic, was not afraid of death we can well believe; the tears so abundantly shed by all present are a little

* The title borne by the King's cousin, the prince de Condé.

more open to question. People, in the seventeenth century, still thought that crying was the normal and proper response to an emotionally trying situation: men and women alike, when parting, for instance, or when they were present at a deathbed, sobbed as a matter of routine, even if the death in question actually suited them very well. Given this, we may especially wonder about the Queen's tears. She never afterward gave any indication of missing her late husband; with his death, she would find herself in a far more agreeable position than before: there can be very little doubt, therefore, as to her real feelings.

Far from really grieving, in fact, she must have been absolutely furious. The King, it is true, had officially appointed her Regent; but then, Monsieur became Lieutenant General of the young King—and, usually, the Lieutenant General was the person who ruled when the King could not. Nor was that all: the government was to be run by a Council of regency led by Cardinal Mazarin, whom the Queen had no reason to trust, and composed almost exclusively of Richelieu's friends. It could not be clearer, therefore: although the Queen might be Regent in name, she would be powerless in fact. She can hardly have been grateful for this final proof that her husband distrusted her utterly, but she had won one great point: her children were not to be taken away from her; and such was the magic aura surrounding even an infant King that whoever controlled him was well on the way to controlling France.

For the moment, however, Louis XIII was still alive, and the way he unexpectedly clung to life must have proved a considerable worry to his future widow. All through April, he held on, and people began to wonder if he might not survive after all, especially when one day he vomited an immensely long worm: perhaps that had been the cause of his illness. Still, at the beginning of May, he grew so weak that he could no longer leave his bed; and then, this peevish, fussy man whose life had been spent in complaining, behaved just the way a King was expected to do. "Séguin, the Queen's First Physician, told me that two hours before [the King's] death, as he passed before his bed, the King nodded to him to come over; then, giving him his hand, he said in a firm voice: 'Séguin, feel my pulse and tell me, please, how many more hours I will live; but feel it properly for I would really like to know the truth.' The physician, seeing how calm he was . . . told him very plainly: 'Sire, Your Majesty cannot have more than two or three hours at most.' Upon which that prince, joining his hands together and looking up at the heavens, answered softly and without showing any emotion: 'Well, Lord, I accept this gladly.' "[8]

Indeed, at the hour of his death, Louis XIII, who was generally disliked, conquered everyone's admiration. "The King died on Thursday [May 14] at three in the afternoon," Turenne, the great general, wrote his sister. "It is true that no one has ever ended so beautifully or so courageously. As for the court's affliction, it is very mediocre . . . there are great intrigues to change the Council as set up by the late King."[9] Turenne was right: no one regretted the death. The great aristocrats felt free, at long last, from the yoke they had borne with such impatience; the rising middle class, officeholders and Parlement men, looked forward to the gain in influence which always resulted from a weak government—and regencies were notoriously weak—and the people hoped for tax relief. Indeed, Olivier Lefèvre d'Ormesson, a magistrate, expressed the consensus in his diary: "He died . . . after having reigned for thirty-three years less two hours. He never had any contentment in his life and always met with crises. He accomplished some things, but only under the leadership of his favorites, especially the Cardinal who, for twenty years, always had to force him to do things so that, during his illness, he said that the way the Cardinal had constrained him had reduced him to his present state."[10] We know today that this is not a fair assessment but at the time it seemed an evident truth. Now, of course, all looked forward to a change.

They were not disappointed: it was a cliché that the Queen was kind; if she ruled, therefore, all expected a new age of plenty; and within twenty-four hours of the King's death, Anne of Austria set out to claim the power her late husband had tried to deny her. Of course, she also pretended a sorrow she cannot have felt: appearances had to be respected; but immediately she put herself in touch with the Parlement. The King had died at Saint-Germaine-en-Laye: the very next day, the Queen moved back to the Louvre and called the Parlement to a *lit de justice.*

What took place next was nothing less than a coup d'état. Louis XIII's will had not only been read to the assembled grandees, it had also been duly registered by the Parlement; this was only a formality, but a necessary one. The Parlement, unlike its English namesake, was not an elected chamber; rather, it consisted of several courts of law composed of judges who had bought their offices. Thus it embodied neither the will of the people nor, indeed, much legal knowledge, but was simply a gathering of rich people whose family had a tradition of holding this kind of office. Only forty years earlier, in fact, the *conseillers* and *présidents* of the Parlement had talked King Henri IV into making their offices hereditary against the payment of a yearly tax.

If the Parlement represented no one but itself, however, it did have one important political function. In order to avoid confusion, and because a record had to be kept somewhere, it had been decided, around 1300, that all royal edicts would be inscribed in its registers. This was merely an administrative convenience; but with the passage of time, the Parlement had arrogated onto itself first the right to make remonstrances,† then that of refusing registration altogether. Since, however, it was an established principle that the King was supreme, registration could still be forced on a reluctant Parlement. Whenever necessary (in practice, very seldom) the King went to the Parlement in person and held a *lit de justice* during which he ordered the registration of the controversial edict; the Parlement then invariably obeyed.

Once before, however, its powers had been expanded. When, in 1610, Henri IV was assassinated, his widow went to the Parlement to claim an untrammeled regency despite the late King's will; and she was given it. She also promptly found that the Parlement, in consequence, had become far more fractious than ever before, and it had taken all the authority of Louis XIII and Richelieu together to put it down again. Now, in 1643, there was a will, which, further, had been well and truly registered—as Henri IV's had not.

That the Queen would follow Marie de' Médicis' precedent, no one doubted. As Voltaire, a century later, commented: "The custom which attributes the regency to the King's mother seemed then to the French almost as fundamental a law as that which makes women unable to bear the crown."[11] And indeed, at the *lit de justice,* as the five-year-old Louis XIV sat on a heap of velvet cushions embroidered

---

† Remonstrances were the process by which a delegation of the Parlement objected to an edict; the King could overlook this or accede to the Parlement's request for changes. Originally remonstrances were made only when a new edict conflicted with an older law.

with gold fleur-de-lis, the late King's will was declared invalid. France was to be governed, without restrictions, by the Queen Mother.

It all seemed remarkably easy. No opposition was expressed; even the one man who had the most to lose kept his peace: Monsieur thought he knew his sister-in-law well enough not to worry. Anne of Austria, after all, was weak, kind, indolent, and not especially clever. She was obviously incapable of governing by herself; equally obviously, she would turn to Monsieur for help: the two had always been close friends and fellow enemies of Richelieu.

"The great cabal [which surrounded her] was composed of all those who were displeased with the former reign, wanted to take their revenge for what Cardinal de Richelieu had done to them on his remaining relatives and friends, and had no doubt that the Queen, who had suffered as much and more than them, intended this to happen. But they found in her the same change that, in earlier times, earned Louis XII so much praise because, once he became King, he refused to take vengeance on the duc d'Orléans's enemies."‡[12]

In this case, however, her own change, far from earning praise, caused first consternation, then anger. Although she did indeed free from prison or recall from exile many of those who had incurred Richelieu's displeasure, she only waited for four days before, on May 18, she announced that she had chosen a Prime Minister—not Monsieur, not Monsieur le Prince, not one of the former ministers dismissed at Richelieu's urging, not even one of the young nobles who had stood by her in her troubles and carried her secret messages: no, the new ruler of France was that fawning Italian whom Richelieu gave to Louis XIII, that man of no birth and no connections, Cardinal Mazarin.

The stupor which greeted this announcement was universal; but while most disapproved of the Queen's choice, none was in a mood to oppose it: Anne of Austria was genuinely popular; she was the King's mother at a time when the Parlement's Attorney General had just described the monarch as a visible deity; and, just as important, it was clear that the spineless Mazarin would do as he was told. The general mood of euphoria was further reinforced when news came of

‡ Before his accession to the throne, Louis XII (1498–1515) bore the title of duc d'Orléans.

a great French victory: at Rocroi, the twenty-one-year-old duc d'Enghien, Monsieur le Prince's son and a great military genius, had just crushed the Spanish cavalry. Of course, there had been French victories before; but this, as people realized, began the final decline of Spain.

*I*N THAT summer of 1643, the first of Louis XIV's reign, the Court and Parlement, while still rejoicing over the great change, looked about them to see where power was to be found; and what they discovered often surprised them. Of course, at the very apex of the pyramid, there was the King, blond, blue-eyed, a little boy with round cheeks and a surprisingly serious disposition. His brother, Philippe, duc d'Anjou, at the tender age of three was dark, animated, joyful. And although they were both treated with enormous respect, although the King, especially, was frequently displayed in public, where he was greeted with adoration, neither mattered much; even a living idol can hardly take over the government before he has learned to write his name. No one forgot the high rate of infant mortality, either: many children died before their teens. That Louis XIV would survive to manhood was, on the whole, not very probable.

Then there was Monsieur, who, as the King's uncle, certainly expected to be in charge. Of course, he was promptly appeased by titles and pensions; but, luckily for the Queen, few men have ever been more unfit to govern. Lazy, shallow-minded, incapable of both exertion and tenacity of purpose, unable to apply himself to the actual tasks of government, Monsieur was perfectly happy to sit in the Council when he did not have anything more amusing to do, attend Their Majesties often, and see to it that his favorites got a variety of plums. Visible influence mattered far more to him than the reality of power; with all that, and putting aside his unfortunate tendency to betray his friends in a crisis, Monsieur was quite a nice man; kind, well-disposed, cheerful; on the whole he liked to please.

Monsieur le Prince, the First Prince of the Blood Royal, was equally unmenacing. Because he cared about money more than anything, he had abased himself before Richelieu and even married his son, the duc d'Enghien, to one of Richelieu's nieces. Now he was just as ready to abase himself before the Regent, but his son was

11

already looking like a very different proposition; still, he was off at the northern border winning battles.

After that, there was a bevy of very distant relatives, the duc de Longueville, the comte de Soissons, and Henri IV's bastard sons, the ducs de Beaufort and de Vendôme; but they, too, were well-disposed; and the grandees were far too busy enjoying the benefits of the new reign to make trouble. Power, therefore, was concentrated in just two members of the Council: Cardinal Mazarin and the Regent herself.

Few statesmen have ever had a more misleading appearance. Although cardinals in the seventeenth century were very grand people indeed, entitled to take precedence over the dukes and be addressed as *"mon cousin"* by the King, Mazarin seemed deliberately to abase himself. Where Richelieu had been proud, haughty, domineering, Mazarin apparently could never be sufficiently humble. He bowed low to people who should have bowed to him, cared nothing for the precedence to which he was entitled, went on at great length about the virtues of most everyone else while making it plain he could not hold a candle to them. Pudgy, unattractive, dark, he altogether lacked physical presence; he was also despised for his lack of sexual adventures in an age when high churchmen commonly had mistresses or minions, especially since he was not even a priest; indeed, there is considerable doubt that he actually believed in God. Finally, his very lack of family and connections seemed to be another weakness: Richelieu, upon reaching power, had been able to use his many relatives in positions of importance. Mazarin was alone.

That, as it turned out, was also his main strength. Anne of Austria, who was far cleverer than most people thought, realized that if she chose a Prime Minister who depended on herself only, then she would have power without fatigue: Mazarin could implement the decisions made by the Regent. The drawbacks of Monsieur, for instance, or a former minister with obligations and a party were obvious: they themselves would rule in the Queen's name. And Mazarin was not only safe—no one would oppose his dismissal, should the Regent want another minister—but he was also extremely clever. His earlier diplomatic successes were a matter of record, as was the fact that, alone in France, he had managed to be Richelieu's man without alienating the Queen. He also had almost superhuman powers when it came to convincing the fractious and appeasing the unappeasable. He knew how to negotiate with a foreign power, but also how to propitiate touchy and difficult men at home; and finally, he made it plain to the Regent that he intended to carry on—less brutally, of course—Richelieu's policies: the war with Spain must go on until France was victorious, and the taxes would therefore stay high. Not only that, but he thought that what his mentor had done by using raw strength, he could achieve by negotiation and compromise.

Had Mazarin been merely clever, he would have advocated the opposite: everyone knew that the Queen was pro-Spanish and a devout Catholic; she was therefore expected to reach a quick peace with her brother, Philip IV, and Emperor Ferdinand III, the head of the Austrian branch of her house; she would lower taxes; she would turn the government to her friends who would reverse the centralizing policies of the previous reign. Only, just as Mazarin had an ironlike tenacity under all his obeisances, Anne of Austria turned out to have the intelligence and spirit of a great ruler. Spanish she might once have been; now, to the general stupefaction, she became an ardent Frenchwoman.

Of course, there was a good reason for this radical transformation. In the first place, she no longer felt oppressed by a dour husband and dictatorial minister, so she could judge their policies on the merits, and she quickly realized that they tended to reinforce the sovereign's authority. Like the good Habsburg she was, Anne of Austria firmly believed kings (and queens) to be of semidivine essence, and she longed for the kind of unquestioned obedience expected, and received, by her brother. Most important of all, however, was her position as the new King's mother. There could be no doubt that she dearly loved both her sons and meant them to have a prosperous future. Then, too, she had been brought up to respect greatness; she lived in a world where honor was all, where Corneille's plays—*Le Cid* was just seven years old—accurately depicted the importance of duty and glory. As the mother of the infant King, her obligation was plain: she must govern so as to ensure the grandeur of her son's realm. Thus, instead of making peace, she became, if not a bellicist, at least an ardent proponent of a victorious peace, and firmly intended Louis XIV to become, in that often used contemporary phrase, *le plus grand roi du monde* (the greatest king in the world). Within the four days that separated Louis XIII's death and his own appointment as Prime Minister, Mazarin was able to show her, first, that these were his very goals, and second, that he could achieve them while eschewing his predecessor's brutal methods.

As Regent, Anne of Austria's duties were numerous: she must govern, oversee the education of her children, decide whether to grant the innumerable favors daily asked of her, make sure that the war was pursued vigorously, and, just as important, hold court in a dignified and splendid manner. Clearly, it was all too much, especially for a woman just freed from almost thirty years of constraint; and indeed, except for rewarding her friends, the Regent was content to leave most of the work to Mazarin while she enjoyed herself. Still, she remained very easy of access; the royal family and great nobles attended her regularly; she was, in fact, the most visible person in France. What, then, was she like?

There are, of course, many descriptions of the Regent; the most trustworthy of these, however, is undoubtedly that of Mme de Motteville, her faithful lady, and perhaps the person at court who knew her best and spent the most time with her. After telling us that "her feelings are all noble: her soul is both kind and brave," Mme de Motteville goes on to describe her. "She is tall and well-built, has a kind and majestic demeanor . . . She [is] one of the great beauties of her century . . . Her eyes are perfectly beautiful; their expression is sweet and serious . . . Her mouth is small and red . . . she can win a thousand hearts with just one of her smiles . . . her hair is beautiful, a light chestnut in color, and very abundant . . . Her hands, which have received universal praise . . . are extremely white . . .

"Her bosom is beautiful and shapely . . . All her skin is equally white, and of a delicateness which cannot sufficiently be praised. The complexion of her face is not as good, and her neglect of its conservation, which means she hardly ever wears a mask,* does not help it. Her nose is not as beautiful as her other features: it is big, but its size goes quite well with her large eyes . . . Her feet are very beautiful, small and shapely . . .

"She is no slave to fashion, but dresses well. She is clean and very tidy."[13] Of course, the Queen was well aware of her reputation for beauty: she never forgot that the dashing Duke of Buckingham had

* Women, in the seventeeth century, usually wore masks when they were outdoors so as to prevent tanning.

fallen in love with her at first sight, and she was especially proud of her hands—which were indeed famous. With all that, however, she was not vain: her lively religious feelings prevented it; and while she dressed in the splendid fashion which became her station, she was never very interested in clothes; similarly, although she owned some spectacular jewels and always wore a necklace of huge pearls, she never tried, once she was Regent, to enlarge her collection. Her main expense, in fact, was her chapel: there, only gold and precious stones were good enough. No doubt she remembered the Spanish churches of her childhood.

"Piety," Mme de Motteville goes on, "is one of the main illustrations of this great princess . . . we constantly see her praying and giving charity. She is tireless in her religious practices . . . she often takes communion; she worships holy relics . . . Her chapel is her favorite place.

"Her virtue is firm, but without fuss; she is modest, without being shocked by an innocent cheerfulness . . . She is quick to believe good reports and unwilling to hear denunciations.

"She is kind, friendly and familiar with all those who are close to her and who have the honor of serving her . . . but that quality does not prevent her from being proud or from discerning very clearly those who do their duty by behaving as they should from those who lack the proper respect . . ."[14]

Her pride was indeed extreme: she never forgot that she was a princess of Spain and a queen of France; and while, on a number of occasions, she was forced to dissemble, she never forgave those who had given her less than what she considered her due. In that sense, her amiability, which was genuine, was also misleading: the smiling woman could easily become an affronted sovereign.

While her elevation as Regent did, in one way, make her life much easier—not least by ending her money problems—it also presented her with new difficulties: government, in mid-seventeenth-century France, required a very firm hand. Luckily, she had many of the qualities needed to face the problems which awaited her. "She likes few people, but devotedly . . . She is firm and discreet," Mme de Motteville tells us. "She hates her enemies . . . and would willingly take revenge on them; but reason and her conscience hold her back . . . She is naturally generous, and capable of giving profusely . . . She is not frightened by great dangers . . . In great occasions, she is fearless, and neither death nor misfortune can move her."[15] These, as it turned out, were precious qualities. Because, within so little time, France had become the cultural leader in Europe, we tend to forget what an uncivilized and violent place it was still in the 1640s; especially since the plays of Corneille, with their exalted and austere feeling, the majestic portraits of Philippe de Champaigne or the seductive early letters of Mme de Sévigné are misleading: far from showing us the norm, they are no more than an indication of things to come.

With the disappearance of the King and the Cardinal, the long-repressed centrifugal forces in French society were released. The King's relatives wanted to rule, the great nobles intended to control the state, the middle class yearned for power and was getting ready to seize it by blocking the Queen's ministers at every turn.

For a little time, the Queen's popularity and Mazarin's humility kept things quiet. Because of this, both Anne and Mazarin have often been reproached with lacking vigor and thus inviting disorder, but the truth is that no other course was possible. The nature of the French government had changed radically under Louis XIII, and only an adult king backed by a minister of genius could keep it going. A female regent simply lacked the power and authority to behave like the late King: compromise was very much the order of the day; and as long as the army remained victorious, it surely was not a bad policy.

Indeed, as the exiles came home, as the royal family appeared to be united around the new government, a new golden age seemed to begin. Smart people did note that while the Queen recalled her old friend, the duchesse de Chevreuse, from exile, she showed herself astonishingly cool when that arch-plotter proved to be at her old tricks again; but when, in 1644, Anne moved from the austere and still fortified Louvre to the brand-new Palais Royal, it seemed like the confirmation that a new era was indeed under way: while the Louvre symbolized the monarchy in all its strength, the Palais Royal was set right in the middle of the city, without walls, moats, or any defensive outbuildings. Erected as the most modern, most sumptuous of palaces by the Cardinal de Richelieu, it had been left, in his will, to the Crown. When she moved into its convenient and cheerful ambiance, the Regent signaled the beginning of a more easygoing, more self-indulgent style of government. Unlike the earlier, war-torn regencies of Catherine de Médicis in the sixteenth century or Marie de Médicis in the early seventeenth, this was obviously going to be a time of good feeling.

II
A Royal Education

*W*HEN, every morning, the Regent rose between ten and eleven, the day officially began at Court: it was all very different from the pattern set under the late King. While Louis XIII liked to rise and retire early, avoided Paris for a variety of country palaces and lodges, and spent much time hunting, Anne of Austria kept Spanish hours, never hunted, and resided most of the year at the Palais Royal. Then, too, while her dour husband had disliked pomp, the Regent was welcoming, amiable, and fond of ceremony. "The Queen," wrote one of her courtiers, "knew all about everyone's birth and merit and liked to notice them: proud and polite at the same time, she knew how to hold a court better than anyone and although virtuous actually enjoyed the atmosphere of flirtation which is essential to make things pleasant and urbane."[16] It was altogether a more civilized atmosphere which now prevailed; but, in spite of this new sophistication, there was no attempt at reviving the interest in the arts which had been so characteristic of earlier monarchs.

That surprised no one. Anne of Austria was basically ignorant; she hardly ever read, had had the most neglected of educations, and was anything but an intellectual. As for painting and sculpture, they meant nothing to her; even architecture, that standard preoccupation of most princes, failed to interest her. The most one can say for her is that when she decided to have a convent built at the Val de Grâce, in what was then suburban Paris, she called on Le Vau, the best architect of his time; but then again, it was, most probably, on Mazarin's advice.

This particular lacuna was an obvious setback when the time came to organize her sons' education: knowing so little herself, the Regent was hardly in a position either to set standards or even to make a wise choice. She showed this when she chose a new Governess of the Children of France. Louis XIII had appointed Mme de Lansac because she was Richelieu's creature. Now the Queen promptly, and understandably, dismissed her. As her replacement she chose Mme de Sénecé, an old friend whose only preoccupation was the defense of her prerogatives at Court and who cared nothing for her charges. The Subgoverness, the amiable and cheerful Mme de Lassalle, loved to play with the two little boys. Wearing black feathers in her hair and a sword at her side, she commanded a company of children in mock military maneuvers to the great pleasure of the young King; and while that may have begun the child's inclination for all things related to war, it cannot be said to have taught him anything. When, at the age of seven, as was the custom, Louis XIV was turned over to the care of a Governor, he was illiterate.

Still, helped, no doubt, by the child's own predisposition, his governess had shown him how to behave with the dignity which became his rank. When, in 1645, the Regent went to the Parlement to announce the victory just won at Nordlingen by the duc d'Enghien over the imperial troops, the King was naturally required to appear. Once in, he "bowed to the whole company; and after having looked toward the Queen as if to ask for her approbation, he said in a clear voice: 'Messieurs, I have come here to talk to you of my affairs; my Chancellor will tell you my intentions.'

"He spoke those few words with a grace which gave great joy to the whole assembly, and that joy was followed by acclamations which lasted for a long time."[17]

That little episode was, in fact, a good lesson for the young King: appearances, he saw, were often divorced from reality. In spite of the public adoration accorded Louis XIV, the monarch was, in fact, a neglected child. After he and his brother Philippe had spent an hour at their mother's *lever,* they went back to their own apartment where they took off the splendid clothes they wore in public and changed into old and often shabby garments; they then passed the time as best they could. And, already in 1645, there was considerable opposition to the government, partly because taxes were higher than ever, partly because Mazarin was generally—and unfairly—hated. Thus, the ovation given Louis XIV meant nothing: the Parlement fought his mother's policies all the same so that, early on, the boy learned all about deceit and hypocrisy.

These lessons were confirmed by the next great event in the King's life. According to custom, royal boys were taken away from their Governess when they reached the age of seven and entrusted to a Governor; this implied a complete change of personnel, an obviously painful moment for a child who suddenly lost all the people he knew. "After the King was taken out of the care of women," La Porte, his First Valet de Chambre, noted, "I was the first who slept in His Majesty's bedroom; that surprised him at first, since he no longer saw the women who used to take care of him; but what upset him the most was that I did not know the fairy tales with which the women used to make him go to sleep . . . I told the Queen that . . . if she allowed me to do so, I would read him French history . . . The Queen agreed . . . The King enjoyed this and was determined to be like the greatest of his ancestors; he would become very angry when told that he would be another Louis the Lazy."*18

La Porte was given his job because he had been imprisoned on Louis XIII's orders for carrying some of the Queen's secret letters— not, perhaps, the best of qualification for someone who was to be constantly with the child King; and, in fact, that little dig about Louis the Lazy was characteristic of the intrigues carried out by the Valet de Chambre: the lesson was, of course, that the sovereign must govern without a prime minister, and its implied consequence, that Mazarin was nothing but a usurper. This often repeated piece of propaganda was so effective that, according to La Porte, "one day, at Compiègne, the King, who was watching His Eminence pass by the terrace of the castle with a large suite, could not help saying, rather loud, 'there goes the Sultan.' Le Plessis told His Eminence, and His Eminence told the Queen, who pressed the King strongly to reveal the name of the person who had first said this, but he never would do so . . . It is true that he was already very secretive."19 La Porte, no doubt, was lucky, since he must have been the author of the comparison between Mazarin and the Sultan; but, in order to indulge his own dislike, the Valet de Chambre was turning Louis XIV against a man who not only ran the country but was deeply devoted to the little monarch.

* Louis the Lazy (986–987) was the last monarch of the Carolingian dynasty.

Almost more important, the Cardinal had also just become Super-intendant of the King's education. "The Queen, who . . . spoke often of her desire to have her children taught all the sciences [i.e., every subject], was completely at a loss when she had to order the way in which it was to be done . . . Princes must know many things: and surely it is not Latin they need most. Politics is the true grammar they must study, as well as history which can give them examples taken from every country . . . but that is unfortunately not a science which can be taught to children . . .

"That is why the Queen, who was sure that M. le Cardinal was the cleverest man in Europe, finally decided to make him responsible for the education of the King. She even left the choice of his Governor up to him, and it was the marquis de Villeroy who was chosen . . . He was the wisest man at Court; he had led armies, but his most important qualification was that he knew the kingdom itself better than anyone, and that he had both capacity for and knowledge of the affairs of state. The tutor who was placed under him was the abbé de Beaumont . . . who was hardly able to concentrate on improving the mind of a great prince. Both said that they behaved according to their superior's instructions . . . The marquis de Villeroy," Mme de Motteville goes on, "told me at the time, talking about the King, whose native intelligence he admired, that he had no control over the way he was brought up; and that if he had had his way, he would not have left so promising a mind without cultivation at the moment it was most needed . . . for he spontaneously liked to learn what he did not know . . .

"At that time, he was taught to translate Caesar's Commentaries; he learned how to dance, to draw, to ride horses, and he was as good at all bodily exercises as a prince, whose profession they aren't, should be . . . The Queen took great care to nurture, in the soul of that young prince . . . feelings of virtue, wisdom, and piety; she preferred preventing the alteration of his innocence by other young men of his age, rather than seeing him more aware of all the things which normally free youth from a certain shyness."[20]

So much for one eyewitness account: Mme de Motteville, indeed, was in a position to know what she was talking about. The facts seem to change, however, when another eyewitness, La Porte, tells us what went on: "M. de Beaumont, the King's tutor, took great pains to teach him and I can truthfully say that, at all the lessons which I attended, he forgot none of the duties of his position; but those who were around the King . . . instead of making him practice the lessons he had been taught kept him entertained with games."[21] Which, then, is it?

When Louis XIV had become a middle-aged man, he complained not infrequently about the poor education he had received; indeed, he went to a great deal of trouble to ensure that his son and grandchildren had the best tutors possible. In 1681, a diarist noted: "The King had all possible qualities of mind and body . . . and if he lacked anything, it was a little education, which Cardinal Mazarin, his governor, was unwilling to give him"[22]; and, a little later, Mme de Maintenon, that born educator, is known to have expressed amazement and horror at the way the King's education had been neglected.

So general a consensus cannot be all wrong; in certain respects, Louis XIV's education clearly left much to be desired; nor is it impossible to place the blame where it belongs: Mme de Motteville and La Porte give us all the clues we need. First, there were the King's attendants. Their attitude was clear: they wanted to please the boy who would one day be in a position to make them rich and powerful, so they flattered him mercilessly—a fact of which, even as a boy of seven, Louis XIV was fully aware—and they did their best to amuse him. It is a rare boy indeed who, when asked what he would like to do, clamors for a little more Latin, or an extra hour of mathematics: so, instead of studying, the little King rode, played, or danced.

Then, there is one persistent myth which must be dispelled, the one according to which Mazarin deliberately sabotaged Louis XIV's education so as to retain power when his charge grew up. That in fact he did the very opposite will become clear later, but he can fairly be accused of neglect. In the circumstances, however, he does have excuses: constant financial crises, violent opposition, a foreign war soon complicated by unrest, then rebellion—all this is enough for any one man. Quite obviously, the Cardinal took on the Superintendent's job in order to prevent someone else from turning the King's mind against him. That is, of course, understandable. Unfortunately, it contributed to the King's ignorance—although one can hardly call anyone who speaks Italian and Spanish, as well as his native language, and knows a great deal of history, wholly uncultured.

*B*Y 1646, the harmony which had marked the beginnings of the regency was only a memory. The two powerful groups which at first had supported the new government, the aristocracy and the Parlement, were now turning against it; and while the two had nothing in common, their united opposition could bring about an impossible situation. That, in the end, the middle class and the great nobles wanted completely different regimes was already clear; but both also began to see that a temporary alliance might at least bring about their common goal, the firing of Mazarin. They also assumed that the Regent was weak and lazy, so that, once she was liberated from the Cardinal's influence, she would follow her new minister's policy docilely. In fact, they were wrong in one essential point: whatever the appearances, Anne of Austria was absolutely determined to stick by her minister because he was carrying out the very policy most likely to make France (and therefore Louis XIV) strong and glorious. The measure of her determination can, in retrospect, be seen clearly in her attitude to Philip IV: she distrusted herself when writing this beloved brother, she told Mme de Motteville, because "she was afraid that her affection might cause her to neglect the interests of her son the King."[23]

Because Mazarin also had great charm, the Queen undoubtedly grew fond of him; and that gave her new enemies just the handle they needed. Resisting the King was always a problem: the monarchy's mystique was so strong that people had a way of falling to their knees before the Lord's anointed; disobeying the Regent was already a lot easier: she was, after all, only a woman, and in power solely because her son was too young to reign; fighting a minister, who was a foreigner† to boot, seemed perfectly normal, especially if his place depended on being the Queen's favorite or, worse, her lover.

There has, ever since the 1640s, been a vast outpouring of publications discussing the exact nature of Anne of Austria's relationship to Mazarin: was she or was she not his mistress? One side, leaning on a letter with a particularly warm ending ("I am dying, and Mazarin knows just why") holds that she was; the other points out that Anne was given to verbal exaggeration, and far too proud of her birth and

† Although Mazarin was naturalized a Frenchman under Louis XIII, most people still thought of him as Italian, especially since he spoke with a strong accent; to have a foreigner rule France was, of course, particularly galling.

position to have an affair with a man of no birth at all; and that she was also too pious to commit so great a sin. That, on balance, seems the most likely; especially since the mechanics of adultery would have proved almost impossibly complicated. The Queen was never alone: at least one, often two, of her ladies slept in her room; and even her private conferences with the Cardinal took place at one end of a gallery with the Court watching from the other end.

Unfortunately, even if, as is probable, Anne of Austria remained chaste, her obvious fondness for Mazarin made the reverse seem likely; worse, it affronted everyone. "The love that the people had felt until then for the Queen began to wane little by little. The absolute power she gave Cardinal Mazarin made her lose her own; and because she wanted him to be loved, she caused him to be hated,"[24] Mme de Motteville noted; and she was right. Not only were royal favorites usually loathed: the Cardinal's permanence drove every ambitious man to a frenzy.

By 1646, one of these was becoming an obvious danger. With the death of the old prince de Condé, the young and brilliant duc d'Enghien moved to the center of the stage. Notoriously proud and bad-tempered (as well as extraordinarily dirty), the new Monsieur le Prince was not only Grand Master of France, the highest post at Court, but also Governor of Burgundy, Berry, and Champagne, and the richest man in the country. Except for the always indecisive duc d'Orléans, he was the King's closest relative; and as if all that were not enough, he had just won a series of great victories. Finally, because he wanted to conquer an independent principality in Flanders, he now demanded full control of both army and navy.

Condé—as he was now called—felt nothing but contempt for Mazarin; but even that satisfying feeling was becoming tinged with impatience: it did not take a clever man to guess that opposition to the Prime Minister would soon have the Prince's support, along with that of his large following. Still, Mazarin was no fool: he promptly appointed Condé Viceroy of Catalonia and sent him off to besiege Lerida.

Even more dangerous at the moment, the Parlement had embarked on a kind of opposition which was rapidly veering from the loyal to the factious. Already in 1645, the *lit de justice* held for the registration of the new fiscal edicts had caused Omer Talon, the Attorney General, to paint a stark and all too accurate picture of the overburdened people's misery. Now the Parlement took on the role of defender of the poor and oppressed; this would have been more convincing if its judges had not themselves been exempt from taxes, but, as it was, it earned an undoubted popularity. More, with a look across the Channel to the English Parliament which, just then, had defeated Charles I, it began, timidly at first, to claim power on the purse strings so as to control the government itself.

Mazarin, safe in the knowledge that he had the Queen's support, simply ignored this: power, he knew, belonged to the monarch, and the notion that these middle-class magistrates might influence the Regent's policies seemed preposterous. As for Anne of Austria, she saw what was happening, but she knew her duty: the prerogatives left her by Louis XIII must be passed on to her son intact. There could be no question of compromise with the Parlement, so she mostly ignored it.

In spite of all this, the life of the Court continued as if all were well. In early March, 1647, for instance, there was a theatrical evening offered by Mazarin, with Commedia dell'Arte players, and especially rich sets and costumes; after which "a ball was given on the stage of the theater; a hall had been created, all gilded and made by large frames filled with paintings whose deep perspective formed a fine sight for those who sat in the audience. This hall was furnished with seats and cushions which were placed in niches . . . At the far end, there was a throne placed on four or five steps with chairs and cushions and a canopy made of gold and silver cloth and tassels worthy of such splendor. Four great crystal chandeliers lit this hall which really looked magical . . .

"The King was dressed in black satin with gold and silver embroidery; the black was only visible to serve as a foil for the embroidery. Scarlet plumes and ribbons completed his costume, but the handsome features of his face, the sweet yet serious look in his eyes, the whiteness of his complexion together with his hair which was then very fair, adorned him even better than his costume. He danced admirably; and although he was then only eight years old, one could say of him that he was one of those who had the grandest air, and certainly the most beauty."[25]

The little duc d'Anjou, of whom the Queen was very fond, was also becoming one of the Court's ornaments; but while Louis was preternaturally serious and dignified, his brother Philippe gave a very different sort of promise. "That prince had wit as soon as he learned how to talk. The clearness of his thoughts went along with two praiseworthy inclinations . . . generosity and humanity. It might be wished, however, that the idle amusements he was allowed had been forbidden him. He liked spending his time with women and girls, dressing them and doing their hair: he knew what would make them look elegant even better than the most curious women . . . He was well built; his features were fine . . . His eyes were black, shiny and beautiful; their expression was sweet, yet grave . . . His black hair, which curled naturally, suited his complexion; and his nose, which looked as if it might become aquiline, was then handsome. One could think that, if the years did not lessen his beauty, he could dispute its crown with the fairest ladies; but it already seemed as if he would not be tall."[26] No doubt Mme de Motteville is right: Philippe's effeminate tastes were strongly encouraged; but then, both Anne of Austria and Mazarin knew all too well that the King's brother could be a permanent menace: better for the duc d'Anjou to care about dresses rather than rebellions.

*I*N THIS unstable situation, with plots and counterplots crisscrossing, a series of startling events made it look as if all might change. First, in late September 1647, the duc d'Anjou became ill, and, for a while, it was thought he might not survive. The Queen, aside from her very real affection for Philippe, had another good reason to fear his death, since the duc d'Orléans would then become heir to the throne, a situation of much greater weight than that of uncle to the King; "but all pretended gaiety for different reasons: The Queen, who would have been desperate if she had lost the prince, pretended to be cheerful; and the duc d'Orléans, who would have been easily consoled, did not dare look sad for fear of being thought too false; but then, he was so frightened of looking pleased that he did not dare to joke or laugh about any topic."[27]

As it turned out, the little boy soon improved, and the disappointed Monsieur was, no doubt, able to laugh again; but then, on November 10, 1647, the nine-year-old King began to feel unwell. "People thought it would not be anything; but the next day, he had a high fever, which frightened the Queen greatly . . .

"Two days later, the disease was seen to be smallpox, which at first reassured the Queen, who had feared it might be something worse. She left her apartment that day and slept in the patient's room.

"As the King's fever continued unabated, the Queen grew more worried with every passing moment and the physicians were unable to reassure her . . .

"The Queen, on this occasion, carried away by her feelings, was unable to put on a public face; and her anxiety showed that she felt a very great love for the King, more so than for her younger son. [The King] was given to her by God, after a thousand unfulfilled longings, and when she had even given up hope. He had rescued her from the wretched state to which Cardinal de Richelieu's persecution had brought her. He had made her the Regent; and finally, he had been the first to claim all her love, so that she had only that left for Monsieur with which nature provides all good mothers . . .

"The King's illness now caused her to become ill herself. The feelings of her heart were plain on her face, and I have never seen her so changed in so little time. Two or three days later, she was reassured when the King's fever suddenly went down and the pustules came out abundantly.

"Until the eleventh day of his illness, the King gave the Queen no worries other than those she had had before the pustules came out. She suffered because he did; but since these were sufferings common to all children, she was consoled in advance for the loss of his beauty as long as his life was safe. On the twenty-first, as she was hearing mass at Notre Dame, suddenly the King felt worse. His fever rose rapidly; he fainted and remained unconscious for three quarters of an hour.

"When the Queen returned and found him thus, she felt the strongest pain, and nearly died herself. For the rest of that day, according to the physicians, he remained in great peril and the Queen never stopped crying. The duc d'Orléans stayed with her, which made her feel even worse; she found neither relief nor consolation in crying in front of him. That evening, until midnight, the King felt a little better; but the next morning, his illness grew far graver again. On the Sunday, the fourteenth day of his illness, he felt so ill that the physicians no longer expected him to live because since the time of his faint, three days before, the pustules had all gone back in; and although he had been bled four times, his fever was no lower . . .

"All that day the Queen was almost choked for she was not much given to crying and kept her sufferings to herself . . . but since no one can remain in that condition without showing it, she fainted that day by the King's bed . . . finally at midnight God gave her back the child who was so dear to her and whose life was so necessary to France. The fever came down and the pustules reappeared; on Monday and Tuesday he was purged; and after that he grew progressively better."[28]

Throughout the King's illness, of course, everyone at Court made plans for a new reign. Monsieur, having caught on too late in 1643, was determined to grab power this time, in either his own name or that of the duc d'Anjou; the Parlement, for its part, was planning to make Monsieur and the prince de Condé co-Regents while preparing a text which would prevent any foreign-born person from becoming a minister. On the evening of the King's fainting spell, Monsieur's entourage gleefully toasted the health of King Gaston I, while the Queen, sobbing, knelt by the bedside of her dying son. That in the end the boy recovered therefore seemed especially maddening: after all their hopes, Mazarin was more powerful than ever; his enemies, who had twice come so close to triumph, now redoubled their efforts; and the ten-year-old King watched it all.

*I*N THIS greedy, violent world, where slander was an everyday occupation and murder not uncommon, all the passions which had so long been repressed by Richelieu now flared up with extraordinary strength. All around Anne of Austria and her children, haughty nobles strutted, avidly looking for an opportunity to grab anything they could while the royal family led by Monsieur and Condé wanted nothing more than to replace Mazarin and the Regent. Throughout it all, the most ardent devotion was professed for the person of the King while his true interests were firmly ignored by all except his mother and his foreigner of a prime minister: it was as sharp a lesson as any monarch has ever been taught. At ten, the unusually secretive Louis XIV already saw that he could count on virtually no one, that everyone was out to weaken his power and impoverish his realm, and that he could expect no pity.

At the same time, he was very aware of his semidivine status. Kings, he knew, were chosen by God, from whom they held their absolute power; thus resistance to their orders was something very like sacrilege. That, at any rate, was the theory; how far it was removed from the everyday reality in France was something the child could see all too well, and it seemed all the more scandalous to him that the very thorough religious education he was receiving confirmed his understanding of what it meant to be a king. Of course, like all his literate contemporaries, he was taught Latin; and the texts he was given to translate in 1647–48 make interesting reading.

"I know," he wrote in his still childish script, "that a Christian prince's first duty is to serve God and that piety is the source of all royal virtues." And again: "I know that hypocrites do not serve God as they should because they worship him with words only. Therefore, I will adore God's majesty not with words but with my heart, as I know that He will not be mocked . . .

"I must command myself before giving orders to others . . . The king who obeys his passions, will do nothing they forbid and refuse nothing they demand is not free . . . I must always remember that I am a king so that I will do nothing unworthy of my name."[29] Lofty principles; but, interestingly, the boy took them seriously. Already, he controlled his feelings and never showed what he thought; as for his duty to God and his people, that suffered no more doubt than its corollary, the obedience that was due him.

All around him, however, he could see challenges to his mother's authority. On January 15, 1648, the Queen held yet another *lit de justice* to force the registration of new fiscal edicts. In truth, the Parlement had some reason to complain: the endless war was ruinously expensive while the government's finances were increasingly mismanaged. Mazarin took no interest in matters such as taxes and expenses; the financiers who, with increasing frequency, lent the state money were thoroughly adept at making huge profits on the backs of the people; and Mazarin himself, who was living in conspicuous splendor, looked as if he were stealing with the best of them when, in fact, most of his very large income was derived from ecclesiastical benefices.

That the Parlement should have refused registration, therefore, was not very surprising. Far more startling was the speech made by Omer Talon during the *lit de justice* in which he came up with a whole new constitutional theory. Edicts, he said, only became the law of the land once the Parlement had discussed them and authorized their registration. Why should the King's presence make an edict legal when Parlement had already voted against it? It was neither logical nor moral; and he then went on to give a stark, moving and all too accurate picture of the people's sufferings.

Laments about the peasants' ruin were nothing new; but when he attacked the very notion of the *lit de justice,* Talon took a giant step away from tradition. By representing the Parlement's registration of an edict as the result of a deliberative act rather than a mere formality, Talon was saying that the judges were co-rulers with the King; that, in fact, the Parlement was a Parliament. As for where that sort of theory was likely to lead, that, too, was perfectly clear: Charles I of England was at that very moment a powerless prisoner of the Commonwealth.

Still, for the little boy who sat on a tall heap of velvet cushions, Talon's words were not only an insult, they were also a clear example of the hypocrisy against which his tutor had warned him: if the Parlement had refused to register the fiscal edicts, it was less because it cared about the fate of the poor than because, in an effort to find money, the government had just created (and sold, as was the custom) twelve new offices of conseiller, the ordinary judges.

After that, the Parlement's rebellion grew apace. First, it ignored the *lit de justice* and still refused registration. The Queen punished it by revoking the edict making its members' offices hereditary. Thus struck where it hurt, the Parlement turned to three other, part judicial, part administrative, chambers, the Grand Conseil, the Cour des Comptes, and the Cour des Aides, and decreed that all four were, henceforth, to be one body. Mazarin forbade this; the courts paid him no attention and, on June 16, the union took place; and in spite of the Queen's fury, that revolutionary step was legalized by the helpless government. The new chamber then set about changing the very nature of the monarchy. The King lost the power to arrest or detain people arbitrarily, taxes were only legal if voted by the Parlement; and, immediately, that assembly proceeded to starve out the armies by decreeing the end of a quarter of the government's income.

Clearly, the situation had become impossible. Since the time for a show of authority was now past, both Mazarin and Anne of Austria resorted to trickery: they pretended to like what was happening, while secretly asking the prince de Condé, who was leading France's largest army, to help; and then, on August 20, the prince won yet another crushing victory at Lens. "The gentlemen of the Parlement won't like this,"[30] Louis XIV commented when he heard the news, so clear had it become to the ten-year-old boy that the magistrates longed for the kind of bad news that would increase their power.

As it turned out, the victory proved exceptionally fruitful in that it led to the conclusion within three months of the Treaty of Westphalia, which finally crushed the ambition of the Austrian Habsburgs while giving France a new province, Alsace, as well as the role of arbiter in a divided Germany; but it also gave Anne of Austria a wholly mistaken illusion of strength. At the end of the Te Deum celebrated at Notre Dame, she had the four most extreme Parlement men arrested.

That very afternoon Paris rose. Its narrow streets were blocked by chains and barricades so that troops could no longer circulate and it became clear that the Palais Royal itself was no longer safe. The Queen, in deep humiliation, had no choice but to release her prisoners.

That quieted the riots, but the situation remained tense and government impossible; so Mazarin tried something new. On September 12, he and the King, with some difficulty, moved out to Rueil, the palace Richelieu had built himself some ten miles outside Paris, and the next day the Queen joined them. Now it was all up to Monsieur le Prince and his army: with his help, Paris could be reconquered and the traditional monarchy restored.

That Monsieur le Prince would play the role assigned to him was hardly in doubt: as a member of the royal family, he believed in the supremacy of kings and had nothing but disdain for those scriveners of the Parlement; besides, if free to rule as she pleased, the Regent could pay for his help generously; and Condé was not only enormously proud, he was also very greedy.

Instead, he chose to play the arbiter between Crown and Parlement, thus showing everyone that he was indeed the essential man. On October 22, Anne of Austria, tears pouring down her face, signed a declaration accepting the constitution invented by the Parlement, adding bitterly that henceforth her son would be no more than a playing-card king. Two days later, her Declaration was registered by an overjoyed Parlement which went on to ignore the signing, the very same day, of the Treaty of Westphalia; and the Court returned to Paris.

Clearly, guile was called for; and luckily for the Queen, Mazarin

31

set out to justify his reputation as a diplomat. First, he sent Condé money which had been put aside to pay the troops. Naturally, Condé kept it. The Parlement, equally naturally, remonstrated. Condé, who felt he had been insulted, now turned against the magistrates and would have nothing more to do with them. It was a first step.

The next was also engineered by the Cardinal, who understood all about human foibles. Both Monsieur and Condé wanted to dispose of a cardinal's hat; only one was available: that was enough to turn the princes into instant enemies, and since Monsieur backed the Parlement, the Queen could now count on Condé if she decided to fight the magistrates.

Still, Anne could do nothing if she remained in Paris; but, obviously, the Parlement was not about to let her go. "On January 5 [1649], I went in to the Queen in the evening," Mme de Motteville wrote. "I found her in her small study, peacefully watching the King at play and nonchalantly leaning on the corner of a table, apparently thinking only of what she was looking at . . . A moment later, Mme de La Tremoille . . . told me in a very low voice: 'They say in Paris that the Queen will be leaving tonight.' This surprised me. As an answer, I merely pointed to the Queen, and the peace of her mind; and shrugging my shoulders, I shared my surprise at this rumor with her." It is perhaps useful to remember at this point that, although not in on state secrets, Mme de Motteville was not only one of Anne of Austria's favorite ladies but an old friend as well. She could be expected, therefore, to recognize any sign of incipient nervousness.

"The Queen spent the rest of the evening in the same quiet mood which accompanied all the actions of her life," Mme de Motteville goes on. "The only thing we noticed was that she seemed more cheerful than usual . . . In a word, we were so thoroughly taken in that we laughed with her at those who said that she would be leaving that same night . . .

"Having seen the Queen in her bed, we went off home . . . As soon as we had left, the gates of the Palais Royal were closed with the command not to open them again. The Queen got up again to think about her situation and confided her secret only to her First Woman of the Bedchamber who slept near her . . .

"The necessary orders were then given to the captains of the guard . . . The maréchal de Villeroy allowed the King to sleep until three in the morning; then he roused him, along with Monsieur,‡ and brought them to a carriage which was waiting for them at the garden gate of the Palais Royal. The Queen joined the King and Monsieur."

From there, it was a very short ride to the Cours la Reine, safely outside the walls of Paris. This was the rendezvous for the rest of the royal party: Mazarin, naturally, and all the other members of the royal family, who all arrived rubbing their eyes as they had had no more idea than Mme de Motteville of the Queen's plans.

"Once all the royal House was assembled," Mme de Motteville continues, "they drove off to Saint-Germain-en-Laye. [Because all the King's household goods moved with him and the trip was strictly secret], the King, the Queen and the Court found themselves there without beds, without attendants, without linens, without any of the things needed for the service of the royal family. The Queen, upon her arrival, went to sleep in a small bed which Cardinal Mazarin had sent out from Paris a few days earlier for this purpose. In the same way, he had provided for the King, and there were, further, two small camp beds, one of which he gave Monsieur and the other of which he kept for himself. Madame la duchesse d'Orléans slept that night on a bunch of straw as did Mademoiselle.* All those who had followed the court shared the same fate; and within a few hours, straw had become so expensive in Saint Germain that it could no longer be found at any price."[31]

At least the Queen and her children were safe. This was no mean achievement, especially since, in February, the news of Charles I's execution arrived at Saint-Germain: the lengths to which a rebellious people might go were all too plain; and while no one expected the civilized French to imitate the notoriously unruly English, still it was best to be protected from the Parisians by Monsieur le Prince's army. That essential safety did not come cheap, however: it is never a good thing for a monarch's prestige to flee in the darkness of night from his people's anger, and no age was more conscious of prestige than the seventeenth century. Of course, by her removal, Anne of Austria

‡ Strictly speaking, the little duc d'Anjou should already have been called Monsieur as he was the reigning King's brother; most of the time, however, the duc d'Orléans, although now only the King's uncle, was still called Monsieur.

* Mademoiselle was the appellation given to the King's brother's eldest daughter; thus here, the daughter of Gaston, duc d'Orléans; she was also known as Mlle de Montpensier.

had preserved the essential—the person of the King and his right to rule as an absolute monarch—since she could now freely repudiate her earlier Declaration limiting the monarch's power; but neither she nor Louis XIV ever forgot the humiliation endured that day and compounded in the following months. It was not only that Monsieur le Prince was now master of the situation, and consequently brusque, haughty, and disdainful: with the beginning of the civil war—for that is what the siege of Paris meant—taxes stopped coming in so that the royal family lived in a state of extreme penury. Pages, for instance, had to be sent away because they could no longer be fed, let alone paid; the crown jewels were pledged to raise funds and still the King often lacked the necessities of life: his kitchen, which was separate from the Queen's, had to be closed for lack of money. The Queen, obviously, minded it all; but it was the young King who felt the deepest resentment. He knew exactly what was owed him as God's representative on earth; he expected to be treated with deep respect and full obedience. Instead, he was now watching his proud cousin deliberately humiliate the Regent and, by implication, himself, while his rebellious subjects forced him to live, almost unattended, in virtual poverty. This unacceptable situation was the result of the government's weakness, and that, in turn, came from the excess of power enjoyed by the grandees. The lesson was clear, and it impressed the boy far more thoroughly than anything ever taught by the abbé de Beaumont.

Within a week of the Court's arrival in Saint Germain, most of the princes moved back to Paris and directed the city's resistance. "The royal army took its quarters around Paris so as to starve it into submission. M. le Prince de Conti,† M. de Longueville,‡ M. d'Elbeuf,* M. de Bouillon† and many other persons remained in the capital because they were sure that during the King's minority one could not undertake something of so great consequence without the help of the princes of the blood. Immediately the Court sent to M. de Turenne to find out how he stood. He made it clear. He even wrote to

† Condé's younger brother, who, at the moment, was in love with his sister, Mme de Longueville.
‡ A very distant cousin of the King's whose wife, Condé's sister, was the leader of the Parisians.
* A prince of the House of Lorraine.
† The owner of an independent principality on the northern border of France and a frequent rebel under Louis XIII.

M. le cardinal Mazarin that his friendship would cease if things went on the same way, and that when he [Turenne] crossed the Rhine‡ with his army to return to France, it would be only to reestablish peace, and not at all to help with a policy which he did not think ought to be so lightly pursued."[32] Turenne, of course, was the duc de Bouillon's youngest brother; and while it was not unusual for one brother to hate the other—Condé and Conti were perfect examples —Turenne was almost unique in his devotion to a rich, complacent, and much less talented elder brother; besides which he detested Condé, and so was not about to enter any enterprise in which the prince had the leading role.

That, however, created a dangerous situation: the Parisians were raising an army with the help of Spain, whose position as the enemy of France in no wise deterred them. If Turenne were now to join the Fronde—the name given the rebellion—Condé's army would be caught between his forces and those of the Parisians with obviously disastrous consequences. At this point, the desperate Mazarin borrowed 800,000 livres from Condé and sent them to Turenne's army so that it would remain in Germany. And when, in the early summer, the Parisians began to think that perhaps they had gone too far, the Regent found herself as powerless as ever. Negotiations started with the Parlement, and the result, as before, reflected Condé's preferences: the Declaration of 1648 remained in effect but no one had any illusions: henceforth, it would be Monsieur le Prince who would rule the country.

On August 18, therefore, Louis XIV and Anne of Austria reentered Paris. "They were received with all the applause, all the cries of gladness usual to these occasions . . . Never had there been such a crowd to follow the King's carriage and, because of this public rejoicing, the past began to look like a dream."[33] Not, perhaps, for everyone: all around the city a wide band of devastation testified to the usual accompaniment of civil wars.

The humiliations which seemed to have become a permanent fact of life to both Queen and Cardinal continued as well. In spite of frantic efforts on Mazarin's part to conciliate Monsieur le Prince, the latter, drunk with pride and power, proceeded publicly and repeatedly to insult "the Sicilian blackguard," as he called him to his face.

‡ His army was then encamped in Germany pending ratification of the Treaty of Westphalia.

There were the many times when Condé pulled the Cardinal's beard, the endless derogatory remarks, and finally a slap: this all happened in front of the Queen and, not infrequently, the King himself. Then, the prince's many demands had to be satisfied, even when he went against the normally unbreakable etiquette, to advance the status of his followers.

Things went even further when Monsieur le Prince decided that the Queen should have a lover, the marquis de Jarzé, chosen by himself. Anne of Austria, very properly, reprimanded the marquis before the entire Court when he pressed his suit. Because Monsieur le Prince had behaved just as arrogantly to everyone else, his downfall began to appear a distinct possibility.

First, of course, some of Condé's friends had to be won over; the most active plotter among the former Frondeurs was an ecclesiastic, Paul de Gondi, the nephew and *coadjuteur* (successor) of the Archbishop of Paris. Gondi, just then, could be bought: he, too, had been offended by Monsieur le Prince's arrogance, besides which he longed to be made a cardinal; so, in the course of several secret meetings, Anne of Austria, who pretended to be half in love with the coadjuteur, promised him the promotion he wanted so badly, as well as influence in the government. Gondi, in return, offered his friends' acquiescence to the Queen's revenge. All was now ready.

Until the very last moment, Mazarin and the Queen behaved as if nothing had changed; then, on January 18, 1650, to the general stupor, Condé, Conti, and the duc de Longueville were arrested and jailed in the Vincennes fortress. Almost immediately, however, it became clear that the Regent had not gone far enough. Condé's wife and mother set off in one direction to rekindle the civil war, his sister, the duchesse de Longueville, in another. As for Turenne, who had been the prince's enemy, he tells us himself what happened. "The very moment the prince was arrested, M. le Cardinal sent M. de Ruvigny to M. de Turenne with the assurance that he was perfectly safe and the promise of favorable treatment . . .

"M. de Turenne, although he believed this . . . and in spite of the fact that he had not been on good terms with Monsieur le Prince for some time, decided not to abandon the prince in his misfortune and left with four noblemen the very night of the arrest . . . He decided to act so as to force the Court to release Monsieur le Prince.

"Accordingly, he sent messengers to all the troops which had been under Monsieur le Prince and to all the Governors who were friendly to Monsieur le Prince or displeased with the Court."[34]

Coming from the general-in-chief of one of the King's armies, this sort of insubordination is nothing short of stunning; so low had fidelity to the Crown fallen that the most vaporous notion of honor had now become more important than the plainest of duties. Of course, Louis XIV's age was always a handy pretext; but even then, it was clear that the government no longer governed anything: rebellion, far from being considered a crime, had become something like a question of good manners. The following letter, written by the young and fashionable comte de Bussy-Rabutin to his cousin, the marquise de Sévigné, is typical of that attitude; it is only one of hundreds: "I have finally declared for Monsieur le Prince, my fair cousin; it wasn't without much repugnance, for I will be serving a prince who doesn't like me against my King. It is true that I pity his [Condé's] condition. I will therefore serve him while he is in prison as if he liked me, and if he ever comes out, I will resign my position and will immediately leave him once again to do my duty."[35]

That really says it all: duty to king and country has become something taken up or put off as easily as a pair of gloves. The ensuing anarchy is not hard to imagine; and as if all that were not bad enough, Turenne—the honest, devoted Turenne, the winner of many battles against the Spanish and Austrians—now turned to the very enemy he had been fighting so as to ensure the liberation of a prince he did not even like. Worse, he offered to give up what France had won with such effort: "The treaty was concluded in which M. de Fuensaldagne [an envoy of Philip IV] promised, in the name of the Most Catholic King, and Mme de Longueville and M. de Turenne promised in their own name not to make peace [with the Court] until Monsieur le Prince was out of prison and a just, generous, and reasonable peace was offered to Spain.

"Things being thus concluded, we prepared to open the campaign."[36]

Because in our own time childhood is often prolonged into the twenties, we forget how very fast people once grew up. In 1650, Louis XIV was only twelve; but he was also king, in an age when Condé, for instance, had won his first great victory at the age of twenty-two. And he knew very well that his God-given authority was mocked, that the realm was ravaged by opposing armies, and that he himself had been reduced to an almost unbearable position. Had he had any doubts, the state of his wardrobe would have enlightened him. "Every year, the King was customarily given twelve pairs of sheets and two dressing gowns, one for the summer, one for the winter," La Porte noted; "in spite of this, I watched him using six pairs of sheets for three whole years and one dressing gown of green velvet lined with rabbit fur in winter and summer alike for that same period so that, the last year, it barely reached half way down his legs; and as for the sheets, they were so worn out that I found him several times with his legs poking through them; and everything else was the same."[37] The King could hardly have had a more graphic reminder of his exact situation.

At least he was growing up to be strong, energetic, and healthy. Already by 1648, his doctors started the treatments which were to last his whole life: once a month he was given an extremely potent enema—it provoked, according to a note in the register, ten violent evacuations—or an equally strong purge; and at least twice a year he was bled. That for so many years this kind of abuse had no ill effect is an eloquent comment on the strength of Louis's constitution, as is an incident reported by La Porte in late 1649. "Once . . . at Fontaine-bleau . . . after having undressed before going to bed, [the King] started to jump and tumble on his bed; and finally, he made such a leap that he hit his head on the tester across the bed; that hit made such a noise that I feared the worst. I immediately ran to the King and carried him back onto his bed, but found that he had suffered only a superficial wound."[38]

In fact, the adolescent was skilled at all physical exercises, a bold and competent rider and a graceful dancer well able to play a role in the elaborate ballets put on at court when the times allowed. He was also clearly intelligent, aware of both events and people, and full of a sense of his own mission. Thus the second Fronde, as it developed in 1650, was not merely an adults' game: he felt directly and painfully involved. That became even clearer in early February.

Mme de Longueville, Turenne's cosigner, was one of the leaders of the rebellion: it was not only that she was Condé's loving—some said too loving—sister, and the wife of the duc de Longueville, the head of the next closest branch of the royal family; she was also proud, ambitious, and eager to play a major political role; so, boldly, she went off to capture Rouen.

This was a major threat: Rouen was the capital of Normandy, one of the largest and richest cities in France and the key to Paris: since it commanded the lower Seine, along which much of the city's food was shipped, anyone who held Rouen could starve Paris. Obviously, something had to be done, but the government now commanded few troops; so, together, the Queen and Mazarin decided to rely on the strength of the average Frenchman's devotion to his King: an expedition was mounted with the King at its head; and Rouen, which would probably have closed its doors to Mazarin and received Mme de Longueville, gave Louis XIV a warm and enthusiastic reception.

While this was just the result for which Anne of Austria had hoped, it could also be seen as a deep humiliation for the young monarch. When major cities were now so close to revolt that only the King's actual presence could keep them within their duty, then, clearly, the situation was almost desperate. Sure enough, worse was yet to come. In July, the Queen decided to try the same method on Bordeaux, and this time it failed: the King was refused entry into the third largest city in his realm. If now the old monarchical mystique failed, then hope was faint indeed.

Indeed, it began to look as if the war begun some twenty years earlier, pursued at such cost in men and money, and at last practically won, would also be lost. Although the maréchal du Plessis-Praslin won a battle at Rethel, in northern France, the Spanish armies were once again marching forward, compounding the devastation wrought by the contending French forces; and Mazarin, who was held responsible for this array of disasters, had undoubtedly become the most hated man in the country. Anne of Austria trusted him just as much as ever, but how long she would be able to protect him no one could tell. Most of the attacks on the government were naturally directed at the Cardinal: the King was too young to be blamed, the Queen still too respected; so Mazarin was traduced in every possible way.

When, at the end of the summer, the Court returned to Paris, the situation deteriorated still further. What had saved the Crown so far had been the conflicts pitting the princes against one another; now Gondi turned against the Queen as soon as he found out she had not nominated him to the cardinalate, and set about reconciling the former adversaries with each other and the Parlement. By December, it was clear that Anne of Austria and her government had lost all support. When, on January 20, 1651, the Parlement's chief magistrate,

Premier Président Molé, came to the Palais Royal, he read the infuriated Queen a violent remonstrance demanding the liberation of the imprisoned princes; it was no surprise, but the King, who was, naturally, present, exclaimed, when Molé had left: "Mother, if I had not feared upsetting you, I would, on three occasions, have told the President to be silent and leave."[39]

At this point, and very understandably, Mazarin lost his temper: during a meeting of the Council, he compared the rebellious nobles and the Parlement to the Englishmen who had just executed their King. That gave Monsieur the pretext he wanted for breaking with the Prime Minister, while the Parlement demanded the freedom of the princes and the dismissal of the Cardinal. It was at this desperate juncture that both Anne of Austria and Mazarin decided that it was time to bring the twelve-year-old King into their confidence. In the deepest secrecy, Louis XIV was told their plan; then Mazarin, disguised as a musketeer and carrying the Crown's remaining diamonds with him, fled to Saint-Germaine-en-Laye, fully expecting the King and Queen to follow him. Unfortunately, as soon as his flight became known, Monsieur, prompted by Gondi, realized he had everything to lose by the King's flight: while he remained in Paris, Monsieur was in charge; once gone, Monsieur was only one more rebel against whom the Queen, with Mazarin's advice, could proceed. Still, as was his wont, he dithered; and when Gondi asked him to sign an order that all the gates of Paris be closed, he hesitated so long that it was his wife who signed.

As for Louis XIV and Anne of Austria, they were now trapped. "On the night of the ninth to the tenth of February, the Queen had intended to flee . . . The duc d'Orléans said very audibly that one of the King's principal officers had warned him about this; and by making his apprehension public, he soon made it spread to all the others . . .

". . . This news soon alarmed the Parisians . . . and the duc d'Orléans decided to use the people's fears . . . for he had good reason to prevent the King's absence from Paris . . .

"The streets immediately filled with armed men . . . The Queen was told that the duc d'Orléans apparently wanted to take the King away from her . . . She was in bed, it was already past midnight . . .

". . . The tumult grew constantly in the streets and the darkness made it all more fearful still." At that moment, M. de Sourches came on a mission from Monsieur to make sure the Queen had not left the Palais Royal. She told him that the King was asleep, and that she herself was in her night clothes; but did not add that she had only just undressed when she realized the people were likely to break into the palace or that the King, though he was indeed under the covers, was fully dressed and only shamming sleep.

"De Sourches went in to the King's room and, following the Queen's order, he lifted the curtain behind which the young monarch was lying, and watched him sleep for a long time . . . Upon leaving the Palais Royal, he did his best to pacify the Parisians." That, however, was a hopeless enterprise. The angry mobs now made their way to the palace gates and demanded that they be open. Anne of Austria, alone and unadvised, ordered that the people be let in. "Thus some of them came into the Palais Royal, shouting that the King must be shown to them, that they wanted to see him. The Queen, upon hearing this, immediately had all the doors opened and the people taken to the King's bedroom. The rebels were delighted with this. They all crowded near the King's bed; its curtains were all open and then, remembering their love for him, they blessed him again and again. They spent a long time watching him sleep and never grew tired of admiring him . . . Their anger was dissipated . . . They left as if they had been the most obedient of subjects."[40] It had been a very close call; only Anne of Austria's coolness had saved the situation, for there cannot be much doubt that, if she had ordered the gates defended instead of opened, all the inhabitants of the palace would have perished that night.

Alive though they might be, however, the King and Queen were unquestionably prisoners. In a last attempt at saving the situation, Mazarin went personally to Le Havre, where Condé had been transferred, and freed the prince himself, but it was all useless: he was left with no choice but flight and retreated to the Electorate of Cologne, across the Rhine, where he settled at the castle of Bruhl and soon refused Philip IV, who offered him anything he wanted if only he would come to govern Spain. Considering the way he had been treated in France, it was no mean proof of his devotion to the country and the Queen; and, of course, he corresponded secretly with Anne of Austria, advising her from afar but well.

From then on, the scene in Paris resembled one of those endless, complicated, and artificial novels which were at that time much in vogue. Monsieur, after much hesitation, decided not to seize the regency, thus apparently consolidating the Queen's position; but his daughter, Mademoiselle, took over as one of the leaders of the Fronde.

The result was a kaleidoscopic shifting of alliances and alignments within the aristocratic element of the Fronde, with Condé, after much wavering, refusing to usurp the crown on the grounds that such actions did not fit someone of his birth; and, of course, the Parlement, realizing that its interests and those of the great nobles were altogether different, pursued its own line even though, and sometimes because, it conflicted with that of the other Frondeurs.

All through this confused and tumultuous year, Anne of Austria had to rely on two divergent sources of advice: far away in Bruhl, Mazarin wrote letter after letter telling the Regent what to do, while, right in Paris, she relied on the newly reconciled Gondi. This time, the cardinal's hat was not merely promised him: the French Ambassador in Rome was ordered to ask the Pope for the promotion, so Gondi helped the Queen whittle down Monsieur le Prince's power and popularity; since he had so recently belonged to the party he was now fighting and knew its weaknesses, he was quite effective.

Then there was Turenne. Now that Condé was free again, he veered back toward the Crown. "Monsieur le Prince came to see M. de Turenne as soon as he knew he had arrived, took him to the Louvre and thence to dinner with him, after which there was the usual gathering at the Hôtel de Longueville; but M. de Turenne, after that day, would go there no more because he had quickly realized that only private interests mattered."[41] As for the King, he too played his part in this imbroglio. Anne of Austria now took him into her confidence, and he helped her by being especially amiable to those—Condé first and foremost—whom she was trying to fool.

It soon began to work: Condé in jail had had great appeal; Condé in person was as haughty and quarrelsome as ever. It was in the midst of this swirl of alliances made and broken that a most important event took place: on September 5, 1651, Louis XIV reached his thirteenth birthday, the age at which the King, in France, ceased being a minor.

*O*F COURSE, there were great and appropriately splendid celebrations. During a grand cavalcade all through Paris, "His Majesty, dressed in clothes so heavily embroidered with gold that one could see neither the fabric nor the color, seemed so tall that it was hard to believe he was not yet fourteen."[42] There was a *séance royale* at the Parlement in the course of which Anne of Austria officially ended her regency and the King having been proclaimed of age, told her: "Madame, I thank you for the care you were pleased to take of my education and the administration of my realm. Pray continue giving me your advice; I wish that, after myself, you be the head of my Council."[43] And once the ceremonies were over, nothing much was seen to have changed; as Mme de Motteville commented: "The King's majority did not give the Queen the peace she had expected; but it gave her strength with which to face a second war."[44]

Ostensibly, Louis XIV was now to begin his rule: all the acts of the government would bear his name instead of the Queen's; disobedience to the government would be an affront to the King's person. That was unquestionably a help; at the same time, it was perfectly plain that, although mature beyond his years, the monarch would do no more than carry out his mother's policies.

Just how well the combination would work was almost immediately put to the test. After much urging from his sister, Mme de Longueville, his brother, the prince de Conti, and his friend, M. de Marcillac, Condé left Paris, signed a treaty with Spain, and started a new civil war: after Turenne, now mercifully back doing his duty, Condé, the First Prince of the Blood Royal, had formed an alliance with the enemy against his own sovereign, all for the sole purpose of forcing the Queen to grant him even more favors than he had been offered in the negotiations held to avert a break.

At first, it looked as if Condé's rebellion would be short-lived; although a number of provinces followed the prince, it was expected that they would return to normal once the King appeared in person; so, at the head of a small army, Louis XIV, Anne of Austria, and the Court set out toward the Southwest, while Monsieur stayed sulking in Paris. That had at least one happy consequence: at long last, and without difficulty, the King was able to leave Paris; nor, expecting as he did to return at the head of a triumphant army, did he foresee any repetition of the humiliating incidents of January 1651.

Those expectations were well on their way to being realized when, yet again, the whole picture suddenly changed. In an effort to solid-ify the peace, the Regent had agreed to outlaw Mazarin as her last official act. With the King fully of age, the rationale for the Fronde had become obsolete, and Condé's latest adventure looked simply like the greed of an overambitious prince; it was thus unlikely to attract much support. If, however, Mazarin were to return, people would feel they had been duped by the government, Condé's cause would become popular, and the war would start in earnest. It would therefore seem that Mazarin's recall was the one mistake to avoid.

But that was just what the Queen and King proceeded to do. It may not seem surprising that Anne of Austria should have recalled the minister she trusted and admired (it says a good deal about her sense of gratitude, since she could have let things remain as they were and turned instead to Gondi), but that Louis XIV should have sent the Cardinal a notably warm letter requires an explanation, espe-cially since he was now in a position to refuse approval to any of his mother's official acts.

The simple fact is that, as they left Paris, the Queen and King faced a crucial choice: Mazarin's exile had been forced on them by the Parlement and the great nobles; if it were allowed to continue, the monarchy would suffer a defeat all the more serious in that the Dec-laration of 1648, transferring many of the King's powers to the Parlement, was still in effect, and, clearly, any future minister who displeased the same people was likely to suffer a similar fate. Under those conditions, Louis XIV, unable to govern as he saw fit, would have been King in name only. Still, had the Cardinal been a dishon-est or incompetent minister, his recall would hardly have been worth its consequences. It is because both Anne of Austria and Louis XIV were convinced of the contrary that they both felt it essential to recall the one man who could help them not only in reestablishing the traditional power of the Crown but also in concluding the kind of peace with Spain for which France had been fighting. Well aware of the risks, they chose present difficulty because it was the best road to future success.

As Mazarin, along with a little army of eight thousand soldiers paid by himself, made his way toward Poitiers, where he was to meet the Court, the expected happened. An anonymous correspondent of Condé's, who reported to the prince from Paris on January 27, 1652, makes the situation very clear: "M. d'Orléans has received a letter from the King in which His Majesty informs him that he could not without injustice deny M. le Cardinal permission to come back and justify himself or refuse the help he was bringing. That is why He asks him to share his feelings, and to join the Court where he would be very welcome. M. d'Orléans answered that he could not go to court if M. le Cardinal returned, and that he would do whatever he could to prevent his presence in office. To that end, I hear that on Wednesday evening a Treaty of Union will be signed by Mme d'Orléans, who has a power of attorney from her brother, the duc de Lorraine, with M. d'Orléans, in which M. de Longueville and Monsieur le Prince will also be parties. It is thought that the duc de Lorraine will come in person at the head of his troops, and that M. de Beaufort* will command those of His Royal Highness . . . Mademoiselle is raising two thousand men and will pay for them herself . . .

"Thursday, at the Parlement, a decree was voted to send the King new written remonstrances and that no peer or marshal of France would be received† until the declaration given against M. le Cardinal had been carried out."[45] The Fronde was, once again, well under way. Worse, it looked as if it might succeed.

The King of Spain, who for once acted promptly, sent troops to Paris even as he reconquered Catalonia, and these met with the little army under the duc de Beaufort, while in Paris Monsieur traded on his prestige as a royal prince to close the capital to his nephew: by May 1652 the rebels could claim, rightly, that their forces were several times stronger than the King's, and that, further, they were led by one of the two greatest generals in France.

Luckily for the Court, however, it, too, had a few important strengths. Turenne, now firmly committed to the King, was appointed to command the royal troops: Mazarin could not have made a better choice; and the rebel troops were led by frivolous, often incompetent officers so that Condé's orders were often poorly carried out. On March 13, 1652, for instance, the prince wrote his friend the marquis de Jarzé: "The comte d'Harcourt came yesterday with all his troops right in the middle of the area where all my troops were

* This handsome, stupid, but popular young man was the son of one of Henri IV's bastard sons.
† Peers and marshals of France, although created by the King, took rank from the date of their reception by the Parlement.

encamped because the guards I had ordered posted did not do their duty; that is why my troops could not be mustered and so I had to recross the Garonne instead of giving battle . . . I write you all this hastily so that you can withdraw your own troops."[46] Obviously, this sort of disorganization gave the King's army a substantial chance. And finally, there was the mystique attached to the person of the King: even at the worst moments, its power could not be ignored.

Still, in June and early July the Court's position was almost desperate. Among the many sources confirming this, we can turn to one particularly expert witness: the young Duke of York, Charles I's second son, who knew at first hand just how monarchies perished. "At the beginning of that year [1652]," he wrote in his memoirs, "the Court was reduced to the last extremities: few subjects were faithful to their King; even those whose very self-interest ought to have tied them closely to the salvation of the state were the main instruments of the troubles which were rending it under the specious pretext, which has ever been that of rebellious men, that they wanted to remove bad advisers from the King's councils. In order to make this complaint more plausible, they especially attacked the minister [Mazarin], shouting that it was shameful to see France governed by a foreigner while so many princes of the blood royal were both more entitled and more able than the Cardinal to carry on the government. These princes led the protesters, and they were followed by most of the nobles and the most important people in the realm. The largest cities and most of the Parlements‡ had joined their ranks; and although the duc de Longueville belonged to no party, it was well known that that he leaned toward the princes, and Normandy* with him, and that he only pretended to be neutral so as to join the strongest party without risk to himself."[47] Obviously, this was an all too familiar situation for the young man.

Turenne himself knew that the situation was well nigh desperate. "The Court was in extreme trouble," he wrote; "the King's army numbered no more than eight thousand men; that of the princes, in Paris, had five thousand, and the Spaniards, together with the army from Lorraine, came up to twenty thousand men. Normandy refused to receive the King. The evening this news reached the Court, M. de Turenne . . . learned that it had decided to retreat towards Bur-

‡ France had thirteen Parlements; that of Paris was the most important one.
* Longueville was Governor of Normandy.

gundy . . . He immediately said that if that was the case, everything would be lost."[48] Turenne was perfectly right: once a Spanish army moved into Paris, it would not soon come out again; as for the fleeing King, he ran every chance of eventual capture by superior forces. Clearly, the time had come for audacity, and it was Louis XIV's luck that the leader of his small army was a man whose extreme coolness in battle was allied to the soundest military judgment of the age. At Turenne's urging, therefore, it was decided to fight Condé's army and move to Compiègne, some fifty miles north of Paris, where the Spanish army could be cut off from its bases in the Netherlands. On April 7, 1652, the battle was engaged near the little village of Blèneau; the forces in presence numbered some fifteen thousand men; only a few hundred men were killed; but by evening Turenne's superior organization had prevailed. Condé retreated instead of the Court, and the monarchy, for the moment at least, was saved. As for Condé, he returned to Paris which he now took over from Monsieur.

Although not yet fourteen, Louis XIV was anything but an idle spectator of all these convulsions. Already he had stunned a delegation of the Parlement by tearing up, without reading them, the remonstrances it had brought to him. Now, when the rebel princes sent an embassy to him, instead of negotiating the kind of peace that would have left them all-powerful, he simply told the ambassadors that they would have to talk to his minister; and when they answered that their instructions forbade their ever meeting Mazarin, he ordered them to follow him and took them in to the minister himself.

The King's intense and personal resentment of the Frondeurs was caused by what he saw, rightly, as their assault against the powers of the Crown; but he was also well aware that, because of the grandees' whims, his people were suffering greatly. Armies, in the seventeenth century, were almost as devastating as the worst of natural catastrophes; looting, arson, rape, murder—these usual accompaniments of all military operation left the countryside ravaged and deserted; nor was the royal army less at fault, in this respect, than that of the Fronde. Already in 1652, Louis XIV felt directly responsible for the welfare of his subjects. His correspondence with Turenne on this topic is all the more eloquent in that his fortunes were at their lowest ebb: he might be forgiven for worrying more about his own future than that of the peasants in the area of operations. That this was not the case, at so desperate a time, says a great deal about his notion of what it was to be a king.

Thus, on April 28 he was writing the commander in chief: "I receive complaints from every quarter about the extreme disorders caused by the troops in my army . . . who pillage through towns and country and do not even spare noble houses."[49] Again in May he tried to protect his subjects: "It is with great displeasure that I have received a complaint from the inhabitants of Melun, which is that on the eleventh of this month sixty to eighty German cavalry men, or some other foreign troops belonging to my army, of which you are in command, took a hundred and fifty cows from the neighborhood of the same town whose inhabitants had already lost several plow horses which were taken from them; and when several of the most notable men of this town went, with the poor people to whom the cows belonged, all of them unarmed, to recover them from the soldiers who had stolen them, offering money, they [the soldiers] killed in cold blood several of the said inhabitants and of the poor people who were with them."[50] For a thirteen-year-old King beset by the most serious troubles himself, this is an impressive letter indeed.

Faced with the seemingly impossible situation which confronted him, Louis XIV might have gone one of two ways: many a boy his age would simply have retreated from the world and let his mother cope with the countless problems which afflicted the government. For Louis, however, this simply was not a possibility: only the other way seemed to him both fruitful and honorable. Now that he was no longer a minor, he felt that the fate of the monarchy rested on his shoulders. Of course, there could be no question of his assuming power alone: he knew very well that he was too young and inexperienced for that; but the very act of retaining Mazarin, whom he had the power to dismiss, spoke volumes. The minister implemented— and determined—the government's policy, but only with the approval of the King.

Still, in spite of all those weighty decisions, he remained an exuberant boy. "At Corbeil," La Porte noted, "the King had Monsieur† sleep in his bedroom even though it was so small that only one person could get through at a time. In the morning, when they woke up, the King, without thinking, spat on Monsieur's bed, who imme-

† Monsieur, in this case, is obviously the eleven-year-old duc d'Anjou.

diately and on purpose spat on the King's. The King, a little angry now, spat in Monsieur's face. Monsieur then leapt on the King's bed and pissed on it; the King did the same on Monsieur's bed . . . and soon after they grappled and started to fight. During this affray I did what I could to stop the King, but since I got nowhere, I called for M. de Villeroy who put a stop to it all. Monsieur had become angry much faster than the King, but the King was much harder to appease than Monsieur."[51] Besides the eloquent comment on the difference between the two brothers' characters, this text is interesting in that it shows how simple, not to say poverty-stricken, the life of the royal family had become.

As spring drew into summer, the situation looked as if it might be improving. Mazarin suggested to the Queen that she agree to his dismissal against the right concessions—essentially the abrogation by the Parlement of the Declaration of 1648. Needless to say, this was to be only a sham and the Cardinal was to be recalled as soon as the government was a little stronger. In the meantime, on July 2, the royal army prepared to fight before Paris. At first it looked as if Condé had been beaten, but the gates of Paris opened just in time to save the prince's army, then closed as the King's troops were reaching them: the King had been deprived of a decisive victory through the intervention of the Parisians led by none other than Mademoiselle, his cousin, who reveled in her newfound military role. More infuriating still, a few hours later, when a charge by Condé's army was broken up by Turenne's troops, and it looked as if victory were finally at hand, smoke was seen to rise from the towers of the Bastille, near which the fighting was taking place: Mademoiselle, once again in charge, had ordered the guns of the old fortress to fire on her cousin's army. This time, there was no overcoming the setback, and the fight ended in failure. The Fronde, which had nearly seen its last day, was given a new lease on life.

As for the King, he never forgot that a combination of his cousins —Condé and Mademoiselle—with most of the great nobles had nearly cost him the throne. Despite what the Frondeurs thought, times had changed. Even the imperious Richelieu had assumed that putting up with the princes' endless plots and rebellions was simply a fact of life: time after time, Monsieur had betrayed Louis XIII and been forgiven. Now, for the first time in French history, the King looked at the games played by his relatives and neither forgave nor forgot.

Bad as the Court's situation might be, however, that of the two princes was even worse. The judges of the Parlement, who had watched their country estates being burned and pillaged by both armies, and who stood to lose even more if the war continued, were willing to submit to the King provided only that Mazarin was dismissed; that would leave both Condé and the duc d'Orléans high and dry, unable to negotiate from a position of strength; so together they provoked riots by accusing the Parlement of having become pro-Mazarin; upon which, after some bloodshed, part of that tribunal fled Paris, settled itself in Pontoise, and worked on a reconciliation with the King, while in Paris, on July 20, the rump appointed Monsieur lieutenant general—i.e. dictator—and Condé commander in chief of all the armies.

Once again, it looked as if chaos were only days away. Voltaire described the situation perfectly: "There was, at this time, no party but was weak; that of the Court was no stronger than the others; strength and money were lacking everywhere; factions were multiplying; the battles produced only losses and regrets on both sides."[52] Clearly, there was only one solution: Mazarin, "whom everyone blamed as the cause of the rebellion but who was only its pretext,"[53] once again left France; only this time he went to Sedan, the independent principality on the northern border which belonged to Turenne's brother, the duc de Bouillon, to the accompaniment of a royal proclamation praising his accomplishments. That was enough. Within days, even the rump of the Parlement started negotiating with the Court; Condé was forced to leave; and on October 20 the King, the Queen, and the Court reentered the city, Ormesson wrote, "with the acclamations of the crowds and shouts of Long live the King from all the people, who surrounded His Majesty's return with all the greater affection that he was bringing them the only possibility of living in peace after so many calamities.

"The next day, the King met his Parlement in the Gallery of the Louvre; he had a general amnesty registered in his presence, as well as the reunion of the two Parlements, that of Paris and that of Pontoise; he decreed the exile of some twelve conseillers who had been particularly violent Frondeurs; he forbade the Parlement ever to discuss the affairs of the state again without his permission; he ordered that no one serve the princes or accept a pension from them; and finally he called on the great nobles to come and render their respects to him within three days . . . The very next day, the Bastille was turned over to the King . . . This return of the King's is a miracle, a work of God."[54] Strong words for someone whose office and family tradition tied him firmly to the Parlement; but the results were too clear for controversy: when, together with the princes, the Parlement had so weakened the Crown as to render it ineffective, the consequence had been civil war, general disorder, and widespread ruin.

As for the chiefs of the rebellion, they, too, were now only anxious for forgiveness. The duc d'Orléans was ordered to retire to his castle in Blois, and he remained there for the next six years; Mademoiselle, who tried staying on in Paris, was exiled to her estate at Saint Fargeau, a week's travel away from the Court; the ducs de Beaufort and de Rohan were exiled as well; and the King, who was clearly in charge, "settled in at the Louvre for good, having learned from the untoward events of the Palais Royal that private, moatless houses were not for him."[55] Only Condé continued the war but, abandoned by most of his former partisans, poorly financed by Spain, he was only able to skirmish in northern Champagne until, finally, he left France to be appointed commander in chief of the Spanish armies, thus putting himself wholly in Philip IV's dependency; in France, his estates were seized and, on March 27, 1653, the Parlement, having tried the prince in absentia, convicted him of treason and condemned him to be beheaded.

As if all that were not proof enough that the Fronde was well and truly ended, the King, obviously in full control, recalled Mazarin, who reached Paris in February 1653. A year earlier, this would have caused the most violent opposition; now, he was received with acclamations and, after being reinstated in his post of Prime Minister by Louis XIV, he proceeded to gather the reins of government once more while his most determined enemies, Messieurs of the Parlement, begged for the honor of visiting him so as formally to request his protection. Never, perhaps, has a minister's situation altered so radically from general rejection to enthusiastic subjection. Just how true this was soon became, if possible, even clearer: that spring, one of the many nieces the Cardinal had brought over from Italy was betrothed, then married to the prince de Conti, Condé's own brother: Mazarin had now scaled the same heights as Richelieu; but, unlike his predecessor, he could govern an obedient country where opposition no longer existed.

III
The Cardinal's Peace

*W*HEN, returning from the wars, Louis XIV at last moved back into the palace of his ancestors, it seemed to almost everyone that he was still a silent partner in a government run by his mother and the Cardinal. He apparently took a less than ardent interest in politics; he rode, he hunted, he danced, he courted women, and pleasure appeared to be his main concern. We know from rather a nasty story retailed by La Porte that, as of 1652, the King was mature sexually; as peace returned he embarked, discreetly at first, on a series of brief affairs, and people predicted that he would need a prime minister for the rest of his life.

This prospect seemed all the more likely as Mazarin's power grew with every month. He now took every major decision himself, often telling the Queen only after it had been implemented. Pensions, promotions, honors, all came from him: he ruled France as if he had been the most absolute of monarchs; and all the while, he grew richer himself. By 1658, when Colbert, his business manager, drew up a summary of his position, he was enjoying a yearly income of 793, 570 livres (about $6.5 million); his fortune had risen to over 8 million livres (about $65 million), all without counting his justly famous collection of paintings, sculpture, rare books, and precious objects[56]; he had been created a duke, with reversion of the title on whichever of his nieces he chose; and as the years passed, the etiquette surrounding him grew ever more demanding: it was a singular turnaround for someone whose humility had been a byword.

Still, while sharp observers noted that the Queen was beginning to resent the Cardinal's new, imperious manner, it was also very clear that the King was perfectly satisfied with what was being done in his name; and in fact, despite all the appearances to the contrary, Mazarin was careful not only to seek Louis's approval but to explain his policy in such a way as to teach the young man all he would need to know about government; thus, from 1653 on, the ill-educated King received his political education as he watched the wiliest of living statesmen.

The winter of 1653–54 was quiet enough; the war continued, but without major battles; France, now happily delivered from civil strife, seemed intent on making up for the wasted years as prosperity reappeared; and on June 7, 1654, the King's coronation confirmed that a new era was indeed under way. The ceremonies were marked by the usual lavish display, Louis XIV was anointed with the balm supposedly brought down by an angel some thousand years earlier, the crown was placed on his head by the Archbishop of Rheims, the scepter and the hand of justice were given him and the people who filled the vast Gothic cathedral shouted: *"Vivat Rex in aeternum."* After that, the King, the Cardinal, and the Court moved on to Stenay, in northern France, which was held by the Spanish and besieged by the French. There could be no doubt now for anyone in the kingdom: Louis XIV was now indeed the Chosen of the Lord, a fact with which he had long been familiar himself.

That knowledge showed: although, in the spring of 1654, Louis XIV was still only fifteen years old, he could already be astonishingly imposing; "His tallness and his handsome appearance were much admired, and his eyes and his entire person bore a look of majesty,"[57] Mme de Motteville noted. At court, this awesome appearance only served to contain the natural exuberance of the younger people within decent bounds; but soon the King showed that he was indeed an absolute monarch.

"The Parlement, which felt humiliated only because it could no longer resist the King's power, tried, now and again, to recover its strength; there were even some occasions when police measures* and the King's service forced it to come together†; but since these assemblies had been so harmful to France, and that very word 'assembly' being odious to the Minister, the King stopped them, and [on

---

* The Parlement was responsible, in part, for maintaining order in the capital.
† The Parlement was composed of several tribunals which sat separately: they had come together during the Fronde in order to fight the government.

April 10, 1653] came from the Vincennes forest [where he had been hunting] wearing his riding boots to forbid these assemblies."[58] That, in itself, was a startling break with precedent. Not only did he dispense with the usual ceremonies, which would have given the several *chambres* time to organize their resistance, he also came booted, spurred and a whip in his hand, as if his anger, on hearing of the Parlement's assembly, had been too great for him to master, while at the same time showing the judges that they were unworthy of a more splendid costume. In fact, that had all been carefully planned with Mazarin.

"As he walked in, His Majesty showed only too clearly in his expression the anger he felt in his heart. 'Everyone knows,' he said in a voice less pleasant and graceful than usual, 'the troubles your assemblies have brought upon the state, and the dangerous consequences they have had. I have learned that you expect to go on with them, taking as your pretext a deliberation on the edicts which have been read and published in my presence. I have come here for the sole purpose [pointing to Messieurs of the Enquêtes‡] of forbidding you to go on with them, as I do now absolutely; and I forbid you, Monsieur le Premier président* [also pointing to him] to allow or grant them no matter how much the Enquêtes may ask for them.' After that, His Majesty having risen immediately before anyone else had spoken a word, returned to the Louvre and from there to Vincennes."[59] That was a tone the Parlement had not heard in a very long time; but even Messieurs des Enquêtes knew the King was right: no one wanted a new series of wars and rebellions.

Even those who were most fully convinced that Mazarin ruled alone had to admit that the King, at the very least, was backing his minister to the full: in fact, Louis XIV, who realized he was not yet competent to govern, knew very well what he wanted. That the Cardinal disliked the Parlement, and with good reason, cannot be doubted; but the King, too, had strong feelings about that anomalous institution and while the nature of his speech had been concerted with his minister, the actual words he spoke, his tone of voice, his

‡ The Chambre des Enquêtes was one of the several tribunals of the Parlement; the judges who sat on it had been among the most extreme Frondeurs.
* The Premier président was the chief magistrate; unlike all the other judges, who bought their offices, he was appointed by the King.

55

imperious pointing, all that was strictly his own: on that day in April 1653, for the first time, we hear the voice of the Sun King.

In one other way, as well, he participated in the tasks of government: the war with Spain continued, not very energetically, because both countries were exhausted; and, year by year, France reconquered all the territory it had lost during the last years of the Fronde. All through the campaigning seasons—mercifully brief in that civilized era—the King lived with his army and learned the art of making war while encouraging his troops in person. Since, however, his life was too precious to risk, Mazarin made sure that he usually found himself in places where the danger was minimal—the very notion which, today, applies to generals commanding an army.

The first major victory came on August 25, 1654. The Spanish army was besieging Arras; Turenne, in turn, besieged the Spanish army, forced its lines and beat it; only Condé managed, briefly, to withstand the French onslaught, but he, too, had to retreat: as Voltaire points out, this general of genius, who never lost a battle when he fought at the head of a French army, never won one when he served against his country. After that, the war became, again, indecisive. Clearly something more was needed, so Mazarin looked toward England.

That in itself required the kind of realism which the minister so eminently possessed: Charles I had been married to Henrietta Maria of France, Louis XIII's sister who now lived, a penniless refugee, at the Louvre. The pretender to the throne, the future Charles II, was Louis XIV's first cousin; he, too, lived in Paris and when, in 1652, the Court had reentered the city, Charles had ridden at Louis's side: there seemed to be all the reason in the world, therefore, to shun the Commonwealth.

Mazarin, however, knew as well as anyone that, under Cromwell, England had become a major power, and that with its help, he could finally inflict a decisive defeat on Spain; as for the Lord Protector, like the good Puritan he was, he detested the kind of Catholicism represented by Spain and still considered it the menace it had been at the time of the Armada: thus, he only needed a little encouragement to join the war on the side of France. This Mazarin provided by offering to take Dunkerque together with him and then turn the city over to him so that England would have a port in Flanders: on November 8, 1655, the treaty was signed. To the scandal of almost everyone at court, one of its clauses prescribed the expulsion of the pretender and his brother, the Duke of York.

In short order, the alliance proved effective. A fleet under Admiral Blake caught up with the Spanish treasure ships near the Canary Islands and sent them to the bottom; for a government already tottering on the brink of bankruptcy, this was a nearly fatal blow, since there no longer was any money with which to pay the troops fighting in Flanders. Then, a British fleet blockaded Dunkerque while six thousand experienced English soldiers were sent to fight under Turenne. On June 14, 1658, at the Battle of the Dunes, the Spanish army under Don Juan of Austria was crushed by the Franco-British under Turenne, and Spain never recovered from the defeat.

Briefly, however, it looked as if the campaign might prove fatal to France as well. On June 22, "the King fell ill at Calais with a continuous scarlet fever which made us fear for his life . . .

"For two weeks, he was in the greatest danger and the Queen felt all the anguish which her great love for him was bound to cause . . .

"Monsieur showed her the greatest affection possible and seemed very frightened of losing his brother. When the Queen told him he must no longer visit for fear of catching his disease, he started to cry and . . . it was a long time before he could say a word . . .

"The King was twice given an emetic wine [and recovered]."[60] As it turned out, the King and France were lucky on two counts: first, that he recovered in spite of the "emetic wine"; and, second, that the education given Monsieur had been so effective: effeminate the prince might be, but he genuinely loved his brother and, in spite of the hopes encouraged by the maréchal du Plessis-Praslin, his former governor, and the comte de Guiche, his closest friend, he absolutely refused to serve as a rallying point for all those who still opposed Mazarin.

That Monsieur should prefer his amusements to politics was just what the Queen and Mazarin wanted; but even Louis XIV, in those early years of his reign, showed all the taste for pleasure that normally characterizes young men of his age; and since Mazarin's nieces were young, smart, and pretty, he began looking at them with more than passing interest. Already in 1653, Mme de Motteville noted, "he grew interested, not in the most beautiful one, but in Mlle de Mancini . . . Her eyes were full of fire; and, despite the defects of her features, her reaching the age of eighteen had its effect: her figure grew, her complexion became whiter and beautiful, her face filled out; she developed dimples in her cheeks which gave her great charm and her mouth became smaller; she had fine arms and hands and both favor and elegance gave a brilliant look to her mediocre beauty. Finally, she seemed worthy of love to the King, and rather pretty to everyone else. He saw her often . . .

"The Queen, who trusted both the King and Mlle de Mancini, was not upset by their attachment because she thought it innocent; but she could not stand it, even as a joke, if someone seemed to think this friendship might lead to marriage . . . Mlle de Mancini herself, who knew that she was not destined to be a queen, was thinking of her future and wanted to become a princess like her sisters . . .

"The King remained for some time in this state which, in truth, seemed more like a feeling which made him enjoy being with this girl than like a great passion."[61]

Mme de Motteville was quite right, Louis XIV was not really in love, but he did find Hortense Mancini both attractive and entertaining: she was lively, cheerful, intelligent, and decorative as well. She soon married the comte de Soissons, a scion of the younger branch of the House of Savoy, bore a son, and became the King's mistress.

Already in the mid-fifties, however, it seemed highly probable to many at court that Louis's marriage would depend on the outcome of the war: there would be no better way to seal a peace with Spain than to arrange for an infanta to become queen of France; and since that was not yet possible, then the King was free to amuse himself; indeed, Anne of Austria encouraged him to do so. There were balls given quite regularly at the Louvre, for instance, and sometimes the King came to them wearing a mask so as to be free of the ever-present etiquette; there were ballets in which Louis, often in the guise of Apollo, took part; there were equestrian performances of all kinds; and sometimes these different modes of entertainment came together as in the first of the great carrousels of the reign, that of 1656, in which three groups of eight riders each competed.

The King, naturally, headed one of the groups, and his colors were crimson and white, those of the second team blue and white, those of the third green and white, all heavily embroidered with gold and silver; for greater glamour, all the knights' costumes were loose imitations of ancient Roman fashions, with beplumed helmets; and all rode lavishly caparisoned horses. To make it all more splendid, there were great troops of pages, spear carriers, and attendants of various kinds, all awash in plumes and ribbons: although a competition actually took place—a ring had to be speared—the point was obviously to give as magnificent a spectacle as possible.

Of course, entertainments like these were expensive; quite where the money came from, only a very few people knew: the war was still draining great sums; worse, the total confusion of the royal finances, which had always existed but had grown altogether spectacular during the Fronde, was now such that the Treasury was perennially empty. Still, the money was not lost for everyone: as taxes began to yield more, thanks to the end of the civil war, the financiers who collected them under a complicated system of contracts with the Treasury simply kept larger and larger sums for themselves; fraudulent operations of all kinds multiplied; and while the King himself almost had to beg Mazarin whenever he wanted a little money, he watched a small group of his subjects grow spectacularly rich. Indeed, his very own Superintendent of Finances seemed to have a marked talent for enriching himself at the King's expense: by 1658, Fouquet had started to build what was obviously a château of unparalleled magnificence. That the sight was galling hardly needs pointing out; nor can Louis XIV have enjoyed seeing the courtiers flocking around the Cardinal in their endless quest for preferment while paying relatively little attention to their sovereign; and it says something for the strength of the young man's devotion to the state that he allowed it all to continue without ever saying a word: as long as Mazarin was the best prime minister for France, then the King was willing to put up with a great deal.

That aspect of the young Louis XIV's character should not, however, be overemphasized: much of the time, he was simply a pleasure-loving young man. There was the time, for instance, when he snubbed his cousin because no young man of sixteen wants to be seen with a little girl of eleven. "One evening [in 1655], the Queen asked the Queen of England to come and see the King dance in private . . . and made sure that the company, though small, was worthy of the royal guests. The King, who was all too accustomed to putting the Cardinal's nieces first, asked Mme de Mercoeur to dance the first *branle* with him. The Queen, who was surprised by this mistake, rose quickly from her chair, pushed Mme de Mercoeur away from him, and told him to go and ask the princess of England . . .

Later that evening, he was again scolded by his mother, but he answered that he did not like little girls . . . The Queen behaved to him with respect and tenderness in public, but when he made some small mistake, she used the prerogatives of a mother."[62] The point, obviously, is that Henrietta of England, as a king's daughter and his cousin, had precedence, even if she was young, plain, and dowdy; and that it was also unkind to ignore her since she lived in exile and poverty with her notoriously difficult mother.

Still, when it came to glamour, there could be no doubt about it: the Cardinal's nieces outshone everyone: not only were they all well able to dress splendidly and in the latest fashions, they had also inherited their uncle's intelligence; and when, in February 1657, yet another of these young women appeared at the Louvre, the King immediately paid attention to her. This time, however, people were surprised: a gawky adolescent hardly seemed like suitable competition for the beauties of the Court.

If, in fact, Marie Mancini had lived in the late twentieth century, she might well have been a model: tall, thin, dark, with huge black eyes and a dazzling smile, she contravened every canon dear to the seventeenth century, when to be fair, plump, and cute seemed far more desirable; but the fire in those disproportionate eyes dazzled the King, as did a kind of fierce intelligence, of stormy emotiveness with which he was wholly unfamiliar.

From the very first, Louis XIV noticed the odd, unusual girl whose conversation was so unlike that of her sisters: at the onset of the age of classicism, the King had come face to face with romanticism, and, for the moment at least, he quite liked what he saw. It was not until some fifteen months later, however, that his feelings underwent a drastic change. During the Court's stay in Fontainebleau that summer, it was noticed that Louis was spending much of his time deep in conversation with Marie; and that, despite what all agreed was her plainness, he seemed attracted to her. Soon, they began to realize that this was not the King's standard flirtation with one of Mazarin's nieces: instead of merely entertaining him as best she could, the young woman had clearly fallen head over heels in love with him.

For Louis, that was a new experience. He was already used to immediate and easy conquests, but these had remained purely physical. Now, for the first time, he was being loved, passionately and devotedly, for himself: there are few young men who would not, at the very least, be flattered by this; nor, under the circumstances, was it very difficult to reciprocate so ardent an offering. That is exactly what happened: by August, 1658, the King was obviously in love with Marie Mancini.

That was all very well up to a point: while the Cardinal might not be very happy about it, if his niece simply had a fiery affair with the King, and if that affair moved along to its predestined end, then all would be well; and that, after all, seemed the obvious outcome. Unfortunately, Marie saw no reason why Louis's position should alter what would otherwise be the result when two young, unmarried people fall in love; so, instead of marrying someone else, then inviting the King to her bed, she proceeded to behave in ways which at first seemed merely odd, then worrisome, and finally almost sacrilegious: princes may marry shepherdesses in fairy tales, but in seventeenth century Europe, kings stuck strictly to their own kind.

The very notion that a girl of no birth, and who was only at court because her uncle was Prime Minister, had set her sights for the sovereign was bad enough; far worse, she would, if successful, ruin the efforts of nearly thirty years: already that summer, the subtle Cardinal knew, through a variety of secret contacts, that the King of Spain was at long last ready to negotiate in earnest, and that the inevitable concomitant of a peace treaty would be the betrothal of King and Infanta. Then, too, Anne of Austria, for all her graciousness, had strict standards. The only bride worthy of her son, she felt, was her niece, and there could be no question of some little Italian standing in the way.

Still, that hardly seemed probable, so the King and Marie were allowed to enjoy their romance. And since Louis was now twenty, his age was used to exert a little diplomatic pressure on Spain: on October 25, 1658, the court set off for Lyon; there, it was to meet with another of the King's cousins, the princess of Savoy,† and it was heavily hinted that a marriage agreement was the likely result. Of course, far away in Madrid, Philip IV heard the news, just as Mazarin meant him to do; and his response was simple. *"Esto no puede ser, y no sera,"*63‡ he said, and promptly sent forth his negotiators.

In the meantime, the King and Marie behaved like two young people in love. They saw each other constantly, rode off together,

† She was the daughter of Chrétienne, Louis XIII's sister.
‡ This cannot be, and it will not be.

laughed, sighed, even cried on occasion; and then, on November 24, they arrived in Lyon. By then, Marie felt quite sure that Louis loved her; and since it apparently never occurred to her that true love is not always rewarded, she took the forthcoming meeting with Marguerite of Savoy very much in her stride. As for the King, he behaved as if nothing was amiss: upon meeting the princess, he rode back to his mother's carriage and told her: "She is very attractive, and very like her portraits. She is a little dark, but that does not prevent her from having a very good figure."[64] Louis's equanimity is perhaps not so very surprising after all: neither Anne of Austria nor Mazarin had ever thought of the meeting as anything but a ploy to soften Philip IV, and the King, no doubt, was well aware of this, especially since it was at Lyon that the Cardinal received a secret envoy from Spain.

Don Diego Pimentel's presence in Lyon meant everything: until then, the Cardinal and Philip IV had communicated via traveling monks and merchants, so as to avoid all appearances of negotiations and the loss of face consequent to their being broken off by the other party, but Pimentel was one of the King's ministers. That night, Mazarin gave the good news to the Queen and the two Savoys, mother and daughter, were let down gently. For Marie Mancini, however, who knew nothing of all this, it simply looked as if Louis had turned the princess down because he was already in love with her; and both the Queen and Mazarin unwittingly encouraged her in her error: when the Court left Lyon to return to Paris, Louis and Marie rode back almost alone.

For Marie, the trip was a triumph: as she passed through towns and villages, the people treated her almost as if she were queen; and, once in Paris, the romance continued to flourish. There were little concerts, with music written by a young foreigner named Lulli; there were balls in which Marie shone with a beauty now generally recognized, and costumed dances, to one of which she came as a shepherdess bearing a silver crook; even more important, there were countless evenings of just sitting and talking; and just in case any doubts still lingered, the King bought a celebrated pearl necklace from the impoverished Queen of England for 70,000 livres (over a half million dollars) and gave it to Marie.

That he should have been able to do so depended, of course, on the Cardinal's providing the money; and the reason Mazarin was willing to do so was that, throughout that winter, Louis's obvious love for Marie was a major diplomatic asset: in his negotiations with Pimentel, he could point out that, as far as he was concerned, the Spanish marriage was only an extra complication. Far from France's asking for the Infanta's hand, Spain was finding itself forced to offer it. Even diplomatic ploys have their limits, however; and in this case Anne of Austria was the one to blow the whistle.

Had Marie become the King's mistress, she would have had no complaints; only, while everyone thought it quite normal to have the sovereign sleep with married women, girls were considered off limits, so Marie was constantly watched by Mme de Venel, her eagle-eyed chaperone. Had Marie agreed to a match of convenience, then she could have loved the King to her heart's content; but when it became clear that she had no intention of marrying anyone but Louis, and, worse, that Louis himself was really in love, and might even consider making Marie his wife, then Anne of Austria began to worry; and just in case the Cardinal was dazzled by the glory of putting his niece on the throne, she made her feelings very clear. "I do not believe, Monsieur le Cardinal," she told him in the spring of 1659, "that the King is capable of behaving like a coward; but if it were possible that he ever thought about it, I warn you that France would rise in revolt against the both of you, that I would put myself at the head of the rebels and would take my [younger] son with me."[65]

The choice was now clear: either Louis XIV could behave like a coward by giving in to his feelings, or he could act like a king by doing his duty. The Cardinal himself had no doubt about which it should be, and, Marie being a minor and his ward, he was in a good position to make his will prevail. Obviously, the solution was to send her away from the Court; and this in June he proceeded to do. "The King," Mme de Motteville tells us, "who loved her dearly, was so moved by her sufferings in being taken away from him that his passion carried him away to the degree that he told Cardinal Mazarin . . . that he wanted to marry his niece . . .

"The minister . . . did himself honor by refusing the King's offer, saying to him that he [the King] was carried away by the violence of a passion which he would soon repent and that he would reproach [Mazarin] for not having stopped him when the whole kingdom rose against him to prevent his being dishonored by so unworthy a marriage. He added that he had been chosen by the late King his father, and then by the Queen his mother, to be his adviser; that he had served him until then with an inviolable faith and that, therefore, he was not about to take advantage, either of the King's admission of his weakness, or of the authority which he [Mazarin] enjoyed over his realm, to allow him to do something so contrary to his reputation . . .

"The King was thus forced to allow so painful a separation, and saw Mlle de Mancini off to Brouage . . . It was not without shedding tears along with her, but he did not give in even when she told him: 'You are crying yet you are the master' . . .

"The King was greatly to be praised because he knew that his sufferings were due to the Queen and realized, in spite of his feelings, that this was like what happens when a surgeon cures an illness with an incision. He cried with her, complained not about her but with her . . .

"The Queen told me: 'I pity the King, he is in love yet reasonable at the same time; but I have just told him that I am sure he will thank me one day for the suffering I have caused him, and because of what I see in him, I do not doubt that will be the case.' . . . The next day, June 22, Mlle de Mancini left . . . There were many tears on both parts."[66]

In fact, convinced though he might be by his mother's arguments, Louis was suffering so badly that he could not bear to give up. He promptly started a secret correspondence with Marie, which was almost as quickly discovered by Mazarin. Clearly, the situation was grave: the Court was about to leave for Saint Jean de Luz in order to sign a treaty with Spain of which the marriage would be an essential clause; so, on July 12, 1659, he sat down and wrote Louis XIV a letter such as few ministers can ever have written to their sovereign.

"You will allow me to tell you, with all the respect and obedience I owe you, that although my willingness to do whatever you wished has always been extreme, when I found myself able to so behave without damaging your service or your reputation, and although I wish that on this occasion I could do the same, still, my reputation is at stake along with that of a person whom you honor with your kindness and it will undoubtedly be irreparably wounded if you do not consent to stop the relationship which you continue so publicly. I beg you to do so. And being, as you are, the kindest and most reasonable of men, I cannot doubt that for those reasons alone you will do me this favor, still, I want to receive it as the greatest reward you can give me for the little services I have been so happy as to render you, and I dare say also that, in the present situation, you also owe it to yourself, you are about to set off to carry out something which cannot occur if you continue the said relationship, which causes you a greater wrong than if the person in question were at court and if you were behaving to her as you did in Paris . . . And since I care even more for your honor than for that which can affect me the most directly, I cannot refrain from telling you all this . . . I beg your pardon if I press you to do something which, at first, will go against your inclinations and hope you will believe I would give my life so as to be able only to suggest things that would be pleasant for you."[67]

The phrasing of this letter tells more, even, than its contents: these endless, complicated, and sinuous sentences show very clearly how difficult Mazarin felt his task to be, and how important it was that he succeed. In fact, he had taken just the right attitude, no doubt in conjunction with the Queen. While the twenty-year-old monarch was beginning to feel that, in all matters, his will must prevail, still the thoughts of honor, reputation, and glory invoked by Mazarin were even more powerful than love. Already, Louis XIV was first a king, then a man; he knew his duty; and while that is a notion which, in our time, we have learned to disdain, nothing could have been more important in the seventeenth century: a man—or a woman—who scorned duty deserved only contempt. And when it came to choosing between Marie Mancini and the Infanta, Louis's duty was absolutely clear. Because he was so very much in love, with the Queen's permission he did see Marie one last time, on August 13; once again, many tears were shed; but when the King left, he was on his way to Saint Jean de Luz and his duty.

That very day, Mazarin, who had gone on ahead, met the Spanish Prime Minister, Don Luis de Haro, on an island in the middle of the Bidassoa, the river which divided France and Spain; but he worried about the King as much as about the negotiations; for while Louis XIV was indeed separated from his beloved, he continued to talk about her and correspond with her, so that the Cardinal, in turn, started writing endless letters, but to the King, in which he criticized his niece so strongly that the proud monarch began to rebel; and when Mazarin found out that M. du Terron, the man he had chosen to look after his niece, was encouraging her correspondence with the King, he exploded. "So a relationship which had altogether ended after all the efforts I made to that end (going even so far as to tell the King I would resign and meant to leave everything and take ship with my nieces to go wherever I could if he did not break with her) is now about to start again, more than ever, because of the said Terron who, in one word, has tried thus to make his fortune,"[68] he wrote Colbert in a rage.

The situation, in fact, was even more dangerous than Colbert, Mazarin's faithful assistant, knew: the King, exasperated by the tone of Mazarin's letters, had well and truly accepted the Cardinal's resignation; at which point, his blackmail having failed, Mazarin had simply gone on negotiating as if nothing had happened. At last, the Infanta was mentioned; and then Marie, whom her uncle had kept informed, realized that all now depended on her. Like the true romantic she was, she nobly renounced her ill-fated love, and so told the King, who promptly gave way to tears. On November 7, 1659, the Treaty of the Pyrenees, matrimonial clause and all, was signed; and Louis XIV, who had just become the most powerful monarch in Europe, felt nothing but despair.

IV
The Rising Sun

*T*O *ANYONE* other than a young man unhappily in love, the Treaty of the Pyrenees would have offered some solid consolations. Mazarin, ever aware that today's enemy was tomorrow's potential ally, had not tried to crush Spain; still, France received two Mediterranean provinces, Roussillon and Cerdagne, thus pushing the frontier over to the mountains, and a key northern province, Artois, which it had tried to conquer for two hundred years, as well as half a dozen fortresses. Most important of all, however, was an innocuous-looking clause. The Infanta, upon marrying Louis XIV, gave up her rights to Spain and its empire, provided that one key condition was fulfilled: Philip IV was to pay France a dowry of 500,000 gold écus.

Nothing could have been more usual—only Spain was bankrupt and quite incapable of producing so large a sum: the door was thus open to any and all future demands; and given the fact that Philip IV was known to be in poor health and that his only son was not expected to live, it hardly took much imagination to see where the nonpayment of the dowry might lead: that Don Luis de Haro, the Spanish minister, should have accepted this clause is an eloquent comment on the weakness of Spain. Equally clearly, France had now become the preeminent power on the Continent.

The King thought only of his broken heart; but, having given up Marie Mancini, he was now anxious to get his marriage over with. Once again Mazarin pointed out this would not do. A formal embassy, led by the maréchal-duc de Grammont, was sent to Madrid to ask for the Infanta's hand and reported that the Spanish Court was extraordinarily formal, the King majestic but silent, and the Infanta attractive but oddly dressed: fashions had not changed in a century. Still, the maréchal reported, Maria Teresa was likely to be a good wife. Brought up in the belief that a person of royal blood could only marry another person of royal blood, and that, in all Europe, only the King of France was good enough for her, she had every expectation of pleasing her husband. Further, she was pious and well educated except for an unfortunate oversight: she did not know a word of French; and indeed, although she learned the language soon enough, she never lost her heavy Spanish accent. Finally, she was highly docile, a quality sure to appeal to her future husband.

From then on, the preparations went forward. In France, the Queen, Mazarin, and Colbert supervised the renovation of the royal apartments and ordered the most sumptuous costumes ever seen, much to the groom's disgust; and, as if to prepare the new era, the face of politics changed as well. Already in the fall of 1659, the all-powerful Mazarin was taking a hard look at the future. "I tried to serve you well," he wrote to the King. ". . . If once you take over, you will do more in one day than a cleverer man than myself could manage in six months; for the actions of a King have a greater weight, are more visible, and make a greater impression than those of a minister, no matter how authorized he may be. I will be the happiest of men if I see you, as I expect I will, carry out your resolve to pay attention to business, and I will die most satisfied and pleased the very moment I see you are able to rule by yourself, using your ministers only to provide you with advice which you will use as you please, after which you will give them the orders which they will have to carry out."[69] Excellent advice, of course; more remarkably, Mazarin meant exactly what he said, and the King knew it: having preferred duty to love, he was beginning to shed his adolescent carelessness: at twenty-one, after a reign of sixteen years, he was discovering the fascination of power.

It all happened at the right time: one by one, the problems facing France were vanishing. Now that the war with Spain was over, the prince de Condé, specifically included in the peace treaty at Philip IV's request, returned home, humbled and obedient. "I will admit that I have wished you very ill," Anne of Austria told him, "and you will do me the justice to admit that I was right,"[70] and the tame lion merely bowed in reply before retiring to his castle at Chantilly. Then, as if to underline his submission, Gaston, duc d'Orléans, died on February 2, 1660, leaving only daughters. Soon, that very title was given by Louis XIV to Philippe, his brother. Henceforth, in a complete reversal, the name stood for complete submission to the King's authority. With this, the Fronde entered an increasingly remote past; and the new prosperity which followed the peace made not only for compliance with the government's policy but for an increase in tax receipts as well.

Even abroad, events favored France. Cromwell's death in 1658 pushed Great Britain into a period of uncertainty which considerably weakened its ability to influence the rest of Europe. Even better, in the spring of 1660, much to everyone's surprise, the Pretender found himself recalled to the throne of his ancestors. Of course, Charles II had some solid reasons to resent the way he had been treated by the French Government; but he was Louis XIV's first cousin, his mother was still living in Paris, and he could blame Mazarin rather than Louis XIV for his expulsion some six years earlier. As luck would have it, he was also singularly able to forget past grudges, especially since it occurred to him, early on, that France might well pay for the privilege of being his ally; so, in April 1661, Henrietta Stuart, Charles II's adored sister, and Monsieur were married: there, too, it seemed, France could do no wrong.

That spring, the Court set off once more to the Spanish border, while on his side Philip IV and the Infanta moved toward France. The Spanish stopped in San Sebastian, the French in Saint Jean de Luz; the ministers resumed negotiations about the last few details while the fiancés remained separated; when Louis XIV sent his bride a letter, it was returned, but not before the Infanta whispered to the messenger that her father had promised her a quick end to the delays. Finally, on June 3, the marriage by procuration was celebrated, with Don Luis de Haro standing in for Louis XIV, after which Anne of Austria was at last able to visit her brother. "In the course of that meeting . . . Cardinal Mazarin . . . came up to Their Majesties and told them that an unknown man at the door was asking that it be opened . . . The Queen blushed when she saw that it was the King, her son, and the young Queen still more as she looked at him fixedly . . . The Queen immediately said in Spanish that she would like to ask [her niece] how she liked this stranger, upon which [Philip IV] answered *'que non ero tiempo de decirlo'* (that this was not the time to say).

" 'And when will she be able to say?,' asked the Queen.

" '*Quanda avra pasado a quella puerta*' (when she has walked through that door),* the King, her brother, answered. Monsieur then said in a low voice to the young Queen: *'Que le parece a Vuestra Majestad de la puerta?'* (How does Your Majesty like the door?). She immediately answered in a lively and cheerful way: *'Muy linda, muy buena me parece la puerta'* (the door looks very good, very handsome to me).

"After [Louis XIV] had looked at the Infanta, he left . . . As he went out, he told M. le prince de Conti and M. de Turenne that, at first, he had been surprised by the frightful coiffure and dress of the Infanta; but that once he looked at her carefully, he had realized that she was quite beautiful."[71]

It would have been, in fact, difficult to find anyone more unlike Marie Mancini: not only was the young Queen as fair as Marie was dark, she was tiny, and while her blond hair, blue eyes, and fresh complexion helped to make her attractive, she also had a large nose and pendulous lower lip. Then, where Marie was quick, intelligent, and fiery, the Infanta was slow, obedient, fanatically pious and obviously stupid. Still, that was just as well: everyone remembered the catastrophes caused by Marie de Médicis, the last Queen of France with a taste for power. In the new era, compliance was all, and there could be no doubt that Queen Marie Thérèse would do just as she was told.

On June 6, the two kings at last met officially and swore to observe the peace they had just signed; on the seventh, the Infanta, dressed in crimson silk embroidered in gold and silver and riding in a golden carriage, crossed the border; on the ninth, walking behind the prince de Conti and the Cardinal, the King, dressed in gold cloth covered with a black veil,† made his way to the main church of Saint Jean de Luz; soon after, the Infanta followed, wearing a silver brocade dress, a crown, and a purple velvet cloak embroidered with gold fleur-de-lis; and Anne of Austria, in black and silver, closed the procession. After so many years of civil and foreign wars, the great object of her life was finally achieved; and remembering the horror of her own public wedding night, she made sure that when the King and his

---

* I.e., once she was in France.
† As a sign of mourning for Gaston d'Orléans, his uncle.

bride were put to bed early that night—Louis was noticeably impatient—they were left alone.

By the next morning, it was clear that history would not be repeated: the new Queen showed that she had fallen head over ears in love, while the King announced that, on the trip back to Paris, he and his bride would share the same room; but if the marriage was well and duly consummated, the two young people had little else in common than sex and a sense of their own dignity: Louis XIV spoke very little Spanish, Marie Thérèse hardly any French. Eventually, of course, she learned the language of her new country; but since her interests were limited to food, prayer, and the collecting of dwarfs, the uglier the better, she could hardly be expected to keep her husband's attention. Never forgetting that duty came first, however, the King, even when he had mistresses, went on sleeping with his wife, a fact attested by the Queen's habit of clapping her hand at her *lever* whenever she had spent the night with her husband.

As it was, the consummation of the marriage, that confirmation of the peace, was everything. On its way back toward Paris, the royal family was greeted everywhere with the most ecstatic acclaim. Fete followed fete, and the King looked ever more delighted. Then, at Saintes, near Bordeaux, Louis announced that the Queens would proceed on to Saint Jean d'Angély while he himself visited La Rochelle—an important port, to be sure, but also a city within a few miles of Brouage, Marie Mancini's former residence. Of course, both the Queen Mother and the Cardinal were horrified, especially when the King refused to be accompanied by anyone other than four of his gentlemen. And indeed, after a brief visit to La Rochelle and its fleet, Louis went on to Brouage, where he spent half the night walking along the shore and sobbing. The next step was all too clear: Marie's sister, Olympe, had become the King's mistress after marrying the comte de Soissons; now Marie, who was to wed Prince Colonna, would follow her example; but while Olympe only wanted favor and position, Marie, the romantic Marie, was likely to make real trouble; so, when Louis arrived in Saint Jean d'Angély, he heard the newest gossip: the future Princess Colonna, people said, who was madly in love with Prince Charles of Lorraine, had thrown all discretion to the winds in pursuing him. That, of course, was enough. It was also a lie, carefully publicized by the Cardinal and the Queen Mother. The innocent Marie never understood why, when she met the King again at Fontainebleau, she received only the most distant of greetings. In fact, the calumny had done its work: Louis XIV's great passion was finally over.

After that, there was the usual ceremonies. On August 26, the King and the new Queen made their state entrance into Paris, he riding a prancing horse, she sitting in an open golden chariot. There were arches of triumph, fireworks, cheers, and speeches in which the King was not only praised but treated more like a deity than a mortal: here, visible to all, was the symbol of the greatness, prosperity, and unity of France, and even the former rebels fell over themselves to worship the very monarch whom they had fought so hard just a few years earlier.

*W*HEN, on that day in August 1660, the King, the Queen, and the Court paraded among the adoring multitudes, they also rode past the one man who had made it all possible: although Cardinal Mazarin's place as prime minister was in the procession, his health made it impossible for him to do anything but watch. Racked by gout and stones in the bladder, afflicted with a failing heart, the Cardinal was declining visibly; but, as is so often the case, no one realized that a new era was at hand. Never, apparently, had Mazarin governed so absolutely; he had grown positively rude to the Queen Mother, and, perhaps more to the point, he still treated Louis XIV more like a pupil than like a king. In fact, appearances were deceiving: almost every day, the declining statesman was giving the young monarch lessons in how to rule, accounts of the state of the kingdom, and explanations about the positions of the different European powers. As for the King, who was as apparently uninterested in politics as ever, he began to feel a growing yearning for the moment when power would actually be his. As it turned out, he did not have long to wait. By December, Mazarin was declining visibly; by January, his doctors informed him that he only had two months to live. It was enough. With some regret—Must I then leave all this? he is reputed to have sighed as he looked at his collections—he prepared to dispose of his power and his fortune. Very properly, the King refused the last; as for the first, shortly before his death on March 9, 1661, the Cardinal gave his last recommendations; and Louis XIV promptly set these down on paper.

"M. le Cardinal, aware that his end was near . . . gave his last moments on earth to the love he has always felt for the welfare of my state and my own glory," the King dictated to his Secretary. "In that condition, he gave me several important pieces of advice . . .

"First, to maintain the Church in all its rights, immunities, and privileges in my capacity as its Eldest Son, without allowing them to be weakened under any possible pretext; that this was an obligation of conscience, as was the making sure that those to whom I give benefices‡ have the capacity, the piety, and the other qualities needed to fill them properly, and that, above all, they must be eager to serve me and the peace of my State."[72]

That the Church should come first was normal enough considering that the Cardinal expected soon to meet his maker; but it is interesting to note that even here his respect for God's service is tempered by practicality. Indeed, the King listened especially to the last sentence: a few years later, he wrote: "Kings are the absolute masters over, and have naturally the full and free disposition of, all goods,* whether they be owned by clerics or by the laity, and must at all times dispose of them as wise managers, that is according to the needs of the State . . .

"These mysterious expressions of franchises or liberties of the Church, with which certain people may perhaps try to fool us . . . exempt no one from obedience to the sovereign."[73]

Still the Cardinal went on. "As for the nobility, [he said that] it is my right arm, that I must prize it and treat it trustfully and kindly . . .

"As for the judiciary [i.e., the Parlement], it is right that it be honored, but it is very important to prevent those of that profession from emancipating themselves, and to force them to remain within their duties so that they will think of nothing but rendering my subjects the justice which I have delegated to them.

"That it was the duty of a good king to relieve my subjects not only when it came to the *taille*† but also to all the other taxes whatsoever, but no farther than the expenses necessary and indispensable to the conservation of my state would allow, since the subjects' prosperity depends upon that of the state.

‡ I.e., nominations to bishoprics, archbishoprics, abbacies and other ecclesiastic positions.
* The King is referring here only to the power to tax as he sees fit.
† The *taille* was a form of income tax paid by nonnoble persons.

"That I had near my person very able and faithful servants; that it was up to me to discern what each will do best so as to employ them according to their talents.

"That I must make sure that all realize that I am myself the [chief] minister; that gifts [and favors] must come from myself alone, and that especially I must grant them only to those who deserve them because of their services or their capacity, and their fidelity to my person.

"That I must make sure that the members of my Council be on good terms with one another lest their enmity harm my service; must hear their advice; always look for the best policy among their several opinions, come to a decision by myself and then uphold it while not allowing the slightest infringement on my authority.

"That if one of those I use in the business of the state was so unfortunate as to act without my orders, I must absolutely dismiss him as unworthy to serve me.

"That I must allow no scandal at court, or tolerate impiety."[74] Once again, the Cardinal had proved to be a great minister. Not only was his advice an impressive effort on the part of a dying man, it also provided the young, still inexperienced King with every principle he needed to govern wisely: here, almost complete, was the charter for a new type of absolute monarchy. Not surprisingly, Louis XIV always remembered the Cardinal with gratitude; more to the point, he applied the principles to which he had listened on that day of March 1661 to the end of his long life.

Already on the evening of the seventh, as the Cardinal began to sink rapidly, the King called his ministers together and briefly heard from them; but as long as Mazarin still lived he would not take over. He did not have long to wait. By the next evening, the dying man had lost consciousness; between two and three on the morning of the ninth, after much suffering, he was finally gone.

"As soon as the Cardinal was dead," Brienne, one of the junior ministers, noted, "the King, with tears in his eyes, came into the wardrobe where I stood waiting with the principal members of the Court and, leaning on the maréchal de Grammont, he told him: 'We have just lost, you and I, a true friend.'"[75] That Louis XIV felt real sorrow cannot be doubted; that he had long been prepared for his loss soon became equally obvious. "No sooner was the Cardinal dead than the King sent for MM. Fouquet‡, Le Tellier,* and de Lionne† and gave to them alone his trust for the most secret part of the state's business."[76] Here, indeed, was the first application of Mazarin's maxims: a small inner group of ministers was to be responsible to the King alone; and we may gather what he told them from what he said, a few moments later, to his full Council. "As soon as we had entered," Brienne the younger noted, "the, King who was already there, said gravely: 'Messieurs, I have gathered you here to tell you that henceforth I intend to rule my state alone. M. le Chancelier‡ and M. le Surintendant will no longer sign any decree or any *ordonnance de comptant** without first telling me, and the Secretaries of State will no longer issue any papers, and I mean not even a passport or a spending authorization of a hundred écus, without having first received my orders to do so. Whenever one of you gentlemen has something to tell me, he may do so freely, and if there is the slightest criticism of my decisions, I mean concerning the legal forms which I have not yet had time to learn, I will gladly listen to the good advice of my faithful servants."[77] Upon which, the King announced that he intended to hold two councils a week, on Mondays and Thursdays, at which the current business would be discussed, and which only the Chancellor, Fouquet, Le Tellier, and de Lionne would attend. As for Brienne the elder, who was directly in charge of the day-to-day conduct of foreign affairs, he was told never to discuss them outside of this narrow group, but to join it whenever he had anything to report. For the rest of the month, however, Louis XIV found himself holding a council every day.

There was indeed much to be done. Every single major group must be notified of the new order of things, and a good many individuals besides; on March 10, for instance, aside from holding court, attending Mass, and approving the ceremonies for the Cardinal's funeral, the King sent for the permanent representatives of the clergy,

‡ The Surintendant des Finances, or Finance Minister, in charge of all the Crown's financial operations.
* Secretary of State for War and the Navy.
† Minister of State with a wide brief and oversight on Foreign Affairs, a department supposedly run by the two Brienne, father and son.
‡ Pierre Sèguier, who was in charge of the judiciary.
* An *ordonnance de comptant* was a slip of paper, signed by the Surintendant des Finances, which ordered the Treasury to pay the sum specified. This was done outside the normal channels and gave rise to many abuses.

who were to be told to attend his *lever* the next day; he asked for a full account of the garrisons in all fortified cities, both under the late King and since the beginning of his reign; and he ordered a message taken to the Spanish Ambassador severely criticizing Philip IV's action in a recent Italian dispute.

All this meant a direct break with tradition. Prime ministers, after all, had ruled France ever since Henri IV's death in 1610; still, most people expected the young monarch soon to tire of business and slowly let one of his ministers take over. More startling and even more unprecedented was the membership of the Council. Virtually without exception, the kings, in France, had called on their close male relatives and the main grandees for advice and support. Now, for the first time, not a single prince of the blood royal, not a single duke, not a single aristocrat, in fact, was allowed to share power with the monarch. A few years earlier, the princes and the great nobles had lost the civil war; now they found themselves excluded from all share in policy-making as well; and there was nothing they could do about it. Monsieur, the King's brother, was far too well trained ever to disobey; the prince de Condé was still licking his wounds in Chantilly; the prince de Conti, alone, could do nothing; and the duc de Longueville was dead. The Queen Mother herself was out, an unpalatable change she accepted after a brief protest.

The new order was announced without delay. On March 10, "the King gathered in the Queen Mother's bedroom, where the Councils had been held, all the people who usually attended them, the princes, the dukes, and the ministers of state; there, he told them that he had decided to rule his state alone without trusting to any cares but his own (these were his very words) and sent them away very politely telling them that he would call for them when he needed good advice."[78] That the former rebels should have been excluded from the new council is understandable, as is the King's feelings that the grandees had already more than enough power without influencing the government's decisions; but most remarkable, the one person responsible for the preservation of the state during Louis XIV's youth, the Queen Mother, found herself excluded as well.

That, in turn, entailed a drastic change in the way the King allotted his time. As long as Mazarin lived, Louis XIV had spent at most an hour of every day on his conferences with the Minister; now that he was really in charge, he found that he must curtail his entertainments.

As a result, "He decided to rise between eight and nine even though he went to sleep very late. When he left the Queen's bed, he went to his own; then he said his prayers and was dressed. His business then forced him to close the door of his bedroom [to the Court] . . . Around ten, the King went in to the Council and stayed there until noon. Then he attended Mass; and he gave the rest of the time before his dinner [i.e., 2 P.M.] to the public and especially to the Queens.

"After the meal, he usually stayed a rather long time with the royal family, then he went off to work with one of his ministers. He gave audiences to those who requested them, patiently listening to those who spoke to him. He took written requests from those who presented them to him and answered them on certain days which were reserved for this; in the same way a day was set apart for the Council of Conscience† which had been set up at the beginning of the regency and which he now revived . . .

"As he set himself to work he began to enjoy it and the desire he had to learn the things he needed to know soon made him very knowledgeable . . . He became politic in the affairs of state, a theologian as regarded the Church, precise when it came to the finances. He spoke well, always made the right decision in Council; he was sensitive to private people's interests but hated intrigues and flattery; he was harsh to the great nobles because he suspected they wanted to rule him.

"In person he was kind, polite, and of easy access to all, but with a serious and majestic mien which made him feared and respected and prevented even those closest to him from taking liberties even in private, though he was friendly and cheerful with the ladies."[79] That description, due to Mme de Motteville, is as accurate as it is thorough: from the very first, Louis XIV displayed so strong a consciousness of his unique position as to reduce most people to terrified silence. This awesome presence was, of course, partly corrected by youth and undoubted charm; but it was clear to all that prompt and willing obedience was the only possible response to a royal command. To all, that is, except the one man at court who thought himself not only far cleverer than anyone else but also indispensable

† The Council of Conscience had been set up to advise on ecclesiastical appointments.

because he was the only one able to make his way through the tangle of the royal finances: the Superintendent, Nicolas Fouquet.

Already on March 11, two days after the Cardinal's death, the King had notified Europe of the new order. Brienne was ordered to write all French ambassadors and ministers, who, in turn, were to tell the princes to whom they were accredited that, henceforth, the King would rule alone. And when it came to the most important message of all, Louis XIV took up the pen himself. "It is because of my confidence in your friendship that I must communicate to you the greatest sorrow ever to afflict me, the fact that it has pleased God to call to Himself . . . Cardinal Mazarin, thus depriving me of the advice of so worthy and faithful a minister," he wrote the newly restored Charles II of England. "I am sure that, as you love me, . . . you will feel some regret for his death especially when I tell you that what he most advised me to do, all through his last and most excruciating sufferings, was to be united to you with the closest friendship possible . . ."[80] As it was, there was not much reason to worry: Monsieur and the princess Henrietta were to be married within three weeks; but this kind of thoroughness, indeed of prudence, was typical of the King's methods.

That was startling enough on the part of a young man who, just a few weeks earlier, had apparently cared for nothing but his amusements; but at least a major foreign policy issue was involved. What the ministers noticed with barely repressed incredulity was that Louis XIV made it a point to follow up even the smallest details of government: on March 21, for instance, he gave orders that a search be made of all titles of nobility. This was typical of the new regime: not only did the King want order—and, therefore, proof that all who claimed to be noble actually were—but also non-nobles were subject to specific taxes; if vast numbers of commoners claimed they were noble, the tax yield would shrink.

This order, and another on April 4, that a tax on drinks levied in Normandy was to be abolished, actually revealed another facet of the King's disposition. Although at first glance Louis was acting only to relieve the overtaxed lower classes in the province, a traditional way of showing royal concern for the welfare of the subject, it was most unusual for the monarch to focus on an imposition so minor that it yielded a mere 150,000 livres a year. What this meant, of course, was that the King was aware of the smallest details of government;

and that, in turn, boded ill for any official who counted on his lack of knowledge or application and planned to go on doing business as usual.

None of the ministers made that mistake—none, that is, except one: the Surintendant. Naturally, he had his reasons: the first, undoubtedly, was his confident belief that the royal finances were so complicated, so opaque to nonprofessional scrutiny, that the King would never find out what he was up to; and he had a point. The irrational accretion of outdated practices, which had long made it virtually impossible for the King to know what he could afford, was rendered even more incomprehensible by the debts contracted during the Fronde. Governments do not scrutinize the conditions of desperately needed loans, so there was an undefined sum in outstanding paper, some of which had been bought at five or ten percent of par, but was now presented to the Treasury for payment in full: this not only cost the state large and unnecessary sums, it also enriched a number of thoroughly undeserving people. Then, too, the hodgepodge of taxes, national and local, was such that the state's income remained largely a mystery, especially since some of the consumption levies were farmed out to groups of financiers.

As it was, Fouquet also felt confident that no untrained young man —let alone a newly emancipated monarch—could long be bothered with tedious details. Finally, because all that had been true of Mazarin, Fouquet had begun to consider himself both cleverer than anyone else at Court and virtually immune from attack since he alone knew what he was talking about; so when Louis XIV announced that he intended to rule, Fouquet smugly assumed that this was no more than presumption and that, just as soon as the young man realized that governing was hard work, a new Prime Minister, in fact if not in name, would be appointed; and when it came to that, the Surintendant had no doubt at all that he himself would be the happy man.

As a result, he vowed obedience while absolutely disregarding the orders which inconvenienced him. Worse, he continued to help himself from the Treasury whenever he felt the need: he could always buy some of that depreciated paper, for instance, and redeem it to himself at full value. This was not only obviously theft, it also went directly against the King's orders: calling in Fouquet, Louis XIV told him that he was aware that the Surintendant's fortune owed much to his depredations; that the past would be forgotten; but that, in future, it must all stop. Without even a moment's apprehension, Fouquet, who was then spending vast sums building a château at Vaux, ignored the King's warning, safe in the knowledge that no one would ever be able to disentangle the mess. Unfortunately for him, he had forgotten Colbert, Mazarin's factotum, a man of immense intelligence and activity. As for the King, he knew just what he was doing: "It may seem strange that I decided to keep Fouquet when, already then, his *thefts* were known to me; but I knew he was clever and had a thorough knowledge of the workings of the government, which made me think that, if he admitted his faults and promised amendment, he might still be of great service. Still, in order to be safe, I gave him Colbert as a controller under the title of intendant [a standard midlevel office]. This was a man whom I trusted completely because I knew him to be very hardworking, intelligent, and honest."[81]

Here was an obvious challenge: if he failed to control his finances, Louis XIV would never reign in fact; still, merely dismissing the Surintendant was likely to have unpleasant consequences. The King thought long and deep about it and consulted with Colbert. In this, the first major decision that faced him, he demonstrated that he knew how to wait and how to keep a secret, but not without anguish. "The sight of the great positions [Fouquet] was preparing for himself, and the insolent purchases he had made‡ convinced me that his ambition was boundless*; and the general sufferings of all my [overtaxed] people were a constant call for justice," the King wrote some ten years later. "But what made him still guiltier toward me was that, far from recognizing the kindness I had shown him by retaining him in my Council, he had thought that proof he could fool me; far from becoming wiser, he merely tried to be cleverer.

"No matter what stratagems he practiced, however, I soon noticed his bad faith. For he was unable to stop his excessive outlays, fortifying his own fortresses, building palaces, forming cabals, and putting under his friends' names important offices which he bought at my own expense in the hope of making himself the supreme arbiter of the state.

‡ Fouquet had just bought the island of Belle Isle, was fortifying it and raising troops for its garrison.
* The Surintendant's emblem, still displayed everywhere at Vaux, was a squirrel with the motto: "How far will I not rise?"

"Although this behavior was unquestionably criminal, I first meant only to dismiss him; but I considered that his ambition would not allow him to withstand this reverse without attempting something new; I therefore thought it safer to have him arrested.

"I delayed the execution of my plan, however, and that gave me great pain for I could see that, at this time, he was using new and subtler means to rob me, and what annoyed me even more was that, in order to seem more powerful, he was also asking for private audiences; I was forced to grant them so that he would not suspect my plans, and I suffered him to make useless speeches to me while I knew the depth of his treachery.

"You† can well imagine that at the age I was then, my reason had to make a great effort to overcome my resentment . . . But I saw, first that the dismissal of the Surintendant had necessary connections with the renewal of the tax contracts‡; and also I knew that the summer, as it was then, was the time of year when these changes can least easily be made; besides which I wanted most of all to have 4 million livres at hand to meet any urgent needs. Thus I decided to await the fall."[82]

As for the other ministers, however, they soon caught on. On April 1, for instance, two letters went out to the provinces. One was written by Brienne, the other by Le Tellier. Both express the same sense of wonder. "The King," Brienne noted, "who since the death of M. le Cardinal has taken over the government, works at it with the most astonishing thoroughness. You would think, when you see him listening, deliberating, and deciding, that he had never done anything else, and the fact is that his subjects, even the cleverest and most critical, and the ambassadors equally admire his qualities of mind. His seriousness, his modesty, and his courtesy bring him a thousand blessings from all; he is straight and sparse in his speeches, deliberate and firm in his decisions and brings to all business a spirit of fairness and justice."[83] And, on his side, Le Tellier told the intendant* of Languedoc: "The King takes care of his business and works

† These memoirs were written as advice to the young Dauphin should the King die while his son was still a child.

‡ Many consumption taxes were farmed out to financiers, and the contracts governing their yield stood to be renewed.

* The intendants were the representatives of the central government in the provinces.

at it without intermission for three hours every morning and two more hours after dinner . . . It is impossible for those who have not seen it for themselves to believe that the King can have so great a disposition for and so deep an understanding of business . . . There is no doubt that he will be the greatest king we have had since the beginning of the monarchy."[84]

There must, of course, be an element of flattery in this appraisal; the King, after all, had only been in charge for some three weeks; but the ministers rightly perceived that the new developments were likely to be permanent. And every day, Louis XIV extended the limits of his personal control, while taking on that imperious tone which was to remain unaltered for the rest of his life. On March 18, for instance, he ordered Le Tellier to tell the widowed duchesse d'Orléans that her daughter (who was most reluctant) could either marry the Grand Duke of Tuscany's heir, as planned, or become a nun. That the young woman, who was in love with someone else, had good reason to resist marriage with a most unpleasant groom was beside the point: it was her duty to France to do as she was told, and her personal feelings were therefore unimportant; a harsh maxim, but one the King himself knew well.

At the same time, Louis XIV asserted his personal control of foreign policy. Early on, he wrote the comte d'Estrades, his Ambassador in London: "I have decided to answer myself all the letters which I have asked my ambassadors to write me . . . when they need to convey information the importance of which requires deeper secrecy" and de Lionne, increasingly in charge of Foreign Affairs, added in a covering letter: "It is a thought he had of himself . . . I have the honor to read him the most secret dispatches which are addressed through me after they have been deciphered . . . He calls me in to tell me his feelings and intentions about the answer which I draft article by article according to his instructions and in his presence, and His Majesty corrects me when I misunderstand him."[85] One by one, the working methods of the rest of the reign were thus established.

Still, it was one thing to impress the ministers and quite another to rule effectively. Ever since Richelieu's death in 1642, the French had grown accustomed to a weak central government, first under the regency, then during the Fronde, and finally under Mazarin, who believed in conciliation and suppleness. The Parlement de Paris, it is true, had been curbed; but in 1661 it was still possible to see that as a purely temporary position. As for the royal family, although it had learned that armed rebellion did not pay, it still considered itself above the law. One moment's hesitation on the King's part could therefore have disastrous consequences, and he knew it; so here, too, he struck fast and hard.

First, he tackled the Parlement of Aix. Perier, one of its conseillers, had led the resistance to the royal government, so he was ordered to come immediately to Paris, there no doubt to be browbeaten into submission. Immediately, in a move highly reminiscent of the Fronde, the Parlement's several chambers met, sent remonstrances to the King, and ordered that Perier stay in place. The royal answer was prompt and striking.

First, the Parlement's decision was annulled by the *conseil d'en haut,* a section of the Council which sat as the court of last resort. This was undoubtedly legal; but it was also one of the royal prerogatives the Queen Regent had been forced to abandon during the Fronde. It was thus highly significant that, within a month of his taking over, Louis XIV should have chosen to use it. Nor was this all: a letter was sent to M. de Raguse, the president of the Aix Parlement, to express His Majesty's displeasure at his having thus assembled the several chambers, and to order him to Paris forthwith; should he delay he was to be arrested and imprisoned in the fortress of Montélimar—the very fate then overtaking Perier.

This quick and effective response quelled any further taste for rebellion. The Président de Raguse came straight to court, where he was reminded at some length that his first duty was to the King, and, a month later, allowed to go home. There was no more trouble from Aix after that.

It was just as important, in view of their still recent behavior, to impress the need for obedience on the several members of the royal family. The most dangerous of them, potentially, was Monsieur; but he had been well trained by the Queen Mother and never dreamed of opposing his brother. Mademoiselle, who had ordered the guns of the Bastille fired on the King's army back in 1652, was thoroughly tamed; and the prince de Condé, just back from seven years in the service of Spain, only longed for peace and comfort. Still, there could be no doubt that they, too, would seize any favorable opportunity.

Thus, when in May 1661 the comte de Soissons† proceeded to misbehave, the King struck immediately.

Dueling had long been forbidden in France, but it was only under Richelieu that the prohibition was actually enforced; under the regency, duels became once again an everyday occurrence, but then Louis XIV announced that he intended the law to be obeyed; so when the comte de Soissons called out the duc de Navailles as a result of a dispute between their respective wives, the King, without a moment's hesitation, exiled Soissons to a remote country house. This was particularly startling, not only because no one had thought the ban applied to royalty but also because the comtesse de Soissons was none other than Olympe Mancini, Louis's former mistress.

In fact, the case brought together several elements sure to arouse the King's displeasure. First, of course, was the comte de Soissons's assumption that he could disregard a royal order; there was, Louis XIV clearly felt, only a very short step from this to political opposition; then, the subject of the dispute had been the claim by the comtesse de Soissons, as Superintendent‡ of the Queen's Household, of prerogatives which properly belonged to the duchesse de Navailles as *dame d'honneur,* and the King was not about to countenance that sort of abuse by a woman trading on their former relationship; finally the dispute had disrupted the good order of the Court, and that, it soon became plain, was something the King would not tolerate.

The comte de Soissons's exile was, in itself, only a minor incident, if a revealing one. Louis XIV's steady work with his ministers might last only a few months; but then, on September 5, 1661, the King served final notice on all possible doubters that he really meant to rule, and to rule absolutely. On that day, the apparently powerful Fouquet was not only dismissed from all his offices but arrested and interned in a fortress while his papers were seized; within days, it was announced that he would be tried on a capital charge.

Because the Sun King has long been the archetype of the absolute monarch, we tend to think of him as all-powerful from the start. That this was not the case during the Fronde and its aftermath is plain enough. It is more startling to see that even after he had seized

† The comte de Soissons was a member of the Duke of Savoy's family, and was closely related to the King himself.
‡ The Superintendent, usually a member of the royal family, was the Queen's chief attendant; next came the *dame d'honneur.*

control of the government, Louis XIV found it necessary to plan and plot in the deepest secrecy before he could dismiss a dishonest and unfaithful minister.

Fouquet's fall was decided by the King on May 3, 1661, according to Colbert; but as has been noted by Louis himself, his immediate dismissal was impossible because it would have provoked a grave financial crisis; then, too, there was the distinct possibility that the Surintendant, once dismissed, would try to start a new civil war: he was known, after all, to be fortifying Belle Isle; many key members of the Parlement de Paris and the royal administration were in his debt and might well rise to defend him while defeating the King's attempt at making himself an absolute ruler. Thus, in the worst possible case, the state would go bankrupt just as a new Fronde began.

Obviously some careful planning was required—something a less prudent monarch might not have realized; so, together, and in the deepest secrecy, Louis XIV and Colbert set about undermining Fouquet's position. Their first step was also the most important. Among the Surintendant's many offices, that of *procureur général* (attorney general) to the Parlement gave him immunity from arrest; he must therefore be somehow tricked into resigning. That was achieved, simply enough, by heavy hints that, as soon as the elderly Séguier died,* the King intended to appoint Fouquet Chancellor of France; and since that great official was at the head of the judiciary, he obviously could not at the same time retain a subordinate office. Amazingly, Fouquet swallowed it all—as clear a case of hubris as can be found anywhere. Now he could be arrested when the time came, and thus prevented from starting a new civil war.

Next, the King and Colbert had to provide for financial stability. This was done not only by accumulating funds in the Treasury, but also by enlisting—still in the deepest secrecy—some major outside help; thus Mazarin's chief heir, the new duc de Mazarin, who was a very rich man indeed, was approached; and being fully conscious that he owed his fortune to the King's refusal of it, he promptly agreed to lend the huge sum of 2 million livres whenever the King should need it. This was most important: since under Fouquet the Treasury lived from day to day on the short-term loans made by financiers

* The Chancellor was appointed for life; and despite his age (he was seventy-three) and his apparent frailty, Séguier survived until 1672.

friendly with the Surintendant, that source of ready money was expected to dry up as soon as the news of the arrest became public.

All through this time Louis XIV went on playing the grateful ruler every time he saw Fouquet; along with the hints about the Chancellor's office, the Surintendant was given to understand that, as had sometimes been the case in the sixteenth century, he would also be the effective head of the government.

He might, perhaps, have begun to wonder about the King's real feelings toward him when in early August, the power to sign the *états de distribution*† was taken away from him; but any misgiving he may have felt was allayed by his triumph on the nineteenth of that month.

Whatever his faults, Fouquet was not only a man of enormous charm but also a remarkably enlightened connoisseur; so when he decided to build himself a château on his estate of Vaux, he not only spent money as if his fortune were endless (and, in the sense that he kept helping himself to Treasury funds, it was), he also hired three of the greatest geniuses in the history of French art. The house itself was designed by Le Vau and turned out to be a marvel of grace, restraint, and majestic charm in a brand-new style; the rooms were planned and often frescoed by Lebrun, a painter and decorator of immense talent; the gardens were laid out by Lenôtre, with straight allées, parterres that looked as if they were pieces of embroidery, and water —in fountains, basins, and canals—everywhere.

The results were as stunning to the contemporaries as they have remained to this day‡: a whole new French style was born made of grandeur and classical measure, and it was soon imitated by the rest of Europe. Naturally, so brilliant, so sumptuous an estate deserved a proper inauguration; so the King, the Queens, and the entire Court were invited to a day-and night-long party on August 19.

It was typical of Fouquet that along with the Court proper, he made sure that wits like Mme de Sévigné (people did not yet realize that she was also a great writer) and poets like La Fontaine were present. There was a play by Molière and music by Lulli, fireworks and endless meals; and although no one quite realized it, on that day

† The forms allowing payments by the Treasury. This was a major obstacle to his continued plundering.

‡ Some forty miles east of Paris, and in superb condition, Vaux is now open to the public.

French art, music, and literature moved to the forefront of European culture.

For the host and most of the guests, the great fete of Vaux proved conclusively that the Surintendant was the most powerful man in France. The King's feelings may easily be imagined. Contrary to legend, however, it was not anger at the magnificence of the display which made him decide on Fouquet's fall: that was already well under way.

Indeed, the whittling-down process continued. Within a week of the fete, on August 25, Louis XIV announced that he intended to put an end to the use, and abuse, of the ordonnances de comptant. These were simple notes in which the King, or the Surintendant, simply ordered the payment, immediately and in cash, of a specified sum to a specified person. That simple process circumvented all the safeguards set up to prevent the looting of the Treasury; when it was used by the King himself there was obviously nothing to be said: the Treasury was simply the repository of his money. When it was used by the Surintendant, it meant that vast sums could be spent without explanation.

The King's announcement should have worried Fouquet: within one month, he had become unable to order the payment of any sum at all by the Treasury; but he was so sure of his power and of his favor that he appears not to have worried; and when, on the twenty-ninth, the Court left Fontainebleau for Nantes, the capital of Brittany, where the King was to address the Parlement de Bretagne, Fouquet went along.

Indeed, Louis XIV kept appearances up until the last moment; on the morning of September 5, he announced that he intended to hunt after holding a Council and that his guards were to be ready to serve as his escort—thus giving himself a reason for gathering enough men to ensure a fast and quiet move against Fouquet. As for what happened next, the King described it himself in a letter he sent Anne of Austria.

"Madame my Mother," he wrote, "I had already written you this morning to tell you that my order to arrest the Surintendant had been carried out; I am now happy to give you the details of the business: you know I had intended it for a long time . . . You cannot imagine the difficulty I had in just finding a means of speaking privately with Artagnan [the commanding officer of the Musketeers];

for I am bothered all day by an infinity of people who are all very wide awake and who, given the smallest clue, might have guessed much: still, two days ago, I ordered him to be in readiness and to use du Claveau and Maupertuis instead of the lieutenant and brigadiers of my Musketeers, most of whom are ill; I felt the greatest impatience in the world for it all to be over, since nothing else was keeping me here. Finally, this morning, the Surintendant having come to work with me as usual, I talked first about one thing, then about another, and pretended I was looking for some papers until, through my study window, I saw Artagnan in the castle's courtyard; I then let the Surintendant go who, after having spoken with La Feuillade for a short time at the bottom of the stairs, disappeared just as Artagnan was greeting the Sieur Le Tellier; so that the poor Artagnan thought he had missed [Fouquet], and sent me word by Maupertuis that he suspected someone must have told him to flee; but he caught up with him in front of the big church and arrested him . . . at about noon. He asked for the papers he was carrying, in which I was told I would find the truth about Belle Isle; but I have so much other business I have not been able to look at them yet. In the meantime I ordered the Sieur Boucherat to seize all the Surintendant's papers, and the Sieur Pellot to do the same at Pellisson's [Fouquet's assistant], whom I had arrested also. I had said that I wanted to go hunting this morning and under that pretext had my carriages ready and my Musketeers mounted; I also ordered the guard companies I have here to be ready for exercises in the meadow so that they would be ready to march against Belle Isle. As soon, therefore, as the business was done, the Surintendant was put into one of my carriages, escorted by my Musketeers; he is being taken to the fort at Angers and awaits me there, while his wife has been ordered to Limoges. Fourille is just off with my guards company to the bay of Belle Isle, whence he will send Chavigni to take the fort over with a hundred French and sixty Swiss Guards; and if perchance the Surintendant's men there wanted to resist, I ordered that the assault be given. I first wanted to wait here for the news of all this, but the orders are so thorough that there is no likelihood of the thing failing, and so I will return [to Paris] without further delay, and this is the last letter I will write you on this trip. I then talked about this event with the gentlemen who are here with me; I told them frankly that I had taken my decision four months ago, that you were the only one who knew about it, and that

I had told the Sieur le Tellier only two days ago so that the orders could be sent off. I also told them I no longer wanted to have a Surintendant, and that I would take care of the finances myself with some trustworthy people who will work under me, since I know that is the only way for me to be prosperous while unburdening my people. You will not be surprised to hear that there are many unhappy faces, but I am glad they see I am not the dupe they had thought me."[86]

Fouquet's arrest struck the Court like a thunderclap in a serene sky: not only were a great many people of every rank part of the former Surintendant's party, they had also written a great many compromising letters and these, along with all Fouquet's other papers, had been seized by the King's orders. As a result, all concerned felt the deepest apprehension: even if they were not arrested, surely they must incur the King's dislike; and in an age when favor could do anything, that was a terrible prospect. In fact, with perhaps a half-dozen exceptions, they had nothing to fear. Enormously vindictive toward those who consciously disobeyed or opposed him, Louis XIV was always ready to forgive those who merely erred. Even Pellisson, Fouquet's assistant, ended his life as royal historiographer.

Still, partly because an example had to be made, partly because the Surintendant had deliberately ignored the King's demand that he change his earlier behavior, there could be no mercy for Fouquet. Not only was he closely imprisoned, he was also to be tried by a special tribunal; and at the same time his associates' books were seized so that they, too, could be made to disgorge their ill-gotten gains. Thus Fouquet, once the most visible sign that it paid to be corrupt, had now become the symbol of the King's unbreakable will to reform the state. It must, however, be said that his was no show trial: the King may have made it plain that he expected the death penalty—in the end Fouquet was imprisoned for life—but the trial was conducted in a thoroughly open and aboveboard manner, with some of the most respected men in France acting as prosecutors and judges.

That was still in the future: but, aside from the arrest itself, what made the most difference, in September 1661, was Louis XIV's decision that henceforth there would be no more Surintendant: the abolition of the office completed that of the Prime Minister. Of course, the finances still required some sort of day-to-day management: even if the King meant to supervise the department, he could hardly take on the thousand and one tasks that must be seen to; so he created a Council of Finances headed by Villeroy, his former tutor, which Colbert attended as an intendant; a fact, it soon became clear that Colbert was the most important man there, in fact the King confirmed when, in 1665, he gave him the title of Contrôleur Général.

Still, Louis XIV meant just what he said when he announced that henceforth he would be his own Surintendant. On that same September 5, for instance, he wrote not only the duc de Mazarin, but also a former official, Hervart: "The late M. le cardinal having assured me, in the last days of his life, that I could always rely on you for an assistance of two or three million livres whenever the good of my service forced me to bring about some change in the administration of my finances, now that I have had, for divers reasons, to order the arrest of the Surintendant, I am writing you this to tell you that you will please me by providing, either alone or with your friends, the largest sum you can so that I may use it in case of need. Upon which I await your answer."[87]

It was not unprecedented for a king to borrow money, far from it; but the whole subject was thought to be somehow contemptible, and at any rate beneath the royal notice. Money of course was necessary, but only merchants thought about it and the great nobles all had people to manage their estates; it was a rare duke who ever looked at the accounts. There was thus something very shocking about a king of France announcing that, henceforth, he would be his own finance minister. That Louis XIV, so near the beginning of his personal reign, should have braved that particular kind of prejudice says a great deal about his notion of kingship.

Here, once again, a few clichés must be explored. We tend to think of the Sun King as a wild spendthrift, who built sumptuous palaces and virtually bankrupted France. Nothing, in fact, could be further from the truth. All through the Fronde the monarchy was, as we have seen, nearly penniless; and even in the late fifties, Mazarin's government had lived from hand to mouth. Louis XIV was thus very well aware of what it meant to have no money; he also knew that neither a spirited foreign policy nor the kind of display essential to maintaining the monarchy's prestige was possible without adequate financing; so, from September 1661 on, he made very sure that his income would always be sufficient; and since there was a long tradition of peculation on the part of a variety of officials and financiers, only royal supervision could improve the situation.

Today, a head of state who vows to watch every penny can count on instant popularity; but when Louis XIV assumed control of his finances, some of the courtiers began to refer to him as a bourgeois monarch, an insult if ever there was one. The King, typically, paid no attention. Already in 1661 he knew how little those kinds of whispers meant, and he had the best of reasons to go right on; at long last, he could count on governing as he thought best without depending on the goodwill of a small group of greedy and often dishonest financiers.

Still, even in the seventeenth century, when national budgets took in a far smaller proportion of the gross national product than they do today, it required a good deal of technical know-how to figure out just what was what. In this, of course, Louis XIV was helped by Colbert, who had precisely the right sort of expertise and was astonishingly diligent besides. Indeed, in the new Council, the key business was discussed with three men only—Colbert, Le Tellier, and Lionne; the Chancellor, who was in charge of the judiciary, was often present but spoke only about his own direct concerns. Lionne, who was increasingly replacing Brienne, was in charge of foreign affairs; Le Tellier, helped by Louvois, his son, looked after all military business; and Colbert, who seems to have had an inexhaustible capacity for work, monopolized the finances, police, navy, public works, commerce, the colonies, the arts, and the King's Household. With all that, however, the King made a point of knowing just what was being done, understanding it all, and reserving all major and many minor decisions to himself.

"People were rightly surprised," he wrote, "that I was so quickly able to penetrate the obscurities which so many clever Surintendants had never been able to solve. But what should explain it is the natural difference between the Prince's interest and that of his Surintendants, for private people have no greater care, in their office, than that of retaining the freedom of disposing of everything as they please; so they use their talents more often in making all this unfathomable than in making it easily understood, while a king brings about clearness and order since he can only lose through confusion."[88]

What Louis XIV found, as he and Colbert started disentangling the many complications carefully set up by Fouquet, was nothing short of appalling. Massive thefts had been allowed, so steps were taken to recover as much of the missing funds as possible; but that was only a one-time operation. Far more important, it became clear, first, that although the taxes were indeed paid by the people, a significant portion of these funds failed to reach the Treasury. Without any rise in the tax rate, the yield went from 54 million livres in 1662 to 88.5 million in 1664.

Under Fouquet, almost a sixth of the already shrunken revenue had been alienated: certain debts were given priority by being assigned the yield of specific taxes; thus, in 1662 over 16 million livres never reached the Treasury. Needless to say, those favored creditors were closely connected to the Surintendant so that, in many cases, the payments were altogether abusive. Finally, adding still further to the confusion was yet another unsound practice, that of the *anticipations*. When the Treasury ran out of money, it would borrow (usually at horrendous rates) against the following year's income, thus creating an even larger future deficit and a greater need to borrow. In 1662, for instance, the sum involved came to some 13 million livres.[89] Add that to the alienations, and it came to almost half the budget. Worse, on the day Fouquet was arrested, all the income for that year had already been spent, along with 26 million in anticipation of 1662, while 9.5 million still remained due: it was little wonder the King was perennially penniless.

Given all this, and Colbert's absolute honesty, the King might well have left it up to him to clear up the mess; instead, he saw to it himself; and to make sure that, henceforth, the state of the Treasury would be clear at all times, a little notebook,* bound in red leather and stamped in gold with the crown and fleur-de-lis, was prepared for him. In it, all the different sources of income, all the known outlays for the year, were listed, so that, at a glance, Louis XIV could be aware of the state of his finances. Since he was determined to balance the budget, he undertook no new expenditure without first seeing whether he had the necessary resources; and, to that effect, he carried the current notebook in a pocket.

One of the consequences of the old system had been that while the King was perennially poor, people were also overtaxed. This Louis

* These little books have been preserved for most years of the reign and can be consulted at the Bibliothèque Nationale.

XIV decided to remedy—as he now could. "Nothing seemed more urgent to me," he wrote, "than to relieve my people . . . The state of my finances seemed to preclude this, and, in any case, made for a delay; but one should always be in a hurry to do good . . . I therefore ignored every other consideration and immediately forgave three millions on the *tailles* which were about to be collected."[90] As it turned out this was the shrewdest of moves: it made for instant popularity without further embarrassing the Treasury, which was now recovering fast. And by 1664 the French finances were the healthiest in Europe: the expenditure for that year, including all the costs of a war, came to 63,071,008 livres; the revenue to 63,602,796—a surplus of over half a million livres. To be sure, that was not a huge sum, but it came within two years of a 30-million deficit. Even better, in the following years, with the increase of prosperity, the surplus grew significantly. For a king who realized that money was strength, there could be no more satisfying result.

All this—the assumption of power, the fall of Fouquet—had happened within a mere six months. By the end of September, it was clear that the King had indeed carried out a revolution. Not only did he control his finances, his was also the last word on every aspect of political and Court life; he alone gave out the plums—pensions, titles, offices, promotions—which had earlier been in the Prime Minister's gift; he alone determined policy and made sure it was carried out. Free for the first time in French history from the pressures of the royal princes and the magnates, the King decided everything in the deepest of secrecy: now there were no leaks from the new, restricted Council. Then, as if all this were not enough, on November 1, at 11:55 A.M., the Queen gave birth to a son. The succession was assured, intrigues by members of the royal family without object. Free from all the uncertainties which had plagued his own father until 1638, Louis XIV now offered his dazzled subjects the very image of the rising sun.

V
Government and the Court

THE CHANGES made by Louis XIV in the first year of his reign amounted to nothing less than a revolution. Even though Richelieu, in his long tenure as Prime Minister under Louis XIII, had shown the way toward centralization and firm government, he had been hampered by three major obstacles: the lack, until September 1638, of an heir, which gave the ever factious princes a very strong position; an endless and sometimes disastrous war which created constant financial strain and widespread dissatisfaction; and the fact that, in France, even the most powerful minister could never be as effective as the King: it was always legitimate to resist "evil advisers."

In the very act of taking over the government, Louis XIV freed himself of all these obstacles. France was at peace and prosperous, so he could reform the finances; there could be no doubt whatsoever that he himself was in charge, and that the ministers merely carried out his instructions; and he had an heir. Then, too, the devastations caused by the Fronde had been so great, and were still so recent, that a strong central authority, able to preserve civil peace, seemed highly desirable; and the Parlement, although anxious to recover its lost influence, was still far too unpopular to offer significant resistance.

The opportunity for reform was there, but it had to be seized. In the end, the King's understanding of the situation and his willingness to move fast may be his greatest claims to lasting glory. A weaker man, one less sure of his goals, might well have wasted the opening offered by circumstances in 1661, but Louis XIV showed that he was not only determined but also remarkably clear-eyed. In spite of the lessons taught him by Mazarin, he was not yet proficient in the arts of government. As it turned out, however, this knowledge, which he acquired quickly enough, was not necessary at the outset, and he realized that himself when he looked back some ten years later.

"A king's function," he wrote then, "consists mainly in letting common sense rule; it always come easily and naturally."[91] Of course, in his case, common sense was helped by the very best of advice. Le Tellier, who had long been in government, was fifty-nine in 1662 and a seasoned statesman; and in the forthcoming—and highly effective—reorganization of the army, he was assisted by Louvois,* his hardworking and brilliant son. Thus, he was able to give the King all the information needed to set the best possible policy in circumstances where really troubling decisions were very seldom needed. Colbert, a master when it came to all financial, industrial, commercial, and artistic questions, was the most devoted of servants, and one who always had the information the King wanted; and finally Lionne, although not, perhaps, of quite the same caliber as his colleagues, was nonetheless thoroughly informed as to the state of Europe; since the King himself determined France's foreign policy, the arrangement worked quite well.

Indeed, in some ways, the King knew more than his ministers. Partly, no doubt, it was because he felt in himself the strength and confidence of youth; but also, almost alone, he realized that at long last France had become the greatest power in Europe; and he prized what he called *ma gloire* above all things. That, in itself, is a misleading expression. What the King had in mind was not glory in the Napoleonic sense, the fame won by famous victories, but rather a kind of high repute, an untarnished name. Boldness was necessary—cowardice being one of the antitheses of *gloire*—but also fairness, and generosity. To his contemporaries and posterity alike, Louis XIV wanted to be known as a great king, if possible the greatest ever to rule France; and that required a great deal: justice, moderation, compassion, enlightenment along with pride.

Still, none of these qualities would be really effective unless they were seen to be so: for the first time a ruler understood the uses of publicity. Of course, other monarchs before Louis XIV had paid

---

* It was possible in seventeenth-century France to buy, with the King's permission, an estate which carried a title; thus Le Tellier had purchased Louvois and its marquessate for his son.

poets, painters, and writers to celebrate their virtues; but that had been done more as a form of flattery; indeed, the praise given, for instance, to Marie de Médicis, the King's grandmother, to her face, was more than counterbalanced by her public reputation. Now Louis XIV saw that the right sort of publicity will, in fact, make it easier to carry through a policy: on a simple level, if you are thought to be a fierce warrior, you are much less likely to be attacked than if you are considered weak and yielding. In this particular case, if the King was thought to be a model monarch, he would clearly be obeyed faster and more willingly; and that, in turn, would create new habits, a new climate in which a repetition of the Fronde would become unthinkable.

This was something Colbert understood thoroughly, so he set about magnifying the King's merits. Writers were pensioned to praise the monarch; painters exalted his rule; historians chronicled his every success; coins were struck to comment on the glories of the reign, and Louis XIV himself made very sure to reward all those who helped bring him renown. In the mid-sixties, for instance, he visited the *petite Académie,* a body set up to study Roman and other historical data and furnish the same kind of concise, laudatory sentences as were to be found on ancient monuments and medals; and he did not spare his compliments.

"You may see how greatly I esteem you, Messieurs," he said, "since I entrust you with the thing in the world I value most, and that is my *gloire;* I am sure you will do wonders; I will try, for myself, to give you material deserving of being shaped by people as clever as you are."[92]

The King's very appellation adds an interesting note to this effort. It had long been the custom in France to give the monarch a qualifying epithet: Louis XIII, for instance, had been the Just. We in the twentieth century tend to think of Louis XIV as the Sun King; and in fact, starting with his role in the *Ballet de la Nuit* in 1653, he had often been identified with the sun. That, in a number of obvious ways, seemed an apposite symbol: as all light and warmth come from the sun, as only cold and dark can be expected without it, so the King brought happiness and prosperity to the realm, and without him all was dark and drear. Then, too, the sun is king of the heavens, dazzlingly bright, golden, and splendid; so, indeed, all through the reign the sun was frequently used as the King's emblem. His appellation, however, was another thing altogether. To his contemporaries, and to posterity as well, Louis XIV was Ludovicus Magnus, Louis le Grand, just as in the next century Tsar Peter of Russia or King Frederick II of Prussia were to be called "the Great"; a title which, in Louis XIV's case, implied achievements in a variety of fields.

A great king, in seventeenth-century France, was naturally expected to win whatever wars he waged; but he also had to foster the arts, encourage trade, build splendid palaces, look after the nobility and, perhaps most important, see that his people prospered. "We must," Louis XIV wrote, "consider our subjects' good before our own. They are indeed like a part of ourselves since we are the head of the body, and they the limbs. We must give them laws for their own advantage only; and we must use the power we have over them only so as more effectively to bring them happiness."[93]

Besides its obvious common sense, that exhortation also nicely disposes of the purely apocryphal remark *"L'état, c'est moi"* (I am the state). Far from being the self-absorbed, self-indulgent tyrant of legend, Louis XIV, all through the reign, cared greatly for his subjects' welfare, and knew that he had even more duties than rights.

The King's obligations, in fact, went further still. His subjects must not only be prosperous, they must also be free. That may seem like a paradox, given the fact that Louis XIV ruled absolutely: after all, he alone determined which taxes were to be paid† and how the revenue should be spent; he alone made war and peace, negotiated and ratified treaties, commanded all the armed forces of the state; he made laws, and they were just such as he pleased: indeed, the obligatory final formula of all edicts was *"car tel est nôtre bon plaisir"* (for such is our pleasure); he could hire and fire every single government employee, from minister to copyist, from soldier to general; he appointed bishops, archbishops, and abbots;‡ he gave out the eagerly sought Court positions which ensured frequent access to his presence, as well as pensions, titles of nobility, and every other reward. He could have anyone arrested, and imprisoned, at will, and for any length of time; he could impose censorship on all publications. How then could the people be called free?

† Certain taxes had to be voted by a variety of provincial estates; but in fact, under Louis XIV, they almost invariably were.
‡ Subject to confirmation by the Pope, in theory; but that had become purely a formality. The Pope never refused his assent.

Liberty, in seventeenth-century France, was a well-understood notion wholly unrelated to what it has now become; it did not imply popular representation or the kind of immunities enshrined in the Bill of Rights; rather it meant, first, the continued validity of a wide array of privileges: freedom from arrest for the Procureur Général of the Paris Parlement or the right, if you were one of its judges, to buy and sell your office; the exclusive right to manufacture specific articles or the exemption from certain taxes; self-government for incorporated cities or the right to be judged only by a specific court. These traditional "freedoms" were as disparate as they were numerous. Just as important was the opportunity to pursue one's life and career safe from the kind of predators who, especially in time of civil disorders, preyed upon the weak: princes and great nobles or crooked moneylenders. In that sense freedom, which was wholly unrelated to democracy, meant protection by the government of all those who were unable to defend themselves: in essence, the guarantee of a fair society. In 1774, the American rebels claimed they had a right to life, liberty, and the pursuit of happiness; to a Frenchman in 1661, the pursuit of happiness was, far and away, the most important thing; and because France was still partly feudal, it was crucial to have a powerful, unrestricted central government, able to right wrongs as they occurred.

In the same way, a reform of the judiciary had become essential. "Its offices," the King noted, "were filled by chance or money,* rather than selection and merit; many judges had little experience and less knowledge; my predecessors' ordinances on age and length of service were almost invariably ignored . . . My Council, even, instead of regulating the other jurisdictions, all too often created confusion by giving out a quantity of contradictory decisions, all equally bearing my name and as if ordered by me, which made the disorder more shameful still."[94] When injustice was done, when equity called for a reversal, only the King could come to the rescue of the subject's freedom.

Molière, always the true mirror of his society, gives a striking example of this in *Tartuffe*. At the end of the play, Orgon, the head of the family, at long last realizes he has been fooled: Tartuffe, far from being a saint, is a lecherous crook; but just when, in a fit of righteous

---

* Anyone with enough money could buy himself an office in the Parlement and thus become a judge, whether he was qualified or not.

anger, Orgon orders Tartuffe out of the house, the impostor triumphantly points to the deed of gift signed by Orgon; this, he says, is *his* house: it is for Orgon and his family to leave. The deed is valid; Orgon and his family are utterly ruined. And just at that point, a law officer comes in. *"Nous vivons,"* he says, *"sous un roi ennemi de la fraude"* (We are ruled by a king who will not tolerate injustice)[95]; and Orgon is saved: that is a perfect example of the kind of freedom the French meant.

Of course, Orgon lived in Paris, close to King and Court. In all likelihood, someone in Dijon or Montpellier would have been too far away for effective redress from the central government. For that reason, and also to promote a more effective rule, the whole system of delegated power was now transformed. Traditionally, each one of the French provinces was run by a governor who received a large salary and was either a member of the royal family or a great aristocrat. In times of unrest, this obviously had disastrous consequences: the governor, leaning on the resources of his province, felt quite able, at best to disregard, at worst to fight, the King's government. Even when all was peaceful, the governor naturally promoted his own interest and that of his family, friends, and followers before that of the King. Already under Richelieu, therefore, a new kind of official, the *intendant,* had been created, as a direct representative of the central government; but with the Fronde the power of the intendants had faded and that of the governors increased. Now, the position of governor became, essentially, honorary. It still carried a large salary; it still entailed grand receptions in the province and all kinds of precedence, but it lost all power. Indeed, most of the governors, instead of residing, at least part of the year, in their province as they had once done, were expected to pay only flying visits every now and again—to open the estates, for instance, and, where necessary, ensure that the requisite amount of tax was voted; but day-to-day effective power belonged to the intendant, appointed by the King from the increasingly large and competent body of middle-class men on which he relied more year by year. Since he had no previous connection with the province, the intendant not only carried out the King's policies without regard to local interests, he could also ensure the freedom of the subject in his area: even away from Paris order was now expected.

Of course, merely ordering the governors to stay at court would not have done much good; for centuries kings had tried, and failed, to do just that. It was Louis XIV's great achievement that he made them want to be there; indeed, he so arranged things that leaving him for any length of time became the greatest calamity imaginable.

There was a variety of reasons for this startling new development. Princes and great aristocrats were just as greedy for promotions, favors, and pensions as the rest of the world; and the King now made it plain that all these were reserved for the people he saw frequently; absence, therefore, was quite exactly self-destructive; then it became clear that, within this golden circle, he handed out rewards precisely as he chose, but that good behavior—i.e., unfailing and prompt obedience—would help; and finally, trading on the frivolity, snobbism, and taste for glamour to be found everywhere and always, he made the Court the one place where all these foibles could be indulged.

"Disorder," Louis XIV wrote about France in 1661, "was everywhere, and my Court, generally, was still quite far from the condition in which I trust you will find it. The *gens de qualité* [the nobles], who were accustomed to continual negotiations with a minister who did not object to them, and to whom they had sometimes been a necessity, always claimed imaginary rights on whatever took their fancy. No governor of a fortress but was difficult to manage; no request but was mixed with reproaches about the past or a future discontent which was to be seen and feared; favors were demanded and extorted, expected by all if given to one man, and therefore received without gratitude, so that they were used only to wound those to whom they were refused."[96]

Even as early as 1661, no one would have dared to behave with Louis XIV as they had with Mazarin; but now the Court gradually became the center of all pleasure. Already in May 1661 the *Gazette de France* gave an example of this. "On the 8th of this month," it related, "Their Majesties, accompanied by M le prince and Mme la princesse de Condé and many other lords and ladies were entertained on the canal in barges while trumpet fanfares sounded and the King gave a splendid supper to all present. That same day, the princess of Tuscany† along with Mademoiselle‡ and several other persons of quality arrived at Court . . . and the next day accompanied

† Mlle d'Orléans, that is, whom the King had forced to marry the Hereditary Prince of Tuscany.
‡ The King's cousin and former leader of the Fronde.

Their Majesties to an outing on the same canal and to the Comédie Française.*

"On the 10th, the King offered her a very splendid dinner . . . The illustrious company then went for an outing and, when they returned, were offered a ball."[97] That, perhaps, was not so unusual a schedule for the Court of a great country; but then, Louis XIII had been notoriously averse to this (or any other) kind of entertainment, and the Fronde had, to all intents and purposes, put a stop to pleasure; thus, these kinds of repeated fetes now seemed especially attractive.

Very quickly, however, Louis XIV realized that more was needed if the Court was to be a center of attraction, so he deliberately gave it glamour by fostering the very latest fashions: at this point they entailed wearing, if you were a man, a short, bolero-like jacket open over a bouffant white shirt liberally sprinkled with lace; a kind of skirt reaching to just below the knee, with stockings underneath; and clumps of ribbons everywhere—on shoulders, sleeves, cuffs, jacket, skirt, knees, ankles, and shoes. It is hard to think of a sillier-looking costume, but, as it was, the King used its constant changes to the fullest. Then, in 1662, he designed a special new coat made of blue silk or velvet embroidered with gold and silver—the *justaucorps à brevet*—which required written permission before it could be worn, and which therefore signaled that its owner was high in the royal favor. And, naturally, he gave increasingly frequent and splendid entertainments which culminated in the famed Carrousel of 1662.

"There are some nations," Louis XIV noted, "where the majesty of kings consists for the great part in not allowing themselves to be seen† and this may be reasonable among minds accustomed to servitude, people who can only be governed by fear and terror; but such is not the genius of our Frenchmen . . .

"These social pleasures which give the people at Court a proper familiarity with us touches and charms them more than one can say. On their side, the people enjoy the show."[98]

The King was quite right; just as, today, some of the Queen of

* This meant that French plays were performed as opposed to the Comédie italienne, the Commedia dell'arte.
† An allusion to Spain, where the King virtually never left his palaces and was only visible, on rare occasions, to the grandees; it is typical of Louis XIV to contrast the free French to the enslaved Spanish.

England's popularity is no doubt due to the splendid spectacle she occasionally provides, so, too, in seventeenth-century France the middle and lower classes, who, after all had neither radio nor television nor stereos and virtually never went to the theater, loved a public and lavish display; it flattered them as well: there was a good deal to be said for having the most dazzling Court in Europe, especially when taxes had just been cut. It is also important to remember that royal parks and palaces were open to all decently dressed persons, and that a good deal of the show often took place outdoors where anyone at all could see it. When the President of the United States gives a state dinner, only the two hundred or so participants get to see it and the White House. When Louis XIV gave a ball, many of his nonaristocratic subjects were able to watch it.

This was even truer of the carrousel because it took place in the large open space which separated the Palace of the Tuileries from the Louvre. A carefully rehearsed tourney, it involved various horseback competitions, but here the sport was only a pretext: what really mattered was the splendor of the costumes. The various teams were each supposed to represent a half-mythical and distant land: there were Persians, Americans, Turks, all of whom were French and wholly unfamiliar with the countries they were supposed to represent. In fact that, too, was a pretext for sumptuous display. The King headed one "nation," Monsieur another; the duc de Guise, the head of the younger branch of the House of Lorraine, another still. And, most important, all the participants, human and equine, shone with finery, whether red and gold like the King or green and gold like Monsieur. Huge bouquets of ostrich plumes waved from everywhere, the costumes, saddles and horse trappings were made of the costliest fabrics, lavishly embroidered in gold, silver, and precious stones. The principals glittered with diamonds and were followed by numerous pages wearing their colors. It was all as splendid a spectacle as anyone could remember seeing; it was also high politics.

Clearly, a great noble engaged in polishing up his horsemanship and planning his costume was too busy to think of plotting against the government; he was also safely ensconced in Paris, far from his estates and his sources of power and income, and therefore markedly more dependent on the King. Then, too, the trappings needed for the carrousel were ruinously expensive—as Louis XIV knew very well. Before deciding to hold that great festivity, in fact, he had consulted Colbert, and been reassured: in the end, the minister said, the Treasury would make more money on the seventeenth-century equivalent of sales taxes than it would spend on the carrousel because of the great influx of tourists into Paris; and, as usual, he was right. What was true for the King, however, was utterly false for everyone else.

Because the Court was more brilliant, because every new ball, every new reception, required increasingly splendid clothes, it suddenly became far more expensive to spend time there. There were also other sources of expense: you could hardly arrive at the Louvre or the Tuileries in a shabby carriage, or with an insufficient number of servants; liveries were costly too; and then, at Court, much time was spent playing cards for very high stakes, so that people sometimes lost half a year's income in just one night.

Of course, they could always go off to their country estate; but because the Court was rapidly becoming the very center of fashion, that was hardly considered a pleasant choice. If, on the other hand, they stayed on, they were likely to spend far more than they could afford. Rather than cut down and lose face, most nobles then went into debt; eventually the debts, having grown, became a problem; and then the obvious remedy consisted in going to the King—who could give you a sum of money or a pension or an office which carried a salary. The aim, then, was to please His Majesty; and that required constant attendance at Court—where life was so terribly expensive. Thus, in a very short time, and altogether peacefully, Louis XIV had begun to domesticate the most dangerous class of his subjects.

He was helped in all this by the glamour which, increasingly, surrounded him. It was not only that he was young, athletic, good-looking, and very sufficiently intelligent: there radiated from him the conviction that he was different in essence from other men. "Our coronation," he wrote, "does not make us kings but it displays our royalty to the people and makes it more august in us."[99] That was a telling remark: kings, Louis XIV thought, were especially chosen by God to be his representatives on earth; they owed their crowns, therefore, not to a mere ceremony, like the Coronation, but to the very fact of being born, and their special relationship to the Divinity began when they first drew breath. A number of consequences flowed from this.

"We lack not only justice but prudence," the King went on, "when we lack veneration for Him whose mere lieutenants we are; our submission to Him corresponds to that which is due to us. Armies, councils, all human activities, would be insufficient to keep us on the throne if every man thought he had as much right to it as ourselves."[100] In an age when men differed as to how God should be worshipped, but never thought that there might not be any God at all, this was a very strong stand indeed. Disobedience to the King became a sin, to be punished in this world but also in the next, an even more unpleasant prospect; and it also stood to reason that God's representative lived on an altogether different plane from the rest of humanity. It was not enough, either, to be a member of the royal family (although, of course, it helped): only the King was semidivine; and human fragility being what it was, you could never tell who would eventually succeed him since his son, for instance, might die before he did.

No doubt Louis XIV's extraordinary majesty was due in great part to all this; but he also knew how to temper what might otherwise have been a frightening distance with the most thoroughgoing politeness and with a taste for pleasure which enlivened the Court, so that the result was an attractive and cheerful grandeur; but no one ever forgot the respect they owed the King.

"The Court, which was attended by a great many, abounded in pleasures," Mme de Motteville wrote. "The prince de Condé held the first rank after Monsieur and the King felt great consideration for him . . . That prince showed that he was as great by his humility and his urbanity as he had been through his victories . . .

"Several times, the King, the Queens, Monsieur, and Madame being in a gilded boat shaped like a galley where, in the coolness of the day, Their Majesties were having a light meal, Monsieur le prince followed them in his quality of *grand maître*‡ with so much respect, and so easy a look that it was impossible to see him behaving thus . . . without thanking God for the current peace . . .

"We could see the duc de Beaufort,* that leader of the *Importants*†

‡ The grand maître was the chief officer of the King's Household.
* The duc de Beaufort was an illegitimate grandson of Henri IV; he had been one of the leaders of the Fronde.
† The *Importants* were an aristocratic element of the second Fronde.

and of the Fronde, the former king of the *halle,* eagerly following the King, his master, and trying to please him.

Besides the princesses and the ladies who attended the Court, the maids-in-waiting‡ of the two Queens and of Madame played an important role, and some of them were very beautiful. There were frequent balls, plays, carriage rides, and hunts. In a word, no amusement was wanting. The different courts and gardens of Fontainebleau seemed like enchanted palaces and gardens."[101]

Multiplied entertainments and a superb decor were an important part of Court life, of course; but they were not enough. Wit and lively conversation became a necessity to fill the long, leisurely hours: even if the King worked hard, most of the courtiers had literally nothing to do. And, as was only right when the monarch was young and strongly attracted to the opposite sex, beautiful women were greatly sought after.

That most of the maids-in-waiting should have been pretty was not really surprising; that the Court should have attracted many aristocratic beauties was also perfectly normal; far more surprising was the transformation immediately noticed in a young woman with whom, only a few years ago, the King had not wanted to dance: Henrietta Stuart, now the bride of the King's brother, Philippe, duc d'Orléans, and generally known as Madame.

"The Princess of England was rather tall: she was very graceful and her figure, which was not free of faults,* did not then seem as spoiled as it actually was; but her whole person, although it was not shapely, was still altogether attractive because of her manner and her charm. She had a very delicate and very white complexion, mixed with a natural blush similar to the rose and the jasmine. Her eyes were small, but brilliant and inviting; her nose was not ugly; her lips were very red and her teeth as white and as fine as anyone could wish; but her face was too long and she was too thin, which seemed to indicate that her beauty would not last.

"She dressed and arranged her hair in the most becoming way . . . and already showed much intelligence and reason."[102] In fact, although she was only seventeen in 1661, she had that kind of myste-

‡ The maids-in-waiting were young unmarried women of good families who surrounded the queens and Madame.

* Because of a malformation of her spine, she limped and had one shoulder higher than the other.

rious attraction which is all the more potent for being indefinable; she knew how to entertain, converse, and amuse; she was full of the liveliest spirit, and the King, who was, after all married to a dull, unattractive woman, promptly fell in love with her.

Indeed, they seemed made for each other: both young, both brilliant in different ways, both fond of the same pleasures, both royal. Of course, there was one awkward little fact: Madame was the King's sister-in-law.† And Monsieur, who soon caught on to his wife's inclination, was not at all happy—a development which became public with great rapidity since he was never one to keep his feelings to himself.

The King was not very tall, but he was imposing; Monsieur was very short and not infrequently lacking in dignity: shrill rages combined with extreme frivolity made him vulnerable to criticism, as, in short order, did his private life. It was not only that he was perhaps too fond of sumptuous clothes, perfumes, and jewelry, or that he was fascinated by women's fashions and gossip; he was also given to falling in love with handsome but undeserving young men, who were generally unfaithful to him (often with women); and all this happened in the constant glare of total publicity. Clearly, when Anne of Austria and Mazarin, together, had decided to make sure that Philippe would never behave like his uncle, the late duc d'Orléans, they had done a good job. No one could imagine Monsieur leading a civil war against his brother.

In spite of all that, however, the prince was not lacking in good qualities. He was quick, intelligent, and witty; he knew how to be amiable and welcoming while retaining his dignity; he was unquestionably kind; he had a sharp eye for painting, architecture, and decor and understood just how to give a successful party; but since, unlike the King, he was only marginally sensitive to feminine charms, he quite failed to fall in love with his wife, a fact of which she was very well aware.

That the young Madame should have been attracted to the King was, therefore, quite natural; the problem was that Monsieur soon noticed and started to behave like the most conventional of jealous husbands. Even worse, after a little delay—she was none too quick—

† As well, of course, as his first cousin: her mother was his father's sister.

the Queen caught on as well; and though she knew better than to make scenes, she made her unhappiness very plain.

That, in itself, was not likely to deter the King, who thought himself above the common law in this respect as well. Marie Thérèse, he readily acknowledged, had certain rights: to be treated with the respect due a queen of France, to be slept with at regular intervals; but he felt perfectly free to be unfaithful to her as frequently as he chose.‡ Whether, in fact, his liaison with Madame was actually consummated is not known, although it is difficult to see why it would not have been; the Queen, for her part, certainly thought that it had. In any event, Madame's attraction soon turned out to be more intellectual than physical. Already as a young man Louis XIV loved intelligent, witty women: that is unquestionably the side of Madame that appealed to him most.

Then, too, there seemed something especially appropriate in having the Court's amusements and festivities led by a princess; and that, in short order, is what Madame's role turned out to be. She had been married in the spring of 1661; by the summer, it was noticed that the King paid particular attention to one of her maids-in-waiting. "Mlle de La Vallière was very amiable, and her beauty was much enhanced by her dazzling pink and white complexion, her blue eyes which had a very sweet expression and the attraction of her silvery blond hair which made her face still more appealing,"[103] wrote one eyewitness, and another added: "She has a handsome figure and a noble look; there is something majestic in the way she walks; her eyes have a kind of languor which must charm all those who have a tender heart. She has the most beautiful hair in the world, and in great abundance. She is kind, has taste, likes books, and is a good judge of them. She is polite, generous, helpful."[104]

At first, both Madame and the comtesse de Soissons encouraged the King's romance with Mlle de La Vallière, Madame because she really thought of it as a way for the King to be around all the time without incurring blame herself, the comtesse de Soissons, whose own affair with Louis XIV was only the first of many, because she favored sex in general. Neither imagined for a moment that the meek, mild La Vallière, a penniless girl from an undistinguished provincial family, would be anything more than a passing amusement;

‡ The Queen, of course, was expected to remain strictly faithful.

certainly it never occurred to them that Louis XIV might begin to give her the time he was still spending with them. As for the Queen, slow as ever, she was firmly convinced that a king could only love a woman of royal blood, so while she had been most upset about Madame, she simply did not worry about La Vallière. Only Anne of Austria, who knew her son and the world, showed her disapproval.

All these intrigues naturally fascinated the Court. Interest in the love life of the great is hardly an unusual phenomenon: in our own day, more than one publication is devoted to precisely that topic. In seventeenth-century France, however, there were no gossip sheets; personal presence was all. Of course, it would be silly to say that Louis XIV fell in love so as to provide the nobility with yet another reason to stay at Court; he was highly sexed and fell in love easily; but there is no denying that keeping up with the latest news was a powerful incentive to many.

With all that, however, the Court, in the early sixties, remained small—larger, to be sure, than under the regency or Mazarin, but still composed of probably no more than two hundred people. Slowly, it began to grow: events like the Carrousel of 1662 brought a number of nobles to Paris, and many of them stayed; and then it became plain that the royal houses were very far from sufficient to contain them all. There were, in fact, two clear deficiencies: one was size, the other shabbiness.

Splendor was very much a part of the royal mystique: God's representative on earth must be surrounded by pomp and glory. That was easy enough to achieve in clothes and party-giving; coming up with suitably impressive palaces was obviously more difficult; and the royal houses, when Louis XIV took over, left a great deal to be desired.

The Louvre, the King's main palace, was in fact an architectural catastrophe. Unfinished wings, some started as early as 1550, ran smack into remnants of the old medieval fortress; there was neither an impressive entrance nor an adequate garden; and inside many rooms were either impossibly shabby or simply unfinished. Because the problems involved were so great Louis XIV and Colbert turned to the smaller Palace of the Tuileries.* Started in the 1560s by Catherine de Médicis, it remained uncompleted in 1661; so Le Vau was

---

* The palace of the Tuileries was used as the main royal or imperial residence after 1789; it was burned by the Commune in 1871, and torn down shortly thereafter.

commissioned to finish it outside and in. By 1662, the King was able to move into new and splendid apartments decorated by Le Brun in the new manner first seen at Vaux, Fouquet's château.

There were painted ceilings, and white-and-gold wood paneling, Gobelins tapestries and Aubusson carpets—both manufactures were just then taken over by the Crown—as well as gilded wood and solid silver furniture: Louis XIV might jail Fouquet, but he knew talent when he saw it; so he simply took over the people who had done such spectacular work at Vaux. Le Vau became his architect, Le Brun his painter and designer, Le Nôtre his garden architect, and new plans for the Tuileries garden were soon put in hand. The results, everyone agreed, were spectacular; still, the Tuileries hardly seemed grand enough for *"le plus grand roi du monde,"* as the King began to be called.

Of course, there were houses outside Paris. Fontainebleau was large but antiquated: no work had been done there since Henri IV's death in 1610, and taste had changed. Compiègne was still more like a medieval fortress than a château; so, while visiting Fontainebleau at regular intervals, the Court spent more time at Saint-Germain-en-Laye. That, too, was an antiquated castle, or rather, two castles, the first built in the early sixteenth century, the other erected under Henri IV, but at least it was in better condition because it had been one of Louis XIII's favorite residences; and it boasted terraced gardens and a splendid view over the Seine and Paris.

Both Fontainebleau and Saint Germain required improvements, and these were soon started; but by 1662 it became clear that the project closer to the King's heart was the new park, naturally designed by Le Nôtre, which was being laid out at fairly considerable expense—close to half a million livres a year—around a little hunting lodge at Versailles; it was, however, nothing more than a good place for a stroll, and the King still lacked a really impressive palace. Together with Colbert, therefore, he decided that a new, grand entrance must be added on the eastern end of the Louvre: this wing would then form one side of a square inner courtyard, of which the southern side had been built by Henri II and the western side by Henri IV and Louis XIII; a northern wing would now connect this to the new constructions and close the courtyard; and because Le Vau, with all his talent, was arrogant and demanding, Louis XIV decided to confine him to the Tuileries and, instead, consulted the western world's greatest and most famous architect, the cavaliere Bernini.

All these apparent indulgences—in buildings, fetes, and women—absolutely failed to distract the King from what he saw as his main task, the government of France; indeed, they were really one of its aspects; and much as he enjoyed them, he cared for politics more. Through a unique piece of luck, it is possible to know exactly how he felt about what one might call his profession.

In 1671, he decided to write memoirs for the use of his son should he, Louis XIV, die while the Dauphin was still a child. These memoirs were strictly confidential; they were dictated by the King to one of his secretaries, the Président Rose, and were first published in 1806. They are well worth quoting at length because they give a true picture of Louis XIV's actions and attitudes at the beginning of his reign, seen from a sufficient distance to ensure a cool and dispassionate appraisal.

It was not, he realized, an easy job to be king. "I have given thought to the situation of kings, which is hard and rigorous in that they owe, so to speak, a public account of all their actions to the world and to posterity and yet cannot provide it to anyone at the time without revealing the secrets of their policy and thus endangering their most crucial interests . . . I therefore want you to have [these notes] so that you can correct the historians if they were to misunderstand or be mistaken for lack of having properly understood my plans and motivations. I will explain it all without disguise even in the cases where my good intentions have not succeeded: as I believe that only small minds, who are usually wrong, want always to be right, and that in those who have sufficient merit to be most often successful, there is, I think, some magnanimity in admitting one's faults."[105]

It is usually the case that people are never more deluded than when they announce they are perfectly willing to admit they sometimes (very rarely) err. In this case, however, because the King was watched by so many clear-eyed observers, we can check his claims against the descriptions of Frenchmen and foreigners alike; and there can be no doubt that what he wrote is true. As for his description of the rationale behind his methods of government, that too is easily verified: the rest of his reign proved that he meant what he said.

"Since the main hope of [the success] of these reforms," he noted, "lay in my own will, the best way to consolidate them was to make my decisions supreme through a behavior that would inspire submission and respect. I was exact in doing justice to all who had a claim; but as to favors, I gave them freely and without constraint when I pleased and to whom I pleased: but in such a way that as time passed people would see that while I needed to justify myself to no one, I still governed rationally and that . . . my awareness of past services, my distinguishing and raising men of merit, in one word my doing good, was not only the most important occupation but also the greatest pleasure of a prince. Unquestionably, two things were necessary: I needed to work very hard, I needed to find a wide choice of people who could help and relieve me.

"As for work, my son, you may first read these memoirs when you are at an age when one usually fears it . . . But I will tell you not only that it is a necessary way of ruling, and the reason we rule, but also that we would show God pride and ingratitude, and men injustice and tyranny, if we wanted the one without the other . . .

"Nothing would be more wearisome than ceaseless pleasure if you were so unhappy as to experience it; first bored with business, you would soon tire of pleasures, then of leisure itself . . .

"I made it a law for myself to work twice a day for two or three hours each time with different persons, without counting the hours I spent alone or those I might give exceptionally to unusual problems if they came up; there was not a moment but [the ministers] were allowed to speak to me about them if they required a prompt resolution . . .

"I cannot tell you how fruitful this new way of life proved to be. I felt as if my mind and courage had grown, I felt like another man, I found in myself much I had not known, and I joyfully reproached myself with having ignored it so long. That early shyness which our judgment always causes in us, and from which I suffered, especially when I had to speak at length and in public, vanished in no time. Only then did I feel like a king and realize I was born to be one. I felt a pleasure I can hardly describe, and which you yourself will never know unless you earn it as I did . . . No satisfaction can equal that of seeing every day some progress in high and glorious undertakings, and the happiness of the people when it has been brought about by one's own plans and goals.

"Whatever is most needed in this work is also most pleasant for it means, in a word, my son, having one's eyes open to this earth; learning at all times the news from the provinces and from abroad, the secrets of all the [foreign] courts and all their ministers, knowing an infinite number of things we are thought to ignore; discovering the most secret views of our own courtiers, their most hidden interests which come to us through the play of contrary interests, so I know of no other pleasure we would not give up for this one."[106]

Hard work, concern for the people, fascination in the workings of the government: it would be difficult to ask for more; but that Louis XIV should have felt that way is all the more striking that it broke with well-established precedent. Even if one disregards the admittedly exceptional circumstances of the regency, the rulers in France had always spent far more time on pleasure than on work; and the better of these kings had made up for that by entrusting an able minister with the reality of power. Indeed, it would be necessary to go back some two hundred years to find in Louis XI† another monarch who ruled himself.

Nor was this most delicate of all pleasures a selfish one. It is striking to see listed among the rewards of hard work the welfare of the people. Although he never forgot his *gloire,* Louis XIV understood very well that the purpose of government was not his own aggrandizement (unlike, for instance, Napoleon or some recent presidents of the United States) but the happiness of those over whom he reigned. While he never doubted that he had been chosen by God to sit on the throne, and that he was His direct representative, that meant he considered himself something like a trustee. France, and the French, did not belong to him: rather, he had been placed at their head so that he might improve their lot.

This kind of mystical attitude is, of course, still completely medieval, and could be found in countless early treatises, some of which were still read in the seventeenth century; but in the Middle Ages, power had been limited by a belief in the inalienable rights of the varying components of society, first and foremost the Church. It is thus perhaps the most striking paradox about Louis XIV that he managed to be at the same time an eminently modern ruler who relied on the power of the state (a clearly nonreligious notion) and the last of the priest-kings.

† He reigned from 1461 to 1483 with conspicuous success.

When his belief in his connection with God gave him the assurance he needed to rule well and fairly, it was undoubtedly an asset; but like all deeply held nonrational beliefs, it could also prove exceedingly dangerous. Not, of course, that Louis XIV was controlled by the Catholic Church; on the contrary, he considered it very much one of the tools of his rule and was at odds with the Pope more often than not; but then there was the vexed question of religious toleration.

In most of Europe, the principle *Cujus regio, ejus religio* had prevailed: the subjects' religion was that of the ruler. In most cases—Spain, for instance, or Sweden—the minority belief had been entirely eliminated. In others—England is the best example—a strong religious minority found itself forced, under pain of extreme penalties, to conform to the established Church. France, however, was a virtually unique case. At the end of the long and ferocious wars of religion that had pitted Catholics against Protestants, each trying hard to exterminate the other, Henri IV had, in 1598, promulgated the Edict of Nantes. This allowed the Protestants public places of worship everywhere except at Court and within the city walls of Paris; schools; universities; special tribunals; and a number of fortified cities.

These last soon came to form a state within the state, and it had been one of Richelieu's great achievements to win them back again; thus, in 1661, there were no more independent fortresses in France, but the Protestants still enjoyed all the other privileges given them by the Edict.

Seen in retrospect this was an eminently sensible solution: while the vast majority of the French was Catholic, the rights of the Protestant minority (probably about 12 percent of the population with a very uneven distribution) were preserved. By 1661, however, there were strong anti-Protestant pressures, and the guarantees of the Edict, while they stood legally, were often nibbled away. Sense, unfortunately, is often vanquished by intolerance; and Louis XIV, who *knew* that the Catholics were right and thought that the Protestants were at best deluded and at worst willful heretics, found the situation almost intolerable.

"As for that great number of my subjects of the RPR,‡ which was an evil which caused me then and still causes me today [in 1671]

‡ The Protestants. RPR stood for *religion prétendue réformée,* or so-called reformed religion.

great pain, I decided right then how to behave with them, and I must have done the right things since God has granted that it result . . . in a very great number of conversions.

"It seemed to me that those who chose to use violent remedies did not understand the nature of the problem . . . which must be allowed gradually to pass and die away rather than exciting it anew by strong contradictions, which are in any event useless when the disease . . . is spread throughout the state . . .

"I thought that the best way to reduce the number of Huguenots was no longer to press them with any new rigor, and to see that the guarantees they obtained from my predecessors were observed; but I granted them no new ones, and saw to it that they be kept within the narrowest limits that justice and fairness would allow. But as for those favors which depended on me alone, I decided to allow them none, and that through kindness rather than anger, so that they would be forced to consider of themselves, from time to time and without violence whether they had good reason to deprive themselves of the advantages which otherwise they would have shared with my other subjects."[107]

Given the King's beliefs, this was a notably liberal stand—far more so, in fact, than that to be shortly taken by the English Parliament. Of course, the "favors" in question included a good many promotions which, today, come as of right, but there can be no doubt that many Frenchmen would have supported a far more rigorous policy. That this moderation was prompted not by tolerance but by the belief that, in the long run, it would prove more effective than persecutions changes nothing: trying to convince or seduce is not at all the same as converting forcibly.

To this it should be added that, had Louis XIV thought that force would be effective, he, no doubt, would have used it: but here as everywhere he showed the most acute instinct for the nature, extent, and limitations of his power. Indeed, just as he had taken naturally to governing, and proceeded to enjoy it almost voluptuously, so he seemed born with an exact understanding of how power can be gained or lost; and while he was soon going to demonstrate this trait in his foreign policy, he also applied his knowledge to the people closest to him, his ministers.

"I decided first never to have a prime minister," he wrote, "Nothing could be more shameful than to see, on one side the functions, on the other the sole title of King. It was thus absolutely necessary for me to share out my trust and the execution of my orders without giving all of it to any one man; and to use these different people for different jobs, this being perhaps a prince's first and greatest talent.

"Because I wanted to concentrate in myself all the authority [of the state], and even though there are, in every sort of field, details to which our occupations and even our dignity do not allow us to lower ourselves, I decided, once I had chosen my ministers, to look after these, now and again, with each of them whenever they least expected it so that they understood I might do the same things at other times and on other subjects.

"I cannot easily tell you, my son, how to choose the several ministers. Luck plays just as great a role as wisdom in this . . . and instinct is often more effective than reasoning."[108]

The King then goes on to explain that, in choosing men of little importance, he was shoring up his own authority since they would depend on him entirely for the realization of their hopes, while princes or great aristocrats would never have the humility or the selflessness required by the new autocrat. What follows is a cry of pride.

"Many thought that, within a short time, one of the men close to me would rule my mind and my kingdom. Most thought that the assiduity with which I worked was a temporary phase which would soon be over . . . Time has shown them up and *this is now the tenth year**** that I have progressed steadily in the same direction, never letting up my effort; listening to the lowest of my subjects; knowing at all times the number and quality of my soldiers and the condition of my fortresses; giving my orders every day for all their needs; negotiating at every moment with the foreign ambassadors; receiving and reading the dispatches; writing part of the answers myself and giving the gist of the rest to my secretaries; regulating the income and expenditure of the state; hearing the direct reports of those whom I place in important offices; keeping all my business more secret than anyone ever had before me; distributing favors according to my own preference and keeping those who serve me, although laden with my kindnesses to them and their families, in a modest condition very different from the power and elevation of the prime ministers.

* Underlined by the King himself.

"As people noticed all of this over time, they began to feel respect for me; and that opinion has greatly contributed to the success of my undertakings."[109]

With this nod to the power of publicity, the King once again shows how very prudent he was: far from rushing ahead at any risk, the triumphs he most enjoyed were those which had cost the least: it was thus typical that when, in October 1662, he decided to recover Dunkerque, which had been the price paid for Cromwell's alliance in the fifties, he went about it in a completely unconventional manner. His predecessors would have laid siege to the city; Louis XIV waited until Charles II needed money even more badly than usual, and then offered to take Dunkerque off his hands for the sum of 5 million livres. This was an irresistible lure; too good to be true, in fact: as a result of last-minute adjustments and some use of a fluctuating rate of exchange between French and British currencies, the actual payment sank to some 3.5 million. Nor was it merely a question of pride: as soon as Dunkerque was French, a formidable set of fortifications began to rise. These had a triple purpose: they made the city a safe harbor for the rapidly developing fleet; they would serve to slow a Spanish attack if the need arose; and they could be used to intimidate Charles II if ever he thought of returning to Cromwell's policy.

In many ways, the purchase of Dunkerque is exemplary, both of the way the King did business—prudently and without shedding a drop of blood—and of the possibilities opened up by his careful watch over the finances. Having a well-filled Treasury meant that money could be spent instead of men in gaining important advantages, while at the same time a stronger army served to deter any possible aggression. Thus, in spite of his solar emblem and proud motto, in spite of what naïve people thought of as his impetuous youth, Louis XIV governed like the most seasoned of statesmen.

That, however, was perfectly compatible with great and visible pride. Already in 1661, the King felt quite sure that France was the first power in Europe; as we know with the benefit of hindsight, he was perfectly right, but most people, including his ministers, had yet to discover this fact. An incident in London now proved it to the world.

On the occasion of the formal entry of the Swedish Ambassador into London, the comte d'Estrades, Louis XIV's Ambassador and his Spanish colleague, the baron de Vatteville, quarreled about whose carriage was to go first. Vatteville, who had provoked the dispute and was therefore prepared for it, had not only brought along an unusually large escort, but also bribed men in the crowd; thus, from the very beginning, he was in a position of strength. First, his people killed the horses which drew the French carriages; then Estrades's gentlemen were attacked and in some cases severely wounded, upon which, triumphantly, the Spaniards rejoined the procession.

As is so often the case in international disputes, both sides were partly right: it had long been understood that the ambassadors of Spain would be given precedence, so Estrades was wrong to dispute it; on the other hand, strong-arming and wounding the French was inexcusable. Here, obviously, was a situation made for a compromise solution, and that is just what Brienne, who was still in office, and Lionne recommended.

The King, however, had a clearer view of the relative strength of France and Spain. Far from negotiating a compromise, he sent a strongly worded letter to Charles II demanding the expulsion of M. de Vatteville. He then recalled his own envoy from Madrid, expelled the Spanish Ambassador, and recalled his negotiators from the conferences then held in Flanders to work out border details not clearly set out in the Treaty of the Pyrenees. More, he informed Philip IV, his uncle and father-in-law, that unless Spain recognized French precedence while offering a public apology, the war would start again.

This seemed the height of imprudence to the French ministers. Because, to a degree, they still lived in the past, because they remembered that, as late as 1636, the Spanish Army had very nearly taken Paris, because finally Spain had been the leading European power for nearly a century and a half, they thought it mad to risk war over a point of etiquette. The King, however, perceived very rightly that Spain was no longer in any state to make war; its long decline, in fact, was already well under way, and the risk, therefore, very small. Ignoring the advice offered by his Council, he proceeded as he pleased; and events soon confirmed his perception. Vatteville was recalled from London, and, in March, 1662, the count of Fuentes, Philip IV's envoy, arrived in Fontainebleau. There, before the entire Court and the diplomatic corps, he announced that henceforth, Spanish ambassadors would give France precedence.

Once again, no blood had been shed; but Louis XIV's triumph shook Europe just the same. For the very first time since the beginning of the sixteenth century Spain had been openly humbled; and France, clearly, had now taken its place as the leading power. More, the King's determination and coolness impressed, and sometimes frightened, his neighbors. If he was ready to start a war on a point of etiquette, it was obvious that he would not hesitate when more substantial French interests were at stake. Of course, Louis himself saw the disputed precedence as a very substantial point indeed: by showing firmness in a minor matter, he avoided many a future conflict while ensuring his *gloire.*

More surprising, this bold new policy was carried out without a murmur from anyone in France, partly because there had been no leaks before the decisions were announced, partly because the ministers had indeed learned to obey. Even under the fearsome Richelieu, disputes and leaks were commonplace: the Court, the royal family, and, to some extent, the government were divided between the strong anti-Habsburg policy practiced by the Cardinal and its reverse, an alliance with Spain against the Protestants. Now, with the ministers absolutely dependent on the King, it was at last possible for France to have a strong, steady, and effective policy.

"Le Tellier, who had studied the King's mind with great care," Mme de Motteville noted, "confirmed what my brother told me about the seriousness and severity which he [the King] added to his natural kindness, so as to create a feeling of respect in all those who saw him and a feeling of fear in those who came closest to him so that they were not tempted to abuse the freedom he gave them of speaking out."[110] That, in fact, was a key element of Louis XIV's new style of government: he expected no flattery, no fawning, from his ministers. They were free, and expected, to defend their point of view or criticize another; but then, having listened to them, the King made the final decision; and after that, the minister's job was to carry out his orders.

"Our elevation," Louis XIV wrote, "removes us in a way from our people to whom the ministers are closer; they are thus better able to see a thousand details of which we are not aware . . . but when, on important occasions, they have argued out all the possible solutions, all the reasons pro and con, and reported what is done abroad in similar cases, then it is up to us, my son, to decide what must actually be done. And that choice, I daresay that if we lack neither courage nor common sense, no one else can make it as well as we. For decisions require a master's mind; and it is incomparably easier to be what we are than to imitate what we are not . . .

"In certain circumstances, wisdom calls for leaving much to chance; reason itself then makes us give in to I know not what blind instincts or reactions, beyond reason and which seem inspired by God† to all men, but which those he has placed in the first rank have the greater obligation to acknowledge. No one can say when we must distrust these instincts, and when we must obey them, that is not to be found in books or taught by experience . . . And although my ministers saw that they would always be just what they should be,‡ they were all the happier in an office where, with a thousand other advantages, they could feel absolutely safe when they did their duty."[111]

The "thousand other advantages" Louis XIV mentions were very substantial indeed. Where, earlier, some ministers had made rapid but uncertain fortunes by robbing the state, and then worried about possible retribution—it occasionally followed—now men like Colbert or Lionne or Le Tellier grew immensely rich legitimately and legally, on the King's gifts. By 1665, palaces were going up which belonged to them; and that, too, reflected the King's policy. Obviously, a happy subordinate will work harder and be more faithful; but also, by giving his ministers the means to live like princes, by seeing to it that their children married into the great noble families,* Louis XIV was also making a point about his own power. The people who carried out his will were rapidly becoming the first in the state because they were a reflection of himself; and in no time at all, base-born men like Colbert or Le Tellier were addressed as *monseigneur*, an appellation heretofore reserved to dukes and the royal family.†

Naturally, the ministers then tried to bring their relatives into the royal service, so that clans developed: Colbert's brother and his son both had important positions, while Le Tellier's son was the equivalent of Undersecretary of War; but these new groupings had no independent power, no connection to entrenched aristocratic families;

† Today, we might replace God by the unconscious.

‡ Not ruling in place of the King, that is, as Richelieu, Mazarin, and Fouquet had done.

* Colbert's two daughters, for instance, each married a duke.

† Richelieu and Mazarin, because they were cardinals, that is princes of the Church, and dukes besides, had been called *monseigneur*; but none of the other ministers was.

they held office solely because the King wanted them to; and while he would have had great difficulty in dismissing a prince of the blood royal from his Council, there were a thousand candidates waiting to replace the ministers, and no one of any consequence to resist their dismissal.

This new method of government was immensely shocking—so much so, in fact, that at Louis XIV's death in 1715, fifty-four years later, the ministers were dismissed and the great nobles put in charge once more. What the outraged aristocracy had failed to perceive, however, was that a modern state required a competent government: in short order, the ministers came back and the system inaugurated in 1661 continued until the end of the Ancien Régime.

Just because the ministers were powerful and respected, however, did not mean that they formed a united, independent cabinet; indeed, a lively enmity soon developed between the Colbert and Le Tellier clans, with their representatives often taking opposing positions at the Council. That, too, was useful: it is clearly better to hear different points of view before arriving at a decision, and the King used the very rivalries between his servants in order to rule better and more effectively. Then, too, for the first time, private interests were unable to shape the Council's decisions. Fouquet, for instance, could always be counted on to defend the Parlement, as had ministers under Louis XIII and Richelieu; Cardinals, whether they were prime ministers or just members of the Council, were likely to favor the Pope's policy. With the removal of these two important factions the King now found himself free to deal with those two states within the state, the Church, and the Parlements.

"It was necessary," Louis XIV wrote, "to abate the excessively great authority of the main Parlements . . . which considered themselves to be so many independent and separate sovereigns. I made it clear that I would not allow their usurpations, and soon acted in consequence. The *cour des aides*‡ was the first to forget its duty; I exiled a few of its members because I thought that this remedy, used immediately, would preclude any need for it henceforth, and so it did.

"Upon this, I made my intentions plainer still in a solemn decision

‡ The cour des aides supposedly oversaw the collection of a consumer tax but was, in fact, a Parlement-like tax court.

given out by my conseil d'en haut* . . . I forbade them all ever to give judgments contrary to those of my Council under any pretext whatsoever . . . It was time to show them that I did not fear them and that the times had changed. And those whose interests made them hope that the Parlements would resist learned from their obedience what was due to me."[112] This may look like another typical instance of antidemocratic despotism; but, here too, hindsight leads straight into error.

Neither in 1661 nor in 1648 did the Parlements represent anyone but themselves: Their name gives the misleading impression that they were a representative assembly; in fact, they were a gathering of rich men who had bought judicial office: it cannot be said too often that the Parlements were tribunals and nothing more; that the judges were people who had bought their offices, so that money, and not competence, determined their membership; that the registration of laws had been started purely as a legal convenience so as to avoid having contradictory statutes; and that nothing in the selection or the training of the présidents and conseillers entitled them to behave as if they had been elected.

The Parlements, in fact, behind the veil of demagogy which they were wont to use, were interested mainly in preserving the rich from the obligation of paying any taxes; thus, even if resistance to taxation can easily be misrepresented as sympathy for the people, they stood for a markedly unfair and retrogressive policy; as for their lack of capacity to rule, it had been amply demonstrated during the Fronde, so that Louis XIV's reassertion of his authority met with nothing but approval: had there been elections in 1662, there can be no doubt that the King would have won them handily.

Louis XIV himself, in his memoirs, made a good case for the utility and justice of a policy which, he claimed, was wholly unaffected by private considerations. "I do not want you to think that [my policy as regards the Parlements] was due to motives of fear, hatred, or vengeance for the events of the Fronde . . . That satisfaction people expect from vengeance is hardly made for us: it can only flatter those whose power is fragile . . . As for us, my son, we are very rarely in that middle state where one takes pleasure in revenge; for, either we can do what we please without difficulty or else we find ourselves, on

---

* The conseil d'en haut was composed of the King, the Chancellor, and a few ministers; it was the supreme judicial organ of the state.

the contrary, in certain difficult and delicate circumstances which prevent us from imposing the fullness of our power.

"Finally, just as we belong to our people, so our people belong to us and I have yet to see a wise man taking vengeance at his own cost by hurting those who belong to him . . .

"The elevation of the Parlements was a danger to the realm when I was a minor; it was necessary to curb them, less because of past evils than because of what they might have done in the future."[113]

Here, for the first time, Louis XIV is less than sincere. His arguments are, of course, perfectly valid; so are his fears for the future;† but there can be no doubt that he nursed a burning resentment for the men and events of the Fronde. When, like Condé, the Frondeurs had turned into obedient courtiers, they could be forgiven; but the Parlement de Paris's humbling of the monarchy, the powerless dissembling when the mob invaded the young King's bedroom, the grinding poverty of the Court during the civil wars, all that was never forgotten. Much of the reign, in fact, consists of policies designed to prevent any repetition of the Fronde, from the reorganization of the King's Council to the Court's eventual removal from Paris. In that perspective, eradicating the Parlement's political power was an essential goal.

Nor was the supremacy of the conseil d'en haut the only step. The King was patient, but persistent. In 1666, after five years of peace, the Parlement began, once again, to resist: it refused to register an edict establishing a yearly production tax, another one in which heavy fines were imposed on the financiers who had stolen from the Treasury under Fouquet and were, in return, granted amnesty, and a third reducing the interest on the debt to 5 percent. Promptly, Louis XIV held a lit de justice and ordered the registration, upon which the chambre des requêtes, always the boldest one, tried to protest; immediately, the King forbade the protest. "There was an assembly of the chambres of the Parlement at which M. le Premier président related the King's prohibition and the order he had received to assemble the chambres. Once he had finished speaking, the whole company remained silent for a while; and after some time, since no one said a word, M. Le Coigneux, président of [the chambre of] la Tournelle stood up; all followed him, one after the other; and thus

† As the Parlement demonstrated amply during the minority of Louis XV.

everyone left without a single word being said, everyone looking abashed. There is no previous example of such an event in the history of the Parlement,"[114] Ormesson, one of its members, noted.

What Ormesson, who had been through the Fronde, forgets, however, is that the very refusal to register was a relative innovation; and that protests against registrations made during a lit de justice had begun precisely when the Parlement was rebelling against Anne of Austria's authority, a time at which orders to be silent were hardly likely to be heeded. In fact, once again, the refusal to register had been purely selfish: many of the fined financiers came from Parlement families; the new tax would raise the price of luxuries; and finally the reduction of the rate of interest to 5 percent once again affected the rich who had lent money to the government at exorbitant rates—i.e., the Parlement families. This time, however, the King had prevailed.

Two years later, in 1668, Louis XIV went a step further. On January 16, the King told the Attorney General that he wanted to see a deputation from the Parlement. "On the seventeenth, they came to Saint Germain. The King spoke to them privately behind closed doors‡ and told them that M. le Chancelier [Séguier] would tell them his intentions; which he did, informing them that the King wanted to have the registers of the Parlement from the year 1645 to the year 1652, inclusively, so as to remove anything concerned with the affairs of state, and that, as for all private business,* that would be carefully copied so that the public would not suffer from this.

"At the same time, the King ordered the chief clerk to bring him all these registers the next day."[115] This was eradicating the past with a vengeance, and removing all possible precedents for future resistance. Only one more change was now needed to ensure absolute compliance: the end of the Parlement's right to refuse registration. In 1668, it began to look as if this might be a likely development.

*T*ACKLING the Parlement was one thing; being virtually at war with the Pope and demanding the humblest of apologies from him quite another. Certainly, by the mid-seventeenth century, the once formidable weapons of excommunication and interdiction had

‡ The King usually received such deputations in public, with the Court watching and listening.
* Private suits and criminal trials, that is.

123

become altogether blunted, but it was a bold Catholic indeed who treated the Supreme Pontiff not like the successor to St. Peter but like the small Italian prince he was in reality. And just as had been the case with the King of Spain, the conflict between Louis XIV and the Pope was provoked by an insult offered the French Ambassador.

As it was, France and the Pope had been at odds for some time, both over matters affecting the Church in France and over the sequestration by the Holy See of territories France claimed for two of its allies—the duchies of Castro and Ronciglione for the Duke of Parma, the town of Commachio for the Duke of Modena. Underlying this conflict was the fact that Alexander VII Chigi had, all along, favored Spain over France. Still, none of the issues at stake was crucial; and thinking that a compromise was possible, Louis XIV sent a new ambassador, the duc de Créqui, to Rome as a conciliatory gesture.

Shortly after his arrival, however, an ugly incident resulted in a complete break in diplomatic relations. Rome, under the popes, was always a badly administered city; in the seventeenth century, the prevailing lawlessness was much encouraged by an odd and unique custom: while embassies are always granted extraterritoriality, in Rome that privilege extended to the entire neighborhood surrounding the embassy; and the practical consequence of that anomaly was virtual anarchy, since the papal police were powerless to intervene. Sensibly enough, the Pope tried to put an end to this; but privileges once granted cannot easily be taken back; so the ambassadors protested and the status quo prevailed.

Perhaps, after all, the duc de Créqui had not been a very good choice: not only was he known for his enormous pride, he had also brought with him an entourage of lively, disorderly young men who proceeded to misbehave as they might have done in Paris, getting drunk, rioting, even beating up the police. Early in August, in fact, several of the duc's footmen attacked a small troop of the Corsican Guards who were supposed to keep order in the city.

Corsicans, then as now, were fond of vendettas; and don Mario Chigi, the Pope's brother, who had been offended by Créqui's domineering manner, encouraged them to seek revenge. As a result, on August 20, 1662, a number of the Guards set siege to the embassy and even shot at a carriage in which the duchesse de Créqui was coming home, killing one of her pages. Obviously, this was a direct insult to France; but while don Mario expected some sort of reaction, both he and Alexander VII, who were used to Mazarin's pragmatism, assumed that the incident would be forgotten within a few months. They had, however, misjudged Louis XIV. Ten days after the incident, a letter such as few popes have ever received went off from Saint Germain.

"Holy Father," the King wrote in his own hand, "our cousin† the duc de Créqui, our Ambassador Extraordinary, having informed us of the murder attempt against his person, that of the Ambassadress his wife, and all the Frenchmen who were in Rome on the twentieth of this month, by Your Holiness' Corsican militia, we have immediately ordered our said cousin to withdraw from the States of the Church so that his person and our dignity will no longer remain endangered by attempts unexampled even among Barbarians; we have also ordered the Sieur de Bourlemont, Auditor of the Rota,‡ to find out from Your Holiness whether you intend us a reparation proportionate to the magnitude of this offense, which has not only violated but shamefully undone the law of nations.

"We do not hereby ask for anything from your Holiness. You have so well-established a habit of refusing us everything, and have shown heretofore such aversion for all that concerns our person and our Crown, that we think it best to leave to your own prudence the decisions which will prompt our own, and only hope that they will be such as to make us continue praying to God that he preserve, Holy Father, Your Holiness to our Holy Mother the Church."[116]

As we read this fulmination, it is Louis XIV's own voice we hear: no minister would have dared address the Pope in so cutting a tone; and actions soon followed. Créqui left Rome for Tuscany and took a group of pro-French cardinals with him; the Nuncio was ordered to remove himself all the way to Meaux, but not before he had received letters promising satisfaction. The French then pointed out that vague promises would not do, and they were further outraged by the news that some of the Corsicans who had been jailed had now escaped, clearly with the connivance of the authorities. By the end of the year, the Nuncio had been expelled from France altogether, Créqui was ordered home, and an attempt by Queen Christina of Swe-

† As a matter of etiquette, the kings of France called all dukes and cardinals "mon cousin."
‡ The French representative before a Church tribunal.

den, who lived in Rome, to suggest that the whole incident should be forgotten was countered by yet another strongly worded royal letter.

Then, at the end of January 1663, Alexander VII decided to resume negotiations through the Venetian and Spanish ambassadors. He now offered the restitution of Castro, Ronciglione, and Commachio to their respective dukes, but no apology; and his offer was promptly turned down: not only was Louis XIV intent on showing that no one could insult him and get away with it, his quarrel with the Pope also served his foreign policy: because he announced that, if necessary, he would send an army to Rome, Spain was forced to keep a large garrison in Milan, one of its possessions, just at the time when it was fighting Portugal; it was thus not until June that negotiations were started in Savoy—the Nuncio was still persona non grata in France. Although most of the French demands were accepted, the talks broke down within a month on the restitution of Castro, about which the Pope had changed his mind.

Clearly, Alexander VII was not frightened enough; so Louis XIV proceeded to annex Avignon and its province, the Comtat Venaissin, which had belonged to the popes ever since the thirteenth century, and he assembled an army near the Alps under the command of the experienced maréchal du Plessis-Praslin. There was no force capable of resisting it; the memories of the sack of Rome in 1521 were still green: on January 19, 1664, negotiations were resumed and this time Alexander VII gave in. Castro and Ronciglione were returned to the Duke of Parma; the Duke of Modena was compensated for the loss of Commachio; don Mario Chigi was dismissed as governor of Rome; a pyramid was built in the City to commemorate the insult and the Pope's humiliation*; a special legate was sent to offer the King a public apology, and Cardinal Chigi, the Pope's nephew, accompanied him. Louis XIV's triumph was complete: by humbling the Pope after the King of Spain, he had shown clearly that he was indeed the most powerful monarch in Europe; that, when it came to his *gloire,* he would stop at nothing; and that, while deeply religious, he had very little respect for the temporal power of the Church. And once again, all this was achieved at minimal cost and without spilling a drop of blood.

Clearly none of these successes would have been possible under

* It was torn down, with the King's permission, a few years later.

the old system: Louis XIV could now show proof that his changes were positive, that the new absolute monarchy could enjoy a position which his forefathers scarcely imagined. And as time passed, the Court began to understand that there would be no backsliding. Anne of Austria could have testified to it: it was not just that she was not consulted, she was not even informed. The affairs of state were transacted in the King's Council, and nowhere else; nor could anyone claim that he was even close to influencing the monarch: Louis XIV actually went out of his way to demonstrate that no one could ever control him.

This exclusion of the royal family was made even more visible because it was not the result of personal conflicts. The King was visibly fond of his brother; he appeared to worship his mother. In April and May 1663, for instance, the old Queen fell ill. "The King stayed up watching her for several nights when it was feared that the fever would be more violent. He had a mattress brought in, which he had put down on the carpet by the Queen's bed, and sometimes slept on it without undressing . . . He also looked after her with the greatest of care, he helped her to change beds and served her better and more gently than her maids."[117]

The very fact that his new policy was so impersonal denoted its permanence: principles, not feelings, were its root. When, however, feeling was manifested, it, too, showed that the King thought he should prevail over everyone. By 1663, it was clear to all that he was very much in love with Mlle de La Vallière; even Marie Thérèse had caught on to the fact. That the wife was hardly likely to prevail over the mistress surprised no one; but when the Queen Mother intervened, the Court was startled to notice that it made absolutely no difference. Because, on a variety of grounds, Anne of Austria disapproved of the affair, she stopped speaking to La Vallière; and when Louis XIV told her bluntly that this was unacceptable, she announced that she would retire to a convent. After many tears, the King persuaded her to stay; but it was also noticed that she had become far more pleasant to the mistress.

Even more striking than the resolution of this crisis is what Louis had told his mother: after admitting that he was wrong to commit adultery and make his wife miserable, he continued: "I know my problem, I sometimes feel sorry and ashamed, I have done what I could to stop offending God and resist my passions, but I am forced to admit that they have become stronger than my reason. I can no longer resist them, and do not even feel the desire to do so."[118] It was a telling admission: whatever the King wanted he must have; and he was so far above ordinary mortals that it no longer mattered if he ignored the laws that bound them.

VI
War and Fortune

A *SUBMISSIVE* Court, talented but obedient ministers, a prosperous Treasury, and an adoring people: in January 1666 the magnitude of the King's achievement was evident to all; and yet, as is often the case with rapid change, the transformation was not as thorough as it might have appeared; by the end of the year, however, two great events had deepened the impact of the reforms: Louis XIV was preparing to attack Spain, and the Queen Mother was dead.

Powerless though she had become even in small matters, Anne of Austria nonetheless represented a survival of the past: to see her was to remember the Fronde and the King's minority; and while her attempt at freezing out La Vallière had been wholly unsuccessful, she still embodied a powerful (even if only potential) moral force; and because she was the only remaining member of the older generation in the royal family, she stood for a certain kind of tradition. Early in 1665, however, it became clear that this, too, was about to change, when she was discovered to be suffering from breast cancer.

Even seventeenth-century doctors, incompetent though they were, understood that a mastectomy was indicated; but the state of medical knowledge was such that the operation would have entailed a far more rapid death than the absence of treatment. In the Queen Mother's case, however, because the patient was so famous, something had to be done, and so the doctors devised a method of unparalleled barbarity. For an entire year, the wretched Anne submitted, at regular intervals, to a sort of semi-ablation in which slices of both breast and tumor were cut off by her physicians; the pain inflicted by this procedure in an age wholly without anesthesia can be readily imagined, as well as the horror of bandages adhering to the raw flesh and removed without regard for the patient's suffering; all, of course, to absolutely no avail. All through the year of her martyrdom Anne behaved with a courage which earned her the admiration of all; and the King spent much time trying to comfort her. By January 1666, however, she was clearly at death's door; indeed, she is reputed to have said, looking at her once beautiful hands which had become swollen with cancer: "I can see it is time I went."

Even then, however, she remained a public figure: there were quarrels about who was to inherit what, the King, in particular, claiming her famous pearls and Monsieur disputing violently about his share of her inheritance; and almost to the last, whether at Saint Germain or at the Louvre, where she was eventually moved, she continued to receive courtiers. Her religious observances, always strict, now came to occupy much of her time, and her attendants, watching her dedicate her sufferings to God, did not hesitate to call her a saint. At last, between four and five in the morning of January 20, Anne of Austria, Infanta of Spain, Queen and erstwhile Regent of France, breathed her last, leaving behind her an apparently inconsolable family.

"I was told by people who slept in the King's bedroom [the next night] that he wept in his bed for almost the entire night," Mme de Motteville noted. "The next day, speaking to the duchesse de Montausier about the Queen Mother, he said that he had the consolation of knowing that he had never disobeyed her in anything of real consequence; and, continuing to extol her merits, he added that the Queen, his mother, was not only a great Queen but that she deserved to be ranked with the greatest Kings."[119] And Monsieur, who cried quite as easily as the King, but whose tears were perhaps the signs of a more affectionate nature, was clearly devastated for weeks. Then, too, he must have realized that there was no longer anyone to whom he could appeal against his brother's decisions.

To say that Monsieur's affection went deeper than the King's does not, however, imply a lack of sincerity on the latter's part; as always, a distinction must be made between the King's personal and public feelings; thus, excluding his mother from the Council or disregarding her admonitions about La Vallière implied not lack of love but an overriding concern for his duties and prerogatives as King. Indeed, when later in the year he reflected about the recent past, the result was a singularly handsome, and unquestionably sincere, tribute.

"Nature," Louis XIV wrote, "had formed the first links which tied me to the Queen, my mother; but the closeness resulting from a kinship of the soul is much harder to end than that due only to blood. To explain both the extent and the justice of my sorrow, I would have to set out here the full merit of this Queen, and that would be a very difficult undertaking. The most eloquent men of this century, whom I set to working on this subject, have scarcely been able to fulfill their task; the simple tale of this princess's actions to be found in history will always surpass all the praise they have given her.

". . . The respect I paid her was not of that forced kind of duty we owe to appearances. The habit I made of living in the same house and eating at the same table with her, the assiduity with which I could be seen to visit her several times a day were not an obligation I imposed on myself for reasons of state but a sign of the pleasure I found in her company; and in fact the way in which she had freely transmitted the sovereign power to me showed me clearly enough that I had nothing to fear from her ambition to allow me to dispense with insincere marks of affection."[120] These words say more than, perhaps, Louis XIV intended: then and henceforth, blood ties meant little to him except inasmuch as they gave certain people certain positions; and he was grateful to his mother less for her many achievements during and just after the regency than for the ease with which she had given up power. In the event, she died just in time: Philip IV, her brother, had predeceased her, dying on September 17, 1665, and leaving as his heir a retarded four-year-old child. The situation was obviously right for further French expansion, a process which would surely have deeply distressed the Queen Mother.

As it was, the King went into the purple mourning reserved for royalty, and the obligatory ceremonies took place. After the reading of the late Queen's will, which immediately followed her death, Louis XIV left for his hunting pavilion at Versailles in obedience to the etiquette which forbade the King's presence in the same house as a dead body. "On the the twenty-first, at 7 A.M., the Queen's surgeon took out her heart through her side as she had ordered; they embalmed her body though she had forbidden it, but it was so gangrened that it had to be done, since the body had to stay at the Louvre for a few days so as to allow enough time to prepare the coaches . . . [She was then put into] a lead coffin, which was put in a covering of black velvet and white satin and . . . topped with a crowned canopy bearing at each corner the Queen's arms embroidered.

"On the twenty-second the coffin was put on a platform . . . with many silver candlesticks holding white candles bearing the Queen's arms . . . All the room, including the ceiling, was draped in black . . . a crown with the fleur-de-lis covered by a black crepe was put on a black velvet cushion at the head of the coffin."[121] All through this time, priests prayed constantly for the late Queen's soul; but, almost immediately, the kind of dispute with which Anne had been all too familiar broke out between the chevalier d'honneur and the dame d'atours as to who would be first to sprinkle the bier with holy water, and that was followed by endless disputes between the duchesses and the "foreign princesses,"* and between the representatives of the various courts, all of which had to be settled, sometimes by referring to precedent, sometimes directly by the King, before, on the twenty-eighth, the body was interred in the Abbey of Saint Denis; all in all, these disputes were so varied and so complex that it takes seventy pages, filled with tiny handwriting, in the Register of Ceremonies to account for it all.

Of course, precedence had always been important and quarrels fierce; but at just about this time, the always complex etiquette begins to undergo a further development, something the King watched with approval: if the nobles had to fight, it was obviously better that it be about the claims to a cushion in church or an eight-foot train. Precedence now began to replace policy as a subject of contention, and that, as Louis XIV knew very well, made his task doubly easy: not only was his government free from aristocratic opposition, but also the quarrels about points of etiquette must in the end be settled by the King, thus giving him yet another way to reward or punish his courtiers.

Had the Queen Mother's death taken place a few years earlier, it would unquestionably have had serious political consequences. As it was, it made absolutely no difference to anyone except the members of her household, many of whom now retired from the Court, and

---

* "Foreign princesses" were the wives, either of members of minor ruling families, like the House of Lorraine, or of former rulers of minuscule states, like the duc de Bouillon, whose erstwhile possessions were now part of France.

Queen Marie Thérèse lost not just an aunt and a mother-in-law but also the only person in whom she could confide her chagrin at her husband's infidelities.

Although she received all the respect that was her due, and was treated with a measure of consideration, the Queen knew that she hardly mattered, but always refrained from the kind of complaining the King would have resented. "The Heavens," Louis wrote, "have perhaps never gathered within one woman more virtue, more beauty, a higher birth, more tenderness for her children, more love and respect for her husband"[122]; but because she had neither charm nor intelligence, she was left to mourn, alone now, her rivals' triumphs.

The King himself missed his mother, not just because he was so used to seeing her often, but because she set a certain grandly polished tone not seen elsewhere in the young, exuberant, but rather unrefined Court; but it was Monsieur who suffered most from his mother's loss. While she lived, he could count on her to see that he was well treated by the King: although she lacked ultimate authority, she still had some influence. Now the King, who undoubtedly felt affection for his brother, simply treated him as a possible rival. His own testimony on this subject is eloquent.

"I must," the King wrote in his *Memoirs,* "tell you about a conversation I had with [my brother] at the most acute moment of our common suffering, and which ought to have been more public because of the warmth of our mutual affection.

"The most important thing that happened then was that I promised him I would in no way abate the closeness with which I had behaved to him while the Queen our mother was alive, even assuring him that I would extend this to his children; that I would have his son brought up and educated by the same governor and the same preceptor as yourself,† and that, whenever he had a just claim, he would find me as careful of his interests as of my very own.

"The moment in which I was telling him all this, and my condition as I was saying it left him in no doubt that it was due solely to my love for him; for it is well known that reason is not strong enough to control our speeches and actions when our hearts are in turmoil.

"But it is however true that, since I must point out everything

† I.e., the Dauphin. This promise was not carried out.

which may help to enlighten you . . . if I had planned this speech in the most cool and considerate manner, I could not have thought of anything more appropriate, since, at the same time, I was doing my brother an honor for which he was bound to be grateful and taking as hostage for his good behavior what was most precious to him."[123]

There is no reason to doubt the exact truth of this statement, written within a year of the Queen Mother's death, and thus before time had, as it often does, altered memory. We may, however, pause and wonder. That the transformation from the pleasure-loving young man into the very incarnation of monarchy had already gone far was clear to all observers; what is more amazing is that Louis himself was so conscious of it: what others might call inhumanity—the use of his mother's loss to bind his brother into greater dependence—he saw as mere duty, well carried out; and his analysis of himself is uncommonly perceptive when he points out that the genuine affection he felt for Monsieur only helped in putting through a political scheme. Here, indeed, is the first clear proof that Louis XIV actually believed that France came first: because it is disguised by such kingly splendor, this revolutionary message is easy to miss, but it is there nonetheless. Earlier rulers had thought of the country as a possession: they owned France much as a lesser man might own an estate; now, for the first time, the King is seen as the first servant of an eternal state to whom he owes an unceasing duty. Pushed a little further, that notion leads straight to ideas of the kind expounded by the revolutionaries in 1789. Obviously, Louis XIV did not go that far: to him, the prosperity of France depended on the strength of its monarch.

"It must be agreed," the King goes on, "that nothing is more useful to the public good, or necessary to the greatness of the state, or advantageous to all the members of the royal family, than the links tying them to he who is its head . . . Then, potential rebels, seeing those princes too bound [to the King], no longer try to seduce them: as they fear that their criminal endeavors will fail and perhaps even be punished, they are forced to remain silent; those who are dissatisfied, finding no one to whom they can rally, are forced to swallow their displeasure in their own houses and the foreigners, deprived of the help given them by the allies who, alone, have made them a menace to this state, are more restrained in their purposes."[124]

This is, obviously, a recipe for preventing the recurrence of the Fronde; and, indeed, in 1666, France had not been at peace long enough for its ravages to be forgotten. Because, after 1661, the princes of the blood stopped rebelling, it is easy to think that their compliance was a natural development, that it was bound to happen. Nothing could be less true: it took unceasing vigilance and a personal reign that continued for over fifty years to end that particular peril.

Still, what may be generally true is often false in particular instances. Louis XIV was obsessed by the memory of his uncle, Gaston d'Orléans, who had provided a rallying point for plot after plot, and so he failed to see that his brother was deeply loyal to him. Although Monsieur was, like his uncle, the King's brother, his personality was altogether different from Gaston's; then, too, Gaston's strength had been that, until 1638, he was heir to the throne while, within a year of his marriage, Louis XIV had already fathered a son.

As a result, Monsieur was, to some extent at least, made to suffer for his uncle's sins. "The prince de Conti's unexpected death," Louis XIV noted, "caused my brother to feel again that he was entitled to the governorship‡ of Languedoc. He convinced himself that since my uncle had once occupied that position, he had an unarguable example proving that it should now be his as of right; but I thought it best not to grant him his request, feeling quite sure that (after the disorders which we have so often seen in the realm) it would show an absolute lack of forethought and reason if I were to entrust the governorships of the provinces to Sons of France* because, for the good of the state, they should have no retreat other than the Court, and no stronghold other than the heart of their elder brother.

"My uncle's example, which was apparently the foundation of my brother's claim, was a great lesson for me."[125] Thus was Monsieur's fate set: this intelligent and brave prince was forced to spend his life doing nothing. Of course, he was given compensations. The King, while denying him every possible power base, was anxious to keep him from being too greatly dissatisfied; so he was given estates and pensions and encouraged to spend his vast income on buildings, jewels, and festivities.

Even that, however, failed to satisfy the King. Because Monsieur was fascinated by etiquette, and vastly knowledgeable when it came

‡ Once the direct representative of the central government, the governor, invariably a prince or a duke, was increasingly superseded by the intendants.
* Son or Daughter of France was the title given the King's children.

to settling problems of precedence, he was usually consulted about most of these disputes; but when he put forth a claim of his own, it was slapped down with all possible speed. "My brother," Louis XIV wrote, "decided, in his leisure, on a request that his wife be given a chair† when she was before the Queen.

"My affection for him was such that I would have wished never to refuse him anything, but seeing how important this was, I told him immediately, in the friendliest tone possible, that I could not grant his request and that, when it came to anything which placed him above my other subjects, I would always do it with pleasure; but that I did not think I should ever allow anything that would bring him too close [in rank] to me . . .

"Those whose think that ambitions of this kind are mere affairs of ceremonial are wholly deluded; there is nothing in these matters which does not request careful thought or which is not capable of having serious consequences. The people whom we rule cannot penetrate into secrets of state, and therefore judge according to what they see on the outside, so that it is most usually by the place and rank that they measure their respect and their obedience . . . One cannot, without harming the entire body of the state, deprive its Head of the least signs of superiority which distinguish him from its other members."[126]

There, in that sentence, Monsieur's position was fixed for the rest of his life. Still, the King did, as he promised, distinguish him from all others at Court. He was, naturally, given precedence immediately following the King and, when he grew up, the Dauphin; and he was also the only one who instead of addressing Louis XIV as *Sire* or *Vôtre Majesté* called him simply Monsieur; while to the King, he was always *mon frère.*

Even more interesting than Louis XIV's attitude to his brother, however, are two brand-new notions. The first is the importance of etiquette, a matter in which the French Court had until then lagged behind that of Spain; and the other that of what the twentieth century has called public relations: the King rules in part because he is seen to rule, just as today, presidents of the United States take great care to look "presidential." Here, too, under the guise of following precedent, Louis XIV was innovating; and as always, for the specific pur-

† As opposed to a stool, that is. The Queen sat in an armchair. A regular chair, even without arms, would have seemed too similar.

pose of preventing rebellion and civil war. By raising the King so high above all others that he would come to seem more than human, he made it virtually impossible for people to think they could disobey him and get away with it.

Stiffening the etiquette might impress the once rebellious princes and nobles; but they were, after all, only a small part of the population. At the other end of the social scale, its overwhelming majority was not expected to have any opinion at all: peasants worked so hard, led such uncertain lives, and were so ill-informed besides that they were simply supposed to obey. Still, that left an ever more significant group, the growing, increasingly rich, increasingly powerful middle class, who did not attend the Court but controlled a good deal of the country's wealth, and that often the most active. In an age without radio, television, or newspapers,‡ the government depended on writers of all kinds for its propaganda, from Racine, who was to become Royal Historiographer, to the humblest of pamphlet writers. Their steady output was also important in that it could be expected to reach foreign courts.

Praise, in fact, whether spontaneous or bought, now became one of the most visible elements of the King's new way of ruling. A wave of pamphlets appeared, all adulatory in tone. There was, for instance, a proposed inscription on the new gate to the Louvre: *"Monde, viens voir ce que je voi / Et ce que le soleil admire / Rome dans un palais, dans Paris un Empire / Et tous les Césars dans un Roi"* (World, come see what I see / And what the very sun admires / A palace worthy of Rome, Paris the heart of Empire / and a King worthy of all the Caesars).[127] There were sonnets, like this one: *"Montrer la majesté peinte sur le visage / Avoir l'air d'un héros, au dessus des humains / Etre plus généreux, plus vaillant et plus sage / Que ne furent jadis les Grecs ni les Romains . . . / Enfin surmonter tout sans rencontrer d'obstacle / La nature, soi-même et tous ses ennemis / C'est dans le grand Louis qu'on voit tous ces miracles"* (His majesty shows in his face / He looks like a hero, above common mortals / He is more magnanimous, valiant and wise / than ever were the Greeks and the Romans . . . / No obstacle stops him, he overcomes all / Nature, himself and all his enemies / All these miracles are seen in Louis the Great).[128] Dreadful verse, and dutiful praise; but even here, a key element of Louis XIV's new style is

‡ Although there was a bimonthly paper, it was essentially an account of the world's main events and the Court's festivities; it never meddled in politics.

noted: "He overcomes . . . himself." This mastery over one's own feelings was well understood to be a key element of greatness; already in 1640, Corneille, who in many ways set the tone for the reign of the Sun King, had Augustus say: *"Je suis maître de moi comme de l'univers"** (I rule over myself as I do over the world). This absolute mastery over self, which never ceased to amaze his contemporaries, was one of most powerful components of the new image.

This is all quite a change: traditionally in France, songs and pamphlets were critical, not laudatory; indeed the *mazarinades* began the Fronde. That this tradition was not quite yet at an end is attested by verse like: *"Le peuple que jadis Dieu governait lui-même / Las de son bonheur voulut avoit un roi / Eh bien, dit le Seigneur, peuple ingrat et sans foi / Tu sentiras bientôt le joug du diadème / Celui que je mettrai á ce degré suprême / Comme un cruel vautour viendra fondre sur toi . . . / Ainsi régne aujourd'hui par les voeux de la France / Le monarque absolu que Dieu nous a donné"* (The people whom, once, God governed himself / weary of happiness wanted to have a king / Well, said the Lord, ingrate and faithless folk / You will soon feel the full weight of a Crown / He whom I will place in the highest place / Like a cruel vulture will prey upon you . . . / Thus reigns today through the wishes of France / the absolute monarch the Heavens have given us).[129] This may well have been the work of a former Frondeur, or that of a friend of Fouquet; in any event, it represents a rare, generally unheard false note in the universal concert of praise.

By the end of 1666, however, there were some criticisms, especially at Court; war, everyone agreed, was the noblest of pastimes; it gave men the chance to show how brave they were, earn some glory, and be rewarded by the King; but while no one doubted that the French army was superior to all others, Louis XIV obstinately refused to use it; and some of the young nobles began to murmur that the King must be a coward. As it happens, they were right, in one respect at least: while Louis XIV appears to have been physically brave, he was very well aware that battles are uncertain and wars expensive. Unlike many of his ancestors, therefore, he intended to refrain from fighting until all the chances were so overwhelmingly on his side, and the campaign so thoroughly prepared, that victory would be all but certain.

* In *Cinna ou la clémence d'Auguste.*

This involved three key elements. The first was money: without it, the army would disintegrate; but by 1666, the King and Colbert together had seen to it that the Treasury was well stocked. The second was military preparedness: France had a long and unpleasant history of disasters brought about by untrained troops and undisciplined commanders; but that had changed because the King had himself been supervising the reorganization and retraining of his army. The third was, obviously, the relative strength of the enemy; but that was now nothing to worry about: Spain was not only in decline but ruled by a weak and incompetent Regent; so the King had every prospect of success.

Even that, however, was not enough. Partly in order to reassure the rest of Europe, partly in order to provide himself with the best possible propaganda, when, in May 1667, the French army crossed the border into the Spanish possessions in Flanders, it was merely, the King said, to claim his wife's property. Because the huge dowry stipulated by Mazarin in the Treaty of the Pyrenees had never been paid—an event fully anticipated by the Cardinal—Marie Thérèse's renunciation to her Spanish inheritance was no longer valid; and as if that were not enough, Louis XIV had his lawyers dredge up a "right of devolution" from the distant past, in virtue of which the Queen was now entitled to Flanders, Brabant, Luxembourg, and the Franche-Comté.

All these precautions were still not enough to reassure the King, however. A secret treaty was concluded with Emperor Leopold I which provided that should Charles II of Spain die without heirs—a likely possibility for a sickly child—the provinces in question would become French while the remainder of the Spanish Empire would go to Austria; so that the war was only the anticipation of what, no one doubted, would soon happen anyway. Then, too, any German prince able to attack France was bribed not to do so; and, finally, a treaty was signed with Portugal on March 31 so that Spain, if need be, could be attacked from the back.

All in all, these were methods that differed sharply from those of Louis XIV's predecessors. Here was no bold attack, carried out in a chivalrous spirit: the famous *furia francese* had been replaced by the most careful, the most thorough of preparations. When it came to going to war, in fact, the Sun King behaved like the most bourgeois of rulers. Predictably, his caution was rewarded: seldom in the history of France has a war been won so easily, seldom have the objects of a conflict been achieved so fully and so promptly.

Because the King knew himself—and his shortcomings—so well, far from trying to set strategy himself, he called on Turenne, the most experienced general in France. The result was a model campaign: one after the other, the Spanish fortresses fell before the French onslaught. By August, the French army had taken Ath, Tournai, Oudenarde, Furnes, Armentières, Courtrai, and Douai. Only Lille, then an even more important city than today, resisted for a while; but even that proved to be a good thing as it gave the King a chance to join his men in the trenches and be exposed to enemy fire before the city fell on August 27. Then, on the thirty-first, the maréchal de Créqui defeated the remainder of the Spanish army and, to the amazement of all, the King stopped the war: he had won enough; now the gains must be made safe; so, rather than strike deeper into Flanders, he ordered a young† but immensely talented engineer, Vauban, to design a new, impregnable fortress at Lille.

Although the results of the campaign can hardly have surprised either Louis XIV or his ministers, they stunned the rest of Europe. Spain had been dominant for so long that it was, erroneously, still considered a major power. In fact, its military organization had been dealt a deathblow at the battle of the Dunes in 1658 and its government was not only virtually bankrupt but also a model of inefficiency. Europe did not yet know all this, but the French government did; the King's restraint may therefore seem all the more surprising. Once again, however, he preferred to run no risks and consolidate his gains before going on to the next campaign.

Just because he chose to stop the war did not mean that he meant it to pass unnoticed. His triumph was widely celebrated, by pen and fireworks, throughout France, as was only normal; but he also inaugurated a new, publicity-conscious style of campaigning. Since Flanders was, after all, part of the Queen's inheritance, and being conquered on her behalf, she, along with the rest of the Court, was invited to come along and watch her husband play the role of the conquering hero. As city after city fell, special ceremonies were organized to celebrate her entry into them; and just so none of the campaign's incidents could ever be forgotten, Le Brun was commis-

† In 1665, Vauban was thirty-two.

sioned to design tapestries, to be woven at the Gobelins, picturing all the great events of the war. In time, engravings were made after the tapestries and broadcast the King's exploits throughout Europe while setting a new trend: from then on, tapestries were everywhere the proper way to enshrine a victory.

This kind of cross-pollination of art and politics was in itself typical of the new, emerging age. While Louis XIV understood painting, and collected it throughout his life, he also, from then on, provided contemporary artists with a stream of commissions, the object of which was to add to the patrimony of France while celebrating the achievements of the King; indeed, at the same time, another series of tapestries, also designed by Le Brun, was celebrating the great moments of the reign, from the Coronation to the meeting with the Nuncio who brought the Pope's apology in regard to the Corsican Guard incident. In 1667, however, Louis XIV still lacked the proper place in which to display paintings and tapestries, a shortcoming of which he began to be acutely conscious.

In one other way, the campaign created a new situation, both at Court and in the King's personal life. Although his affair with Mlle de La Vallière had long been public knowledge, she still lacked an official status; and her children—by 1667 there were two daughters, one of whom died in infancy—were listed in the register of births as of unknown parents. Since even the best-planned war is not without danger, Louis XIV decided to revive his grandfather's custom: La Vallière was made a duchess in her own right, and the surviving daughter, Marie-Anne de Bourbon,‡ was officially declared, before the Parlement, to be the King's issue.

This was an important move: once again, the King set himself above the rules observed by ordinary mortals. He now, besides his wife, had a *maîtresse déclarée,* an officially recognized mistress; and the position, once created, proved to be long-lasting: the last holder of that office was Mme du Barry, more than a century later. As for the legitimization of the little Marie-Anne, precedents had been created by Henri IV. Still, circumstances were very different: Henri IV had not only come to the throne late in life, and after a bitter civil war which had taught him to live less like a king than like a marauding general, he was also notoriously averse to etiquette. Given his grand-

‡ The future Mlle de Blois (1666–1739).

141

son's high regard for his own position, it was an easy guess that his bastard children, once they were recognized, would be given a far more important place than had been customary.

Far from taking the new duchesse's elevation as a sign of increased favor, however, most courtiers assumed that it signaled the beginning of the end, and that she was, in effect, being pensioned off—a cynical but not unnatural view, since the King's eye was visibly roving. La Vallière herself, by 1667, realized that the King no longer loved her as passionately or exclusively as had once been the case; indeed, it is not unlikely that the Queen Mother's death may have helped weaken Louis's attachment to La Vallière, because it meant that the mistress was no longer forbidden fruit. Of course, she still suffered from Madame's very visible hatred: the princess, who had longed to be, if not the King's mistress, at least the sole partner of his amusements, still loathed and resented her former maid-in-waiting; but, in spite of her intellectual qualities, she no longer held the royal interest, and so, fuming in vain, she consoled herself by making Monsieur's life as uncomfortable as she could.

What everyone failed to realize, however, was that Louis XIV liked to keep what he had once had, and that he was also quite able to love several women at a time. While, in the course of his life, he became devoted to only a few, very special, ladies, he was eager, and because of his position, able, to have sex with virtually any young and pretty creature he happened to see; thus while the list of his official mistresses is, in itself, not inconsiderable, that of his conquests, while it has never been drawn up, would, no doubt, easily surpass Don Giovanni's *mille e tre.* This self-indulgence, so notable from then on, was, however, still new; and La Vallière began to worry.

That, unfortunately, was calculated to alienate him further. Had the duchesse become his mistress simply because she was ambitious or greedy, she would, no doubt, have coped far more easily with the new situation and traded on the King's affection and periodic appetite for her. Instead, because she loved him, she entered a period of almost unalloyed suffering, torn as she was when Louis was paying attention to another woman, and full of apprehension that his returns to her would not last; so she cried, looked visibly wan, tried her clumsy best to regain his undivided love, and irritated him instead.

At first, she expressed herself in moderate ways. There was the sonnet written for her by Benserade, for instance, and addressed to the King, who was using the war as a pretext for neglecting her: *"Tout se détruit, tout passe, et le coeur le plus tendre / Ne peut d'un même objet se contenter toujours. / Le passé n'a point vu d'eternelles amours / Et les siècles futurs n'en doivent point attendre. / La raison a des lois qu'on ne veut point entendre, / Jamais de nos désirs rien n'arrête le cours, / Ce qu'on cherche aujourd'hui déplait en peu de jours / Notre inégalité ne saurait se comprendre. / Tous ces défauts, Grand Roi, sont joints á vos vertus. / Vous m'aimiez autrefois et vous ne m'aimez plus. / Ah, que mes sentiments sont différents des vôtres! / Amour de qui depend et mon mal et mon bien / Que ne lui donniez vous un coeur comme le mien / Ou que n'avez vous fait le mien comme les autres!"* (All is destroyed, all passes away, and the most tender heart / cannot always be satisfied with the same love. / The past has seen no eternal loves / and future centuries can expect none. / Reason has its laws that we do not wish to know / Nothing ever stops the burgeoning of desire / what we seek today will soon cease to please / Our inconstancy passes understanding. / All these failings, great King, are joined to your virtues / You loved me once, you love me no longer / Ah, how different my feelings are from yours! / Love on whom depends for me good and evil / Why have you not given him a heart more like mine / Why have you not made mine more like everone else's!).

A touching plaint; but, like so many such, wholly ineffective. The King, polite as always, and fond of verse as he was, promptly replied through Benserade's pen; but the answer, using exactly the same rhymes, was hardly what the first sonnet demanded: *"J'ai le coeur, belle Iris, aussi constant que tendre / Ce que j'ai droit d'aimer, je l'aimerai toujours; / Mais dès que mon devoir condamne mes amours / De ma fidélité l'on ne doit rien attendre. / L'honneur a des raisons et je les dois entendre / Bien que de mes plaisirs il arrête le cours, / J'immole á ce tyran le repos de mes jours / Par un effort sur moi que je ne puis comprendre. / Je renonce á l'amour qui ternit mes vertus / N'alléguez pas ses lois, je ne les connais plus, / Ma gloire a des appats qui triomphent des vôtres. / Après tout, belle Iris, ne savez vous pas bien / Qu'un héros dont le coeur est fait comme le mien / Donne á l'amour des lois que l'amour donne aux autres?"* (My heart, fair Iris, is constant and tender / She whom I may love I will love always / But when my duty condemns my love / No more can be expected of my fidelity. / Honor has its reasons and I must heed them / even if it interrupts my pleasures / I sacrifice my peace to that tyrant / through an effort on self beyond understanding. / I give up love when it tarnishes my virtues / Do not cite its laws, I know them no more / Glory has attractions even greater than yours. / After all, fair Iris, do you not know full well / that a hero whose heart is made like mine / rules love as love rules all else?).[130]

Quite admirable, no doubt; but, for someone who knew better, not very convincing. It was, in fact, in the summer of 1667 that the King became, secretly at first, the lover of the duchesse's best friend, a development which the lovelorn woman no doubt promptly guessed. Still, from her point of view, not all was lost: the lady in question was a married woman with a jealous husband, an awkward situation at best, and one of which the King might soon tire. Had his attraction to her been purely physical, that might well have been the case; but in the marquise de Montespan the King had found not just great beauty and the most enormous gusto for life, but also dazzling intellectual gifts, a well-known characteristic of the Mortemarts, the marquise's family. There could not have been a sharper contrast to the retiring and docile La Vallière; but that did not mean that the latter's unconditional adoration had lost all charm for the imperious monarch.

La Vallière had been left behind when the Court joined the army because she was again pregnant; but, frantic and desolate, she ordered her carriage and drove as fast as she could to the front, only to be met with universal blame when, to the Queen's fury, she appeared before the walls of the besieged La Fère. The next day, "when Mme de La Vallière was on a hilltop from which she could see the army, she had her carriage cross the countryside at top speed. The Queen saw this and became dreadfully angry . . . When the King reached the Queen's carriage, she urged him to join her; he refused, saying he was too muddy. After the Queen had left her carriage, the King stayed with her for a moment, and then went off to Mme de La Vallière, who was not seen for the rest of the evening."[131] This time, it had worked; but as the wretched duchesse soon found out, one evening of ardor changed nothing at all. True, the King did not send her away from Court; but he did not return to her either. Neither wholly loved nor wholly neglected, she found herself in that bitterest of positions, that of having to share the man she adored with a victorious rival; and she suffered accordingly. As for the King, who was seen to spend all his evenings with Mme de Montespan, he had no intention of giving up either of his mistresses; and that fall, Mme de La Vallière gave birth to a son.*

N EITHER his new conquests, feminine and territorial, nor the usual cares of government were enough, that year, to occupy Louis XIV. The Court, in residence, first at Saint Germain, then at the newly completed Tuileries, was as brilliant as ever; and the King saw to the least details of his new system; so thorough was he, in fact, that on January 1, 1667, he wrote the duc de Chaulnes, the senior member of one of the great French families,† the following letter: "My cousin, I have arranged the marriage of the sieur de Chevreuse [Chaulnes's nephew] with the sieur Colbert's elder daughter, and since, through this means, I tie the head and sole heir of your House to that of a man who serves me in my most important business with zeal and success, I have wanted to give you myself the notice of this alliance and feel sure that you will take part in the satisfaction felt by both families."[132]

This seemed to be mere courtesy; in fact, it was also a warning to the duc de Chaulnes that he had better toe the line: the marriage of a girl from a bourgeois family—her grandfather was a mere clothier— to the heir of a duke was virtually without precedent; and in an age of aristocratic pride, not to say arrogance, it seemed immensely shocking; but once again a piece of the new system was being put into place. The King, in fact, was taking care of three matters at once: he was rewarding Colbert, that exemplary minister, by raising his daughter to a level of which she could never have dreamed, and thus making it a virtual certainty that Colbert's grandson would be a *duc et pair;*‡ he was, for the first time, advertising the fact that, in his eyes, all who represented him were ipso facto placed in the very first rank of society so that achievement in the royal service counted as much as noble birth, a revolutionary notion; and he was, finally, lowering the

---

* Later titled comte de Vermandois (1667–83).

† The duc de Chaulnes was a member of the House of d'Albert de Luynes, and the son of Louis XIII's early favorite. The Luyneses not only cumulated three dukedoms, they were also immensely rich.

‡ There were three kinds of dukes in France. The first, the *ducs et pairs* had the right to sit in at the Parlement and were the grandest; the next, the *ducs héréditaires* or *vérifiés* could transmit their titles to their sons, but were not peers, and thus could not sit in the Parlement; and the third, the *ducs à brevet* held the title for their life only. Precedence at Court reflected this division.

status of the great nobles who now became mere cogs in the machinery of state, with the corollary that, the more independence they lost, the less likely they were to rebel.

Because the Court was so brilliant and the etiquette so important, the King's purpose was not immediately apparent; indeed, Mlle Colbert's marriage was seen, at the time, as just another example of royal indulgence to a favorite. In fact, a new division of French society had begun, in which the King was no longer barely more than *primus inter pares:* now, below the throne, all owed equal, prompt, and unquestioning obedience.

Indeed, it seemed as if no matter was unworthy of the royal attention. Converting the Protestants was, obviously, one of the government's goals, so the King could be expected to set up a system of incitements. What is more surprising is that he kept track of individual conversions; thus, for instance, on July 9, 1668, he wrote the marquis de Théobon, a minor noble: "M. le marquis de Théobon, having learned that the comte de la Motte, your grandson, after having been fully apprised of the Christian and Catholic truths, has, without any pressure, given up his heretical beliefs and at the same time has professed his faith to the Lord Archbishop of Paris, I am pleased to appoint him one of the pages of my Grande Ecurie and to assure you myself, by this letter in my own hand,* of the care I mean to take of him. As for you, I feel sure that you will not love him less than you did before this happy change since he alone decided on it."[133] Whether the young man's conversion was, in fact, spontaneous may well be doubted, although it is possible it was due, simply, to ambition: Protestants, after all, were not likely to rise in the King's service.

All conversions, even that of even so unimportant a young man as the comte de la Motte, seemed, to the King, a proof that, politically and religiously, his endeavors were approved from on high; but when Turenne, who lacked neither glory nor honors, and who, furthermore, belonged to one of the greatest families in France, decided to convert, Louis XIV felt that here, indeed, was the justification of his system. No one could claim that Turenne acted as he did out of an ignoble motive: he was, it seems, genuinely convinced that Catholicism was the true faith. Since he was the most visible of all the

---

* In fact, it was probably written by the Président Rose, the King's secretary, who could imitate the royal script perfectly.

Protestants, it seemed almost certain that most of his co-believers would follow him.

Turenne's conversion was a matter of state; but so, in the King's eyes, were the particulars of the Dauphin's education. On May 21, 1667, when the boy was only six, he wrote to the maréchale de La Mothe, his governess: "I am very glad that my children should have arrived at Compiègne in good health and that my son should be well-behaved; use the time in which you are alone with him to make him fear you. I can see nothing more needed at the present time . . . Please write me without ceremony."[134] And two years later, in another letter to the maréchale, he added: "Your letters need no excuse: it is enough that they are from you to be always welcome and besides, they give me such good news of my children that you cannot doubt that I read them with joy."[135] Those two letters define the King's attitude to his son, the only one of his legitimate children to survive infancy. On the one hand, he cared a great deal about him, and not only because he ensured that the throne would descend in his direct posterity; on the other hand, the child was to be made obedient to authority. No doubt Louis XIV realized that the King's heir can also be his enemy and offer a rallying point to all potential opponents, and he was thus trying to prevent the development of a very real problem; but in this case, the personality of the Dauphin, not a forceful one at best, was ignored: it is difficult to escape the conclusion that Louis was treating the boy as if he had been a miniature version of himself. This not being the case, it was soon noticed that the Dauphin was not only terrified of his father but also possessed of a wholly passive disposition.

*B*ECAUSE the King had so unexpectedly suspended the war in Flanders, it was generally assumed that he meant, in fact, to have peace. In any event, the winter of 1667–68 was bound to be calm: seventeenth-century armies did not campaign in winter, partly because supplies were generally unobtainable, partly because sieges required the digging of trenches, a virtual impossibility when the ground was frozen, partly because the generals liked their comfort. It was therefore truly startling when, suddenly, on February 2, 1668, in the middle of the Carnival festivities, the King went off to war.

As usual, Louis XIV moved only after the most deliberate preparation. This time, he was relying on a young man who was to become one of his greatest ministers, and was himself the son of a minister: here, indeed, is the first example of the King's propensity to rely on succeeding generations of the same families.

The marquis de Louvois, who was only twenty-nine in 1668, was the son of Le Tellier, the Minister of War; he had already proved his competence and relieved his father, whose attributions extended to a variety of domains, by taking responsibility for supplying of the army during the Flanders campaign; and the King, who watched carefully, noticed that he was doing an outstanding job. Competent as he was, however, Louvois was even more ambitious: he wanted to succeed his father, of course, but also to surpass him; and his pride was soon notorious. Obviously, managing the Flanders campaign had been a step up for him, but he had found himself repeatedly frustrated in his desire for greater control by Turenne's resistance. In the fall of 1667, therefore, he looked around for an ally against the often bad-tempered maréchal and found him easily in the person of Turenne's old rival, Monsieur le Prince.

Although by this time Condé had resumed his full role at Court, the King, whose memory was faultless, still did not quite trust him; so the Prince was left behind while Turenne covered himself with glory, and of course resented it. He responded all the more eagerly, therefore, when Louvois suggested that, together, they could offer the King a plan to conquer the Franche-Comté swiftly and easily. This had the advantage of bringing Louvois to the King's notice in the most positive way, thus virtually ensuring that he would become Minister of War while giving Condé the revenge for which he was yearning. And when they brought their plan to the King, the expected consequences followed: easy wars were very much what Louis XIV wanted.

That the Franche-Comté should still, in 1668, be Spanish was itself an anomaly, the last remnant, in fact, of the division of Europe in the early Middle Ages. Burgundy had then been divided into two distinct lordships: the duchy and the county, or Franche-Comté; both belonged to members of the French royal family. Then, in the early fifteenth century, the Duke of Burgundy, himself an uncle of King Charles VI of France, had, through his wife, inherited the county, thus reuniting in his person the two separate lordships. With the collapse of the Burgundian realm in 1477, Louis XI took over the duchy, while the Franche-Comté remained the possession of Mary of

Burgundy, the last Duke's daughter; through her marriage with Maximilian of Habsburg, it was transmitted to her grandson the Emperor Charles V, from whom, via his father, grandfather, and great-grandfather, Charles II of Spain had, in turn, inherited it. Thus, although unquestionably Spanish in law, the province was French-speaking, observed French customary law, and is today, in fact, well within France.

This anomaly now presented a double opportunity: helped by a number of generous gifts from Louis XIV, the notable men of the province had no trouble convincing themselves that they really ought to be French; and because it bordered on France, Switzerland, and Lorraine (then still occupied by French troops), it was virtually inaccessible to Spanish armies. Thus, the result of the campaign was a foregone conclusion. Following Monsieur le Prince's plan exactly, the army, headed nominally by the King, conquered the province in just three weeks.

At that, France's neighbors began to worry: if, apparently, nothing could stop the French armies, there was no telling who might be next; so Holland, within five days, signed alliance treaties with Great Britain and Sweden, and the Dutch Ambassador to the French Court, Van Beuning, asked the King to end the war. Naturally, Louvois's advice was to ignore this *sommation,* but both Colbert and Lionne, aware that France might find herself at war not only with those three countries, who were nominally her allies, but also with the Emperor, who was probably bribed to support Spain, pleaded for peace. To anyone who knew the King well, the result of this conflicting advice was a foregone conclusion: he sent an embassy to Madrid offering to make peace, and in the Treaty of Aachen returned the Franche-Comté to Spain while keeping the slice of Flanders he had conquered.

His moderation, however, was nothing but a trompe-l'oeil. Having once conquered the Franche-Comté, he knew just how easy it would be to attack it again: here, it was simply a question of biding his time, especially since Spain was clearly getting steadily weaker. As for Flanders, this new addition to the kingdom had a double advantage: first, for the first time ever, France now had an easily defensible northern border; second, although he did not show it, the King greatly resented the intervention of Holland. Poised on his new fortresses, he was now in a position to attack the Netherlands whenever he chose. Whatever the appearances might be, therefore—and there was a good deal of grumbling in France about the return of the Franche-Comté—the Treaty of Aachen constituted a French triumph.

Triumphs must be celebrated: so, on July 18, the King gave a great fete at Versailles; his father's hunting lodge there had already been transformed into a rather more sizable castle, complete with elaborate forecourt; more important, Le Notre's gardens were, if not completed, at least well under way. Water played in round basins, sculpture was everywhere, long straight alleys led to circular plazas, pavilions, and latticework structures; and closer to the castle brightly colored flowers were arranged in abstract patterns copied from embroidery. It was in these gardens that the fete took place.

Such were its splendors that an observer needed sixty closely printed pages to describe them. There were specially built fountains everywhere; at one place, a cabinet de verdure, a room made of greenery, was built to house five tables set up for a light meal. One of these tables looked like a mountain pierced with many grottoes which had been filled with cold meats; another, which looked like the façade of a palace, was made of cakes and candies; another held up pyramids of candied fruit, another still was covered with vases full of every kind of liquor while the fifth offered a composition of caramels. On the small lawn separating these tables, orange and other fruit trees, in silver planters, bore their own candied fruit, and in the center of all this was a thirty-foot-high jet of water.[136]

All through the gardens, the alleys were lined with fruit trees and sculpture arranged in latticework niches. There was, of course, a theater made entirely of greenery but lined, inside, with tapestries, and lit by crystal chandeliers, with an amphitheater seating twelve-hundred. The stage itself, lined with jets of water, offered a variety of sumptuous architectural sets during the performance of a Molière play—Le Paysan enrichi—with music by Lulli. After that, the King, Queen, and Court set off to a dome-topped octagonal temple, adorned, inside with vases, fountains, sculptures, and bas-reliefs. There, a table for sixty-four bore in its center a sculptured rock from which ran a fountain: that was decorated with sculptures, vases, shells, and figures. This table was surrounded by gilded dolphins, shells, and fountains; crystal chandeliers hung from the roof on scarves of silver gauze linked by festoons of fresh flowers. Interestingly, this was only for the King, Monsieur, and sixty-two ladies. The Queen was in a nearby tent, where tables each seating twenty had been arranged; as for the ambassadors, they had their own special table set up in an artificial grotto. The supper was followed by a ball in an elaborately decorated pavilion, and that in turn by fireworks; and throughout the entire evening, both gardens and castle were brightly illuminated.

All these splendors seemed only fitting for the ruler whom all now compared to Augustus because, like that emperor, he brought his country power, order, and prosperity. There can be no doubt that Louis XIV himself thoroughly enjoyed it all, and Monsieur, who loved a good party, must have been in heaven. This, in fact, was one of the last occasions when the King danced in public, not the sort of stately dance appropriate at a royal ball, but the intricate steps, then thought of as ballet, in which he was accustomed to shine. Within two years, he had given up performing in ballets and carrousels. This was partly because he realized that what befitted a very young man would not look well for a more mature monarch, but also because, at the first performance of *Britannicus,* one of Racine's masterpieces, he heard the following lines: *"Pour toute ambition, pour vertu singulière / Il excelle á conduire un char dans la carrière / A disputer des prix indignes de ses mains / A se donner lui-même en spectacle aux Romains"*[137](As his chief ambition, as his main achievement / he excels in driving in a chariot race / in disputing prizes unworthy of himself / In making a show of himself to all Rome). These lines applied to Nero, but the King took them also for himself.

Splendid as the fete was, however, one of the guests found it the bitterest of torments: the duchesse de La Vallière, now maitresse déclarée, was expected to be highly visible, decorative, and cheerful; but she knew very well that, although the King still occasionally slept with her, he was in love with Mme de Montespan; and that lady saw to it that her predecessor was constantly made aware of the fact. To make her situation even worse, she must have compared her situation that night, officially honored when her heart was broken, to the one she enjoyed during the other great fete, the *Plaisirs de l'Ile Enchantée* some four years earlier; then she had had neither title nor position at Court but she was the heroine of the occasion: Louis XIV was passionately in love with her and, for the first time, was making it plain to all eyes.

Indeed, it is difficult not to feel sorry for La Vallière: unlike most of her successors, under both Louis XIV and Louis XV, she had not a particle of ambition; she cared nothing for money or honors, had no grasping family to establish. She had become Louis's mistress after the hardest-fought resistance and only because she was desperately in love with him; now, and for the next few years, she was made to endure a long drawn-out calvary as, remaining at Court, she watched her rival's triumphs.

As for the King, who was unquestionably cruel to her, he had, as usual, good reasons to behave as he did. The first, and most honorable, is that he still loved her and did not want to do without her; the second was that Mme de Montespan was a married woman. A double adultery, openly displayed, had not lost its power to shock; so La Vallière served as a screen behind which the King could indulge his passion.

Except for that inconvenient and not infrequently obstreperous husband, however, Mme de Montespan seemed far more suited than the shy and tender La Vallière for the post of royal mistress. In the midst of a splendid Court, she was herself the most dazzling of creatures: beautiful, blond, with an admirable if abundant body, she knew how to outdress and outshine all the other ladies. She loved magnificence, in herself, her jewels, her apartments. She enjoyed life on a large scale, eating, drinking, gambling, making love. She could be majestic or uproarious, severely brilliant or extraordinarily funny. Just as the King himself had begun to seem larger than life, so Mme de Montespan seemed bolder and brighter than all her contemporaries; as for her rages, which did not spare Louis XIV himself, they were justly celebrated.

With all that, however, appearances were respected, at least minimally. Mme de Montespan's apartment, for instance, was behind La Vallière's, so the King would, visibly, go in to the duchesse's and send away his attendants, only to cross over, privately, to Mme de Montespan's. When, in 1669, she became pregnant, the fact was carefully concealed and she gave birth in the deepest of secrecy.

No matter where he looked, in fact, the King had reason to be pleased. His Court was the most brilliant in Europe, and now began to be copied: the great leonine wig, for instance, soon spread from France to the rest of Europe, as did fashions in clothes and decor: what might aptly be termed the French century had begun; for the next hundred and twenty years, the fluctuations of politics notwithstanding, France was the lodestar which the rest of Europe followed; and why not? Mansart in architecture, Le Brun in painting, Lulli in music, Molière and Racine in the theater, all contributed to the supremacy of the French style. New, becoming fashions for men replaced the oddities of the early sixties, and, with only slight modifications, they lasted until the end of the eighteenth century. Knee breeches were worn with stockings and buckled shoes; a coat open in front came almost to the knees, with a closed waistcoat worn underneath and a lace cravat around the neck; while women adopted straight lines: tightly corseted waists, straight but sumptuous underskirts with an overskirt open in front and looped at the back; and jewels were everywhere, sewn to men's coats and women's dresses, worn on hats and shoes, as buttons and tiaras, so that the overall look was both dignified and dazzling.

All this was based on an upsurge of prosperity, reflected, in turn, in the yearly budget. When Louis XIV looked at his little notebook in 1670, he could see that his revenues had risen from 63 million livres in 1664 to 74 million now while keeping taxes at the same level; and because of the financial reforms, the percentage taken up by the service on the debt was minute. Indeed, that year, a number of categories rose substantially: the military establishment was given 16 millions more; nearly 2.5 additional millions was spent on fortifying the newly acquired northern cities; the navy, under Colbert's impulsion, was given 9.5 more millions; and finally the King saw to his own pleasures: his outlay for buildings went from 2 to 5 million. Best of all, all this was done on a balanced budget. In fact, as it turned out, 1670 ended with a 4-million deficit due to the lack of accuracy of certain estimates; but that sum was made up the next year.

None of this, certainly, would have been possible without Louis XIV's constant efforts; but he was also helped by ministers of genius. Colbert, the universal man as always, watched over every aspect of the economy, oversaw the King's rapidly increasing constructions, and also took care of details; on May 5, 1670, for instance, he was writing the King: "Sire, Mlle de Blois [the King's illegitimate daughter] has had smallpox . . . the Sieur Bruger looked after her: she is now, thank God, almost over it. M. le comte de Vermandois [her brother] has a bad cold, which has upset him. Your Majesty may be sure that my wife is taking good care of him."[138] Colbert's many achievements, however, did not exempt him from the exact obedience the King demanded of all his servants. Thus, in the spring of 1671, he chose to disregard Colbert's advice in regards to the army; the minister reiterated it forcefully and complained that his master was listening to other people. This assertion of superiority by one of his ministers was precisely what Louis XIV was determined to prevent, but he was also aware of, and grateful for, Colbert's unceasing efforts; so off went a letter that, in its blend of firmness and kindness, was absolutely typical of the King. "Do not think that my regard for you can be abated as long as your services continue, that will never happen, but you must render them such as I wish, and believe that I do all for the best.

"The preference you fear my giving others must not worry you. I only wish to avoid injustice and work for the best of my service. That is what I will do when you will all be near me.

"Believe in the meantime that I have not changed in my feelings toward you and that these are such as you can wish."[139] It might almost be a letter to a jealous lover; and indeed, that was one strong element of Colbert's devotion to the King.

Louis XIV, too, felt strong ties to Colbert: absolute master though he was, he knew very well that only the best advisers allowed him to function successfully; and while his other ministers each played an essential role in a limited area, it was Colbert who saw not just to his very extensive official duties but also to all the awkward events which fell outside regular jurisdictions. An incident which took place early in 1670, and which, twenty years earlier, would have had the gravest consequences is a perfect example, both of the minister's usefulness and of the King's power.

This involved no less a personage than Monsieur. Still utterly without occupation, although he had behaved with conspicuous bravery during the Flanders campaign, the duc d'Orléans, married to a wife he detested and who did her best to annoy him, had fallen passionately in love with the chevalier de Lorraine, a penniless youngest son of a younger son of the illustrious Lorraine family. Entitled by birth to attend the Court, he counted on his good looks and seductiveness to supply his lack of funds; and looking, as he did, to both sexes for support, he was already eminently successful when Monsieur, who had always been attracted to handsome young men, fell head over heels in love with him. That the chevalier immediately responded hardly needs saying: Monsieur might not be powerful, but he was very rich and able, intermittently, to obtain favors from the King; and since jealousy tends to ensure continued love, Lorraine, beside his affair with the prince, was seen to court—some thought successfully—Madame as well.

Naturally, Louis XIV was well aware of all this; and since it was his policy to keep Monsieur satisfied, he occasionally granted his brother's requests regarding the chevalier. Ormesson tells us what happened next: "The news of the death of the Bishop of Langres having reached St. Germain, M. le duc d'Orléans, who had promised the chevalier de Lorraine the two abbeys† belonging to M. de Langres, went to ask the King for permission to proceed. The King answered that his conscience would not allow him to do so, and despite [Monsieur's] repeated pleas, refused him, so Monsieur, gravely annoyed, ordered that his apartment be packed up as he was leaving the Court. The King [sent], in the meantime, M. Le Tellier to see Monsieur and try to convince him to stay, but he was unable to, Monsieur saying that if he had had a house that was a thousand leagues away, he would go there."

That the King should have refused was due not just to religious scruples, although the notion of that kept man, the chevalier de Lorraine, owning two abbeys, was indeed a little shocking. Just as important, it was part of Louis XIV's policy toward his brother to keep him aware that his position depended entirely on the royal goodwill; thus, this was an ideal occasion in which to refuse a request. That the usually docile Monsieur should have left the Court, however, was wholly unexpected, and no doubt awakened memories of the late Gaston d'Orléans, who, under similar circumstances, would have started a civil war.

That catastrophe was unthinkable in 1670, a true measure of Louis XIV's achievement; and Monsieur, although capable of rages and sulks, was, at bottom, absolutely loyal; but the King was not inclined to take chances. As it was, he had the perfect hostage and immediately took advantage of that fact. "The King, who was told this, and thought that it was M. le chevalier de Lorraine who had encouraged

† Their income, that is; they would then have been run by an underpaid ecclesiastic. This was common practice, but Louis XIV, in other instances as well, was beginning to amend it.

Monsieur, had him arrested. The guards were doubled around Monsieur's apartment, where the chevalier de Lorraine then was. M. Le Tellier went to inform Monsieur of the King's decision and M. le chevalier de Lorraine, after being embraced by Monsieur and treated by him as the dearest of friends, went out and . . . was arrested by the Captain of the Guard, and sent . . . to Montpellier. Monsieur left St. Germain at midnight with Madame, stopped for a day in Paris . . . and went on to Villers-Coteret.‡"[140] All this happened on January 30.

Three days later, the distraught Monsieur, anxious to find a way out of the crisis, appealed to Colbert: the choice was obvious; and his letter gives a clear picture of the minister's situation, and the relationship between the royal brothers.

"Monsieur Colbert," the duc d'Orléans wrote, "since for some time now I have thought you one of my friends, and since you are the only one among those who have the honor of being close to the King who also showed concern for me in my present dreadful circumstances, I think you will not be sorry that I ask you to tell the King: that I have come here feeling the greatest pain at having either to go away from him or to be covered with shame if I remained at his Court. That I beg him to think of what the world would say if I were observed cheerful and at peace in the pleasures of St. Germain during Carnival while an innocent prince [the chevalier de Lorraine], my best friend on this earth, and one truly attached to me, languishes for the love of me in a wretched prison; further, the manner in which he was seized was an insult to me, uncertain as I was whether it was not myself who was to be arrested, as my room was, for quite some time, surrounded by guards, both at the doors and at the windows, and my servants terrified because they did not know whether this was being done against my own person." It is worth noting here the very fact that His Royal Highness the duc d'Orléans, a Son of France, is addressing Colbert, the bourgeois minister as a friend, something which, even ten years earlier, would have been unthinkable; and that he thought it possible the King would, for no reason, order his arrest. Then, too, the tone of the letter, in its breathless garrulity, is typical of its sender: this is really Monsieur's voice we are hearing.

"Further," the letter continues, "the King sent to ask my wife

‡ One of his castles, situated some twenty miles north of Paris.

156

what she wanted to do; this shows he was inclined to allow her to fail in her duty to me by deserting me. In spite of all this, I would not have left the King if I had thought myself useful to the good of his service; but the way in which he has always treated me has convinced me of the reverse. I know that my mood is such that I could only be an unpleasant sight to him, and that he might even be distressed if he had constantly before him a brother he has reduced to the deepest despair. This would be painful for him and shameful for me, and my only purpose is to hide my sorrow until he allows me to be cheerful again. If I dared, I would ask the King to put himself in my place, . . . to give me the best possible advice so that the world can see he has given it to a brother who, throughout his life, has only tried to please him, as my behavior has always shown. I would rather open my heart to you because . . . you have no interest other than the King's . . . If M. le chevalier de Lorraine were guilty, I would be the first to send him away, but he never thought of anything but deserving [the King's] good graces and esteem; I can answer for this, knowing the bottom of his heart better than anyone; and I will show, to the shame of my enemies, that I love the King better than myself if only he will give me the means of reconciling my love for him and my honor, and in this I beg him to remember I am his brother."[141]

It is difficult to imagine a more perfect contrast with the behavior of earlier princes; no doubt, the prospect of the utter dullness of life at Villers-Coteret, made worse still by Madame's acrimonious presence, was reason enough to wish for a reconciliation; but there can also be no doubt that Monsieur was genuinely distressed at going away from the King.

Given all this, a solution was obviously not far away, especially since, here as always, Louis XIV did not hesitate to use other people's feelings. As a result, a compromise was soon worked out: Monsieur would come back to Court unconditionally, so that a dangerous precedent might be avoided; but then the King would listen to his plea; and, indeed, by March 3, it was all done: Monsieur and Madame arrived at St. Germain and in short order the chevalier de Lorraine was freed. It was a while, however, before he was allowed at Court; and when Louis XIV finally gave him permission to return, Monsieur was pathetically grateful.

There could have been no better illustration of the new state of things: not only was no one powerful enough to challenge the King, it never even occurred to them that they might attempt it. Still, that wholly satisfactory situation might not last: as the writing of his memoirs so clearly shows, Louis XIV knew he could die at any moment, leaving, yet again, a minor on the throne. Then, again, even if he lived to be fifty or sixty, the limit of extreme old age for most everyone in the seventeenth century, his successor might well lack his qualities. What was needed, therefore, was an institution strong enough to carry a weak monarch; and since the potential danger came from the aristocracy, the remedy was a court so expensive and so absorbing as to neutralize that once dangerous class. That this went together with a further exaltation of the monarch's status cannot have displeased the King; and he now set about creating the proper framework for the new monarchy.

Anne of Austria, engraving after her portrait by
Mignard.

Cardinal Mazarin, Prime Minister, exile, Prime
Minister again, with views of Rethel and Arras,
two cities taken under his administration.

The wedding of Louis XIV and the Infanta Thérèse in 1660; tapestry cartoon.

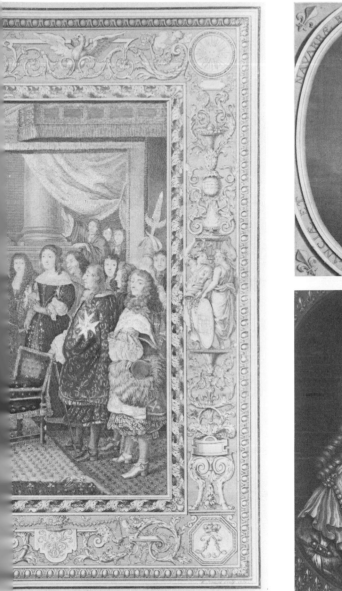

At right, Louis XIV in 1664, engraving by Nanteuil; Queen Marie Thérèse soon after her marriage.

Monsieur as King of Persia in the Carrousel of 1662.

Mme de Montespan, an engraving dated 1694 but taken from a portrait of the 1670s.

The crossing of the Rhine, 1672. The King is in the right foreground.

The Palace of the Tuileries seen from the Gardens.

The Palace of the Tuileries seen from the Louvre. It is within this esplanade that the King's great carrousels took place.

VII
The Golden Hive

"*THOSE OF THE* arts which do not depend entirely on the mind, such as music, painting, sculpture, and architecture, had progressed little in France before that period we call the century of Louis XIV,"[142] Voltaire wrote in 1751. That bold statement neatly—and wrongly—disposes of architects like du Cerceau and Salomon de Brosse, or the painters of the second School of Fontainebleau, although Voltaire goes on to praise Poussin, whom he credits for the beginnings of painting in France. What Voltaire, that incarnation of the Enlightenment, really means, though, is that the sort of integrated decor for which France became so famous, and so envied, was begun under the Sun King.

That Louis XIV, always with the advice of Colbert, only picked up on a preexisting trend is certain: already during the Fronde, a few rich Parlement men were feeling their way to a new kind of splendid environment that owed more to art than to the sole use of precious materials; then, at Vaux, it all came together, so effectively that the King and Colbert simply took over Fouquet's team: within weeks of the Surintendant's fall, Le Brun, Le Vau, and Lenôtre were at work on the royal houses; but even then their achievements, with the single exception of the Palace of the Tuileries, remained fragmentary. A façade here, a few rooms there, a piece of garden elsewhere, did not yet amount to a revolution in taste: as so often, it took politics to give the arts the wide field they needed.

The King himself fully realized that being a patron was part of his image; indeed, when it came to music, he had no trouble at all. Gifted himself, and highly appreciative of composers and performers

159

alike, Louis XIV promptly enlarged the royal orchestra and had it play not just at concerts, but also during all his meals. Opera, under the overall direction of Lulli, was given new impetus, so that performances multiplied; by 1680, it elicited as much interest, and occasionally controversy, as the theater, and Louis himself was the most enlightened and appreciative of critics.

Painting, however, clearly held less appeal for him; indeed, there is good reason to think that he reacted more strongly to beautiful objects—which he collected avidly—than to great art. Not that he was a Philistine: but while he could not live without music, and was therefore constantly commissioning new pieces, it seems very probable that he only bought paintings so as to have a collection worthy of a great king. Indeed, there is something almost impersonal in the orders sent to a variety of agents in Italy throughout the seventies. Buy a lot of the best, they were told, an exhortation not unlike those uttered by certain turn-of-the-century American millionaires. Clearly, rather than satisfying the King's yearning for the work of a particular master, these purchases were meant simply to bolster his reputation. Even when he bought every Poussin that came on the market, as he did throughout the reign, it was less an expression of personal taste than an effort at gathering the work of the man who was widely acknowledged as the only painter of genius France had ever bred.

In the end, however, whether or not the King was deeply moved by art did not matter: he knew very well that encouraging the best painters and sculptors of his time was a good way to make himself illustrious; and the connection between art and architecture, which he had discovered at Vaux, served as just the right kind of spur. Even better, one member of the Vaux triad, Le Brun, was the very man to underline that connection; already in 1663, therefore, the painter was granted a patent of nobility—his arms included a golden sun and a fleur-de-lis—and within a year, he had become Chancellor of the Académie de Peinture and Director of the Manufacture des Gobelins. Both posts were eminently suitable for this gifted man who, besides being a talented painter, was, first and foremost, a designer and organizer of genius.

Here, the Gobelins played a particularly important role. Set up by Colbert, who had regrouped a number of small, independent tapestry makers, the Manufacture Royale soon branched out into all aspects of the decorative arts, producing furniture, mostly made of solid silver, and various objects—vases, ewers, boxes, etc.—as well as the tapestries for which it has remained famous. Now that Le Brun was, in effect, its chief designer, the Gobelins could achieve just the sort of integrated look which was that artist's great contribution.

Still, there can be no good decor without good architecture, and, here, Louis XIV was lucky: during the first forty years of his personal rule, from 1661 to 1700, he was able to work with two architects of genius, Le Vau and Mansart. For a king with a passion for building, this was the ideal situation; especially since Mansart was able to function equally well whether the project was a huge palace or a tiny pavilion. Still, it would be a mistake to assimilate all the successive construction campaigns undertaken from the very beginning of the personal reign. Before 1668, piecemeal projects dominate: the Tuileries were completed, a new façade was added to the Louvre, some small expansions took place at Versailles and Fontainebleau; after 1668, and for almost twenty years, one massive concern, the creation of the most splendid palace in Europe, takes over; and finally, starting in the eighties, the King's pleasure pavilions—Trianon, Marly—introduce a new style altogether, even as work continued at Versailles, where the chapel, begun in 1701, was only completed in 1710.

Versailles itself, the huge palace with its sumptuous decor and majestic gardens, began to fascinate from the first day it was open. It still does today; but while it has been much admired, it has also been described as an act of monstrous self-indulgence, the expression of a grotesquely inflated ego. Its cost, countless critics have charged, bankrupted the nation; its very splendor ruined the monarchy because its gilded salons created so artificial an environment that Louis XIV lost touch with his people.

None of these accusations, in fact, will stand up to examination. Far from being the caprice of a luxury-mad monarch, Versailles probably saved France not just treasure but blood as well, for it was in itself a major political venture, and one which proved to be wholly successful. Between 1540 and 1652, France had been ravaged by six civil wars; any pretext—religion, the minority of the King, or plain, unvarnished greed—had sufficed; and even when the monarch won out at the end—not an unvariable occurrence—the cost was enormous. After Versailles, the civil wars were over.

Nor was it so very expensive. Luckily, all the records have survived, so that we know, in great detail, just what was spent on even a doorknob or a lock; and adding it all up over the years, the grand total comes to exactly 25,725,836 livres (about 112 million of our dollars)—a large sum to be sure, but one which France could well afford since it was spent over some thirty years. Clearly, however, comparative figures are in order. We do not know, obviously, what the French gross national product was in the seventeenth century; not only was the very notion some two hundred and fifty years in the future, but it would also be well nigh impossible to establish for a preindustrial society where many transactions were still in kind. The yearly budget, though, can provide us with a standard, remembering always that taxes took in a far smaller proportion of the national wealth than is the case today.

In the 1670s, a time when war had not yet radically inflated government expenditure, the yearly budget hovered between 85 million and 90 million livres; and during the two great construction campaigns, those of 1670–72, and 1677–1682, expenses ran as follows: 1670: 1,632,800 livres; 1671: 2,481,408 livres; 1672: 2,022,499 livres, with 1673 coming in at a mere 491,171 livres. This represents at most, in 1671, a little less than 3 percent of that year's income of over 87 million livres. By 1680, receipts were up to 91 million livres, and the amount spent on Versailles, 5,640,804 livres, was higher than any other year; but even then it came to only 5 percent of income; and there were many years when the outlay was minimal. Thus, whether it is analyzed year by year or taken as a whole—25 million against well over 2,600 million budgeted—it is clear that Versailles was very far indeed from bankrupting the state.

That was due in great part to Colbert's ceaseless endeavors. "You do marvels about the money and every day adds to the satisfactions you give me. I am pleased to tell you this,"[143] the King wrote Colbert in 1678; and in truth the minister saw to it that Versailles was built as inexpensively as if it had belonged to the most penny-pinching of private owners. Competing bids were almost invariably solicited; the army, instead of being left idle in peacetime, was used for some of the rough labor; estimates were strictly adhered to; fluctuations in prices were watched with care. As a result, what struck most observers as unrestrained lavishness was in fact the result of what might almost be called scrimping—with the consequence that, often, chimneys drew poorly, windows did not shut tight, and discomfort was the rule in winter.

Colbert, of course, oversaw much of the work; but even he could not at the same time be at Versailles and in Paris, where he was running an assortment of ministries; so, in the late seventies, he appointed one of his sons, the marquis d'Ormoy, as his representative on the site. The resulting correspondence is vivid and instructive: its subjects run from delays (Versailles, too, was brought in late) to cost overruns to precise descriptions of a section of decor; and always the King looked, judged and ordered changes. On October 20, 1679, for instance, Ormoy wrote his father: "I have just had the honor of following the King everywhere. He went into the grands and petits appartements* and into the Hall of the Ambassadors where His Majesty stopped for refreshments and ordered me to have the said hall gilded, along with the following small room, and to have gold initials put on the ceiling. Put wooden panels above the doors. Put marble mantelpieces above the fireplaces; that does not have to be done quickly. On the staircase,† fix the shell of the fountain because it is leaking on one side . . . Fix the broken windowpanes in the salon . . . have a door opened between the antichamber of the Queen's grand appartement and her guardroom. Hurry the construction of the Queen's small staircase . . .

"The King did not want to see the water of the pipe to Trianon because . . . the rainwater silted up the wells."[144] This was all typical, as were Colbert's ceaseless exhortations to his son because his questions were not always answered the very same day.

That Louis XIV took the most personal interest in Versailles is beyond question: every single detail was first approved on the plan, then checked once it had been carried out, and often modified. As a result, the palace was almost as much his work as it was the architects' and the designer's—so much so that the building of Versailles became an essential part of the King's life—but first the reasons behind the whole huge enterprise require elucidating.

Far from being the result of the King's own taste for building, as had been the case with the construction of Louis XIV's ancestors, Versailles is in fact both the embodiment of a policy and the machin-

---

* The grands appartements were the state apartments and included the King's bedroom; the petits appartements were the King's private rooms.
† The Escalier des Ambassadeurs; it was torn down in 1751.

ery through which it can be applied; far from being frivolous or self-indulgent, it is nothing less than an act of state. That it should also be so beautiful is one consequence of its purpose for which we have reason to be grateful. For, essentially, the palace is a golden trap in which to catch the princes and the great aristocrats.

Already in 1662, the Court's increasing splendor was doing just that; but, clearly, occasional festivities were not enough. The King's goal was to attract the once dangerous grandees, not for a few weeks, or even months every year, but for good. That, in itself, would sever them from their power bases in the provinces and keep them where they could be watched: the posts were controlled by the government and all interesting mail opened, read, and reported on. Further, the expenses inherent in the ever glamorous life of the Court were likely to put the nobles even deeper in the King's dependence: once their income proved insufficient, they would have to rely on pensions and salaries as a supplement; and that implied being where the King saw and remembered them. Naturally, Louis XIV was careful to emphasize the necessity of actual attendance at Court by saying "I don't know him" in freezing tones of people whom he had not seen in a while.

Still, constant presence had to be made bearable, so the setting and the entertainments must be magnificent; most important, the King had to have a palace large enough to house this suddenly much larger Court. Then, too, the increased size of the Court, and the permanent presence of its members, meant that the etiquette could become both more all-encompassing and more complicated. By multiplying the positions around himself, the Queen and the Royal Family, Louis XIV could catch many more great nobles; by exciting constant jealousy between the different officeholders and the different ranks of the aristocracy, he could also ensure that the energies which had once provoked civil wars would be spent in quarreling about the right to a stool or the order of entrance into the royal bedroom.

As if that were not enough, the very existence of the palace bred yet a new kind of preoccupation for the Court. For the first time, there was room enough to house, if not quite every courtier, at least most of them, so the competition for apartments was fierce, and more than one duke had to make do with a small, dark, all-purpose room. Not being housed at Versailles, however, was considered to be catastrophic: since only constant attendance on His Majesty put one in a position to ask for favors, and since a prerequisite for this was a lodging, all of a sudden even the richest of grandees were glad to exchange their own vast châteaux and sumptuous town houses for a garret; although, from the 1680s on they began to build themselves residences in the town of Versailles.

None of this would have been possible without Versailles. Seen in that light, of course, its cost becomes insignificant; better still, it is very much more than just a successful political machine. Here, for the first time, we see the enriching of a country by its buildings. The castles built by François I or Henri IV, the palazzi ordered by the Farnese or the Orsini, were all expressions of personal achievement. Versailles belonged to France as much as the King, as was made plain by the fact that, from the very beginning, its state apartments and gardens were open to all decently dressed visitors; and it is a measure of the King's success that the palace's power of attraction has only grown with the centuries.

Nor is it merely a question of splendor: without question Versailles is also a major artistic achievement. Not only was a new style born there, it also remained a center of artistic growth throughout the reign and set new and dazzling standards. Magnificence, of course, was ever the order of the day; marble, gold, and silver were everywhere; but, far more important, the quality of every visible element of the decor reached unprecedented heights, so that the rest of Europe, henceforth and until the Revolution, looked to France for guidance in all artistic matters; indeed, from Caserta to Schönbrunn, from Aranjuez to Tsarskoe Selo, the progeny of Versailles is scattered all over the continent.

As it is, what we see today is only the latter Versailles, version number three, so to speak, and precious little of it at that, since it was modified throughout the eighteenth century, then, more drastically still in the nineteenth.

It all started with Louis XIII's hunting lodge, slightly embellished and enlarged in the early 1660s; then, in 1668, Le Vau was commissioned to design a new façade on the park side which would greatly expand the palace. At this stage, however, only what is now the central part of the building was built: neither of the two vast lateral wings was yet contemplated; and where the Hall of Mirrors is today there was an open terrace. After Le Vau's death, in 1670, his plans were carried out by François d'Orbay; and then, in 1676, Jules

Hardouin-Mansart, at the King's order, drew up a whole new palace which, incorporating the existing building, made it immensely larger; and although there have been later additions—the Chapel, the Opera, the two outermost wings in the Cour d'Honneur—from then on, seen from the outside, Versailles looked much as it does today.

Of course, the interior changed as well; but already in the seventies, splendid enfilades existed in which the King held court. That in itself helped modify the very nature of the monarchy. Even before Versailles, of course, the King had stressed that he stood above all other men. Bossuet, that inspired orator and obedient subject, made it all very clear already in 1662: "[Kings] are gods, although they die, but their authority does not," he said in a sermon on the duties of Kings, adding, a little later: "The royal throne is not the throne of a man but the very throne of God."[145] Still, had the King been tiny, undignified, or reclusive, these comparisons would have seemed absurd.

In this case, however, fate was generous: even as a young man, Louis XIV was astonishingly majestic; he looked well in public and had perfected a way of never granting or refusing a request on the spot—*"Je verrai"* (I will see), he always said—which prevented unpleasant moments. He knew just how to speak to everyone, how to be polite without being condescending or short. And most important, he was quite happy to live out his life in public. Except when he was working with his ministers, or actually having sex with one of his mistresses, therefore, he lived out his entire life in the open, and ordered his occupations so that they followed an invariable schedule.

"Never was a prince less ruled by others," Primi Visconti, an Italian observer noted in 1673. "He wants to know everything: through his ministers the affairs of state; through the présidents those of the Parlements; through the judges the least little things; through his favorite ladies the latest fashions; in a word, there seldom occurs, in the course of a day, an event of which he is not informed and there are few people whose names and habits he does not know. He has a penetrating glance, knows everyone's most private business, and, once he has seen a man or heard about him, he always remembers him.

"Besides that he is very orderly in all his actions. He always rises at eight, remains at the Council from ten to twelve-thirty, at which time he goes to mass, always together with the Queen and his family. Because of his intense and persistent desire to control all the state's business, he has become very clever . . . He has an extraordinary talent and can often resolve problems which neither the ministers nor their secretaries could understand . . . At one, after having heard the mass, he visits his mistresses‡ until two, and then he invariably dines with the Queen in public. During the rest of the afternoon, he either hunts or goes for a walk; most of the time, he holds another Council when he returns. From nightfall until about ten, he talks to the ladies, or plays cards, or goes to the theater, or attends a ball. At eleven, after his supper, he visits his mistresses again. He always sleeps with the Queen . . .

"In public, he is full of gravity, and quite different from the way he is in private. Having several times found myself in his bedroom with other courtiers, I noticed that if the door chances to be opened, or if he comes out [from his private apartments] he immediately changes his attitude and his face takes on another expression, as if he were walking on to a stage: in a word, he always knows how to be a king . . . If one wants something, one must ask him directly, and not others. He listens to all, takes the memoranda, and always answers 'I will see' in a graceful and majestic way . . .

"He is helped by a robust state of health and a strong constitution . . . It is a fine show to see him coming out of the castle with the bodyguards, the carriages, the horses, the courtiers, the footmen, and a multitude of people in a mass running all around him . . . The King is almost always alone in his carriage. Sometimes, however, when he goes hunting or walking, he brings a few courtiers with him."[146]

Other men were kings; Louis XIV was monarchy incarnate, in an age where, England always excepted, it was an accepted idea that the celestial hierarchy was mirrored on earth at the royal courts; and as, increasingly throughout the seventies, the Court resided at Versailles, the King moved through his day as majestically, as predictably, as the sun through the heavens. Still, although he was incomparably above even the closest members of his family, he was surrounded by lesser stars; and they, too, helped set what was to become a universal pattern for the Court of a great king.

‡ Mmes de La Vallière and de Montespan.

The Queen, in her way, was as unchanging as her husband; she was, however, a good deal less impressive, and, of course, completely powerless. Louis XIV unquestionably respected her; he did his duty as her husband with great frequency, a fact we know because, invariably, the next morning Marie Thérèse would be seen to pray much longer than usual, no doubt in order to thank the divinity. Her amusements were few—attending religious services, eating, surrounding herself with dwarfs and small dogs—but they satisfied her, and she would have been perfectly happy had it not been for the King's mistresses, whom she always, and ineffectively, hated. Still, she did just what was expected of her and always behaved in public with perfect dignity.

That had not been true of the second lady at Court, Madame. As the sixties passed into the seventies, the princess had become all too aware that the King was no longer interested in her; she retaliated by making her husband's life as miserable as she could. There were constant scenes, after which Monsieur, never given to hiding his feelings, would lament his fate before one and all. Then, not only was Madame involved in intrigues with various factions at Court, she was also, most probably, unfaithful to her husband. In 1669 and early 1670, her position improved because Louis XIV used her as an intermediary between himself and her brother, King Charles II of England; it was in fact largely through her good offices that the Treaty of Dover, which linked the two nations, was concluded. Being needed, she also suddenly had a greater weight at Court, and the King, who, before, had most often sided with Monsieur, now started to defend his sister-in-law.

Here, once again, was a demonstration of Louis XIV's apparent remoteness from normal human feeling. Not only was Monsieur kept absolutely in the dark as to his wife's activities—he was notoriously indiscreet—but also Madame, in whom Christian charity was not the most visible of virtues, now prepared to make his life a living hell; all, of course, under the King's detached but all-knowing eye; and when the poor duc complained about this, he found that he could expect no help: as long as Madame was useful, she could behave just as she pleased.

That was the situation when on the afternoon of June 29, 1670, Madame, who was strolling on the terrace of St. Cloud, asked for, and drank, a glass of chicory water. Within an hour she was seized by the most dreadful stomach pains; she was quickly carried to her bed, but the pains only got worse and were soon followed by convulsions; within hours, amid the most excruciating suffering, the princess breathed her last.

"Poison was immediately suspected," the austere Ormesson noted, "because of all the circumstances of the illness and because of the bad relations between Madame and Monsieur which Monsieur, with reason, found offensive. That evening, the body was opened [for the autopsy] in the presence of the English Ambassador and several physicians of his choice, some of them English, as well as the King's physicians. They reported that Madame's body was severely diseased; one of her lungs adhered to the ribs and was completely spoiled, the liver was all dried up, bloodless, and with a great quantity of bile filling the body and the stomach, from which the conclusion was that no poison was used: if it had been, the stomach would have been pierced and spoiled."[147] The physicians' report notwithstanding, the rumor that Madame had been poisoned, probably on her husband's order, continued to spread, so much so that it has not completely died down to this day. In fact, no such supposition is necessary to explain her death.

Tuberculosis had long been a scourge of the English Royal Family; not so many years before, one of Henrietta's brothers, Henry, Duke of Gloucester, had died of it; and the description of the state of her lungs is in itself eloquent. That she died of peritonitis, probably of tubercular origin, is the most likely explanation, although acute appendicitis is also a possibility. In any event, Madame had long been in very bad health, coughing, losing weight until she was only skin and bones. The rumor that she was poisoned was, of course, provoked by the startling rapidity of her death; but, in truth, she had already been wasting away for a long time. It should also be said, in all fairness, that Monsieur, in spite of his quick temper, would have been incapable of killing a fly, let alone his wife. There is a great distance between complaints and murder; for Monsieur, that distance was impassable.

"Many people, at Court and in Paris, much regretted Madame's death," Ormesson added. It is easy to see why: odiously selfish as she could be on occasion, Madame radiated the sort of charm we have come to expect of movie stars; and with that she was lively, intelligent, interested: a striking contrast to the dull, limited Queen. That, perhaps was what spurred Bossuet when he came to write her funeral oration; what is at any rate certain is that he wrote one of the finest texts in the French language, one which has been quoted from that day to this.

It is, of course, impossible to reproduce it in full: Bossuet, after all, spoke for over an hour, but even a few brief quotes will show the heights eloquence could reach in the seventeenth century.

"O vanity! O emptiness! O mortals ignorant of their own destinies! Could she have believed it ten months ago?* And you, Messieurs, could you have thought, when she shed so many tears in this place, that she would so soon gather you here to mourn her? . . . No, after what you have seen, health is but a word, life but a dream, glory mere appearance, graces and pleasures a dangerous amusement only . . . All that fortune and a high birth, and also the greatest qualities of mind can do to raise a princess high was brought together, then annihilated in her . . .

"O disastrous night! O fearful night in which, suddenly, like a thunderclap was heard that astonishing news, Madame is dying, Madame is dead . . . Everywhere cries resound; everywhere suffering, despair, and the image of death are present. The King, the Queen, Monsieur, the Court, the People, all are stunned, all are desperate . . . In most men, changes come slowly and death usually prepares them for its last stroke, but, like the flowers of the fields, Madame passed from morning to night."[148]

The Court, however, was too self-involved to be really moved by this admirable flight of eloquence: Madame was mourned only by Charles II; as for the King, after shedding a river of tears, he forgot her before the week was out; and negotiations were started to find Monsieur a new wife. Indeed, all observers noted that this lack of feeling was typical: people were useful only as long as they lived; once dead, someone else had to be courted; and Louis himself, after all, had long since stopped loving Madame.

By the early seventies, in fact, he had also just about stopped loving La Vallière, although she was still the maîtresse en titre. "The duchesse de La Vallière's influence was greatly diminished," Visconti noted, "and the marquise de Montespan was high in favor . . . She had fair hair, large azure-blue eyes, a well-shaped aquiline nose, a

* When her mother's funeral service was celebrated in the same cathedral.

small, red mouth, very fine teeth, in a word a perfect face. As for her body, she was of medium height and well-proportioned, but when I first saw her, she had already put on weight. Her greatest charm was a special grace, wit, and way of turning a joke which so pleased La Vallière that she could not bear to be parted from her and was always praising her to the King . . . which made him curious to know her better."[149]

That was soon done: Mme de Montespan and the King were clearly made for each other; just as La Vallière had appealed to a younger, less emancipated monarch, so Montespan, this splendid creature whose appetites matched Louis's own, was the perfect mistress for the next stage of the reign. There was a problem, though: Mme de Montespan was married; and it was not only that the King's double adultery seemed far more sinful than an affair with the unmarried La Vallière: the husband would not cooperate, much to every one's surprise. After all, as Visconti noted in 1674, "there is not a single lady of quality who does not yearn to become the King's mistress. Many women, whether married or not, have told me that to be loved by one's monarch was no offense to their husbands, to their father or even to God himself . . . and the worst is that the families, the mothers, the fathers, and even certain husbands would be proud of this."[150]

M. de Montespan's steadfast refusal to see the light quickly proved an embarrassment: sin was one thing, scandal quite another; and the marquis did all he could to make himself obnoxious. In 1673, for instance, he retired to his estate in Gascony, where he had a requiem mass celebrated for his wife's soul, put himself, his children, and his servants in mourning, and went about deploring his loss. Another time, he took to displaying himself in Paris with horns, the cuckold's symbol, attached to his hat; and most of the time he went about, insulting his wife in language so unrestrained that "whore" was the very least of it.

That, as well as the annoying business about the double adultery, was the reason why the chroniclers, at this period, constantly write of the King's visits to his mistresses, in the plural: Mme de Montespan's apartment was reached through La Vallière, who was thus made to serve as a screen: Louis XIV appeared to be visiting the former mistress when, in fact, he had merely walked through her rooms on his way to the marquise, showing, typically, virtually no concern for the duchesse's feelings as she was thus left behind.

By 1674, however, no one had any doubt at all that Mme de Montespan alone mattered. Her very appearance proved it. On June 6, for instance, from Dôle, which he was busy conquering for the second time, the King wrote Colbert: "Madame de Montespan absolutely refuses to let me give her jewels; but so that she will not lack them, I would like you to order a handsome small coffer in which you will put what I will list hereafter, so that I can easily lend her whatever she would like. It seems extraordinary, but she will not listen to reason when it comes to presents.

"You will put in that coffer a pearl necklace, which I want to be fine; two pairs of earrings, one in diamonds, which I want to be fine, the other of mixed stones; a box and some links of diamonds; a box and some links of mixed stones which can be taken apart and used with the diamonds as well. We must have stones of every color so that they will be available. We must also have a pair of pearl earrings.

"We must also have four dozen buttons, of which the stones can be changed in the middle, the outside being made of small diamonds, that will go with everything; we must have stones ready for this . . .

"You must spend freely on this, it will please me."[151] And five days later, the King ordered an even more significant (and expensive present): an estate having been bought at Clagny, some three miles from Versailles, work was begun on a château designed by Mansard; and although it was torn down during the Revolution, we know from seventeenth-century engravings that it was both large and splendid.

Still, the anti-Montespan pressures were strong: the Church, respectfully but firmly, deplored the double adultery. Because Louis XIV normally took communion at Easter, that was an especially sensitive time: if the affair continued, the Most Christian King must stay away from the altar; and, in 1675, Bossuet finally convinced him the scandal was too great. Not for nothing was this the century of Corneille and Racine: Louis and the marquise parted in public, both weeping torrents and expressing the most edifying sentiments. She then moved to Paris while he duly took communion; and after some six weeks, the bishops decided that it was safe for her to return to Court; so, in order to avoid any possible awkwardness, a meeting between the former lovers was arranged in the presence of a group of elderly and respectable ladies. At first, all proceeded according to plan; then the King took the marquise off near a window; he was seen to whisper in her ear; she whispered back in his. At this, they came back to the middle of the room. Facing the ladies, Louis bowed, the marquise curtseyed, and having done so, both moved into the next room, closing the door behind them. In short order, unequivocal noises filtered through the panel, and nine months later, when Mme de Montespan gave birth to a baby girl, any last, lingering doubt the ladies might have felt was finally eradicated.

By May, the marquise was back at the peak of favor. On the twenty-eighth, the King wrote, "Mme de Montespan wrote me that you had ordered the purchase of some orange trees [for Clagny] and that you always ask her what she would like; continue to do as I have commanded you in this as you have done until now"; on June 5, he reiterated: "Go on doing whatever Mme de Montespan wants"[152]; and on the eighth, he amplified this order: "A great deal of money has been spent [on Clagny] and that proves that nothing is impossible for you in order to please me. Mme de Montespan has written me that you have carried out my commands perfectly and that you are always asking her what she wants: always continue to do so. She also tells me that she went to Sceaux† where she spent a pleasant evening. I have advised her to go some day to Dampierre‡ and have assured her that Mme de Chevreuse and Mme Colbert would be happy to receive her there. I feel sure that you will do the same. I will be pleased to have her amused, and these [evenings] will be very apt to entertain her.

"Confirm that this will happen. I am pleased to let you know all this so that you can see, inasmuch as it is in your power, that she is entertained."[153]

What these letters reveal, however, is not just that Louis XIV was anxious to please the marquise: typically, all these orders were addressed to Colbert, whose many responsibilities included everything connected to the King's private life. Just as Monsieur had written to him when he wanted to be reconciled with his brother, so he was expected to look after the mistresses and their illegitimate children as well as the building of Versailles, the smooth operation of the state manufactures, what, today, we would call the Department of the

† Colbert's country house near Versailles.
‡ The large and splendid château which belonged to Colbert's son-in-law, the duc de Chevreuse.

Treasury and the Bureau of the Budget, international trade, the navy, and just about anything else which was neither War nor Justice.

Naturally, this only happened because he carried out his many functions with spectacular efficiency and honesty; and as a result he developed a very particular relationship to the King, one in which real affection existed. While Louis XIV, in the course of his reign, grew to feel respect for the capacities of certain other ministers— Louvois, Colbert's great rival, is an example of this—he always kept them at a certain distance; they knew they pleased only because they were useful. With Colbert, however, the tone is very different, perhaps because Louis, who never forgot anything, remembered that it was in part to him that he owed his triumph over Fouquet; so he sometimes sounds more like a concerned friend than an imperious master. On April 15, 1671, for instance, he wrote: "Madame Colbert has told me that your health is not too good, and that the speed with which you intend to return [from Rochefort] might harm you.

"I write you this note to order you not to do anything that would make you unable to serve me, when you arrive back, in all the important business with which I entrust you.

"In a word, your health is necessary to me, I want you to preserve it and to believe that I speak to you like this because of the trust and friendship I feel for you."[154] Friendship! that was not a word Louis XIV used casually and here it gives the full measure of the minister's importance.

No less instructive, however, is a letter the King wrote Colbert just nine days later, because the minister, during a Council meeting in which the navy's position had been discussed, had argued on after his master had announced his decision. In its mixture of reproof, domination, and care, it expresses the very essence of the new monarchy. "I was sufficiently master of myself the day before yesterday to conceal from you that it pained me to hear a man whom I covered with favors speak to me in the way you did," Louis wrote on April 24. "I have felt much friendship for you, my actions have shown it, I feel it still today and believe that I show it clearly enough when I tell you that I constrained myself one single moment for you and that I did not want to tell you what I am now writing you so as not to put you in a position where you might displease me still further.

"That feeling is due to my remembrance of the services you have rendered me and to my friendship for you; be glad of it and do not risk annoying me any more, for after I have heard your arguments and those of your colleagues, and then decided on all your requests, I never want to hear another word on those subjects.

"See if the navy does not suit you, if your position is not what you wish, if you would prefer something else; speak freely. But after the decision I will take, I do not want to hear a single argument.

"I am telling you what I think so that you can work on a sound footing and will not take the wrong measures."[155]

It would be difficult to state the position more clearly: the King was always willing to listen to advice *before* taking a decision; but because he was absolute, God's representative on earth, his decisions, once taken, must be obeyed without further discussion. In this particular case, Colbert's trespass had been due to jealousy: Louvois was getting more money for War than he was for the navy; and in his answer to the erring minister's apology, Louis XIV made his position clearer still. "Do not think that my friendship for you will lessen, if your services continue it cannot happen, but you must render them such as I want them, and believe that all I do is for the best.

"The preference you fear I may give others must not pain you. I only want to avoid injustice while working for the good of the state. That is what I will do when you are all with me.

"In the meantime, believe that I have not changed toward you and that my feelings for you are such as you may wish."[156]

Louis XIV had just made himself very plain, and Colbert heard the warning: never again did he discuss a royal decision; but as we look back with the full benefit of hindsight, we are entitled to ask whether that, in fact, was the most productive of attitudes. The King's reasons are clear: he would do whatever was necessary to avoid having a dominating minister and rely on God to inspire him with the right choice. Still, time after time, he chose to ignore excellent advice simply because it did not please him: when, for instance, Colbert pleaded that it was not possible to fight frequent wars, run the most splendid Court in Europe, and build Versailles, Trianon, and Marly all at the same time, he undoubtedly had a point. By 1671, for the first time in the history of the monarchy, he was producing a large surplus, 3,625,353 livres, while the debt was being retired at a steady rate. Already in 1680, the surplus had given way to a deficit of 4.5 million livres—very manageable still, but obviously alarming; and that was due to the King's refusal to curtail his expenditure. As a result, French historians have blamed Louis XIV for creating a lasting financial mess.

In fact, even a 4.5-million deficit still represented only 5 percent of the budget—a negligible figure to our modern eyes; and the King got good value for his money. When his wars resulted in the acquisition of important provinces (which, indeed, have remained French ever since), when his buildings turned out to be masterpieces admired throughout Europe, then the money cannot be said to have been wasted. Thus, it is a surprising, but real, fact that, when he relied on his instinct and ignored Colbert's representations, Louis XIV was doing a great deal for the ultimate glory and welfare of France. There are, in the end, more important goals than a balanced budget, something the uneducated monarch understood better than his enormously competent minister.

Just because Louis XIV reserved the decisions to himself, however, does not mean that he was unaware of the details of his government: besides determining policy, he watched jealously over its implementation. More, he took pride in his unrivaled knowledge of even the most distant parts of his realm. It is, for instance, interesting to read a letter he wrote in May 1671 to M. de Baas, Governor of the Isles of America, as the French Caribbean islands were then called, partly because of the care it denotes, partly because of its note of tolerance.

"Having learned that the Jews who have settled at Martinique and in the other islands inhabited by my subjects have incurred considerable expenses for the cultivation of the land, and that they are still fortifying their towns, which is useful to the population, I write you this to tell you that I want them to enjoy the same privileges as the other inhabitants of the same islands; they are to be given their full freedom of conscience, while the necessary precautions will be taken so that their religious ceremonies will not offend the Catholics."[157]

This letter, obviously, has a double implication. The first and most obvious is that nothing was too inconsiderable for the King's attention; the second, and more surprising, is that he was no enemy of toleration. A clear distinction can thus be made between his attitude to the Protestants, on the one hand, and his understanding of religious freedom on the other; and, as usual, this was based on politics. The Protestants had formed almost a separate country within France; and even in the 1670s, they represented a potentially dangerous minority, not by their power to convince but by their eventual ability to resist the royal government. Since it was the King's great goal to ensure that his writ was unchallenged, he had an obvious reason to wish the Protestants converted to Catholicism. No such resistance was to be feared from the Jews, however, and so no attempt was made to convert them: more, their religious observances were to be protected. Coming from a monarch who eventually became almost a byword for fanatical Catholicism, this openmindedness needs to be noted.

Again, because Louis XIV became so radiant a symbol of monarchy, he is now often seen in modern terms as the first of a long line of dictators. In fact, precisely because he was the King, and thus secure, his method of ruling and of presenting himself was the very opposite of that adopted by someone like Mussolini. While modern "great leaders" have been reduced to pretending universal competence, Louis XIV invariably required, and usually deferred to, the opinions of experts; nor did he ever downplay the importance of those that served him. To take only one example among many, his behavior when Turenne died in July 1675 was typical.

"That evening, when all the courtiers were crowding around the table at which the King usually dines, he had barely appeared before he said gravely: 'We have lost the father of the country' . . . The next morning, so that people could see that the realm was not short of generals, and to lessen the effect of this loss, the King made Schomberg, d'Estrades, Navailles, Rochefort, Luxembourg, La Feuillade, Duras, and Vivonne marshals of France. Since this last was the brother of Mme de Montespan, people said that seven had been raised by the sword and one by the scabbard."[158] In fact, Vivonne was a brave, experienced, and effective general; and Louis XIV's regard both for Turenne and for France's position after his death was eminently sensible.

Common sense, that often despised quality, may well have been the King's greatest boon. That he should have retained it in the midst of constant flattery is all the more admirable: the first consequence of his new system was that he had now become the target of every ambitious man and woman at Court, and that his smallest word was taken as gospel. In 1674, for instance, there was the story of the duc Mazarin, the Cardinal's nephew by marriage, and the man who had lent the King money at the time of Fouquet's dismissal.

"It is enough," Primi Visconti noted, "for the King to speak of someone for that person to be eagerly sought or completely rejected. On that subject, I have heard that when Mlle de La Vallière was the favorite, the duc Mazarin had told the King that he had had a revelation that night that His Majesty was to behave better; to which the King answered: 'Well, I dreamed that you were mad!' Immediately everyone, down to his own footmen, treated the duc as if he had been a madman so that he no longer dared show himself at Court. Several years later, the duc understood his mistake. He told the King how low he had fallen and begged for help. The King, at his *lever,* first talked about hunting with Mazarin, then, turning to the courtiers, he said that the duc had wit. Hardly had the duc left the bedroom before more people crowded around him than around the King."[159] It was, however, part of Louis's extraordinary psychological stability that he saw through these marks of adoration; indeed, throughout the reign he occasionally made fun of his flatterers.

One of these, the maréchal de Grammont, repeatedly suffered from these demonstrations. There was the time, in 1664, when, according to Mme de Sévigné, the King showed him a sonnet, commenting that he thought it very poor. The maréchal wholeheartedly agreed, upon which the King announced that he was its author. Some ten years later, one day at the King's dinner, he offered Grammont a piece of a pear he was eating, saying it was delicious; once again, the maréchal concurred, only to watch as the King told several other courtiers to taste the pear, which was, in fact, no good. Certainly, these stories show a lack of respect for Grammont; but then again, they were testimonials to the fact that the King demanded respect and obedience, not flattery.

Indeed, he could on occasion be positively ingenious in giving pleasure to the people close to him. In 1673, "His Majesty gave* M. le prince de Marcillac the office of Grand Master of the Wardrobe in a manner which charmed everyone. He had one of his pages take him this note: 'I am sending you La Hébertye from whom you will hear some news which will, I think, please you. I rejoice with you, as your friend, for this gift I make you as your master.' "[160] And far from disdaining his subjects, he insisted that anyone of particular

* A double gift was involved: the permission to be Grand Master; and the price of the office. All Court offices were venal: the King chose their holders, but they had to pay their predecessor or his heir a very large sum.

interest come and see him: "Although His Majesty is ordinarily busy with affairs of State, he still gives some moments to things worthy of the curiosity of his great mind, especially since he wants to be aware of everything. That is why when he found out that the Sieur Denis had made discoveries relating to magnets and the weight of air, he had several of his experiments carried out before him, which he admired and he thus caused the Sieur Denis to receive much praise."[161]

Under these circumstances, it seemed quite normal when the King continued to raise his illegitimate children to a high rank. In 1673, three of Mme de Montespan's offsprings were acknowledged and raised to the peerage by letters patent: the three-year-old Louis-Auguste, who was created duc du Maine, the one-year-old Louis-César, who became comte de Vexin, and the newly born Louise-Françoise, now comtesse de Nantes,[162] while in 1676, one more of these offspring, Louise-Marie-Anne was in her turn named Mlle de Tours.

That, obviously, was a first step, but not an uncommon one: across the Channel, Charles II was proceeding in much the same manner. Soon, however, Louis XIV went a good deal further. In July 1675, he told Colbert that the comte de Vermandois was to be given the same rank as the prince de Conti, "just below that of the princes of the blood royal"[163]; and 1680, he signed letters patent signifying to all that henceforth these four children would bear the family name of Bourbon, as if they had been legitimate.[164] Within the next decade, it became clear that the *légitimés,* as they were known, were being moved closer to the position of genuine members of the royal family. Inasmuch as the King saw himself as above the constraints of mere mortals, this made sense: in his eyes, it was more important to be descended from him than from the brother of his great-grandfather, as was the case of Monsieur le Prince. Indeed, the constant identification of Louis XIV with Greco-Roman deities may have finally begun to alter his perception of himself: the bastard children of Zeus-Jupiter, after all, peopled the ancient world and were themselves demigods.

This quasi-divine status, of course, fits in nicely with what might be called the Versailles Plan: the domestication of the once ferocious aristocracy now took place in mythological surroundings, and André Félibien caught that note when he described a garden pavilion, the Grotto of Thetis, which was built there in 1672. It is, of course, impossible to quote in extenso from the forty pages of small type Félibien needed for a full description, but even then, an impression can be given.

"One can say of Versailles," Félibien wrote, "that it is a place where Art alone is at work, and that Nature seems to have forsaken it so as to give the King occasion to bring forth, in a sort of Creation, so to speak, several splendid places . . . Nowhere has Art been more successful than in the Grotto of Thetis . . .

"This building, square in shape, is placed near the palace . . . it is a mass of rusticated stone opening by arcades closed by iron gates that are even more cleverly worked than they are rich. Above the central door there is a golden sun whose spreading rays form the bars of the three gates . . . three large reliefs adorn the front of this building; the central one shows the sun setting into the sea, the other two are full of tritons and sirens rejoicing at his coming; there are also other, smaller round reliefs showing maritime cupids playing with dolphins."[165]

As usual, all these mythological allusions were meant to be easily understood: the Grotto of Thetis was the place where the Sun—i.e., Apollo and, by extension, the King—takes his rest once he has come to the end of his daily ride through the heavens. Magnificence and novelty were also important, however. The grotto's only light came in through the three doors; inside the walls were covered with small, rough stones, contained, however, within strips of marble; and while the statue bases were also of rusticated stones, all the rest of the decor was made of mother-of-pearl. In the vestibule and the three salons alike, there were "paintings" worked in shells and various ornaments of coral, enamel, and mother-of-pearl; the fleur-de-lis, crowns, and "L" motifs were picked out in gold against a blue ground while various aquatic symbols were carved in amethysts. Nor was this all; the pilasters marching around the walls were made of shells with a central panel in which two large L's were picked out in pearls on a ground of amethysts while, just above their capitals, were baskets filled with shell fruit and flowers from which a jet of water fell in one of the many black marble basins that had been positioned through the rooms. Then there were festoons of fruit and flowers framing sirens, tritons, and dolphins spouting water, along with mirrors, cornucopias, and sculpture-filled niches. In the center of the main room water sprang up from a jasper table, struck the ceiling, and fell into a basin, while at the back, the Girardon group of Apollo and the Nymphs,† one of the masterpieces of French sculpture, was seen for the first time. And as if all that still weren't enough, each room also had its chandelier.

"It is," Félibien tells us, "an azure globe on which three branches, forming the sides of a triangle, are joined at the top to make three lyres complete with strings of gold thread. These branches are azure, but bordered with small yellow shells which are like a gold cord. At the bottom they are enriched with big mother-of-pearl leaves each with a large pearl in its center. At the top, the lyres are joined by festoons of different shells holding up a gold crown; at the bottom there are six mother-of-pearl dragons whose tails twine around the azure globe; their wings are spread and they look as if they might fly away except that their necks are chained by more festoons. Each holds in its mouth a candleholder made of shells where candles can be fixed at night but from which water can also spring up to the vault."[166] Nor were the surrounding gardens neglected. The *Mercure galant,* whose magazine format precluded it from describing the grotto as completely as Félibien, added: "The miracles wrought by M. Nautre [sic] are no less considerable. The great numbers of orange trees planted right in the ground [i.e., not in pots] prove this as well as the fully grown trees which have been transplanted to widen the main allée, something which had never been done before now."[167] Outdoors as indoors, dazzlement was the order of the day.

(O)RDERING a splendid court, domesticating the aristocracy in Europe's most splendid palace, exacting the most unquestioning obedience from all his subjects, all that only represented one aspect of the King's life. Just as important, just as carefully planned, was war. Because, in our own century, war has taken on such a devastating character, the word very properly evokes fear and abhorrence: there can be no excuse, ever, for starting an aggressive war. None of this, however, was true in the seventeenth century. Wars were not only shorter and far more limited—guns still most often missed their target, rifles were cumbersome and inaccurate, and took a long time to reload—but they were also only fought part time: there was a

† That admirable group was repositioned in an open kiosk when the grotto was torn down in the late 1680s, then transferred on Marie Antoinette's orders to her own grotto in the garden of the Petit Trianon. It is there today.

campaigning season, from April to November; and in winter the contending armies went into their winter quarters, there to be safe until next spring.

Then, too, the act of fighting was still considered praiseworthy: there was glory to be earned, bravery to be displayed. Great generals were widely admired; and conquered territory seemed highly desirable. This last, no doubt, was especially true in France: not only was it the strongest and most populated country in Europe, but it had also failed to reach what have been since considered its natural limits, the Alps, the Pyrenees, and the modern border with Belgium. That the Franche-Comté, that French-speaking, French-surrounded province, should be Spanish clearly made no sense; and while Louis XIV never forgot his *gloire,* the wars of the seventies, with one exception, aimed at giving France more reasonable borders.

Unfortunately, the exception was a very sizable one: in the entire course of his long reign, Louis XIV never made a worse foreign policy mistake than when he decided to attack Holland: vanquished, it had nothing much to offer him; and if it should resist effectively, it could only damage his reputation. To the King himself, though, the reasons seemed good enough: the Dutch had been instrumental in forcing him to make peace in 1668; by crushing them, he would remove a menace from his flank when the war with Spain resumed; and it is impossible to deny that he had been irked by the Republic's pride.

As it was, he did not move until he felt sure of victory. Madame, just before her death, had been instrumental in concluding a treaty of alliance with Charles II, thus ensuring that the Dutch would also be opposed by Europe's greatest maritime power. The princes whose possessions were near the Rhine were bribed into acquiescence. The Treasury was prosperous and Colbert was ready to provide more money when needed. Finally, the army was superbly trained and supplied thanks to Louvois's tireless efforts; with generals like Condé, Turenne, and Vauban, the great engineer, it was clearly invincible.

Having thus carefully prepared his victory, the King left St. Germain on April 29, 1672. On June 12, the King and the army reached the Rhine and crossed it, defeating the Dutch in the process, and raising the reputation of France to the skies. Indeed, a century later, the crossing of the Rhine was still celebrated. "That air of grandeur which heightened all the King's actions," Voltaire wrote, "the rapid success of his conquests, the splendor of his reign, the idolatry of his courtiers, finally the people's, and especially the Parisians', taste for exaggeration . . . all that made the crossing of the Rhine seem like something prodigious."[168]

The first results of this victory were themselves brilliant. On June 20, Utrecht surrendered; within a few days the French had reached the suburbs of Amsterdam. Had they taken Muyden, the little town which controlled the sluices opening or closing the dikes, Amsterdam must have fallen; but the commander of the regiment sent to seize it, the marquis de Rochefort, failed to realize the importance of his mission and was defeated by its defenders. At that point, much against the advice of William Prince of Orange, their new commander in chief, the Dutch government, led by Jan de Witt, petitioned for peace; and it was then that Louis XIV, drunk with his own power, made a costly mistake. First, Louvois, a man famous for his arrogance as well as his effectiveness, was chosen to treat with the Dutch envoys; the Foreign Secretary, Arnauld de Pomponne, had only been in office a year, feared Louvois, and was generally timid; and finally the King himself, encouraged by Louvois, decided to demand exorbitant terms. The results were swift: on July 1, William of Orange became Stathouder, a position of great power; and on August 20, De Witt, who symbolized the peace party, was massacred, under the Prince's indifferent eye, by an enraged mob. At the same time, all the sluices were opened and Amsterdam became an island: it could no longer be taken; indeed, by allowing even its richest land to be flooded, Holland made itself a purely maritime power; and there, it was superior to all. Already, at the battle of Sole Bay, Ruyter, the great Dutch admiral, had defeated the combined French and British fleets; now a stalemate was reached, and the war which was supposed to be short, easy, and victorious dragged on. Since no more spectacular victories could be expected, the King went home to be present at the celebration of his conquests, and the army was left to hold a hostile and inundated country.

He was greeted with rapture. In Paris, monuments went up in the tradition of the Roman arches of triumph; Boileau celebrated the crossing of the Rhine in an epic poem while van der Meulen painted it; and, always obliging, the *Mercure galant* printed a variety of laudatory verse of which this is a fair sample: *"Quoique vous puissiez attenter*

/ *Louis de votre sort sera toujours l'arbitre/ Et se donnant à vous sous cet illustre titre / Il vous rendra bien plus qu'il ne peut vous ôter; . . . / En vous soumettant à sa loi . . . / Vous perdrez vingt tyrans pour acquérir un Roi"* (No matter what you may try / Louis will always be arbiter of your fate / And as he gives himself to you under that illustrious title / He will give you far more than he can take away; / As you bow to his law / You lose twenty tyrants and gain a single King).[169] Not exactly a sparkling poem, but, no doubt, sincerely meant: never was the praise given the King more fulsome than on his return from this useless campaign.

Of course, with Holland underwater, but unwilling to treat, and the French army settling down to a blend of sieges and antiguerrilla warfare, the conflict, which was supposed to end with the fighting season, dragged on; and naturally, Louis XIV's enemies joined in: along with Emperor Leopold I and the Elector of Brandenburg, the Spanish governor in nearby Flanders sent troops to help the Dutch. As for the people of the occupied areas, they, too, turned against the French with a deep, burning hatred, not so much because of the invasion, but because both the maréchal de Luxembourg, a great strategist who was given to the most rapacious looting, and Louvois, who always thought fear a good ally, ravaged towns and villages alike. The King, when he heard about this, was horrified and ordered it stopped, but it was too late: all over Europe, the French were seen as a present danger.

In January 1673, as if to mark a change in the course of the reign, the man who had written so many plays and divertissements for the King's pleasure died suddenly. In Molière, France and Louis XIV were losing one of the greatest playwrights ever to set pen to paper; perhaps the time for comedies had passed: now grander themes demanded attention; and, in the spring, the fighting resumed. Since, clearly, it was time for some new triumph, the King decided to besiege Maestricht, one of the Netherlands' key fortresses; and in doing so, he scrupulously followed the advice given him by Vauban, the greatest living military engineer. It turned out to be yet another progress in the art of war.

"Vauban used for the first time the parallel trenches invented by Italian engineers serving in the Turkish army before Candia," Voltaire noted. "He added mustering centers the better to gather the troops and rally them in case of enemy sorties. Louis, during this siege, showed himself more exact and harder-working than ever before. By his example, he accustomed to patience and hard work a nation which had until then been accused of having only that fiery courage which fatigue soon dispels. After an eight-day siege, on June 29, 1673, Maestricht surrendered."[170] Unfortunately, the world had changed: not even the fall of the city could bring the Dutch to terms. Only eight days before, Ruyter had once again beaten the Franco-British fleet; and within days, Leopold I of Austria and Charles II of Spain (or rather his Council‡) declared war on France. Since, at the same time, the King of England, prudently heeding his aroused Parliament, was preparing to negotiate with the Dutch, and the small Rhenish states were defecting as well, Louis XIV now found himself without significant allies just when he was opposed by the old Habsburg coalition. The results came soon enough: on September 14, the small fortress of Naerden, which was held by the French, was forced to surrender to the Prince of Orange. Militarily, it was an insignificant setback; but as the first French defeat since 1661, it seemed to many a taste of things to come.

If 1672 had, despite the conquest of so many Dutch cities, ended at best in a draw, 1673 seemed less promising still: with Europe leagued against France, the fall of Maestricht hardly mattered any longer; and because wars are expensive, the winter was marked by a series of small tax rebellions: for a monarch who had prided himself on lightening the tax load while balancing the budget and maintaining the most splendid court in Europe, this was a serious setback. In this case, however, appearances were partly misleading: although the new military expenditures (somewhat diminished by the contributions exacted from occupied Holland), added to the subsidies paid both the King of England and his opposition, came to an unexpected 25 million in a year when the deficit was meant to have been an insignificant 1,376,971 livres,[171] the money could still be found easily thanks to Colbert's excellent management. As for the uprisings, which were repressed with great firmness, they soon subsided.

Most important, however, was the attitude of the King himself. In the twelve years preceding 1673, partly through talent, partly through chance, he had known nothing but success—and perhaps been carried away by it into attacking Holland. Now, as the game

‡ Charles II was only thirteen.

became more difficult and defeat a real possibility, people watched to see what he would do; and far from showing fear, or even worry, he proceeded to give the example of calm assurance. All through the winter of 1673–74, the Court was as festive as ever; and if Louis XIV worked even harder than before, that could surprise no one. What did cause considerable astonishment, however, was his next move: just as he seemed about to be faced with adversaries far more powerful than himself, he went on the attack. Condé was sent off to fight William of Orange in the Netherlands; Turenne was stationed on the Rhine where the Emperor's troops were expected to attack; and the King himself, at the head of yet another army, proceeded to conquer the Franche-Comté for the second time.

As usual, however, this apparently dauntless monarch was taking minimal risks. The key to the Franche-Comté was the attitude of the Swiss: without their cooperation neither Spain nor Austria could send in enough troops to defend it; and they simply counted on the fact that the fiercely independent cantons would prefer not to have Louis XIV as a neighbor; the King, on the other hand, paid them to refuse passage to the Habsburg troops. The conquest, after that, was a foregone conclusion: the siege of Besançon, the province's capital and chief fortress, lasted a mere nine days; and six weeks later, the entire Franche-Comté was annexed to France. It has remained French to this day, "a monument to the weakness of the Austro-Spanish ministry and the strength of that of Louis XIV."[172]

Attacking Spain, especially under these conditions, was easy; the Franche-Comté was geographically isolated, the Spanish army slowly disintegrating for lack of money and generals, and the government itself divided and weak. Austria, however, was a very different proposition. Leopold I was energetic, if not very bright; he had competent advisers, and his troops were led by Montecucculli, one of the best generals of the age. As a result, it took all Turenne's talent, and after his death in 1675, Condé's, to resist the imperial armies. For the first time under Louis XIV, France itself was invaded, but the enemy incursion into Alsace was soon repulsed: not only was Turenne a master tactician, he went on fighting when all sensible men put their troops into winter quarters, and so he won a major battle against the imperial army at Turckheim on January 5, 1675.

That allowed him to cross the Rhine once more, and conquer most of its right bank, with utterly disastrous consequences for its inhabitants. The Palatinate, which had been the Emperor's ally, was utterly and systematically ruined on Louvois's orders. This was meant as a warning of what Leopold's other allies could expect if they continued the war; instead, it stiffened their will to fight—they knew what to expect if they were defeated—and caused hatreds that lasted for more than a century, all without bringing an end to the conflict.

Indeed, it was increasingly clear that the war, never in real danger of being lost, apparently could not be won either. Turenne's death in July 1675—he was killed by a cannonball—was immediately followed by a new invasion of Alsace, at which the King gave Condé the command of the army; the imperial troops were swept away once more then, at the end of the campaigning season, Monsieur le Prince, who was only fifty-four years old but already declining, retired to his castle of Chantilly. Luckily, Montecucculli did the same on his side, so that, by the end of 1675, neither army could boast a general of genius.

Once again, however, appearances were misleading. Just as Turenne lay dying, the duc de Vivonne, Mme de Montespan's brother, attacked and defeated the Spanish fleet near Messina; and starting in 1676, the French began to accumulate victories. In April and May 1676, Bouchain and Condé were taken; in March and April 1677, Valenciennes and Cambrai followed; in March, 1678, Ypres and Gand fell in turn; and all the sieges had been conducted by the King in person, so that, every year, he could point to new conquests. In Germany, after losing Philippsburg in 1676, the French army went on to win battle after battle in 1677 and 1678; and, on April 11, 1677, at the battle of Mont-Cassel, in Flanders, William of Orange, who was accustomed to being defeated by Louis XIV, was now beaten by Monsieur, "who charged with a courage and a presence of mind that no one expected from this effeminate prince. Never has there been a clearer example that bravery is not incompatible with softness; that prince, who often dressed in women's clothes and had a woman's tastes, behaved like a general and a soldier."[173] These remarks of Voltaire's, accurate as they are, need perhaps still more emphasis: Monsieur did indeed dazzle everyone. The *Mercure galant*, naturally, published a poem by Isaac de Benserade, a fashionable author of plays, libretti and occasional verse; it was addressed to the King. *"Un frère généreux par ton example instruit / Cherche tes ennemis, les combat, les détruit / Et vient mettre à tes pieds sa brillante victoire. / De*

l'encens qu'il mérite il n'est point satisfait / Il veut qu'on te le donne . . ."
(A courageous brother learns from your example / He seeks out
your foes, fights and destroys them / And put his brilliant victory at
your feet. / He is not satisfied with the praise he has won / He wants
you to have it . . .).[174]

That was enough for the King. He ignored the fact that Monsieur
was absolutely loyal to him, and that his habits made him a laughingstock. Primi Visconti, for instance, could not refrain from commenting on them: "Monsieur," he wrote, "looked after his toilette and
dressed during the campaign exactly as if he were on his way to a ball
. . . He went, all made-up and languid, to the most perilous and
exposed places . . . He is so naturally brave that he seems unaware
that he is risking his life and yet he looks like a woman because he is
always repairing his make-up; he covers himself with ribbons and
jewellery, he never wears a hat so as not to muss his wig and because
he is short, he wears very high heels on which he is perched so that I
really do not know how he keeps from falling. The King, on the
contrary, dresses richly and conveniently, without all those unnecessary adornments."[175] Still, Louis refrained from visiting or even con-
gratulating his brother and saw to it that Monsieur never again commanded an army: the very last thing he wanted was a brave and
popular brother who might, even now, become a rallying point for
the opposition. Similarly, he ignored Monsieur le Prince's pleas that
his son succeed to his command: henceforth, no member of the royal
family would ever again be in a position to become a hero.

By the spring of 1678, it seemed clear that France had the upper
hand; so, on April 9, the King made new offers for peace. Because,
after all these years and all these battles, the Dutch had come to seem
relatively unimportant, the conditions he offered them were lenient;
most important, he gave up Maestricht and his other conquests; but
Spain as usual was to pay for all: France demanded a large slice of the
Spanish Netherlands (Flanders), including the towns and cities of
Bouchain, Condé, Ypres, Valenciennes, Cambrai, and Maubeuge,
along with the Franche-Comté; from the Emperor, he wanted a free
hand in managing Strasbourg, then an imperial fief; the Elector of
Brandenburg, who had attacked Sweden, France's old ally, was to
disgorge his conquests; and finally, the Duke of Lorraine, whose
states had been occupied by the French, was allowed back only on

condition that France retain the right to move its army through the duchy how and when it chose.

Given the military situation, these were not unreasonable conditions but they obviously fell short of a complete French triumph, something the King was very unwilling to admit publicly; so he masked this by transforming what should have been a negotiation into an ultimatum and, amazingly enough, it worked: on August 10, at Nijmegen, the Dutch signed a treaty which embodied all the French demands; Spain and the Emperor soon joined them.

*F*RANCE, as defined by the Peace of Nijmegen, was unquestionably the first power in Europe: the alliance between Holland, Spain, and the Empire had been unable to prevent it from gaining a significant accretion of territory, and while the allies disbanded their armies as soon as the war was over, Louis XIV kept his at full strength. Even the costs resulting from this, which had always been too heavy for his predecessors, could now easily be borne: in 1680, in spite of the vast sums spent on six years of steady campaigning, in spite of the building of the third Versailles, the deficit was only 4.5 million in a budget of over 96 million,[176] and that last number was, in itself, a major achievement: in 1675, the budget had risen as high as 113 million livres.[177] Well might the King write Colbert, on March 10, 1678: "You are doing wonders with the money and I am more pleased with you every day."[178]

As for the King himself, never had his glory been so brilliant. In 1680, the Paris municipality awarded him the title of *Grand:* henceforth, in all public inscriptions, on all public buildings, in every document, he was to be known as Louis le Grand; and indeed, for the rest of the reign the medals bear the words *Ludovicus Magnus.* The praise offered him all through the war was—in France, at least—universal. In 1674, for instance, the *Mercure* was reporting: "[During the siege of Maestricht] nothing was ever seen to equal His Majesty's activity. This great monarch seems to be everywhere at once; he goes himself to check every posted troop; he is always on horseback; he spends his nights under the tent. All follows his impulse, he gives the orders for everything; and there is so much prudence, wisdom, and experience in everything he orders that the greatest generals . . . never displayed more."[179]

Three years later, it was: *"Grand Roy, porte en tous lieux la guerre /*

La Fortune guide tes pas / Le dieu Mars te prête son bras / et Jupiter te prête son tonnerre" (Great King, take war everywhere / Fortune guides your steps / the god Mars lends you his arm / and Jupiter lends you his thunder)[180]; and when prose succeeded verse, the *Mercure's* readers were told: "The King's vigilance, intrepidity, and tirelessness cannot be expressed. He was within the trench two hours after it was dug and went all the way . . . to its head. A few days earlier, a cannonball went just past the Sieur de Givry, Equerry of the Petite Ecurie, who is never far from His Majesty"[181]; and again, a month later: "Never has a monarch given so many orders himself or spent so many days on horseback than [Louis XIV] before Cambrai. He visited everything, acted immediately, ordered everything, was everywhere."[182] And by May, verse was once again required: *"Miraculeux héros, vainqueur inimitable / Par tes fameux exploits tu te fais admirer . . . / L'Alexandre orgueilleux qui se fit adorer / Se verrait s'il vivait réduit à soupirer / D'être moins grand que toi . . ."* (Miraculous hero, inimitable victor / Your famous exploits have made you admired . . . / That proud Alexander who had himself worshiped / would be forced to sigh, if he lived to day still / that he is not so great as you).[183]

That is only a small sample; and at Court, naturally, the praise was as exaggerated as it was ceaseless, although there was an occasional discordant note: the nobles, after all, followed the King to war and they had occasion to notice that he was often less than heroic. To us, accustomed as we are to generals in chief sitting in perfect safety well away from the battlefield, this is hardly surprising: no greater catastrophe could have befallen the army or the country than the King's death; but to many aristocratic officers, who still believed in the medieval tradition of dauntless (if often disastrous) charges, this very necessary prudence sometimes seemed like cowardice, and there were rumors to that effect of which Louis was very well aware. As it was they were unquestionably unfair: given the occasion, the King showed his courage clearly enough. In one of the trenches at the siege of Lille, for instance, "he [provoked] by his bravery a fine retort from a soldier who saw that he was exposed to enemy fire and that a page of the grande Ecurie had been killed behind him. The man took him roughly by the arm and said to him: 'Go away, is this your place?' "[184]

Even the King's victories struck those courtiers as less than admirable: taking city after city by means of superior siege techniques was perhaps good enough for an engineer—a sort of person for whom they had nothing but contempt. A monarch, however, should lead his troops into battle: Henri IV, Louis's grandfather, had been famous for telling the army to rally around the white plume on his helmet.

Of course, these mutterings, which were restricted to a tiny circle, hardly mattered in the real world; but they showed that the old spirit of rashness and rebellion was not dead, merely contained. The King expected no less: the very fact that such rumors still circulated proved the success of his policies, and the need to continue them: far from relaxing because the war had ended, he applied himself to his tasks as a ruler with even more energy.

The construction of Versailles was pushed forward and the Court, now thoroughly convinced that pleasing His Majesty was the only path to success, was more servile than ever. Not a penny was paid by the Treasury without the King's authorization, not a place given, not a promotion granted, and an observer could legitimately note in 1680: "Thus the King had reached the height of power: all obeyed him inside and outside the realm. He only had to wish in order to obtain; even the weather seemed to favor him; when he wanted to hunt, or to go for a walk, if it was raining, it stopped, which I have noticed particularly since I have been in France. Besides all this, he had wealth, glory, and above all perfect health: in a word he only lacked immortality."[185] And another observer noted: "King Louis the Great, by making peace at Nijmegen, had reached the apex of human glory . . . Satisfied with his conquests, he had given peace to Europe in just the manner he pleased."[186]

It was, in fact, at about this time that the King's identification with the sun, and Apollo, the sun god, came to seem less like a piece of hyperbole than a factual description. Like the sun, nothing could stop him, like the sun, he dazzled all who looked at him. His very appearance was bound to confirm this: as his face had changed from the slightly rounded shape of his youth to the hawklike mask of maturity, he had adopted the great leonine wig which gave him still more presence and majesty. "The King is not handsome," an observer wrote, "but he has regular features; his face is marked with smallpox [a common defect in the seventeenth century]; the eyes are as you will have them: majestic, lively, cheerful, voluptuous, tender, or awe-inspiring; in a word, he has presence and . . . a truly royal look: even if he were only one of the courtiers, he would stand out among them."[187] And then, the splendor of the Court added yet another element to his semidivine state.

During a stay at Fontainebleau in August 1677, for instance, the King was seen to wear, besides the usual number of new suits, twelve especially splendid costumes ordered for him by the prince de Marcillac, his Grand Master of the Wardrobe. We know at least what one of these looked like thanks to the slightly breathless reporting in the *Mercure galant:* "[At a ball] the King appeared with a suit of gold lamé embroidered with gold and silver. His jewels were shaped like so many buckles and besides these, he carried a sword on which the precious stones were worth more than 150,000 livres.

"The Queen seemed covered with jewels of an extraordinary size. Because her gown was black, and its fabric used only to make them brighter, one can fairly say that they dazzled. Monsieur's costume was covered with jewels arranged like the long buttonholes of the Brandenburg coats . . . . The time spent at Fontainebleau was so full of pleasures that, on the nights of *médianoche,* * when the opera or the play ended too early, there were small private balls until midnight."[188] The operas in question, the *Mercure* tells us, were all by Lulli—his *Thésée, Alceste,* and *Athis;* the plays were by Molière—*L'Avare, Le Misanthrope, L'Ecole des femmes*—Racine, and, more surprising since he had long been out of fashion, Corneille. Hunting, of course, was a major amusement; but nothing was more impressive than the balls: splendid though the royal family looked, the courtiers did almost as well. After a minute description of the newly fashionable hairdo—a complex arrangement of curls and one very wide braid—the *Mercure* goes on, as was its wont, to describe every detail: "All the coiffures were adorned with jeweled clasps with a pearl center. All kinds of pearl or jewel bows, replacing the usual ribbons, were set on the sides . . . Their gowns were all covered with jewels, especially on the scarves, and the seams, along with big bows on the front. Their sleeves were adorned in different ways with ties, buttons, or just cabochons of precious stones. The whole front of their skirts was also similarly adorned and the [overskirts] were held back by big diamond clips. Several more jewels formed a bow be-

* Midnight suppers.

hind . . . The undersleeves were made of lace, slashed along the length, and turned up at the bottom with a different sort of lace, which held more jewels above and below . . .

"The buffet after the first ball was superb . . . The four tiers had, at the bottom, eight large baskets of fruit; in the corners there were little circles of candied fruit; the next level had four more baskets and the corners were the same as below. At the top was a large square of fruit that was two feet high. All the rounds and ovals were full of fruit and candied fruit filled all the squares that line the table . . . everywhere . . . there were torches and candlesticks . . . along with crystal saucers bearing quantities of goblets full of iced waters, and there were rare porcelain vases filled with all kinds of compotes . . .

"Imagine then this dazzling array of lights which were reflected one in the other as the torches were reflected in the crystal adorning the candlesticks and the candles in the gold of the torch holders; this was made brighter still by the sheen of the caramels and the candied fruit. Add to that the colors of the fruit, the ribbons in the baskets and the crystal of the saucers and the effect produced by the jewels worn by Their Majesties and the forty ladies who sat around the table."[189] We forget, in this age of electricity, how magical night lighting could be: the scene as described by the *Mercure*, must indeed have been awe-inspiring.

Just as the Court became increasingly more splendid, so the King's private life assumed almost the dimensions of a matter of state: besides his official mistresses, he had always had brief, often unknown affairs that might last less than a week; others might prove enduring but equally discreet, that with the princesse de Soubise being a perfect example. The princesse was beautiful and, naturally, willing; her husband, a member of the ambitious Rohan family, was the soul of tact; as a result, the King slept with Mme de Soubise now and again over the years while showering her family with favors; but the liaison never became fully public.

In the late seventies, however, all that was changed, and the King's new amours became quickly and fully known. First, there was Mme de Ludres. "The King went off to war on March 1 [1677] at the very time when the courtiers thought him occupied with nothing but games, ballets, and a new love. That happened because Mme de Montespan, who had first persecuted Mme de Ludres, believing her influence definitively at an end, has called her back near her. That return, however, renewed the King's desires so that he was seen, more than once, followed by Chamarande, his *premier valet de chambre,* who was in charge of the negotiations, going in a private† sedan chair from the *château vieux* at St. Germain to the *château neuf* where Mme de Ludres was lodged."[190] That he was now tired of Mme de Montespan was perhaps not surprising: the lusty marquise had become enormously fat and even more demanding; worse, she made the most dreadful scenes when she failed to get her way; so the King, whose eye never ceased roving, now began setting up official rivals. Unlike La Vallière, however, Mme de Montespan was firmly determined to stay at Court, partly in the hope that she would recapture her lover.

In the meantime, however, there was no doubt at all that a new star had risen. "Solely because they believed her to be loved by the King, all the princesses and the duchesses stood up when she came in, even in the Queen's presence, and only sat down again when Mme de Ludres asked them to do so, just as it was done with Mme de Montespan. And it was through this mark of distinction given to Mme de Ludres that the Queen learned about the King's new infidelity . . . The Queen, then, had grown accustomed to these affairs but Mme de Montespan was enraged by them. I watched, at the Tuileries, Mme de Ludres and Mme de Thianges‡ exchanging venomous glances. They bumped into each other when they met.* Mme de Montespan did everything she could to hurt her rival but Mme de Ludres was herself responsible for her downfall. She had as her sole adviser a certain poet called Benserade† and as her sole confidante a certain Marianne, the daughter of an apothecary who was married to one Montataire, a wretch with neither influence nor friends. In order to make him more valued, [Marianne] thought of using him as an intermediary between Mme de Ludres and the King. This last, who had already given the job to Chamarande, was so surprised to find himself face to face with Montataire that he stopped seeing Mme de Ludres and ordered her to retire to a convent, offering her 200,000

† Without the royal arms on the side panel, that is.
‡ Mme de Montespan's sister.
* Because each tried to precede the other.
† Far from being "a certain poet," Benserade was one of the King's favorite writers and the author of much occasional verse read during Court festivities.

livres which she did not accept."[191] In one respect, however, Visconti misunderstands the King: what caused Mme de Ludres's dismissal was not surprise: there was nothing Louis XIV hated more than indiscretion, and that applied as well to an affair as to matters of state. Chamarande, obviously, could be trusted to keep his mouth shut; Montataire was likely to talk: no more was needed to make Mme de Ludres expendable.

This was especially true in a court filled with young and pretty women whose greatest ambition was to become the King's mistress; sure enough, within a few weeks, Louis XIV fell in love with a blonde whose dazzling complexion and lithe figure were enhanced by her youth and obvious willingness. "Mlle de Fontanges . . . was tall, with a good body and very pretty but, as she was fair-haired, those who were jealous of her said she was a redhead, for there is in France a prejudice according to which red-haired women are nasty and smell bad. Red-haired men are also supposed to be nasty, but they save themselves by wearing a wig,"[192] the Italian Visconti noted.

Not only was Mlle de Fontanges a perfectly genuine blonde, she was also quiet, pliable and not terribly bright—the very opposite, in fact, of Mme de Montespan, whose legs, according to a sharp-eyed observer, had now reached the girth of an average man and whose temper was worse than ever; then, too, the King had reason to suspect she was slipping him a variety of love potions which were giving him fits of dizziness. There was also that old matter of the double adultery, made more annoying still by M. de Montespan's provocative behavior. Colbert, the indispensable man as always, was set to watch over him. The result was an abundant correspondence of which the following is a fair sample. From Colbert to the King: "I received yesterday, Sire, Your Majesty's letter of the seventeenth and will carry out punctually Your Majesty's orders as regards M. de Montespan. Upon which you must know that some three or four years ago, when you ordered me to see to it that a suit he had before the Parlement be judged so that he would no longer have any reason or pretext to remain in Paris, I carried out Your Majesty's order. The suit was tried and I believe he left.

"About two weeks ago, M. de Montespan came up to me and asked me to recommend to M. de Novion a suit he was engaged in, and the outcome of which he awaited before retiring to his province, but I did not do so because I did not think I should be mixed into his business without orders. If Your Majesty thought it necessary to thus press the said M. de Novion, perhaps he [Montespan] would then leave."[193] This was written on May 28, 1678. The orders were no doubt given, but on June 15 the King was writing Colbert: "I hear that Montespan is talking indiscreetly. He is a madman and you will please me by having him closely followed . . . I know that Montespan threatened he would come and see his wife. As he is quite capable of doing so, and as the consequences of this are to be feared, I rely on you to prevent him from appearing. Do not forget the details of this business and above all let him leave Paris as soon as possible."[194] It was not only that Montespan was quite likely to barge into his wife's apartment and make a dreadful scene: even in Paris, he behaved as scandalously as possible; and obviously none of this fit in with the image of Olympian detachment the King was anxious to preserve.

There was no such drawback with Mlle de Fontanges, but then again, she lacked those intellectual qualities Louis apparently found indispensable; so, from the first, the Court watched for signs that the affair would not last—especially since another star was rising on the horizon. Already in 1675 it was noticed that the King liked to spend time with the lady in question; nor, given his habits, did anyone doubt that she had become his mistress; indeed, from the moment in January of that year when he had created her marquise de Maintenon, the gossips had watched the two with great care.

Still, the new marquise was not likely ever to become really important. Her title, after all, was not unconnected with her functions as governess of the King's illegitimate children. Real *Enfants de France,* born of the Queen, could only be watched over by a duchess; given the way Louis XIV was beginning to feel about his bastards, it was clear that they, too, should have a titled lady in attendance. Then, Mme de Maintenon was Mme de Montespan's protégée; the two ladies were friends, partly because they were both brilliantly intelligent and each appreciated the other's mind. Besides that, Mme de Maintenon was unquestionably devoted to the children placed under her care; the more so, no doubt, because she was wholly unattached. All this was duly appreciated by the King; but the notion that the former widow Scarron could ever play a major role at the most splendid Court in the world was simply laughable.

It was, in fact, the very modesty of the then Mme Scarron's position which had led to her being chosen as governess of Mme de Montespan's growing brood of royal children: because of the double adultery, the King had, at first, been anxious to keep these children a secret; but then, times had changed. The children had become légitimés; they were seen at Court, publicly acknowledged as what they were even by the Queen; and their governess had also come out of the shadows.

She was, as Louis XIV was quick to appreciate, altogether an exceptional woman. The abbé de Choisy, who liked her, gave this picture of her: "She had looked after the education of M. le duc du Maine‡ which had given her a thousand occasions to show what she could do, her wit, her judgment, her straightforwardness, her piety and all the other natural virtues which do not always win hearts as fast as beauty, but which settle their conquests on a much sounder, indeed almost indestructible, base. She was no longer very young but her eyes were so alive, so brilliant, and there was such sparkling wit in her expression when she spoke, that it was difficult to see her often without feeling an inclination for her. The King, accustomed since his childhood to being surrounded with women, was delighted to find one who only spoke about virtue; he did not fear that people would say she ruled him; he had seen that she was undemanding and incapable of abusing her close connection with him."[195]

In 1675, when she began to be noticed, Mme de Maintenon was forty—well past maturity in seventeenth-century terms—but she looked very much younger than her age and was indeed highly attractive. To her intellectual qualities, she added one that she had learned in the course of her difficult life, one the King prized especially highly: absolute discretion; and the fact that she behaved with the greatest modesty helped put her in contrast with the flamboyant Mme de Montespan. Even her appearance made her unique: in a court where women dressed in sumptuous, brightly colored materials and were covered with jewels, she never wore anything but black.

Finally, she was not only pious but intelligently so, and capable both of sustaining a lengthy theological discussion and of making it lively: for a monarch who was genuinely pious himself, and who was increasingly worried about the sins entailed by his liaison with Mme

‡ The duc du Maine, who was born on March 31, 1670, was the King's favorite among his illegitimate children.

197

de Montespan, this, too, was a powerful attraction. As for the lady's less attractive qualities—a certain hypocrisy, a definite thirst for power, a tendency to complain at enormous length—they were not yet in evidence; thus what the King saw, as he came from one of Mme de Montespan's frequent scenes, was an attractive, intelligent, and serious woman with whom he could have a real conversation.

That he did so is the best proof that he cared more for merit than birth or position; for Mme de Maintenon's career had been checkered in the extreme. She was born in a family, the d'Aubignés, who belonged to the very small nobility; but her father, who was essentially a crook, had gone from jail to jail so that the little Françoise was raised by relatives, first in faraway Martinique, then in the Poitou, where she served as maid-companion to her cousins. Any sort of reputable marriage was obviously out of the question since she was absolutely penniless: clearly she would have to earn her living as a companion to some noble lady or governess to her children.

Had she also been plain, or dull, that, no doubt, would have been her fate; but from the first, she was extremely attractive and wonderfully bright. When she followed her aunt to Paris, she quickly gained the reputation of being excellent company; and then, in 1652, at the age of seventeen, she launched herself into the most unexpected and the most grotesque of marriages. Paul Scarron, her groom, was a well-known comic poet, the author of the first burlesque novel in the French language, and a man of culture and wit. He was much appreciated in Paris and counted many nobles among his friends; but he was also, at the age of forty-two, utterly crippled by rheumatism, unable to walk even a few steps by himself and in constant pain. As a result, of course, he looked very much older than his age and was impotent though by no means uninterested in sex.

There was every reason why the marriage should have been disastrous; in fact, it was highly successful. The new Mme Scarron liked her husband and admired his talent while he, on his side, enjoyed his wife's looks and intelligence. She made a comfortable (but not at all luxurious) home for him and in short order found herself at the head of a salon frequented not just by intellectuals, but also by a few dukes and some of the great ladies who ruled Paris society. This was a not unenviable position and Mme Scarron made the most of it. Unfortunately, the seventeenth century was not a good time for authors, financially, at least: they depended on patronage for their living, and during the years of the Scarrons' marriage, the Fronde's aftereffects dried up that source of income. Still, when the poet finally died in 1660, his widow was so well esteemed that Anne of Austria, who knew her to be utterly penniless awarded her a pension.

There followed a period we know almost nothing about; and then Mme Scarron was recruited to take care of the King's illegitimate children. Her antecedents were such, therefore, that she could be no menace to Mme de Montespan, a fact of which that lady was very well aware and which no doubt figured largely in the two women's friendship. Facts of that nature, however, have a way of changing; and while his feelings for Mlle de Fontanges were not affected by those he entertained for Mme de Maintenon, the King nonetheless was seen to pay more and more attention to the governess; by 1679, Mme de Montespan was beginning to find herself in the same position as La Vallière some ten years earlier. Of course, she fought back —with tears and scenes, then, more startlingly, with religion. The sight of the marquise visiting churches at odd hours of the day and spouting the scriptures must have seemed irresistibly comic at first; and there can be no doubt that it was all a maneuver to regain the King's love by preempting Mme de Maintenon's favorite topic. Oddly enough it worked, if in an unexpected way: it did not gain her the King but she did become genuinely pious.

Before she settled for regular attendance at mass, however, Mme de Montespan had tried a few less orthodox methods. In due course the King found out what they were and the knowledge offended and frightened him: neither the marquise nor, indeed, France was quite what he had thought them.

VIII
Palaces and Poison

FRANCE, in the late 1670s, was not unlike a volcano after an eruption: a cold crust had formed over the lava, and the ash had settled, but underneath, the magma continued to boil; in the same way, while the King had apparently imposed his new order and transformed the very spirit of the nation, the disruptive forces he had defeated lived on; only, now, they were hidden.

Still, their effects became noticeable when too many people began to die suddenly and unexpectedly; and in short order, Louis XIV learned that the entire top layer of French society was indulging in a variety of criminal practices.

The aristocracy, after all, had long enriched itself illegitimately by starting civil wars which it was then bribed to stop. Under Louis XIV, the King's favor, that source of potentially endless benefits, had to be deserved rather than conquered. Then, too, life had become enormously more expensive; elder sons, who once had put in only brief appearances at Court, now spent most of their life there and greatly resented having to wait for the day when, at their fathers' death, they would succeed to the family fortune.

Even among those closest to the King, the old instincts for rapine remained: the close confinement of life at Versailles, where Louis XIV now spent more and more of his time, exasperated the rivalries between the different clans. The death of a rival was always a boon: how much more convenient if it could be procured at will. And when love faded, how gratifying if something could be done about it: no aging woman likes to lose her lover; when that lover was the King, the loss was even more devastating.

200

Palaces and Poison

Some of the means used to rectify these various situations were eminently practical, as murder can be as long as it remains undiscovered; others, deemed to be equally sure, relied on old superstitions which were still widely believed to be fact. French civilization, at the end of the seventeenth century, seemed to be one of the most advanced in Europe. The power of reason, the need for demonstrable proof, extolled by Descartes among others, had apparently been accepted; and while religion remained strong, it was based on faith and works, not on the accretion of pagan rituals and demonic beliefs which had marred it at the end of the Middle Ages, or so the most eminent bishops, men like Bossuet and Fénelon, claimed.

In fact, old beliefs die hard, especially when they appear to offer convenient shortcuts. As recently as the beginning of the century, James I of England had written a book, the *Daemonologie,* in which the power of witches was taken as fact. Besides, if a soul was such a very valuable commodity, it stood to reason that the Devil, in whose existence everyone still believed, would pay a high price for it; so it was a trade: hell in the hereafter against instant and easy success in this life.

A need will always create a service. If rich, powerful people needed the help of the Devil, then others were bound to come forward as intermediaries. And if the continued existence of a rich but penny-pinching father was a major inconvenience, then means were found to get rid of him; so it was that arsenic and black magic came together to perform all these necessary functions.

That it should have been so, given the age-old nature of the French upper classes, is perhaps not very surprising; murder, rape, and looting in a civil war were hardly more moral; but they had always been perfectly acceptable. Now similar activities were used more discreetly, and often on relatives instead of rivals; but the basic principle remained the same. Only that persistence of the bad old ways was just what the King thought he had ended. In 1677, he began to discover that instead of the well-ordered society he had been trying to establish, greed, corruption, and crime were everywhere.

It all began, apparently, with a single, isolated criminal affair. The marquise de Brinvilliers was the daughter of a rich, upper-middle-class father whose inheritance she awaited eagerly; and she was married to a man of whom she had grown quite tired. That, in itself, was a fairly normal situation; but, this time, there was a difference. The latest and most entrancing of Mme de Brinvilliers's lovers was a chemist called Sainte-Croix, and he eventually offered to provide her with a powder which would dispatch both husband and father.

The marquise, who was nothing if not practical, listened carefully, explored all possible objections, then decided to make sure the powder would work as predicted: it was one thing to kill her relatives while making it look as if they were dying of some illness, quite another to have them survive and suspect; so she looked around for convenient subjects and, under the guise of charity, found them easily. The Hôtel Dieu, the main hospital in Paris was run by the Church but depended on private help; and in 1676, people noticed that Mme de Brinvilliers seemed to spend much of her time helping the sick, caring for them and feeding them. She was apparently unlucky, though: most of her patients died within a very few weeks.

Having thus made sure that the powder—in fact a variety of arsenic—worked well over time, the marquise then started using it on her family. In one case, that of her husband, she changed her mind after she had already been poisoning him for a while, gave him antidotes and let him live; but several other relatives were duly dispatched, with no one the wiser. There seemed no reason why she should ever be caught, in fact, since she was careful to give her victims small, repeated doses of arsenic, so that their decline simply looked like a normal illness; but then Sainte Croix was found dead in his laboratory, poisoned, apparently, by the accidental breaking of a glass retort. His connection to Mme de Brinvilliers was well known; the deaths in her family now began to look less natural, and, in short order, she was arrested.

"As to the business of Mme de Brinvilliers," the King wrote Colbert, "I think it important that you tell the Premier président and the Attorney General, from me, that I expect them to do all that honorable people like them must do so as to pursue everyone, no matter what their rank, who are involved in such wickedness. Write me what you hear; it is said that there are many solicitations and that much money is being spent."[196] Still, at the moment, Mme de Brinvilliers's crimes, while fascinating for the Parisians who flocked to her trial and execution, seemed only the actions of one perverse woman. In fact, they proved to be the tip of the iceberg.

It is, of course, possible that Mme de Brinvilliers's example stimulated others; but, already before she was caught, poisoners and sorceresses had been offering needy heirs what came to be called "inheritance powder," while at the same time they produced a variety of magical potions to ensure love, or impotence, or any condition, just about, required by the buyer. In some instances, when the case proved especially difficult, black masses were celebrated to enlist Satan's help.

Chief among these sorcerers-poisoners-abortionists were two women, Voisin and Vigouroux, the former's lover, Lesage, and, finally, two priests, the abbés Mariette and Guibourg; and when, in the spring of 1679, they were arrested, terror descended on the Court. On April 10, the King created a special tribunal, the *chambre ardente,* to look into the multiplying accusations; and in short order, 442 upper-class men and women were arrested. Worse, the poisoners now accused some of the people closest to the King, first among these the comtesse de Soissons, Mazarin's niece and Louis's mistress in the 1650s, who now held the first of the great Court offices, that of Superintendent of the Queen's Household. She was by no means alone, however: great ladies like the duchesse de Bouillon, a relative of Turenne's, the princesse de Tingry, the maréchale de La Ferté, and the marquise de Polignac were also denounced by the prisoners.

Some of them, led by the comtesse de Soissons, simply preferred to flee; others, like the maréchal de Luxembourg, asked to be sent to the Bastille, and duly were. Of course, Voisin, Vigouroux, and their accomplices were tried and, early in 1680, executed.

That these wholesale murders should have taken place at all was, obviously, a grim indication as to the real state of society, and a sad comment on the solidity of the new order. The King had, from the very beginning, ordered the police to do its duty fearlessly, no matter how powerful the people involved; but then, in April 1680, a new accusation was made by Marguerite Voisin, the poison maker's daughter; and this time, the person named was none other than Mme de Montespan.

"With an air of naïveté which, if she is telling lies, can fool anyone,"[197] the horrified head of the police reported to his master, she accused the favorite of having used potions to keep or regain the King's love; of having lent herself to the celebration of black masses with the same object; and finally, of having ordered the King poisoned. Worse still, these assertions were corroborated by several other prisoners, including the abbé Guibourg.

Sensibly, Louis ordered that the affair be held absolutely secret; but the inquest continued. Soon, Mme de Montespan's maid, Mlle des Oeillets, was implicated as well; and there was a distinct possibility that the favorite was indeed guilty. Still, parts of the accusation seemed more plausible than others. Even in a fit of jealous rage, it is hard to see why the marquise should have wanted the King poisoned in 1679: after all, she would have been much worse off under the reign of the Dauphin, who, no doubt, would have allowed the Queen to take revenge on the former favorite. The very means to be used, a poisoned pair of gloves, the odor of which was supposedly lethal, hardly compels belief.

There were other improbabilities as well. The marquise was said to have become Voisin's client as early as 1667, a time at which Louis XIV was passionately in love with her and she certainly needed no help from a sorceress; again, the black masses were supposedly celebrated in 1673, a time when her hold on the King was undisputed. Still, an element of doubt remains.

Both Marguerite Voisin and Guibourg, for instance, were specific and precise about the black masses. These were rites held at night in a deserted church where a mass was celebrated, with Satan's name replacing Jesus, a naked woman replacing the altar, and the blood of a freshly killed child (or sometimes an animal) replacing the consecrated wine; thus murder was added to sacrilege. What does seem probable is that the black masses were celebrated; that a woman whom Guibourg and Marguerite Voisin believed to be Mme de Montespan served as the altar; but that the woman in question was Mlle des Oeillets and not the marquise. Confrontations between Mlle des Oeillets and the poisoners were not absolutely conclusive—two recognized her immediately, a third was not sure—but, on balance, the odds are against her.

As for the love powder—on the eye of newt, wing of bat order— that Mme de Montespan is supposed to have bought and slipped into the King's food, the probabilities are overwhelming: giving the desired person magic potions was a far from uncommon course in the seventeenth century and the marquise really had no reason not to try it.

Because the affair, watched over by Colbert as usual, was so very grave, it was allowed to end inconclusively. There was, of course, always the possibility that the poisoners had invented the whole thing to save their skins; but, then, the risks of that course were immense: capital punishment could take on relatively quick and easy forms— hanging, strangulation—or excruciating ones like quartering or burning alive; and the consequences of a false accusation against Mme de Montespan were hardly likely to be pleasant.

On balance, therefore, and without any degree of absolute certainty, a mixed verdict seems called for: Mme de Montespan was probably partly guilty and partly innocent; but, in any case, the blow to Louis XIV's reputation, had all this become known, would have been terrible. To set yourself up as a model of monarchs, as the greatest king in the world, who was, at that very moment, busy enlarging his conquests, and then to be revealed as the adulterous lover of a sacrilegious poisoner, was hardly to be contemplated. The affair remained secret, and Louis went on treating the marquise as if none of this had ever happened.

What does seem certain, however, is that these revelations finally severed the two lovers' ties. As it was, the King was having an affair with Mlle de Fontanges all through 1679; that, in turn, ended in 1680, when a pregnancy was followed by a miscarriage from which the new mistress never recovered; and, more visibly than ever, he turned to the new marquise de Maintenon.

It was no wonder, really: at forty-two, Louis XIV was no longer a young man; scandals which a few years ago had not mattered now worried him more, especially since, with the onset of middle age, he was becoming markedly more religious. Mlle de Fontanges had been unmarried; Mme de Maintenon was widowed; Mme de Montespan was still married to another man. Then, too, both her physical attractions (she was enormous) and her intellectual brio had faded: the marquise was now mostly a fat woman who made scenes; and, right next to her was a quiet, composed, decent, attractive woman with an exceptionally brilliant mind. Much as he liked women physically, Louis was never lastingly attracted unless the object of his desire could also think and talk intelligently: Mme de Maintenon fulfilled all these requirements. Nor should the fact that she was visibly pious be underestimated: as Louis began to turn more toward religion, it could only help to have the woman he loved show him the way.

Then, too, it was in 1680 that the King began to concentrate his affections on his illegitimate children at the expense of their mothers. Royal bastards had long had a place in Court and society: Charles

IX's illegitimate son was created duc d'Angoulême, a title previously borne by princes of the royal house; Henri IV's sons had also been given duchies; but they customarily took rank as of the date of the creation of their peerage and were treated as great nobles, not members of the royal family. Now, to the horror of all traditionalists, Louis XIV, who clearly thought descent from himself was all that counted, began raising the status of his illegitimate offsprings so as to bring them, little by little, closer to that of princes of the blood royal.

Because this was such a new and shocking notion, the King proceeded slowly; but his intentions became unmistakable, when, in January 1680, he arranged the marriage of the fourteen-year-old Mlle de Blois, his daughter with Mme de La Vallière,* with the prince de Conti,† the great Condé's nephew, and a legitimate prince; and the fact that Conti agreed to what, until then, would have been considered a disgrace shows clearly how powerful the King had become. From then on, the policy was pursued relentlessly: by intermingling his bastards and the royal family, Louis XIV made sure that, in the next generation, most distinctions between the two would have faded away.

Just as typical as this exaltation of his children from the wrong side of the blanket was the fact that not once during the elaborate marriage festivities was the absent mother of the bride mentioned. It was not only that, to the King, anyone who left the Court ipso facto ceased existing—and the repentant La Vallière had immured herself in a convent—but also that, henceforth, the emphasis was to be on the father—himself—while the mother, with her taint of lower birth and adultery, was to be forgotten; and Mme de Montespan, who remained all too visible, understood very clearly what this was all about.

By 1680, therefore, the aspect of the Court had changed a good deal. The Queen, whose looks did not improve with age, was as self-effacing as ever: ever ready to demand every last ounce of deference due her by her ladies, ever obedient to all her husband's wishes. The Dauphin, who had reached his nineteenth year, was now given not only his own establishment, but a wife as well, the daughter of the Elector of Bavaria, a Catholic prince and France's ally, most of the time, against the Emperor.

* She had retired to a convent in 1674.
† He was Louis XIV's first cousin three times removed.

The Second Chamber of the Apartment on one of the three weekly reception days at Versailles: Monseigneur, holding cards, sits next to his half-sister, the princesse de Conti; his other half-sister, the duchesse de Bourbon, is across the table.

The Third Chamber of the Apartment: the King playing billiards, one of his favorite pastimes.

The Fourth Chamber of the Apartment: the duc de Chartres dancing with his sister, the future duchesse de Berry; standing, the young duc de Bourgogne; sitting, Madame; the duchesse de Chartres; the duchesse du Maine; the princesse de Conti.

The temporary ballroom built in the Park of Versailles in 1678. The King and Queen, seated in armchairs, watch the dancers.

The Grotto of Thetis, at Versailles.

Versailles in 1674 seen from the Park.

Versailles with its two wings in 1682.

A temporary dining hall in the Park of Versailles, 1678.

The Fountain of the Baths of Apollo at Versailles in 1688.

Mme de Maintenon carrying her Bible.

"The Dauphin," Primi Viconti noted, "took a wife as obediently as he learned his lessons . . . His governor was the duc de Montausier, an elderly man of austere mores and severe principles. The Dauphin seemed to have become wholly passive; no one could say anything in his ear.‡ There were even some who said that the little marquis de Créqui having taught him a certain bad habit, Millet, his undergovernor, would stand with a rod near the bed, and when he saw the Dauphin move his hands under the blanket, he would strike him.

"For his wedding, his First Valet de Chambre, a friend of Mme de Beauvais, who had given the King his first love lesson, was ordered to enlighten him."[198] In fact, although as a child he had seemed lively enough, the Dauphin took after his mother's side: a large, blond young man early given to fat, he had absolutely no intellectual interests: food, the hunt, and, a little later, a low-born mistress were sufficient for his happiness. He knew nothing of government, was never consulted or taught by his father, whom, indeed, he feared greatly. The very appellation Louis XIV gave him at this time was significant: *Monseigneur,* a rough equivalent of Your Lordship, was a term of respect used to a superior: princes and ministers were called Monseigneur by courtiers, and courtiers by their servants. As for earlier Dauphins, they had always been referred to as Monsieur le Dauphin, Your Royal Highness, or, by the King, *"mon fils"* (my son). Now the King started, ironically, to call his son Monseigneur, just as a father reproving a little boy might say sarcastically: "And what has Your Lordship done this time?" In no time at all, the Dauphin became known, simply, as Monseigneur, in the same way that Condé was Monsieur le Prince; and with the passage of time, the original sarcasm was forgotten; still, it was typical of the King's attitude to his only (legitimate) son and heir.

The Dauphin's marriage released him from the unwelcome attentions of the duc de Montausier, a man widely credited with breaking his pupil's spirit, but it did not raise him in his father's esteem: the King expected prompt and absolute obedience; the Dauphin gave it; and that was all. At first glance, this rather dreadful relationship seems to reflect on Louis: so stern, so unloving a father deserves nothing but blame; and yet once again an exception must be made.

‡ The only way to speak to a prince without being heard by the courtiers who always surrounded him.

There was a long tradition, in France and elsewhere, of rebellion from the crown prince or, as was the case under Louis XIII, of the next heir to the throne. Given the very recent taming of the aristocracy, it would have been the most normal of things for dissatisfied nobles to have formed an alliance with the Dauphin to fight the King; and that, of course, is what Louis was determined to prevent. He was undoubtedly helped in this by his son's stupidity—but then no one had extolled the duc d'Orléans's intelligence in the 1630s; what really mattered, however, was that the young man was much too frightened of his father ever to think of rebelling. Just as he had with Monsieur, the King had made very sure that no member of his family would ever again serve as a cover for civil war.

Of course, that achievement—and it was one—had its drawbacks: no one could tell what would happen when the slow, passive, lazy Dauphin's turn came to rule. Still, in 1680, with Louis in vigorous early middle age, that was hardly a pressing problem; and there was always the possibility the prince would be ruled by his wife.

From the beginning, in fact, it was clear that she was, at any rate, cleverer than her husband. "The Dauphine," Primi recorded, "from the moment she arrived, seemed to know all about the Court, ready to flatter the King and obey all his wishes . . . The offices of her Household were sought in preference to those of the Queen's.* The duchesse de Richelieu, who was dame d'honneur† to the Queen, became that of the Dauphine, thus incurring a lowering of her rank, and her husband the duc became chevalier d'honneur,‡ but that was all the result of an intrigue of Mme de Maintenon's, the governess of Mme de Montespan's children, who was made a lady of the wardrobe, first under the maréchale de Rochefort, and was then declared her equal, which infuriated the latter; but the most furious of all was Mme de Montespan, who, as a result of Mme de Fontanges's illness, had hoped the King would come back to her."[199] In fact, there had been a quiet revolution; and it was a while before all those eager spectators realized just what had happened.

Because Mme de Maintenon came from so humble a background, it was long assumed that her rising eminence was due only to some

---

* Because it was hoped the Dauphine might have the King's ear. The Queen, as everyone knew, did not.
† The chief lady of the Household after the Superintendent.
‡ The chief gentleman of the Household.

service she was performing for the King—some thought her his procuress, others the scribe to whom he dictated his memoirs. In fact, Louis had fallen well and truly in love with her; and his feelings grew in intensity as the time passed. The positions in the Dauphine's Household were proof of that: the duchesse de Richelieu was made dame d'honneur not only because she was extremely respectable but because she was one of Mme de Maintenon's closest friends; and the same was true of her husband's appointment as chevalier d'honneur. Equally significant was Mme de Maintenon's own position: first as a lady of the wardrobe, then as the equal of the maréchale de Rochefort, who, socially, was immensely superior to her. Finally, there was a hint of things to come. Mme de Maintenon, as she had shown with her erstwhile charges, Mme de Montespan's children, was a born educator; she was also more than clever enough to understand the importance of conciliating the next generation of the royal family. By placing her in the Dauphine's Household, the King was enabling her to ingratiate herself with the future Queen of France while, probably, taking a hand in the education of the children she was confidently expected to bear.

As for the Dauphine, she found her place as easily as if she had been brought up to it. Fairly tall, noble-looking, she had fine eyes, a good complexion, and perfect teeth, which helped to make up for rather undistinguished features; she could speak several languages and was a gifted musician, something sure to endear her to her father-in-law. "She had a lively mind," an observer noted, "but she did not allow its full extent to be seen on many occasions. She always paid attention to the King, having determined to behave entirely according to his wishes and to avoid anything which might annoy him."[200] In spite of that, it soon became clear that she was hardly capable of influencing anyone: a woman of mediocre intelligence, she much preferred the ease of her private rooms to the festivities of the Court. Still, she fulfilled her most important task. On August 6, 1682, she gave birth to a son, Louis, who was titled duc de Bourgogne; on December 19, 1683, came a second son, Philippe, titled duc d'Anjou; and on August 31, 1686, the Dauphin's third son, Charles, titled duc de Berry, was born. The succession was safely assured.

By 1683, on the other side of Louis XIV's family, the illegitimate, three of the children had died: the sixteen-year-old comte de Vermandois, Mme de La Vallière's only son, the eleven-year-old comte de Vexin, and Mlle de Tours: aside from the princesse de Conti, that left the King two sons and two daughters by Mme de Montespan, and as the years passed they grew more and more visible.

As for the royal family proper, Louis XIV's early goal was fully accomplished. The Queen's death in 1683 made no difference to the life of the Court. The King cried, announced that this was the first sorrow she had caused him, and promptly forgot her. Monsieur, more frivolous than ever, was hopelessly in love with the chevalier de Lorraine, a greedy young man of good family, who exploited him ruthlessly while making very sure that he never opposed the King. The second Madame Elizabeth-Charlotte von der Pfalz, who had married Monsieur in November 1671, was also a Bavarian princess, but of a different branch from the Dauphine's. A large, hearty woman, she developed a passion for the hunt, and (although she did not quite know it) fell in love with the King; the very opposite of her predecessor, Henrietta Stuart, she was incapable of intrigue: there, too, the King could feel safe.

Even that erstwhile rebel Monsieur le Prince was now a dead volcano: after years of total submission, he had slipped into semisenility and stopped mattering for several years before his death in 1686, while his son was an obedient mediocrity. Now, wherever he looked, Louis XIV saw that he had succeeded: there was no one even remotely capable of opposing him.

As a result he became, it seemed, even more awe-inspiring. It was in the eighties that the myth of the Sun King became firmly and finally established: he was, everyone agreed, the greatest monarch in Europe; he ruled the strongest and richest nation, lived in the most beautiful palaces, presided over the most splendid and obedient Court. Here, indeed, was a new paradigm of monarchy.

*A*S IF the state of France had not made the King's triumph plain enough, he now determined to make Versailles the visible expression of the new monarchy: the great building campaigns of the early eighties made the palace into what we see today, at least from the outside, since the most of the interior was transformed repeatedly after Louis XIV's death. Luckily, however, the State Apartments remain much as he made them, and they give us a clear image of what it was all about.

The main changes came on the park side. The two huge side wings were added, the central terrace closed and roofed in became the Hall of Mirrors, and the order of the reception rooms was fixed once and for all, although it was not until the 1690s that the King's Bedroom was shifted to its present location, right at the center of the great hive. All, in fact, was much as it is today with one significant exception: the Escalier des Ambassadeurs, the palace's most splendid staircase, with its marble, gilt bronze, and Le Brun frescoes, was torn down in the eighteenth century, so we can only imagine this awe-inspiring introduction to the Grands Appartements.

From then on, however, the long enfilade of salons was just as we know it. From the Escalier des Ambassadeurs, through doors sculpted and gilded against a white ground, the visitor passed through the salons of Abundance, Venus, Diana, Mars, Mercury, and Apollo, some clad in marble, others lined with rich, and often changed, gold-embroidered velvets or brocades. This enfilade, in which the rooms were separated by white and gilt boiserie doors, led to the Salon de la Guerre, all marble, mirrors, gilt bronze, and frescoes by Le Brun representing the triumphs of the Sun King; then came the Grande Galerie, the Hall of Mirrors, with its wide, arched windows opening onto the park all along one side, and the mirrors, made in the new manufacture created by Colbert, on the other, with at the far end the Salon de la Paix which led to the Queen's Apartments, running along the south side of the central pavilion.

If the geography remains, however, and the ceilings are intact, so much else has changed since the seventeenth century that it now requires a real effort of imagination to picture the Versailles of Louis XIV. Of course, we may still look up to see the gods of Olympus disporting themselves in the heavens or, in the Grande Galerie, the various glorified episodes of the King's life, from the crossing of the Rhine to the making of wise laws; the parquet floors remain; the doors are unchanged; but all the rest is gone.

In the rooms which were given marble walls, at least, more of the original look survives, but in those where the walls were covered with fabrics or tapestries, the twentieth-century replacements can only make us yearn for the lost glories of the originals. The paintings are gone, too, which once hung on those walls, and the fact that they can be seen at the Louvre does nothing to obviate Versailles's impoverishment. Just as significant, the furniture now in place is sparse and,

211

almost without exception, belongs to later periods. In the 1680s, besides all its other treasures, Versailles could also boast solid silver furniture—tables, consoles, chests, candelabra, and large square planters holding miniature orange trees. Add to that the gleam of the silks and velvets worn by the palace's occupants, and the fire of their jewels, and the result is quite a different Versailles from the one we know.

The park, too, its structure roughly intact, is only a ghost of its seventeenth-century self. To be sure, the grand canal is still there, as are the main fountains; but many others are gone, and the plantings are not only virtually shapeless but also dreadfully simplified; and, of course, the rule according to which flowers fresh from the hothouses were planted before the palace at dawn every winter's day is no more. Just as, indoors, the palace seemed like a fairytale castle, so outside the gardens, filled with carefully tended rare trees and flowers, were nothing short of an enchantment. Indeed, Louis XIV took enormous pride in them; he invariably led his more distinguished visitors around them and even went so far as to write a guide book for them, the *Manière de visiter les Jardins de Versailles,* in which the visitor is given the best possible itinerary and told when to stop and where to look.

The final settling of the Court at Versailles, while it did not exclude yearly visits to Fontainebleau, virtually eliminated the stays at Saint Germain, Chambord, or Compiègne which had marked the earlier part of the reign; and, of course, it entailed a permanent and definitive removal from Paris. Now at last the young King's humiliation, when he had had to feign sleep before the invading mob, was expunged. At Versailles, connected to Paris by one single easily defended bridge, Louis XIV knew he was forever safe from the great city's hot temper; and he never again stayed at either the Louvre or the Tuileries.

It is also at this time, the early eighties, that the liveliness of the Court began to wane: as the King settled into middle age, his courtiers were expected to behave more sedately; magnificence increased with the complication of the etiquette, while the monarch's semidivine character was tirelessly emphasized. The resulting look was no doubt impressive, but life at Court became both more tiring —all those long hours of standing and waiting—and more tiresome. In one respect that was all to the good: the courtiers' ferocious disputes about minor points of precedence, bred in good part by their idleness, only consolidated the King's power; new customs, like that of bowing to the royal food as it came from the kitchens, only made rebellion more unthinkable; and the ever increasing cost of living in this gilded environment made the nobles still more dependent on the King's bounty.

At the same time, this kind of hothouse atmosphere had real drawbacks: gambling, for instance, became an almost universal addiction, with huge sums being won and lost daily, and scenes of uncontrolled joy or unrestrained despair enacted daily around the tables. More important, perhaps, cliques formed and intrigued ferociously, while libel and calumny blossomed. Still, it hardly seemed to matter: Louis was apparently endowed not just with astonishing majesty but also with the power of seeing through lies and ambitious plots.

It was in the 1680s also that new notes began to appear in that essential record of etiquette, the Register of Ceremonies. Until then, great ceremonies—marriages, funerals, important receptions—are recorded along with their order of precedence and the various activities pertaining to them; but in 1683, for instance, the following entry appears: "The marquis de Vardes, after a twenty-year exile, returned to Court on May 22; he made his bow to the King in his cabinet where Monseigneur the Dauphin was also present. The King asked him whether he knew Monseigneur the Dauphin, the marquis turned to go to Monseigneur, but the King said to him: 'Vardes, you have probably forgotten that no one else may be acknowledged in my presence.'

"This is not to note the marquis de Vardes's return but to render manifest the respect due to the King."[201]

Still, what might have become a crushing dignity was always leavened by Louis XIV's perfect manners: to the end of his life, he took his hat off to every woman he encountered, even if she was only a maid; he knew how to say the right thing at the right time, how to praise so as to awaken lasting gratitude; and although well aware of the uses of flattery, he was capable of saying to Racine, the great playwright, after having heard the latter's reception speech at the Academy: "I would praise it more if you had praised me less."[202] Then, too, a single remark could change his courtiers' behavior. On April 3, 1684, for instance, "the King, at his lever, talked a great deal about the courtiers who were not taking communion at Easter and said he felt great esteem for those who did, saying he wished them to think seriously about it, and adding that he would be pleased with those who did."[203] Of course, this was more likely to produce hypocritical compliance than true faith, but it was typical of the King's way of controlling the courtiers' way of life.

That Louis XIV should have paid such close attention to something—taking communion—which might well be considered a purely personal matter also shows the increasing importance of religion in his view of the world. He had always been a devout Catholic, of course, but now he began to behave as if he were also in charge of his subjects' souls. In the early eighties he still used suasion; but from there to coercion it was only a short step.

No doubt, this answered to deeply felt, and on the whole benevolent, beliefs; but it can only have been encouraged by the fact that, to all intents and purposes, Louis XIV had become pope within his kingdom. It was not only that he appointed all deans, abbots, and bishops, and selected those French ecclesiastics whom the Pope created cardinals; the clergy was now absolutely obedient. In 1682, for instance, it unanimously subscribed to the so-called four articles: "That Saint Peter and his successors, the Vicars of Jesus Christ, and that the entire Church itself have received power from God only over spiritual matters concerned with salvation, and not over temporal matters . . . We declare in consequence that the kings and sovereigns are independent, by God's order, from all ecclesiastical powers in temporal matters, that they cannot be deposed, directly or indirectly, by the authority of the Head of the Church, that their subjects cannot be dispensed from the submission or obedience they owe them."[204]

These so-called Gallican principles were combined with a radical extension of the *régale*. This was the King's right, first, to select all ecclesiastical dignitaries, subject to canonical ordination by the Pope; second, to deal with the regular orders as he pleased, in some cases suppressing convents and abbeys and seizing their property, while also regulating them independently of the Pope; and, finally, to appropriate the revenues of all benefices while they were unoccupied, i.e., between the death of one holder and the appointment of the next. Taken together, these rights made Louis XIV virtually absolute in Church matters; and that was a good deal more than the Pope could bear.

Innocent XI, who had been elected in 1676, was everything the King was not: austere, opposed to pomp, and more than a little influenced by the Jansenists,* the sect Louis XIV fought throughout his reign. Worse, he saw it as his principal duty to resist any and all diminution of the Church's power; and Popes had long claimed the very rights—over temporal matters, over sovereigns, to depose, to dispense from obedience—denied them by the Assembly of 1682. Naturally, then, Innocent refused to accept the French bishops' declaration, even as he objected to the King's extension of the régale, most particularly where it affected the regular orders; so from April 1682 on, he refused to ratify Louis XIV's appointments to vacant sees. By January 1688, thirty-five bishoprics were (at least theoretically) vacant.

In other, less settled times, this conflict would have been an almost impossible weight for the government to bear; now, it simply demonstrated the thoroughness of the French Church's submission: not one bishop took the Pope's side, and all went on as if the elderly gentleman in Rome counted for nothing. Even more remarkable was the peace in the King's conscience: the early eighties, after all, were marked by a strong increase in Louis's piety; but, firmly separating dogma and administration as he had been taught to do by Mazarin, it never occurred to him that opposing the Pope or extending his power over the Church even began to put his salvation in danger: in this as in all else, he governed his realm as he thought it best.

Indeed, he was almost alone in remembering what had now become the distant past: the new dispensation had come to seem the normal order of things; and the many panegyrics which emphasized the King's absolute power praise him more for exerting it wisely than for conquering it. Nothing, no one, it seemed, could resist him: this was proved yet again when his government invented a brand-new form of war.

Because peace treaties over the centuries had deprived France of various towns Louis XIV wanted, and because it was unquestionably easier to swallow them one by one, a new organization, the *chambres*

---

* The Jansenists, who took their name from a Dutch bishop, believed that salvation came from God's grace and not works, as the Jesuits thought. The implacable enemies of the latter, they advocated leading an austere life as divorced as possible from worldly ambition and pomp. Jansenism had been condemned, most recently, in February 1665, by Pope Alexander VII following Louis XIV's request.

215

de réunion, was created: its task was to search the archives in order to make lists of territories in or near the *Trois Evéchés* (Metz, Toul, Verdun) and Alsace which, though they had once belonged to France, were now lost to it. Once these compilations were completed, Louis XIV cited the various foreign sovereigns and in short order simply reappropriated the lands in question; for the most part they had belonged to small German princes like the Elector of Wurttemberg; but they also included, on September 30, 1681, the thriving city of Strasbourg, which had been an imperial fief.

Taken one at a time, these aggrandizements, which also included the purchase of the fortress of Casal, in northern Italy, from the Duke of Mantua, were not enough to justify a European war; besides, while, after the Peace of Nijmegen, Louis XIV had kept his army intact, the Emperor and his allies, including William of Orange, had disbanded theirs. It would thus have required a major effort to resist these successive nibbles; and it was not made. That, of course, confirmed the prevalent opinion, in France at least, that there was nothing the King could not do; while, abroad, he came to be regarded as the most dangerous and insatiable of conquerors. There was never any telling how or where he would strike next: the only certainty was that he would surely strike; and so, grave and lasting enmities were created.

Even if Louis was aware of these, however, he regarded them simply as the unavoidable consequence of his success, a feeling constantly reinforced by Louvois. Wholly in control, now, of the War Department, that admirably intelligent, effective, and hardworking minister was also mad with ambition; and clearly, he mattered more, had greater influence and power, when France was at or near war. Very naturally, then, he encouraged the King's expansionist tendencies, and presented constant aggrandizement as the easiest of policies: when, for instance, Strasbourg became French without a single cannon shot, it was in large part because the unprepared city woke up one morning to find itself surrounded by twenty thousand French troops: the operation, which was wholly successful, had been planned by Louvois to the last detail; and short, perhaps, of invading Holland again, the King began to believe that no one could resist him.

Oddly enough, even Louis's distrust of prime ministers helped Louvois's ascendancy: because he made the decisions himself, because Colbert, whom Louvois hated, remained a powerful minister, the King thought himself uninfluenced; but he never came closer to abandoning his independence of judgment.

It was at this time, in fact, that he almost began to believe his own myth: for twenty years all had gone well; his achievements were immense; he had created a new form of monarchy to which his people had responded with wild enthusiasm: he was, after all, a little more than human. No wonder he announced that he wished his timetable to be so inflexible that anyone, in the remotest reaches of Europe, would know at any time what the King of France was doing. Like the sun, his course was even, dazzling, and unchanging; and not by coincidence, a new kind of Court memoir now appears, wholly centered on the King's every movement and every word. Never before in the history of France had the person of the monarch been considered interesting enough to warrant a day-by-day, hour-by-hour account of his life; now a devoted courtier, the marquis de Dangeau, started to do exactly that; and in 1690, he was supplemented by a writer of genius who, being a duke, also lived at Court, Louis de Rouvroy, duc de Saint-Simon.

That Dangeau should have decided to set down a typical day in 1684, therefore, is hardly surprising; and today still it is well worth reading: here, detail by detail, is what so fascinated Louis XIV's contemporaries.

"He usually rose between eight and nine; as soon as he was dressed, he closeted himself with his ministers and stayed with them until twelve-thirty; at that hour, he came out of his study, had Mme la Dauphine† warned that he was ready to hear the mass, and the whole royal family went to mass, where the music was very beautiful. The mass usually ended between one and two and the King went to visit Mme de Montespan‡ until his food was ready. His Majesty then took his dinner [sitting at the head of a square table] in Mme la Dauphine's antichamber [the Salon de la Paix]. The appointed noblemen served him. Monseigneur, Mme la Dauphine, Monsieur and Madame, Mlle and Mme de Guise* ate with the King and so, occasionally, did the princes of the blood royal.

† The Queen had died in 1683, so the Dauphine was now the first lady and lived in the late Queen's apartment.
‡ He often just walked through, out a back door, and went to see Mme de Maintenon.
* The daughter and granddaughter of the King's uncle, Gaston, duc d'Orléans.

"After dinner, the King visited with Mme la Dauphine for a moment, then he either closeted himself to work or went out. At seven or eight, he went to Mme de Maintenon's and stayed there until ten; then he took his supper at Mme la Dauphine's; as he arose from the table, he spent a few moments with her, bade her good night, and went to Mme de Montespan's, where he usually stayed until midnight; and the *petit coucher* was ordinarily over by twelve-thirty or one at the latest.

"On the days of *appartement,†* one went into the [State] Apartments at seven. The King played at billiards until nine with M. le duc de Vendôme [an illegitimate grandson of Henri IV], M. le Grand [the Grand Equerry, a prince of the House of Lorraine], the duc de Grammont and M. Chamillard [one of the secretaries of state]; after billiards, the King went into his *cabinet* with Mme de Maintenon or visited her in her apartment until supper. Mme la Dauphine watched the King play for a few minutes, then went and listened to the concert for a quarter of an hour and then opened the ball. Monseigneur usually played at lansquenet or cul bas [card games]; and on days when there was not *appartement,* Monseigneur played cards with Mme la Dauphine or attended a play with her.

"On Sundays, there was a meeting of the Council of State attended by the King, the Chancellor [in 1684, Le Tellier, Louvois's father], M. de Louvois, M. de Croissy [Colbert's brother, in charge of Foreign Affairs] and M. Pelletier,‡ Controller General of the Finances. On Mondays, again Council of State. On Tuesdays, Council of Finances [of lesser importance], attended by the King, Monseigneur [who never opened his mouth], the Chancellor, M. le maréchal de Villeroy, the Controller General, M. Pussort, and M. Boucherat. Wednesday, Council of State. Thursday, Council of State. Friday, Council of Conscience [concerning Church affairs] with the Archbishop of Paris first, then with the Père de La Chaise [the King's confessor], each separately. Saturday, Council of Finances. Every other week on Monday was held a Council of Dispatches [once the most important Council, it was now concerned with secondary current affairs], and on those days there was no Council of State; this Council was attended by the King, Monseigneur, Monsieur, the

† I.e., those days when the King officially entertained the Court—normally, three times a week.
‡ Colbert died in 1683; Pelletier was his successor.

Chancellor, M. le maréchal de Villeroy, the four secretaries of state, who present reports, and the Controller General. On Sunday, a quarter of an hour before the Council, the Controller General brings His Majesty a list of disbursements, which the King authorizes. On Tuesdays, the Chancellor hardly stays at the Council of Finances because that day he holds his own [High] Court. M. de Seignelai [Colbert's son and the Minister of the Navy] alone attends with the King the Council of the Navy after dinner; twice a week in ordinary times, sometimes more often, M. de Louvois is granted private audiences after dinner during which he accounts for the army, the forts, and buildings in general. On Monday after dinner, there is a Council for the Affairs of the Protestants; the King does not attend it, but he is given an account of any important business transacted there."[205]

Because Versailles is so huge, we tend to imagine it filled with crowds; but while that was certainly the case on special days or evenings, the numbers, on the evenings of *appartement* that Dangeau describes generally did not exceed three hundred or so; on July 19, 1684, for instance, there was a "big supper to which forty ladies sat down at two tables."[206] Of course, the men, and some of the less important ladies, simply stood; but it is a good indication of size nonetheless. Again, at Marly, the following year, the King was surprised because the unusually large number of a hundred and eight ladies showed up; to those, of course, we must add the men; then, the royal family, the princes of the blood, and their households, numbered some fifty more people.

On those evenings, besides the music, the dancing, and the card-playing—a major occupation—there were also special events: now and again, for instance, the King held a lottery at which every ticket carried a prize; or there might be the first performance of a play or an opera. Even so, for courtiers who spent their entire days and nights at the palace, this immovable succession of predictable pleasures palled, and boredom was often the order of the day, a fact which was carefully concealed from the King. In 1685, for instance, the letters opened as a matter of course by the Post office included one from the princesse de Conti, the King's daughter, to her husband in which she complained about the deadly boredom of the festivities at Court.[207] The King, naturally, read it, called in the princesse, and gave her one of those scoldings which inspired such abject terror in his children: it was almost as if she had betrayed her country. And in a way, she had:

complaining about the dullness of the Court undermined the effectiveness of one of Louis XIV's most important tools of government.

One other element comes out very clearly in Dangeau's account, the number of hours the King actually worked with his ministers. The Council of State was the mainspring of government, the place where major problems were debated, and it met four times a week; but that in no way precluded Louis XIV from meeting with individual ministers, sometimes as often as every day. In any event, unlike most modern leaders, he never took a day off. That would have been hopelessly exhausting had he not so enjoyed the exercise of power, but, of course, he did, all the more that, on the whole, he had had over twenty years of virtually uninterrupted success.

Working is one thing; but even after Louis had spent several hours, every day, dealing with the affairs of state, he still had unceasing obligations. A president of the United States, at the end of the afternoon, can retreat to the privacy of his second-floor quarters; the Queen of England, busy though she may be, has long holidays and more than a few free evenings; but the Sun King, once he had finished governing, remained permanently on show. All his meals were taken in public, as were his *lever,* his coucher, his walks, his hunts, and virtually all his amusements, a practice his less robust successors found harrowing in the extreme.

That this most secretive of men enjoyed being constantly on display, however, cannot be doubted, especially because it also served a useful purpose. Since to be seen by the King was everything, ambitious courtiers were obligated to be constantly present; and there was no such creature as an unambitious courtier. Still, the unchangeable rhythm, as well as the pomp of life at Versailles, took its toll; and so did the golden palace's discomfort. In those days when all the heat came from large, ineffective wood fires, the great, high-ceilinged rooms were freezing in winter, especially since many windows let in icy drafts. Conversely, in the summer, Court dress was immensely heavy and hot; and by 1685, the park itself, which was open to the public, had become intolerably crowded. "The King, who could no longer walk in his gardens without being mobbed by the multitudes which came from everywhere, and especially Paris, ordered the guards to allow only the courtiers and their guests to enter. The populace which had come in before had spoiled many statues and vases."[208]

Even this new restriction, however, was not enough. Louis XIV now decided he wanted occasional moments of relative privacy. He had always liked pavilions: there had been the Grotto of Thetis and the *Trianon de Porcelaine,* a small house clad, on the outside, with Delft tiles. Both, however, aged badly. By 1682, the King badly wanted some new retreat; and, this time, he decided it must be a place where he could actually stay overnight if he chose. Of course, the privacy he was to enjoy there would still be our idea of a crowd: there would be his Household, his large family with their households, and a number of especially favored courtiers; but that still meant, obviously, far fewer people than at Versailles and, most important, some of the more inflexible constraints of the etiquette could be relaxed. There was obviously to be no change in the respect shown the monarch, but, otherwise, he would treat his guests almost as if he were just the owner of a country house.

*I*T WAS Louis XIV's gift that he knew how to bring together architects, artists, and craftsmen so as to create an integrated look in which the harmony of the ensemble was reinforced by the perfection of the details. Almost more important, perhaps, his buildings were timely as well as dazzling: to see them (or hear about them) if you were a foreign prince was to yearn for their equivalent; and, surprisingly, this was as true of his smaller projects as it was of Versailles. All monarchs, after all, could feel they needed a grand and impressive palace; but Marly, the King's next project, was built purely for pleasure—a pleasure the rest of Europe (including William of Orange) soon realized it could not live without.

Aside from Marly's new and different kind of splendor, one that was seen even more outdoors than in, what most amazed the contemporaries was the site the King had chosen: a small, dank and unpromising valley. Saint-Simon, for one, never got over it. In his love-hate relationship with Louis XIV, the madness of building at Marly loomed large; but it is significant that when, after the King's death, the government considered razing the site to save on upkeep, it was the then influential duc who saved it on the (wholly rational) grounds that it was one of the nation's great artistic treasures.*

In fact, unpromising as the valley must have originally looked, it

* Most unfortunately, Marly was torn down by speculators during the Revolution; a small part of the gardens has survived.

221

had a good deal to recommend it. It was close to Versailles—only some four miles away; it was near the Seine, from which water could be drawn; and it had abundant springs of its own. Given the fact that Louis XIV wanted a garden with pavilions, as opposed to a palace with a park, and that, in seventeenth-century France water was an essential and ever-present element of any good garden, Marly made sense; as did the fact that the very shape of its valley kept it private.

What, by 1684, had become visible, in fact, was a vast and ornate garden in which water slept (in basins), ran (in cascades) and spurted (in fountains), all in a decor of sculpture lightened by carefully shaped trees and bushes; and, as usual, there were flowers everywhere. It was a place to stroll, amid the sweet scents and melodious plashings, so much so that carriages—unlike at Versailles—were not allowed in the gardens, only sedan chairs or little three-wheeled chairs pushed by one of the Swiss Guards. It was also in a constant state of flux. Improvements never ceased, but they were thoroughly tested before being carried out. First, a watercolor rendering would be made and modified until the King was satisfied; then a full-scale model would be built; and only then would the new design be implemented.

On the entrance side, Marly began as a court with a chapel on one side and the Guards' house on the other, with the castle in the middle; on the park side, six pavilions on either side of a wide alley served as lodgings for the Court—women on one side, men on the other; indeed these were built before the château itself; and Louis XIV rejected Le Brun's more elaborate design in favor of Mansart's simple rectangular pavilions adorned on the outside with polychrome frescoes and linked by arbors of jasmine.

Even the King's own, central house remained simple. It was a square building, with a frescoed exterior, pilasters, and a triangular pediment; behind the façade, however, at roof level, a shallow dome rose above a windowed drum, so that the central salon, the main, octagonal, reception room, utterly windowless at ground level, was lit entirely from above.

This was reached by four antichambers, one in each side; then, along the façades, there was, in each angle, a three-room apartment, with, behind, two service rooms; these were used by the King—he had red damask on his walls, Mme de Maintenon (in blue), Monsieur (in green), and Madame (in pink). All the mantelpieces were made of carved marble topped with a mirror; between the windows was carved and gilded paneling.

In the central salon, where the King met his guests to chat, listen to music, play cards, or even dance, the walls were given a rhythm of pilasters with composite capitals; above the doors, the arms of France were held by trumpet-playing figures of Fame. There was an elaborately carved cornice above the pilasters, and from it rose carved figures. At that level, there were windows on four of the sides held up by spread-winged eagles and surrounded by carved attributs, while on the other sides were paintings of the seasons by Delafosse, Coypel, Jean Jouvenet, and Louis Boullongne: these, in fact, hid the flues, since, unlike earlier pavilions, Marly was meant for winter use; then, at the base of the ceiling, four more large oval windows opened in line with the doors.

Of course, the floor was parquet, here with a marble edge; a huge chandelier, surrounded by eight smaller replicas, hung from the ceiling, and the furniture consisted of card tables, banquettes, ottomans, and armchairs (for the ladies) upholstered in crimson damask. A stage could be rapidly set up or taken apart and fit on one side of the salon.

The King's own bedroom had walls covered with panels of crimson damask and gold-ground brocade with gold flowers and multicolored arabesques; the curtains were of white damask with gold fringes. Upstairs, the four apartments were reserved for the Dauphine (and later the duchesse de Bourgogne), the princesse de Conti, the duchesse de Chartres, and the duchessse de Bourbon.

All this was both cheerful and grand: color, in fact, was the key element at Marly, indoors, with its profusion of carved gilt furniture and its intense damasks and brocades, on the polychrome frescoed façades and in the gardens where the flowers vied with the changing tones of the waters, the white of the stone and the gold of the bronze sculptures. No wonder even Saint-Simon was impressed: it must all have looked very like paradise.

All that cost money, of course, but, as usual, not as much as people thought. In 1681 and 1682, when work was mostly done on the gardens, the total came to a mere 300,000 livres a year; with the building campaigns of 1683 and 1684, the yearly total hovered around 460,000 livres, while in 1685, the highest year of all because of the interior work, the expenditure reached 677,000 livres; but in

1686, it dropped to 418,000 livres, and in 1687 to 246,000. By 1690, the figure was down to some 80,000 livres; and it remained fairly constant after that. Given the fact that the budget accounted for some 100 million livres yearly, even the highest figure, 677,000 livres, only took two thirds of 1 percent; and if the cost of building the houses and gardens is added up over a period of ten years, up-keep being included in the figure, it still comes to only 3,381,000 livres, not a very large sum at all.

That this unique blend of ease and luxury should have immediately appealed to other European monarchs is hardly surprising; in France itself, Marly became not just the King's retreat but yet another way of rewarding certain courtiers. Any person presented at Court could be present at Versailles; only those specially chosen by the King as his guests ever came to Marly; an invitation there was a clear proof of the royal favor, but it was not to be had without humiliation. When the King had decided to go to Marly, the fact was announced. Ambitious courtiers then gathered near the King's bedroom; the door would open; Louis XIV would look out as the would-be guests shouted: "Marly, Sire, Marly!"; the King would then retire and dictate the list of the elect. By June 1684 already, the gardens were almost complete; in 1685, the King started the frequent visits, lasting from two days to two weeks, which, henceforth, were such a part of his life.

It was also typical of the change in Louis's feelings that while Mme de Maintenon was from the first given an apartment on the same level as the Dauphin, Monsieur, and Madame, there was no room for Mme de Montespan at all. It was now her turn to endure what La Vallière had once suffered; but, more and more, she retreated to Clagny, until, by the nineties, she had virtually given up appearing at Court. Already in December 1684, she lost her apartment on the main floor at Versailles and was moved downstairs and away from the King: there could have been no more sure or visible signal of disgrace.

As for Mme de Maintenon, her situation was becoming clearer day by day. On May 29, 1684, the Dauphine's dame d'honneur, the duchesse de Richelieu, died. That very evening, the King offered the office to Mme de Maintenon. That in itself was startling enough: normally, only a duchess, and a very grand one at that, would be considered for so considerable a position. Offering it to the widow

Scarron, recent marquise de Maintenon though she might be, was nothing short of revolution. That, however, was only the beginning of it: to everyone's stupefaction, Mme de Maintenon refused the position. At that, "Mme la Dauphine went to Mme de Maintenon's room to ask her to accept the office of dame d'honneur, but was unable to sway her. Mme de Maintenon received with respect this obliging request but remained unmoved; she had asked the King not to mention the honor he had done her in offering her this office, but His Majesty was unable to refrain from talking about it and told the story after his dinner."[209] And as if these startling events were not clear enough an indication, the King then appointed the duchesse d'Arpajon, whose only qualification was that her brother had once been a very close friend of Mme de Maintenon's.

Although there can be no doubt that the marquise had been the King's mistress for a while, the relationship changed dramatically as a result of the Queen's death on July 30, 1683: although a simple adultery was better than a double, still the King was unquestionably sinning with Mme de Maintenon. Given his new, stronger religious feelings, not to mention the marquise's extreme piety, this was, to say the least, awkward. It is true that Mme de Maintenon had been encouraged to give in by her confessor since she was to be the instrument for ending the scandal of the King's liaison with Mme de Montespan while steering him closer to the arms of the Church; but the situation was far from ideal. With the Queen's death, however, new, dazzling possibilities opened up. There was only one problem: a marriage between the King of France and the widow Scarron, aside from making Louis the laughingstock of Europe, seemed, to the rigidly stratified society of the seventeenth century, quite impossible, even if it brought about no issue.

The marriage, however, would appease Louis's conscience and his sensuality at the same time, not a minor consideration. There seems little doubt that Bossuet, still the most influential of the bishops, strongly urged the King to remarry; and it is quite certain that the proud autocrat himself was truly and deeply in love with Mme de Maintenon. Here was no mere sexual attraction: the King respected Mme de Maintenon for her psychological and intellectual qualities.

Given all these problems, one solution, and one alone, was possible: the King must marry, but in secret. Thus he would sin no longer; he would give the woman he loved a far more secure position; but by never acknowledging the marriage, valid though it was in the eyes of the Church, he also precluded the devastating mockery which would have followed an openly declared union. Obviously, every possible advantage was found here; and so at an unknown date, most probably in 1684 since Louis would not have offered the marquise the position of dame d'honneur if they had already been married, the Sun King, in the deepest of secrecy, before Louvois, his confessor, his valet de chambre, and the marquis de Montchevreuil, one of Mme de Maintenon's relatives, was at last wed to the widow Scarron.

Of course, Mme de Maintenon kept her name; but it was noticed not only that the King paid more attention to her than ever but that she remained sitting in an armchair in the presence of the royal family, something which, until then, only the Queen could do, and that she attended mass sitting in the Queen's box. As for her scoldings when the princesses misbehaved, they were to become as feared as they were famous; but even so, the marriage was never acknowledged.

Among Mme de Maintenon's many attractions—physical beauty, unfading, perennial youth, intelligence, wit, common sense—one, no doubt, counted for much with the King: she was the most discreet of women. It is, in fact, posterity's irrecoverable loss that, after Louis XIV's death, she destroyed every scrap of paper she had ever received from him; but in the 1680s, and indeed for the rest of the reign, the King knew he could rely on her never to reveal a secret; as a result, he soon developed the habit of working with his ministers in her apartment and in her presence. That, however, did not mean that she influenced policy: although he frequently consulted her, Louis almost never followed her advice, a fact of which she was painfully aware. It was, for her, the most difficult of positions: with all the appearances of power, she had none; although treated by the King with the utmost respect, she was nothing. Only a woman of exceptional gifts could have prospered as she did.

That she now had influence when it came to Court appointments is, however, clear. The King had always felt this was one of his mistresses' perks; thus, the elevation of the duchesse d'Arpajon to the high office of dame d'honneur was typical. In the same way, Mme de Maintenon's old friends tended to do well; but in all other respects the Court remained unchanged. The Dauphine moved into the Queen's apartment and took over most of her duties; and the etiquette surrounding the King was, if anything, reinforced, while the person of the monarch appeared more splendid than ever. On December 2, 1684, for instance, Louis XIV changed after the hunt, into a suit sewn with over 12 million livres' worth of diamonds, which must indeed have been as dazzling as the sun.

There were other ways of celebrating him, too. In 1685, two new city squares were started in Paris. In April, "it became known that the King had bought M. de Vendôme's house in the rue Saint Honoré in Paris, and that it was to be torn down and replaced by a square something like the Place Royale [today, Place des Vosges] in the middle of which there will be his statue in bronze; and that His Majesty would give the plots around the square to build houses of similar design."[210] Today we know that square as the Place Vendôme; and it is one of the most handsome in Paris.

Inspired by this, the maréchal de La Feuillade, a most assiduous courtier, decided to build a square of his own and adorn it with a statue of the King. As it turned out, La Feuillade was too cheap: the square, although it exists (it is the Place des Victoires) was never completed; but the statue was. On March 28, 1686, "a most extraordinary ceremony was seen before the face of God and man. The maréchal de La Feuillade carried out the consecration of the King's statue in the Place des Victoires. The King is on foot and Fame holds a laurel wreath above his head . . . La Feuillade rode three times around the statue at the head of the Guards regiment, whose colonel he is, and indulged in all the prosternations that the pagans of old dedicated to the statues of their emperors."[211] More than ever the King was coming to seem godlike.

That impression could only be reinforced by the arrival, in May 1685, of the Doge of Genoa. That maritime republic, once as strong as Venice herself, but now somewhat fallen, had shown itself unfriendly to a French expeditionary corps in Italy. Louis XIV demanded that its doge come in person to beg his pardon in spite of the city's constitution, which forbade the Doge to leave it; so the constitution was changed and the Doge traveled to Versailles.

"The Court . . . was lined up in two rows from the second salon to the end of the Hall of Mirrors where the King was sitting on a thronelike silver chair, and that was on a platform covered with a Persian carpet. On this platform were Monseigneur, Monsieur, M. le duc de Chartres [Monsieur's son], M. le duc de Bourbon, M. le duc du Maine, and M. le comte de Toulouse†; and behind the King were all the officers of the State and of his Household who were entitled to be present,"212 Sourches recorded; and Dangeau goes on to describe the ceremony.

"At noon, the Doge came in with four senators and many other people who were part of his suite; he was dressed in red velvet with a hat of the same, the senators in black; he kept his hat on while speaking to the King, but often took it off and put it back on; he did not seem embarrassed . . . After the King answered him, each senator spoke in turn . . . In the afternoon the Doge visited Monseigneur, Madame la Duchesse, M. le duc de Bourgogne, M. le duc d'Anjou, M. le duc de Berry [the King's three grandsons], Monsieur, Madame, M. le duc de Chartres [and all the other princes of the blood]. He did not see the King's illegitimate children."213 For the King, it was a real apotheosis.

This exaltation of himself and those who derived their status from him continued apace. On July 24, 1685, one of Mme de Montespan's daughters, the thirteen-year-old Mlle de Nantes, at an age remarkable even for this century when women married young, was wed to the duc de Bourbon, the grandson of the great Condé. This brought the King's illegitimate children a step closer still to the throne, since the duc de Bourbon was higher in the line of succession than his cousin, the prince de Conti; it also made the bride the third lady in France, right after the Dauphine and Madame.

The celebrations themselves underlined the royal character of the new duchesse. First, the King gave her a dowry of a million livres, a sum so huge that not many legitimate French princesses had received it, as well as 300,000 livres' worth of jewels, and a yearly pension of 100,000 livres, while the groom received his own 100,000-livre pension, the governorship of Burgundy—a largely honorific position—and the reversal of the chief office in the King's Household, that of Grand Master. And as if that all was not clear enough, it was at the wedding banquet that, for the first time, the princes of the blood royal—as opposed to the immediate royal family—were allowed to eat with the King because that gave him an opening to spread the same promotion to his illegitimate children: from that moment on,

† This was the first time that the King's illegitimate sons were treated as if they were part of the royal family; a difference was preserved, though, when the Doge failed to visit them later.

although their official status was still that of peers, his illegitimate sons, the duc du Maine and the comte de Toulouse, were given the same precedence as princes of the blood. It seemed clear that, in time, the position would be granted them in full; and, needless to say, Mme de Maintenon, their erstwhile governess, was delighted.

The festivities, too, were exactly those to be expected at a proper royal wedding, complete with illuminations, fireworks, a musical gondola ride on the grand canal, and a banquet in the gardens of Trianon. There had been no king like him before; no precedent could bind him.

When it came to diplomacy or finance, these feelings of exaltation did not impinge upon Louis's common sense; but it is hard to believe that they did not play a major role in the first irreversible disaster of the reign. Ever since 1661, it had been accepted policy to try and convert as many Protestants as possible; the key word here being convert. To be sure, all kinds of enticements were held out if they did, while, if they did not, they could expect short and unsatisfactory careers; still, no force was ever used. Up to a point, this policy worked: there had indeed been a steady flow of conversions; at the same time, it was clear to those who were willing to look that there remained, and would remain, an irreducible Protestant presence concentrated mostly in the Southwest of France.

This relative tolerance—rare enough among seventeenth-century rulers—was noticed. In a pamphlet entitled *Parallel of Louis the Great with the Other Princes Who Have Been Called Great*, published early in 1685, the author praises him as follows: "He alone united all the qualities all the others have separately: an ardent and tireless zeal for the welfare of the Church, *but a zeal without excess,‡* a justice without riguor, a clemency without weakness, a courage without temerity, an open mind, a clear memory, a well-controlled imagination, a serene watchfulness, and success without pride."[214] It is worth noticing here that the author praises not only the King's great qualities but most of all his moderation, a quality then seen as essential to true greatness.

At the same time, the balance in the government had been destroyed: on September 6, 1683, Colbert died, largely of exhaustion. Seignelai, his son, was given most of his offices, but there was a very significant difference: a voice to which the King always listened atten-

‡ Added italics.

tively, and which invariably spoke for reason and moderation, was gone. Le Pelletier, Colbert's successor as Contrôleur Generale of Finances, was a mediocre minister and quite unable to make himself heard; and Louvois was given the job of Superintendent of the King's Buildings, thus coming much closer to Louis. Worse, in the Council, not even the close alliance of Seignelai and Croissy could oppose Louvois successfully: his was now the preponderant voice.

The King, of course, was aware of this, and he only trusted Louvois so far; but the very knowledge that he was doing this predisposed him to accept Louvois's information, if not always his advice; and in the middle eighties there can be no doubt that the War Minister had become the most influential man in the Council. Unfortunately, that influence was used in one direction only: highly authoritarian in his private and official lives, Louvois believed in force as a matter of policy. So long as he was only in charge of the War Department that did not matter: indeed, there is much to be said for a forceful—and highly effective—leader as organizer of the armies; only Louvois tried to solve the far more complex issues of civilian politics as he would have those posed by a strong enemy.

This predilection for the use of force was especially dangerous because it was allied to a clear perception of the King's deepest desires. In one case, in particular, Louvois found that Louis tended to believe what pleased him: convinced as he was that the Protestants were wrong, resentful as he remained of the existence of a semi-independent minority (at least in theory) within his kingdom, he was quite ready to accept that, convinced at last by his efforts, they were massively converting to Catholicism; and thus, the usually suspicious monarch swallowed whole the many exaggerated reports submitted by Louvois. Had he not thought that only tiny Protestant minorities remained, he might well have shown more tolerance—thus removing the question from Louvois's grasp; and the minister knew it.

As a result, exaggerations gave way to outright lies, and the King still believed. On October 9, 1685, for instance, he told the Papal Nuncio that, like Nimes and Montpellier, the entire town of Uzès had just turned Catholic. On the thirteenth, he announced, at his *lever,* that the province of Poitou had followed suit along with the town of Grenoble. On the sixteenth, it was announced that Lyon, too, had given up the Reformation: so Louvois had informed the King. In fact, of course, none of this was true; scattered conversions had taken place only in response to the strongest pressure and in expectation of worse to come.

Louvois, in fact, had needed no new permission to use force. It was the custom, in France as in most of Europe, to quarter regiments with private people, and it was obviously a hardship for those who were chosen as hosts. In 1681, Louis XIV had signed an ordinance excepting recent converts from this obligation; so all Louvois had to do was give the Protestants a choice: either they converted and were safe; or they would be forced to take in dragoons whose brutality was notorious.

When the King heard about this, he was horrified and ordered it stopped; so the persecutions now took the forms of interminable lawsuits which ruined those who refused to convert. No overt force was used, of course, so the King failed to discover what was actually happening. Then, too, in June 1681, a royal declaration had been published giving seven-year-old Protestant children the right to convert despite their parents' objections: the King had simply meant to make it easier to save souls, as he saw salvation, but the declaration was now used literally to tear the children away from their parents under the wholly fallacious pretext they wanted to convert.

It must also be said that mass conversions, besides pleasing the King, also suited him very well: with Colbert gone, the deficit was growing; and as Protestant religious houses and churches closed for lack of congregations, the government appropriated their endowments. Finally, God seemed to be on his side: across the Channel, the avowedly Catholic James II had succeeded Charles II on the throne of England without even a ripple of opposition.

Once all this has been said, however, and a fair share of blame apportioned to Louvois, the fact remains that Louis XIV knew that, in the end, Protestantism could only be eradicated by force. The Council at which the situation was discussed recognized it so well it split right down the middle, with Louvois leading the anti-Protestant party. The decision, therefore, was the King's alone: indeed he had always pointed out that he would listen to all sides with an open mind, but that he alone would set the government's policy.

On October 19, 1685, he did just that: on that day was abrogated the Edict of Nantes, given out by Henri IV in 1598 as the close to the Wars of Religion, and guaranteeing the Protestants' right of worshiping as they pleased within certain numerical limits. All Protestant churches were to be razed; all ministers were to leave France within two weeks; all newborn children were to be baptized as Catholics.

At Court, and in the Catholic Church, the reaction was one of unalloyed delight. The old and failing Chancellor, Le Tellier, Louvois's father, who had spent his life serving the King, exclaimed "sincerely and from the bottom of his heart that he was no longer sorry to die since he was so happy as to seal the revocation of the Edict of Nantes"[215]; and, indeed, eleven days later, he was dead. As for the person now closest to the King, Mme de Maintenon, although she remained as discreet as ever, her known positions were such that she could only have approved of the Revocation.

Because, no doubt, he had been so readily obeyed in everything else, it simply did not occur to Louis XIV that this was one order which might not be followed; still, he took the precaution of sending out missions in which the priests' eloquence was backed up by platoons of soldiers; and the most appalling persecutions were unleashed on the southwest provinces where, in spite of everything, Protestantism had remained strong. There were tortures and murders, as has invariably been the case when a Church tries to impose itself on a reluctant population. All Protestants caught in the act of holding a service were sent to row, and die, on the King's galleys; and although they had been forbidden to leave the Kingdom, over three hundred thousand Protestants fled, many of them to Brandenburg, where the Elector was only too glad to take them in.

The magnitude of this disaster can scarcely be overestimated. Although, in this century, we are all too familiar with religious persecutions, there can be no excuse for Louis XIV's decision to force his own brand of Christianity on his unwilling subjects: all rulers make mistakes, but this is an ineradicable moral stain. In this case, furthermore, it was bad policy, a mistake as well as a crime: the three hundred thousand who left—a huge number out of a population of slightly under 20 million—were among the most valuable of the French, hardworking artisans, skilled craftsmen, busy merchants. This was an almost crippling blow to the French economy, and one from which it took decades to recover. Vast regions in the Southwest became virtual deserts; and abroad, strong, proselytizing minorities were formed whose main desire was for revenge: that, too, had a devastating effect within just a few years. With all that, however, and despite a few exceptions among whom we can count Saint-Simon, there is no doubt that the Revocation was an immensely popular act among the vast majority of the people. Louis XIV was reproached for much during his lifetime; but for the Revocation, almost never.

E VEN as scenes of horror were being enacted against the Protestants, however, the Court itself was more splendid and more peaceful than ever. On September 1, 1686, the fame earned throughout the world by the King was confirmed in the manner most pleasing to him: for the first time ever, a Siamese embassy arrived in France. Naturally, it was received at Versailles with the greatest pomp: Louis XIV, dressed in a suit of gold cloth covered with huge diamonds, sat on his silver throne; silver tables and candelabra lined the platform on which it had been set; and all watched admiringly, Sourches commenting characteristically that the diamonds were worth more than the entire kingdom of Siam.[216]

Even Mme de Montespan contributed to the new order. Reconciled, at least outwardly, to her new position, she swallowed her pride and asked for her former rival's protection. In December 1685, "she told Mme de Maintenon that she would very much like to see M. d'Antin, her son,* given the office of *menin* [Gentleman of the Bedchamber] to Monseigneur, and that evening, the King went in to Mme de Montespan's and told her he was happy to grant her that wish."[217] From then on, although she not infrequently retreated to Clagny, the once possessive marquise enjoyed a place at the same time close to the King and distant from him: without power or influence, she remained as a familiar figure in the first rank of the Court. On January 4, 1686, for instance, "the King and Monseigneur went to Marly for dinner. Mme la princesse de Conti [Montespan's daughter], Mme de Montespan, and Mme de Thianges [Montespan's sister] were with them . . . Monsieur and Madame arrived around five with many ladies and courtiers; the house was brightly lit; and in the salon, there were four shops, one for each of the seasons of the year.

Monseigneur and Mme de Montespan kept that of autumn; M. du Maine and Mme de Maintenon that of winter; M. le duc de Bourbon and Mme de Thianges that of summer; Mme la duchesse de Bourbon and Mme de Chevreuse [Colbert's daughter] that of spring. There

---

* The marquis, later duc, d'Antin was Mme de Montespan's only legitimate child.

were splendid fabrics, silver, and what is proper to each season, and the courtiers played cards for them and were given whatever they won. It is thought that there was at least 150,000 livres' worth of clothes; playing went on until supper and after that the King and Monseigneur gave away whatever was left in the shops . . . Those who won took their winnings, those who lost were forgiven their debt."[218]

In this perfectly ordered world, however, the principal actor was soon reminded that he was just a man after all. The King's unvarying good health had long been noticed: in 1685, he was already forty-seven, an age at which most of his contemporaries suffered from a variety of infirmities. And, indeed, in October, illness struck in the form of a sharp pain in the foot caused, most probably, by gout; and, for the first time, he was forced to remain indoors for several days. That had followed a disastrous piece of dentistry: the botched extraction of a tooth had caused an abscess, upon which d'Aquin, the King's First Physician and a man of startling incompetence, decided to remove all his patient's upper teeth. This major—and exceedingly painful—operation proved catastrophic: while he was at it, d'Aquin accidentally removed part of the King's palate, and, of course, new abscesses formed, which were then cauterized with a red-hot iron.

All this, of course, was done without any anesthesia; and, throughout, Louis XIV kept his routine unaltered, much to the Court's admiration. Still, neither gout nor extractions were life-threatening. In February 1686, however, that changed as well. "At the beginning of the month the King fell ill with a tumor [probably a large abscess] which came out where the thigh meets the buttock, and since it was so painful as to prevent him from riding, he had it examined by Félix, his First Surgeon, and began to think seriously of having it treated.

"Since he was unaccustomed to pain, he decided against an incision and his physicians and surgeons obeyed him, perhaps too readily. They tried to treat the tumor by inducing sweating, which all those who knew about this disease thought both ridiculous and dangerous."[219]

That, of course, was right; but physicians, in the seventeenth century, had reached a nadir of ignorance: medical treatment killed frequently and almost never cured. There was no antisepsis, so most surgery was followed by gangrene; so the King's dilemma was a very real one: if the tumor were opened, it might drain; but the incision might also become infected and, eventually, deadly.

In early February, however, "since the King's illness continued, the tumor was cut open to help Nature, which was pushing the infection out . . . and Félix used a cautery to widen the wound."[220] That, as it turned out, was still insufficient; by early March the abscess was still there, along with the open wound. Yet another cut proved useless, so a cautery was used again, but still the disease continued. The King spent most of March in bed, as he was no longer able to walk without great pain; and finally, on the thirtieth, the abscess broke and the King started to heal, although, still some three weeks later, the last of the infection had to be cleaned out.

The King, the abbé de Choisy commented, "suffered great pains but never ceased holding his Councils . . . His illness did not sour his temper; he wanted the Court to enjoy itself in his absence."[221] Once again, Louis XIV proved how thoroughly he was master of himself: physical pain was no more able to shake his equanimity than political pressure. Of course, there was more to this than just courage: well-established though it was, the new order was still recent enough to be fragile; and all depended on the King. Had he stopped governing, either the ministers or his family—the incapable Dauphin and the frivolous Monsieur—would have taken over; and that was not a possibility he was willing to allow. As for the amusements of the Court, if they proceeded unalterably on, it was because Louis XIV feared the end of his system of concentrating the aristocracy at Versailles where it was powerless.

Stoicism, however, is not without cost: it was in 1686 that, physically and psychologically, the young, ebullient monarch was replaced by the formidable figure we see in the later portraits, with its hawk-like nose and deep vertical wrinkles. The young King was impressive, but amiably effulgent; the older Louis XIV became terrifyingly majestic, a living icon more than a man. Psychologically too, that detachment from normal emotions which had always characterized the King, that willingness to cause suffering among his family and friends for the good of the state, became even more marked. There is a visible hardness, now, a lack of humanity, which shows up all too clearly in the way the Protestants were treated, an absolute refusal to allow even the slightest dissent. At the same time, while always retaining a measure of selfishness—Mme de Maintenon often deplored

235

this—Louis XIV, as the years passed, devoted himself ever more completely to the state he had created, so that the identification between man and function became virtually total.

This transcending of normal human feeling was, in one sense, only an extension of that semidivine status the King had long enjoyed; and just as gods never die, so Louis XIV went on to surmount illnesses which would have either killed or incapacitated most of his subjects. In this, if he wanted to maintain his system, he had no choice: from 1686 on, his health failed on repeated occasions.

Sometimes the illnesses were relatively harmless. "The Court was greatly worried because of the King's fever," Sourches noted in August 1686. "Although it was never very high, it still caused the King to become much thinner and changed his face visibly."[222] The fever may well have been an early symptom of a much more serious disorder. By September, it had become clear to Louis and his physicians that he was suffering from an anal fistula. Not only was this inconvenient and extremely painful; like all such wounds in the seventeenth century it entailed a possibility of generalized and fatal infection. Amazingly, considering the state of medical knowledge, an operation had recently been developed that was known sometimes to effect a cure; but it was also highly dangerous: one way or the other, there was no guarantee of survival.

"The King, who was suffering more and more from his fistula, had been resolved, for two months, to undergo the great operation; but he had confided this secret only to Monseigneur, Mme de Maintenon, M. de Louvois, his First Physician, Félix, his First Surgeon and the Père de La Chaise, his confessor; and even so Monseigneur did not know the King had decided that it would take place on November 19.

"On the seventeenth, he strolled in several places in Versailles and finding himself in great pain, although he did not show it, he decided to have the operation the next day . . ." Already for the past few weeks Félix had been practicing on prisoners with fistulas and corpses so as to know exactly how, where, and how deep to make his incisions. "On the eighteenth, at eight o'clock, those who entered the King's bedroom found that he was sleeping soundly, which showed the tranquillity of his soul on an occasion when others would have felt great fear. Once he had been awakened, he asked whether everything was ready and whether M. de Louvois was in his antichamber;

and when he was told that M. de Louvois was there and that all was ready, he got out of bed and started to pray.

"After this, having risen, he said aloud: 'Lord, I place myself in your hands,' and, getting back onto his bed, he ordered Félix to begin the operation, which he did, in the presence of Bessière, the cleverest surgeon in Paris, and of M. de Louvois, who held the King's hand throughout the operation; for Mme de Maintenon was standing near the mantelpiece.

"The King did not cry out and only said once 'Oh, God!' when the first incision was made. When the operation was almost done, he told Félix not to spare him, and to treat him just as if he were the least important private person in France; which forced Félix to make two more incisions; after which he put on the first bandage and bled him from the arm and there he was not as successful as during the operation, which he had carried out perfectly, for he cut a muscle in the arm and caused the King much pain . . . Around ten [the First Gentleman of the Bedchamber and the King's other attendants] were allowed in . . . and the King held a Council after dinner."[223]

It is difficult for us to imagine just what this sort of operation meant to the patient, the blend of terror and racking pain which accompanied it. It was not uncommon for people to withstand both in silence; but then, within less than two hours of the operation, to have the First Gentleman and the other courtiers come in, and to hold a Council that very afternoon, is so stoical as to be well nigh incomprehensible: if Louis XIV demanded much of others, he expected no less of himself.

This iron front was kept up unfailingly. Four days after the operation, when the King must have been in agonizing pain, he saw the prince de Conti, "and said to him: 'People who do not know me think me very ill, but as soon as they see me, they can easily notice that I am not suffering much.' "[224] That was on November 22; by December 7, it had become all too plain that the wound was not healing.

"The surgeons looked very thoroughly for the cause of this and finally discovered that certain hard bodies had formed at the bottom, and that they absolutely prevented a cure. They decided, therefore, to make new incisions to tear out these hard bodies, and in fact did so; but that could not be done without causing the King inordinate pains, and it even gave him a fever; but even so he continued to see [the Court] two or three times a day, refusing to give this up even on the day of the operation . . . One could see clearly that he suffered extremely and constrained himself not to show it; but the more he suffered, the longer he kept the courtiers in his room."[225] That he should have done so was due in part to his insistence on seeming more than human; but he also had sound political reasons. Any hint that he was likely to die soon would have encouraged certain members of the royal family to start plotting for control of the future King. Everyone knew that the Dauphin was perfectly incapable of ruling alone; and there were many people who longed to be the power behind the throne. Almost worse, France's enemies abroad would have felt encouraged: with Louis XIV removed, the kingdom would become more vulnerable. Thus, when he refused to admit to feeling pain, Louis was also defending his country.

His agony was long drawn out. On December 9, the doctors decided to make a new incision. On the thirteenth, they cut again, and, deciding the wound was scarring over too quickly, they applied a cautery to reopen it, a process which pained the King horribly. Finally, a week later, the recovery began: on December 22, Louis left his room for the first time in over a month; but he was not able to mount a horse again before the middle of March.

That he should have survived at all was virtually a miracle; but the fact that he did only strengthened his image. Clearly, just as his armies could not be defeated, so ordinary disease could not kill him, or, indeed, prevent him from attending to the government of his realm; and as if to underline this, he embarked on yet another building project.

Marly, by the summer of 1687, was just what Louis XIV had wanted, a retreat away from Versailles; but now he decided he wanted a small country residence within the great park itself; and since there had already been a pavilion at Trianon, he decided to build a house which could be used for festivities and an occasional stay. "Since the year was well under way when he gave orders to begin this, and since he wanted it finished before the winter, he pressed the work and often went to spend the afternoons under a tent, where he worked with M. de Louvois and looked at the work from time to time so as to make it go faster."[226]

It was during this summer that the King had a famous difference with Louvois. One day, as the monarch arrived at Trianon, he noticed that one window was out of true and pointed it out to his minister. Louvois looked and, feeling no doubt that his thoroughness was being doubted, swore that this was not the case. Measuring tools were brought and, in short order, it was discovered that while the error was very small, the King had been perfectly right. Indeed, he not only had the visual equivalent of absolute pitch, he was also a thorough perfectionist; and walls were torn down several times when they failed to come up to his very exacting standards.

The result, as usual, was a building which princes throughout Europe admired and copied. A cross between a palace and a garden pavilion, Trianon—the work of Mansart—embodied a completely new concept, that of a subsidiary building, placed close enough to a main palace for convenience yet remote enough for privacy, small enough to exclude most of the Court as a residence, yet large enough to contain most of it for specific festivities, and, with all that, quite as refined and luxurious as the palace itself while remaining almost completely open to the gardens outside.

When, in 1688, the King inaugurated Trianon in the company of Monseigneur and Mme de Maintenon, what the Court saw with wonder was a fairytale palace of blond stone and pink marble. The main courtyard, flanked by two wings, led—as it still does—to an open, arcaded peristyle with, on the far side, paired pink marble columns. On the court side, the tall, arched windows of the wings, repeating the pattern of the peristyle, were topped by carved shells and trophies, and separated by pink marble pilasters; then, above came a band of stone, topped by a band of marble, with, crowning the building, a stone balustrade adorned with vases, trophies, and groups of children. On the garden side, the same pattern was repeated.

Even today, when the balustrade ornaments are gone and nothing is left of Louis XIV's sumptuous interiors, Trianon has lost none of its magic. This long, low building, almost hugging the ground, looks like nothing so much as a jewel placed in a sylvan setting. Versailles had majesty, Marly had charm; Trianon seemed a dream made real, and it quickly became a part of the King's life.

It is one of the paradoxes inherent to any account of the Sun King's life that those surrounding him pale by comparison; thus, unquestionably, much credit must be given to Jules Hardouin-Mansart, who designed the wings, and Robert de Cotte, who was responsible for the peristyle. And yet the King, too, deserves credit—not just for providing the commission and footing the bills, but for his close and constant involvement with architects and builders. Here as elsewhere, Louis XIV was deeply and personally involved with every detail of the building, so that it is no exaggeration to speak of a collaboration between the monarch and those who worked for him; and, like Versailles, Trianon directly reflects the personality of its owner.

This direct involvement did not, however, in any way serve to diminish the artists' merits. Louis XIV's reaction when he received a new work of Le Brun's, the *Elevation of the Cross,* in June 1685, is typical of his constant and visible appreciation. The painting was taken in to the King's bedroom in the morning, "and although the King was holding the Council, since he had given orders that he was to be warned promptly, as soon as it came he came out of the Council to see it and seeing that it was as beautiful as he had hoped, he said a thousand obliging things to M. Le Brun; then returning to the Council, he told the Chancellor and all the others that he had just been brought a painting which was worth their getting up and coming to see it. All the Council came and applauded it and the King showed great joy to all."[227] It is, in fact, one of the Sun King's most endearing features that, while capable of being pitiless to family and friends, he never stinted in proclaiming and rewarding merit of all kinds.

Indeed, he seemed to move about in a golden light of success and splendor. Masterpiece followed masterpiece: to have created the new Versailles, Marly, and Trianon all within ten years is a mind-boggling achievement; Lulli was reinventing music; Molière was dead, it is true, but Racine lived and spent much time at Court, as did Boileau and La Fontaine; Le Brun, perhaps not a great genius, but certainly a painter and designer of the very first rank, was endlessly busy; Puget was sculpting masterpieces. On a different plane, Louvois, for all his shortcomings, was an exceptionally able minister; and over all, enveloped in splendor, shone the King.

As if all that were not enough, the great Court festivities took on a dazzling splendor. The Carrousel of the Civil Wars of Granada was typical of these. "Two trumpets led the parade," we are told, "and were followed by Dumont, Monseigneur's equerry . . . dressed in crimson embroidered with silver.

"Then came eighty pages of Monseigneur's troupe, dressed in black embroidered with gold, in purple embroidered with gold and silver, in grey embroidered with silver, in crimson embroidered with gold and silver, and they carried their master's coat of arms . . .

"M. le duc de Saint Aignan, the leader of the carrousel, rode a splendid horse and wore a Roman-type armor made of silver blades, with gold and ruby ornaments. His helmet was similar, with a golden sphynx holding a quantity of white feathers, and others spotted with black and crimson . . . The harness of his horse was similar, and it wore a quantity of the same feathers on its head . . . His trumpeteers, pages and footmen were in crimson embroidered with silver . . .

"Monseigneur wore a crimson suit, embroidered in silver, with large gold buttonholes and a mosaic of black velvet cut and embroidered with gold and laden with a great number of rubies and diamonds . . ."[228] Then came twenty knights in black and gold, with the same diamond- and ruby-laden black velvet mosaic and black plumes sprinkled with pink; and ten knights in gold and purple with ruby-and-diamond buttonholes; and another ten in gray and silver with emeralds: the description goes on and on, and, on a printed page, the very accumulation soon becomes tedious. How very different it must have been to see the reality: the gold and precious stones sparkling in the sun, the plumes waving, the horses prancing, the music playing. Here was a spectacle on the grandest scale, but not so grand that it was not appropriate to the Court of Louis XIV: for, during these years of peace and power, the sun of France shone so brightly as to dazzle the world.

IX
Useless Victories

*A*S THE 1680s drew to a close, Louis XIV seemed more powerful than ever, if only because his personal rule had lasted for a generation. With the death of the people who had known him when he was a young man, the King's eminence seemed both formidable and natural. In his family, too, he was a feared and uncontested master. It was well understood that everyone's convenience had to give way to his, and that it was better to endanger one's health than to annoy him: in October 1685, for instance, the Dauphine, who was pregnant, began to feel unwell during the performance of a play. There could be no question of leaving before His Majesty, so the poor woman waited; and when she finally reached her room, she miscarried before she could even reach her bed. That sort of behaviour deserved no more than a brief note in Dangeau's memoirs; and there were many similar scenes in the next few years.

Until now, luck had always favored Louis; it had been helped, of course, by his own exertions and that of his ministers, and by the fact that France was the richest and most populated country in Europe; but even so, when fate seemed briefly undecided, it had, in the end favored him. From 1688 on, however, the reverse seems true: time after time, events for which he was not responsible and over which he had no control brought severe setbacks with them. Between 1661 and 1688, his only real failure had been during the attempted conquest of Holland; and even then, peace had been made on his terms. From 1688 on, the limits of his power were made very evident; and so was the scope of his character. Repeated triumphs, at worst, make for overweening pride; appalling difficulties, on the other hand, require persistence, courage, and discernment if they are to be overcome; and those were the very qualities which were now tested in the King.

Friendship with England had always been one of the bases of Louis XIV's foreign policy. Charles II's death in 1685, although it removed a wise and friendly monarch, did not alter this amity. The new king, James II, a kind, brave, honorable, but exceedingly dense man, was himself a Catholic; but in spite of their now traditional hatred of Rome, his subjects, who looked to the succession of his Protestant daughters, Mary, Princess of Orange, and Anne, Princess of Denmark, were content to let him rule. As for Louis XIV, he had every reason to expect that James would be, if anything, friendlier than his late—and Anglican—brother.

Still, James, all unknowing, faced dangers from outside: William of Orange, France's implacable enemy and James's son-in-law, longed for a league uniting the Emperor, Spain, certain German princes, and England. Clearly, however, there was very little chance of that as long as England, no matter how Protestant, was ruled by a Catholic. Equally clearly, the solution lay in a well-conceived coup d'état: if James were replaced by the next heir, William's own wife, then England's accession to the league would be a certainty.

William was as clever as James was dumb; but all his stratagems would have availed him nothing if it had not been for an unexpected quirk of nature: after fifteen years of marriage and several miscarriages, James's second wife, Mary of Modena, unexpectedly gave birth to a healthy boy. Faced with the prospect of a Catholic heir, the English began to feel very differently about their Catholic monarch, and they were further alienated by what looked very like an attempt at importing a French-style absolute monarchy to their country. Whether or not that was in fact James's intention—it most probably was not—hardly matters: it looked as if it must be, and that was enough; so when, in November 1688, William of Orange landed in England, James found himself virtually deserted; in a state of rage and confusion, he fled with his wife and son, throwing the Great Seal overboard into the Thames as he sailed away.

The overthrow of a Catholic monarch was, in itself, bad news for Louis XIV: as an ardent Catholic himself, he had hoped James might bring England back into the Church. Far more devastating, however, was the accession of Mary II to the throne, especially since she re-

243

fused to rule alone and insisted that her husband become King—as opposed to merely Prince or King Consort. Mary herself showed little interest in policy-making and was content to leave it to William; and while his powers were restricted by Act of Parliament, still, he could and did join the anti-French alliance known as the League of Augsburg. Sweden, formerly an ally of France, and several of the more powerful German princes were added to that combination, so that, with England, it included virtually the whole of Europe.

Although history seems to offer many examples of the contrary, it did sometimes happen that a king was simply too stupid to rule: this was unquestionably the case of James II. Louis XIV, who had a first-rate intelligence service, had been aware of William of Orange's intentions, and of his plans to land in England; he had actually warned James of them and offered his assistance, only to be told to stop meddling. Whether, even with the help of the French fleet, James could have kept his throne is obviously an unanswerable question; but, at any rate, Louis had every reason to wash his hands of the exiled James. In fact, he did exactly the opposite, partly because he did not approve of the people dethroning a King, partly because James was obviously a useful weapon against William and Mary. When, in January, the exiled couple arrived in dispersed order—first James's wife, then James himself—they were met as if they had never been dethroned. The King went to greet her at Chatou, near Saint-Germain, and promptly offered her the use of the latter palace. "I render you a sad service, Madame," he told her, "but hope soon to render you greater and happier ones,"[229] an obvious allusion to future military aid.

The "sad service," in fact, was as magnificent as might have been expected from the Sun King: on arriving at Saint-Germain, Mary of Modena found herself surrounded by the same luxury—furniture, plate, clothes even—as if she had been Queen of France, with, on her dressing table, ten thousand gold louis (240,000 livres); and when James arrived, besides similar appurtenances, he was informed that he would henceforth receive 600,000 livres a year. "Never," Voltaire commented, "did the King seem so great; but James seemed small"[230]: his lack of intelligence and his inordinate passion for the Jesuits soon became all too clear. Whether, under these circumstances, it was wise to be so very welcoming to the dethroned King is a question that needs asking: no amount of force could make up for

James's own deficiencies, after all. It might therefore have been wiser to give up the hope that he would one day rule England again.

Louis XIV was certainly not responsible for what the English call the Glorious Revolution; but it is impossible not to feel that his new piety was one of the substantial causes both of the Revocation of the Edict of Nantes and of the support he gave to James II. Of course, the King felt, not without reason, that William III was an irreducible enemy; that he had become king of England solely so that he might attack France; and that any effort to reach an agreement was foredoomed; still, it is significant, and regrettable, that no attempt was made. By January 1689, the once cautious monarch who had only gone to war when he was quite sure of winning was beginning to feel that he could not be beaten: it was more important to look magnanimous by taking James in and, a little later, launching him on an attempted reconquest, than to conciliate William, whom, in any event, the French generals had defeated with absolute regularity. And, of course, James's triumph would also have been that of the Catholics.

At the same time, the King's chief adviser, Louvois, provided him with inaccurate information. Not only was the War Minister convinced that a civil war would break out in England, but he also encouraged Louis XIV to attack the Emperor at what he considered a well-chosen moment.

We may suppose that Louvois was less than honest in his appraisal of the situation in England: operations there would have been the province of Seignelai, the Navy Minister and a member of the Colbert family, and that was reason enough to advise against them. As for a war against the Emperor, Leopold I, he pointed out that the Turkish peril was receding—the siege of Vienna had been lifted in 1684 and by the fall of 1688, the imperial army under a general of genius, Prince Eugene of Savoy, was about to beat the Turks before Belgrade. It therefore seemed wise to attack the Emperor while he was still fighting Turkey, a state of affairs which looked like ending soon; and if that meant war with the Emperor's allies, well, it could be managed also.

Of course, a pretext was needed. Louvois found two. One was exceedingly simple: he claimed that Madame was entitled to part of the Palatinate as an heiress to her late father. Of course, upon marrying Monsieur, she had renounced all such rights; but equally of course, her dowry had not been paid in full; so, without consulting the princess, who had no wish to claim anything, Louis XIV demanded a share of the Electorate.

The other had to do with the traditional French influence on the Rhine area. The Bishop of Cologne was, ex officio, Prince Elector of that small state; and he was chosen by the chapter. First, Louis XIV put pressure on the chapter until it appointed his nominee, Cardinal von Fürstenberg, as coadjutor, i.e., successor designate to the Bishop; then, in September 1688, he demanded that the cardinal be elected and that the Emperor officially approve the election. This, together with Madame's claim, formed the object of an ultimatum which was dispatched on September 24, and gave Leopold three months to comply.

So far, the King, while making inordinate demands, was still playing the normal game of power politics; but then, just one day later, at Louvois's instigation, he behaved in such a way as to unite Europe against him: without the customary declaration of war, indeed without any warning at all, a French army, led nominally by Monseigneur —whom the King could trust neither to outshine nor to disobey him —but really by the maréchal de Duras and Vauban, the great engineer, marched on the Rhine. Almost immediately, it occupied the whole left bank of the Rhine and set siege to Philippsburg, which it took on October 22. The King received the news while he was attending mass at Fontainebleau; in a paroxysm of pleasure and pride, he interrupted the sermon and, tears streaming down his cheeks, he announced this latest triumph.

Nor did it stop there. After Mainz and Heidelberg, Mannheim was taken on November 11; Speier, Trier, Worms, and Oppenheim surrendered on the fifteenth; and it was clear once more that the Sun King was invincible; indeed that whatever he wanted was his to take.

That the fortresses of the Palatinate should have surrendered so quickly was perhaps not so surprising after all: they belonged to a small, not very warlike state; but the French successes, like Hitler's blitzkrieg in Poland, made it quite clear to the rest of Europe that it could either cooperate now to resist or submit later, and that Louis XIV's territorial greed was insatiable. In fact, the invasion of the Rhineland was simply a preventive attack in a war which was obviously going to be declared on France at one point or another; but the chambres de réunion were not forgotten, and, without the benefit of hindsight, the main European powers can well be forgiven for believing that the borders of France would keep creeping forward unless something were done to stop that alarming phenomenon.

The manner in which the Palatinate was invaded only confirmed these fears; as for the way in which the conquered state was treated, it evoked—and rightly—horrified anger. That it was Louvois's policy and not the King's made no difference, nor did the King's anger when he discovered what had been done in his name: the fact remained that an innocent people watched in terror as their cities were burned to the ground, their fields devastated, and they themselves attacked and often killed. The purpose of this apocalypse, according to Louvois, was to create such fear that, henceforth, there would be no resistance in the occupied territories while other potential enemies, aware of what was awaiting them if they were beaten, would think twice before attacking. It must also be said that these methods suited the undoubtedly brutal minister, who, no doubt, enjoyed giving his orders.

To us, at the end of the twentieth century, such horrors seem all too familiar; in the less sophisticated 1680s, they branded France the enemy of all mankind; and much of the energy displayed by her enemies in the ensuing wars was due to this alone. Nor is the fact that the King stopped this barbaric treatment of the Palatinate when he found out about it any excuse: he took special pride in controlling his ministers, in being aware of all that was done in his name; he was, therefore, responsible for all. When he gave Louvois powers extensive enough to rape and ravage, he became, by his own standards, an inadequate king. It had not happened before; it never happened again; but, in this particular case, and no matter how great his repulsion when he finally heard the horrors committed in his name, there can be no denying that the ultimate responsibility was his.

Almost as important, this morally indefensible policy also turned out to be useless. In the spring of 1689, much of the Palatinate rose against the French; at the same time the armies sent by the Emperor arrived. They were commanded by the Duke of Lorraine, whose state had been appropriated by France: to his very considerable talents as a general he added the anger of a man ruined, and he proceeded to beat the French. Mainz was retaken in June, Bonn in November, while, on France's northern border, the maréchal d'Humières was defeated by the Prince of Waldeck, also in June.

Once again, the King saw that Louvois was fallible: Humières, the minister's favorite, was an incompetent commander.

That Louvois's position must have been eroded in the long run is certain: he had tried hard to stop the King from marrying Mme de Maintenon, and the lady knew it; and now, in the year extending from the early summer of 1688 to that of 1689, he had made a number of very serious mistakes. As a result, Louis XIV became himself again: Humières was replaced by the maréchal-duc de Luxembourg, one of Louvois's most violent enemies.

Luxembourg, in fact, was also everything the King disliked: a former Frondeur, he was a notorious debauché who liked to scandalize the faithful; he had been so severely implicated in the Affair of the Poisons as to be sent to the Bastille; and he was the head of one of the oldest and most powerful aristocratic families in France. On the other hand, he knew how to win battles, and the time was no longer when Louis had the choice between Turenne and Condé. Luxembourg, who refused to communicate with Louvois, demanded and was given the unheard-of privilege of writing the King directly, instead of going through the minister, and receiving orders only from him; Catinat, a newcomer of talent, was sent to command on the Italian front; the elderly but highly competent maréchal de Lorges went to Germany; and the equally competent duc de Noailles took charge of a small army whose orders were to invade Catalonia.

Fighting all Europe in this way was, everyone agreed, glorious; it was also extremely expensive. By the spring of 1689, Louis XIV had three hundred thousand men under arms and no money to pay this unprecedented number; so he called in the head of the *Garde-meuble,* the man in charge of all the furnishings of the royal palaces, and ordered that all his silver, including the admirable furniture of the Grands Appartements at Versailles be sent to the Mint, there to be melted down into coin.

That this is a major tragedy hardly needs saying: we know the silver furniture from contemporary illustrations and a few examples sent to Charles II of England. It seems hard to accept that so great an artistic treasure should have disappeared just to pay for yet another war; and yet this, too, had a highly positive side. Since Versailles could hardly be left empty, new, gilt-wood furniture was made; and that, in turn, started an art form which, from its very beginnings, proved superior to anything else that was done in Europe. One can fairly say, in fact, that if, in the eighteenth century, French furniture set new standards of perfection, it was in good part because Louis XIV melted down his silver.*

Still, aside from the loss of beautiful pieces, the move had another meaning: after all those years when the budget had been wholly or nearly balanced, it had once again become a bottomless pit. Colbert might have prevented it, but he was dead; Le Pelletier, his successor, was an incompetent; so now the King replaced him with Pontchartrain, an energetic and effective minister, but one who unfortunately lacked Colbert's almost instinctive understanding of finance. Pontchartrain knew how to tax and make sure everyone paid; but he never realized that taxes are only productive when the country is prosperous.

He was, at any rate, much admired by the King and Court. When Seignelai died in November 1690, the King gave Pontchartrain the Navy, so that Colbert's combination of offices came near to reviving —the new Contrôleur Generale was never in charge of the King's Buildings—and he eventually became Chancellor, remaining in office until shortly before his death. "He was," Choisy wrote, "as faithful and at least as disinterested as [Le Pelletier], a tireless worker, seeing all, able to do all, who, for the last eight years [this was written in 1698] has raised 150 million a year with parchment and sealing wax by imagining offices and other nonsense which sold very well. He remained modest in spite of his success, received no gift from the King except an office as conseiller at the Paris Parlement for his son; he reached decisions easily, finishing more in a day than his predecessor in six months; believing firmly that it is always best to go ahead even if that sometimes entails making a mistake, and then, if need be, mending without blushing the errors due to a little too much speed . . .

"People complain that he does not empathize enough with their difficulties, and that when a poor man, ruined by a tax, comes to ask for relief, he answers with a smile: 'Monsieur, you must pay.' "[231]

It all sounds very modern, but must be read with a grain of salt. It is quite true that taxes went up as a result of the war, and that even the nobility was required to pay something like 5 percent of its income; it is also true that, as always, the main burden was borne by the

* All in all, it produced 2.5 million livres. Silver church furniture went next.

peasantry; but Choisy's "poor man" is, of course, a courtier: the actual poor did not have access to the Controller General. Seen in hindsight, therefore, Pontchartrain's efforts seem, on the whole, praiseworthy. In one respect, however, he created a fatal precedent: the sale of sinecure offices of every kind—there was even a Wig Carrier to the King who, of course, never carried anything—was certainly profitable; but while it raised money on the instant, it meant that salaries would henceforth have to be paid; so when Pontchartrain remarked with satisfaction that no matter how absurd the offices he created, there would always be some fools to buy them, he was being less clever than he thought: year by year the burden of the unnecessary offices grew heavier and heavier.

For a while, at least, the King's sacrifice seemed to pay: a French fleet returned James II to Ireland—"The best I can wish you is never to see you again,"[232] Louis told his English cousin—where he was greeted, by the predominantly Catholic population, with cheers; and promptly showing once again that he had understood nothing, he appointed a Jesuit as his secretary of state. Even better, on July 10, 1690, for the first time ever, a French fleet under Tourville crushed the Anglo-Dutch navies off Beachyhead. That triumph, however, was short-lived: the very next day, at the Battle of the Boyne, William III, powerfully helped by exiled French Protestants, trounced his father-in-law's army. True to precedent, James immediately fled to France. Louis XIV's great project had failed.

At least on the northern front the war was going well; the French won the Battle of Fleurus; and in August Catinat beat the Duke of Savoy near Saluzzo. These victories, however, reinforced Louvois's position, with one disastrous consequence: since England was virtually bare of troops, Seignelai advocated an invasion. The French fleet had command of the sea, and the troops once landed would meet no real army. Of course, Louvois objected. The fleet was expensive, Ireland a failure, the army victorious: Louis XIV listened to the war minister and ordered his ships back into harbor until the next campaigning season.

In spite of the financial strain, nothing at Court was allowed to change. The *Mercure* for January 1690 noted: "The King has, as is his custom, given splendid suppers since the beginning of Carnival and no evening was spent at Versailles without a masquerade or some other amusement. Monseigneur the Dauphin also attended several balls in Paris and having particularly enjoyed the first one Monsieur gave him asked His Royal Highness to give him another one.''[233] If there was anything Monsieur loved (and Madame hated) it was a good party; so, of course, he carried out his nephew's wish. In February, "Monseigneur the Dauphin came to the ball given by His Royal Highness Monsieur. From the beginning until the end at four in the morning, eight to ten thousand masked dancers were counted. Monseigneur was given yet another ball on the last Sunday of Carnival. On Monday there was a ball at Versailles at M. le duc du Maine's [the King and Mme de Montespan's eldest son] where the entire Court was present, and on Tuesday at the King's where Monseigneur the Dauphin appeared in four different costumes. On that same Tuesday, M. le duc de Chartres [Monsieur's son] gave a ball for Mademoiselle at the Palais Royal.''[234]

Amusingly enough, in the very same issue, the *Mercure,* after marveling at the quantity of silver brought in to the Mint by private people who were following the King's example, went on to comment about the successful efforts made at curbing luxury: we may justly suppose that the balls given by the King, Monsieur, and the duc du Maine were not exactly examples of austerity.

Unchanged also was the King's desire to advance his illegitimate children. Those of his daughters who were of age to be married were now part of the royal family; it was time to do something for the nineteen-year-old duc du Maine: the comte de Toulouse, the youngest of his sons, was only eleven in 1689.

That, however, was not so very easy. To begin with, the duc du Maine had not grown up quite straight in spite of Mme de Maintenon's best efforts: one hip was a little out of line, one leg a little shorter than the other, so he had a slight limp; and partly because of this infirmity, he was greatly beloved by his former governess whose special charge he had been and whose protégé he now became. This physical disadvantage, however, made two key royal activities, hunting and leading soldiers to war, markedly more difficult, and to this was added an equivalent—and visible—lack of moral backbone. Given to intrigue, he had few friends and fewer sympathizers. Something, obviously, had to be done, and the King decided that military prowess was the answer.

"I am sending my son, the duc du Maine, to the army you command," he wrote the maréchal d'Humières on May 21, 1689. "You

251

know how fond I am of him and how very much I wish him to be worthy of his position. I have ordered him always to believe what you tell him, as I feel sure you will advise him to do what he must and even a little more," adding, however, "Allow the duc du Maine to see everything, but avoid whenever possible his fighting in small engagements where he might be captured."[235]

What the King was really saying was that he wished his son to acquire glory without taking risks. Humières, who was an excellent courtier, carried out his instructions; but he quickly found that, while it was easy to keep du Maine safe, getting him near the fighting was a more difficult proposition. For the moment, at least, this uncomfortable fact was discreetly kept quiet, but it was likely to emerge one day.

That, all through 1689 and 1690, Louis XIV should have preserved the Olympian calm for which he was now famous surprised no one; but the cost of the Court, added to that of the war, caused considerable resentment. There now appeared, once again, the kind of critical pamphlets which had largely disappeared since the middle sixties. Of course, they attack that most vulnerable target, Mme de Maintenon, whose first marriage to the impotent Scarron was always good for some ribald fun; but, more significantly, she is also usually depicted as sold to the Jesuits. As for Louis, he is said to support James II only because Mary of Modena has become his mistress; and Mme de Maintenon is represented as countering this by procuring a young and virile abbé for the exiled Queen.[236] All nonsense, of course; but indicative of a growing disaffection.

It might, however, have been better if it had been true: James II, back from Ireland, was once again received as the true King of England. On October 11, 1690, he came to Fontainebleau on a visit, was invariably given the place of honor on the King's right and treated like a reigning monarch.[237] It was perhaps wise not to abandon the wretched James in the middle of a war with William III—or, at least, it would have been if William had been allowed to think that support to James might be part of a general trade-off. Unfortunately, it was the very opposite message he received: a French victory would also mean the restoration of his father-in-law; and he naturally fought all the harder.

At the same time, a mild annoyance to both Louis XIV and the Dauphin was removed: on April 20, 1690, the Dauphine, who had never really recovered from her last confinement, finally died. She was missed by no one except her maid, a Piedmontese named Bessola, with whom she appears to have been having an affair. The King had disliked her ever since, four years earlier, she had ventured to criticize his policies; the Dauphin, who spent most of his time with his brilliant half-sister the princesse de Conti, had taken as his mistress one of the princess's maids of honor, Mlle Choin, a large-breasted, stupid young woman whom he seems to have really loved. Still, the Dauphine's death opened the terrifying perspective that the twenty-eight-year-old Monseigneur might be found a new wife; and so, in the only act of his life which was not authorized by his father, he secretly married Mlle Choin. Outwardly, nothing was changed; the lady remained in the princesse de Conti's Household, and many years passed before the secret leaked out; but, immediately, the Dauphin informed Mme de Maintenon. "I feel that I might start sinning," he wrote her. "I know of no princess who would suit me, I realize that the one thing the King would mind the most would be if I slid into debauchery. Tell me when I may see you so that we may speak a little. Once again, absolute secrecy . . ."[238]

In fact, cautious as always, Mme de Maintenon waited until 1694 before telling the King, and even then did it in a characteristically indirect way: a letter to the Dauphin in which she mentioned his wife found its way, apparently by mistake, into the King's pouch. We know nothing of the royal reaction; but given the parallel between the two secret marriages, and the fact that neither the Dauphin nor Mlle Choin was punished, we can only suppose that Louis took it fairly well; it may even have seemed like an inspired act of flattery, imitation being the sincerest form of admiration.

Still, the fact remains that at the proudest and most splendid court in Europe, the King and his only legitimate son had made morganatic marriages: amid all the pomp and the etiquette, and even as the monarch seemed to rise above the rest of mankind, both he and his heir had wives a small nobleman would have scorned. Nor were things much better in his immediate family. Monsieur, who had always had a taste for handsome young men, now openly depended on the chevalier de Lorraine: there were constant scenes, motivated either by the chevalier's greed or, much worse, by his affairs with women; and, up the backstairs, a stream of good-looking lackeys came up to serve Monsieur when the chevalier was busy elsewhere.

The King's grandchildren were still too young to matter; but already his married daughters, the princesse de Conti (widowed in 1685) and the duchesse de Bourbon, irreverent, antireligious, and mad for amusement, gave rise to repeated scandals. As a result, the latter half of the reign cannot be understood if one disregards the constant tension between the stately appearances and the far less admirable reality.

In one aspect of his personal life, however, Louis XIV felt nothing but satisfaction: year by year he grew to love Mme de Maintenon more. In the summers of 1690 and 1691, he continued an earlier tradition by going off to command his army in person; and from the north letters streamed to the marquise, to give her news of a naval battle,[239] tell her that James II was leaving Ireland[240] or that the King himself was preparing to return to Versailles[241]: on reading them the sense of closeness is very evident; and there are also love letters. "I take advantage of Montchevreuil's departure," Louis wrote in April, 1691, "to assure you of a truth which pleases me so that I can never tire of telling it to you; it is that I always cherish you and care for you beyond expression; and that, in a word, no matter how much you may love me, I love you still more, my whole heart being yours."[242]

The corollary of this great love was the advancement of the duc du Maine and the final departure of his mother. In March, 1691, Mme de Montespan's apartment at Versailles was taken from her and given to du Maine; after one last scene, she finally gave up the court and thereafter divided her time between Clagny and her apartment in the Convent of Saint Joseph. With her departure, every last vestige of the King's profligate youth was gone: Mme de Maintenon had good reason to feel triumphant.

*A*LL through 1691 and 1692, the war continued. The French armies went on winning, William III went on being defeated: indeed, the only battle he ever won is that of the Boyne; but it made no difference. The Coalition refused to give up; and no victory was ever thorough enough to prevent the enemy from being again ready to fight within a short time: it was, in fact, a new kind of war, fought not for a specific object, but simply to reduce the power of France. Thus, it hardly mattered that the King in person took Mons in April 1691 or Namur in 1692. These sieges were just as carefully planned, and just as successful, as those of the earlier wars; only now, they made no difference at all.

Still in 1692 the maréchal de Luxembourg proved his mastery of the art of war: at Steinkerque, the French won a major victory in which the eighteen-year-old Philippe, duc de Chartres, Monsieur's son and thus the King's nephew, fought with extraordinary courage and skill. Because Chartres outshone the duc du Maine, and because his behavior gave him added prestige, the King was displeased; and he saw to it that the young man was not given a significant command. At the same time, one last attempt to put James II back on the throne failed: on May 30, 1692, the French fleet, which was to secure a landing in England, was beaten by the British navy; and although by no means destroyed, it was never again strong enough for so difficult an enterprise.

One event, at least, seemed to make a difference: on July 16, 1691, Louvois died suddenly. It was clear that the King was relieved; but he immediately appointed the marquis de Barbezieux, the dead man's son, in his place, so that it began to look as if the ministries were hereditary: this was the third generation of the Le Tellier family to be in charge of the army. Barbezieux, who was as bad-tempered as his father, had neither his love of work nor his genius. With the death of the last great minister of the reign, everything was now, more than ever, up to the King. More and more, he governed directly rather than through aides he trusted; less time, every day, was spent on pleasure, more on the endless details of ruling. Louis XIV had been an effective king for thirty years, but after 1691 he became the government.

The endless paperwork which resulted from this increased involvement did nothing to distract the King from the gravity of the situation; thus it was that he gave up his best chance of crushing William III once and for all. Early in June 1693, William found himself trapped before Louvain by two vastly superior French armies; but instead of giving battle, Louis sent one army off to Germany under Monseigneur's nominal command while he himself returned to Versailles: news from Germany made it seem likely that a great effort on that front would force the Emperor to sue for peace. "I gave in to the strong remonstrances which were made and to the conclusions of my own reason," the King wrote Monsieur, "and I sacrificed with pleasure my own preference and my satisfaction and what would have been most flattering to me to the well-being of the state."[243]

In fact, the King had misjudged his enemies. It was William who was the moving spirit of the Coalition, not the Emperor; and so the war went on, as usual with no decisive result. On July 29, 1693, the maréchal de Luxembourg defeated William III at Neerwinden, and on August 18, Catinat beat the Emperor's army at La Marsaille; but the war went on as if nothing had happened.

The way in which the King had chosen to fight it, however, seemed, for a moment to bring back the past: his refusal to give battle before Louvain was widely attributed to cowardice; the princes began to criticize as if the days of the early Fronde were to be revived; and Louis XIV took due note. One consequence was his refusal to use the duc de Chartres's talents; another was the continued promotion of the bastards: in 1693, while firmly ignoring the princes of the blood, he appointed the duc du Maine Grand Master of the Artillery and the comte de Toulouse Grand Admiral of France, two positions which had, heretofore, been reserved for the royal family.

Even before this, he had taken a major step to fuse his two families; and the young Saint-Simon, who cared greatly about etiquette and rank, was a horrified witness. "The King, preoccupied with the position of his bastards whom he raised higher day by day, had married two of his daughters to two princes of the blood royal," he wrote. "For a long time already, Mme de Maintenon, even more than the King . . . had wanted to wed Mlle de Blois, the King and Mme de Montespan's second daughter, to M. le duc de Chartres. He was the King's only nephew, and much above the Princes of the Blood, both by his rank as Grandson of France† and by the splendid Court which surrounded Monsieur. The marriage of the two princes had scandalized everyone. The King knew it and realized the effect to be expected from a marriage so much more dazzling."[244] So, Saint-Simon tells us, he decided first to sway Monsieur, who was likely to resist his only son's misalliance; and that was done easily enough: both the comte d'Armagnac, the King's Grand Equerry, and his brother the chevalier de Lorraine were given the order of the Saint Esprit with precedence over the dukes on the grounds that they belonged (if distantly) to a ruling family; and the chevalier, whom

† A king's son was called Fils de France, Son of France; Chartres, being Louis XIII's grandson, was called Grandson of France.

Monsieur loved passionately, saw to it that the prince agreed to the marriage.

There remained Madame, who was violently opposed, and the groom himself, the duc de Chartres; but the latter's tutor, the abbé Dubois, was made to see clearly where his advantage lay, and he convinced his pupil, at the last moment, that he must carry out the King's wishes. "Madame heard about it. She spoke to her son about the indignity of this marriage with all her strength, a quality in which she was not deficient, and made him swear he would not give in . . .

"One early afternoon, as I was walking through the Upper Gallery, I saw M. le duc de Chartres coming out of one of his apartment's back doors, looking very sad and embarrassed . . . I asked him where he was rushing to at this odd hour. He answered, with a hurried and unhappy look, that the King had sent for him . . . M. de Chartres found the King alone in his cabinet with Monsieur, whom he had not expected to see there. The King was friendly to M. de Chartres, told him he wanted to take care of him; that the war which was raging on every side made otherwise suitable princesses unavailable; that when it came to princesses of the blood, none was the right age; that he could not better show his affection than by offering him his daughter, whose two sisters had married princes of the blood; that this would make him not just the King's nephew but his son-in-law as well; but that, although he wanted this marriage with a passion, he did not wish to force him, and left him free to decide. This speech, spoken with that terrifying majesty so characteristic of the King, to a prince who was both shy and not prepared to answer, placed him beyond his depth. He thought to escape so slippery a situation by turning to Monsieur and Madame, and answered that the King was the master, but that his (the duc de Chartres's) answer, depended on his parents'. 'You are quite right to say so,' the King told him, 'but if you consent, your father and mother will do the same'; and turning to Monsieur: 'Is that not true, brother?' Monsieur consented to the marriage, as he had done beforehand when alone with the King, so the King promptly said that the only question now lay with Madame; and he had her sent for . . . Madame arrived, and immediately the King told her that he expected she would not be opposed to a proposal which Monsieur desired and to which M. de Chartres had agreed: that it was his marriage with Mlle de Blois, that he wanted it passionately, and he then added all the same

things he had just told M. le duc de Chartres, all in the most imposing way, but looking as if it had not occurred to him that Madame
might be anything but delighted, although he knew very well the
opposite was true. Madame, who had been counting on the refusal
her son had promised he would make, and which, in fact, he had
tried to carry out by his embarrassed and conditional answer, found
herself trapped and speechless. She looked furiously at Monsieur and
M. de Chartres, said that, if they were agreed, she had nothing to say,
curtsied and left. Her son followed her, but she carried on with such
vehemence that he was not able to tell her what had happened.''[245]

There is every reason to believe that this extraordinary scene happened just as Saint-Simon describes it: because he was a close friend
of the duc de Chartres, it is clear that he received his information
from the unhappy young man. As for what happened next, he was
himself an eyewitness. After the betrothal was made public, he
wrote, he saw "Madame, walking in the Hall of Mirrors . . . her
handkerchief in her hand, sobbing openly, speaking quite loudly,
gesticulating, the very image of Ceres, after the rape of her daughter
Proserpina, looking for her with fury and asking Jupiter to give her
back . . . Nothing could have been more ashamed than Monsieur's
expression . . . His son looked desolate and even his fiancée
seemed extremely sad and embarrassed . . .

"The next day, the whole Court visited Monsieur, Madame, and
M. le duc de Chartres, but without saying a word: we merely bowed
or curtsied in the deepest silence. After this, we went to the Hall of
Mirrors as usual, to await the end of the Council and the King's mass.
Madame was there. Her son came to her as he did every day to kiss
her hand; at that moment Madame slapped his face with such
strength that the noise was heard a little distance away, dreadfully
embarrassing the poor prince and causing the countless spectators,
among whom I was, an indescribable amazement.''[246]

As usual, Louis XIV had had his way; and as usual, he was generous: Mlle de Blois received the unprecedented dowry of 2 million
livres, a pension of 150,000 livres, and jewels worth another
600,000 livres—a great deal more than her sisters, and at a time
when the Treasury was nearly empty; and Monsieur, who had merely
been living at the Palais Royal, was now given that splendid building. As for the new duchesse de Chartres, her rank was further underlined by the Household the King gave her: it included a dame

d'honneur, a dame d'atours, and a chevalier d'honneur, all attendants who, until then, had been reserved for a King's legitimate daughter. The marriage itself, which was celebrated on February 18, 1692, gave rise to the standard festivities. Nor was this all: a month later, on March 19, the duc du Maine was married to one of Monsieur le Prince's daughters, Anne Louise, whose diminutive size concealed great wit and a ferocious ambition. Since, in 1692, the comte de Toulouse was only fourteen, all the King's illegitimate children were thus moved over to the royal family proper.

All in all, this was little less than a revolution. In a country, and at a time, when society was rigidly stratified, where the right sort of ancestors made all the difference, and where bloodlines were the key to position and success, integrating the bastards into the royal family subverted all custom. It is, of course, true that the King's illegitimate children were a finite quantity; but a precedent was being set, and the law gave precedents enormous weight. Then, on May 4, 1694, the bastards' status was elevated still further: the King created for them an intermediary rank which left them below—just below—the princes of the blood royal but placed them above the dukes. Except for one or two details of etiquette, the main difference now between the duc du Maine and the comte de Toulouse, on the one hand, and the ducs d'Orléans, de Chartres, de Bourbon, the princes de Condé and de Conti, was that the former could not succeed to the Crown.

This alone would have been change enough; but there was also the concurrent promotion of the middle class. It was quite as clear to Saint-Simon as it is to us today that, by and large, Louis XIV distrusted the aristocracy and, having removed it from most positions of power, was leaning on the bourgeoisie instead. It might still take a duke to be first gentleman of the bedchamber, but the ministers who exerted power in the King's name were, with a single exception, middle-class men. Of course, they bought titles: Le Tellier's son was marquis de Louvois, and his son marquis de Barbezieux; Colbert's son was marquis de Seignelai and his nephew marquis de Torcy; the comte de Pontchartrain, who became Controleur Général, and then Chancellor, was the son of plain Louis Phelypaux; and all not only gave orders to men who considered themselves their betters but were treated practically as if they were royalty: even dukes were expected to address the ministers as Monseigneur.

The reasons for all this will come as no surprise to the reader: the legacy of the Fronde, the greed of the aristocracy, the knowledge that obedience came more easily from a man whose ascension owed everything to the Crown, these were Louis XIV's basic motivations. It is, however, interesting to see how the King extended these principles within his own family: here, the bastards were as dependent on his goodwill as the ministers in another sphere; by raising them progressively to the status of a real princess, in the case of the girls, or to one almost indistinguishable from that of the real princes, in the case of the boys, he merely made them depend on him the more: because they hoped to become actual princes of the blood royal, the duc du Maine and the comte de Toulouse had every reason to behave as well as possible. And at the same time, by marrying the royal bastards, the princes showed clearly that the King's wish was law. It must be added, however, that these marriages also pleased Louis because he loved his illegitimate children; but, clearly, affection came second to deliberate policy.

These events at Court also went together with changes in the structure of the government; but while the first were highly visible, and therefore the object of endless comment, the second passed almost unnoticed. The Parlement had been firmly confined to its judicial duties many years before; now, for those who cared to see, the extent of its obedience was clearly revealed. Taxes had traditionally been imposed with the consent of that body; indeed, the Fronde had started with the Parlement's refusal to register the new taxes Mazarin wanted. Yet when in 1694 Louis XIV instituted a tax that was not only new but revolutionary, not a peep was heard: for the first time, an income tax, the *capitation* (head tax), was imposed on nobles and commoners alike. Although set at an unvarying 5 percent, so that it fell much more heavily on the poor than on the rich, it broke with the hitherto sacrosanct principle according to which nobles were, by definition, personally tax-exempt. Most of the conseillers and présidents of the Parlement, although socially middle-class, were in law noble, either by individual patent or through the possession of a so-called noble estate, a fief which carried a title of nobility. That they failed to oppose this new tax which affected them directly shows the extent of their submission.

The capitation was instituted in answer to a pressing financial need; but it, too, fitted in with the King's general policy of entertaining the nobility at Versailles, and focusing its attention on quarrels of etiquette, while steadily diminishing its privileges: the new tax implied that, in the government's eyes, all the French were equal, a truly revolutionary proposition in a country which thought of itself as divided into three eternal orders, nobility, clergy, commoners. By treating the nobles as if they were commoners, the King was affirming the primacy of the state and the individual's duty to obey, of course, but he was also beginning an evolution which led to the abolition of all privileges in August 1789.

*P*ARADOXICALLY, these radical transformations were accompanied by a growing inefficiency in the actual mechanism of the government due largely to the King himself. It was not power that was lacking here but the effective means of wielding it, and that, in turn, resulted from Louis's belief that he could do practically anything better than the men who worked for him.

It is, no doubt, one of the great drawbacks of an absolute monarchy that all depends on the person of the sovereign, and that the prolonged exercise of power tends to induce personality changes. In 1661, the young King, while intent on deciding all the great issues himself, was content to follow the practical advice of ministers like Colbert, men of devotion, age, and experience. By the 1690s, Louis XIV had been ruling for over thirty years; the first generation of his ministers was gone; their replacements—usually their children—were not only mediocre but also younger than himself; and so, very naturally, it began to seem as if the King always knew more. As a result, he took over more and more of the details of government; and while, on major questions, his splendid instincts remained unimpaired, his ability to deal with minutiae was not equal to his self-imposed task; and all this happened at a time when France was faced with increasingly difficult problems.

That the King should have chosen to put the sons of earlier ministers in office was due in part to his extraordinary sense of fairness: the fathers, having deserved well of him, had earned the right to have their children succeed them. It also satisfied his sense of order to have the generations thus following each other; but it is also quite clear that he put up with mediocrities because he thought himself capable of supplying their deficiencies. Indeed, it gave him a certain satisfaction to do so: all could see that he, alone, ruled.

Barbezieux, Louvois's son and his successor as War Minister at the age of twenty-one, is a good case in point. The young man, who did not lack intelligence or force, was also tactless, often brutal, and more interested in his own pleasures than in his official duties. While his father had lived for his work, Barbezieux was given to spending his evenings, his nights, and frequently his mornings as well, at wild parties in Paris; and since all this took place in the middle of a European war, his work suffered. Of course, the King knew this; but instead of simply dismissing him—as he would surely have done at the beginning of the reign—he chose to keep him in office, while making it plain that he thought little of him.

"I was at the King's dinner on [March 27, 1693]," Saint-Simon noted. "Suddenly the King said, looking at those present: 'Barbezieux will learn about the promotion of the marshals of France on the roads.' Nobody answered. The King was displeased with the frequents trips [Barbezieux] made to Paris in quest of his pleasures. He was not sorry to give him this warning and to advertise how little [the minister] had to do with this promotion."[247] The creation of a marshal of France, who enjoyed the very highest military rank, was a major policy decision, since it predetermined, to a large extent, who would be leading the armies in the next campaigns. That this should be done without the knowledge of the War Minister showed how very little power he had; and in a Court where personal advantage counted for everything, it meant that Barbezieux's following would dwindle away.

Since the King had become aware of the enormous power yielded by Louvois, this obviously fitted in with his long-established decision to be the only fount of honor and advantage. Debasing Barbezieux was an excellent way of elevating himself, hence the remark made at a moment—his dinner—when Louis could count on maximum attention; but at the same time he was unwilling to put up with the young man's laziness. There, a public sally would have done no good; so the King expressed his annoyance in a letter to the Archbishop of Reims, Louvois's brother and Barbezieux's uncle.

"I know what I owe to the memory of M. de Louvois," he wrote the Archbishop some time in 1693,‡ "but if your nephew does not behave better, I will be forced to make a decision [i.e., to dismiss him]. I will be sorry to do so; but I will have to. He has talents but he

‡ The letter is undated.

does not use them well. He asks the princes to supper too often instead of working, he neglects business for pleasure; he keeps the officers waiting too long in his antechamber; he speaks to them with disdain and sometimes with cruelty."[248] Choosing the Archbishop as recipient of this letter was quite shrewd: not only did it avoid a personal unpleasantness with Barbezieux, it put the whole Le Tellier family on notice that it was in danger of losing position and influence. Needless to say, the Archbishop, upon reading this reproof, called upon his nephew. We do not know what he said; but Barbezieux's attitude improved, for a time at least.

By 1695, however, the Minister had clearly forgotten his warning and reverted to his earlier habits. Once again the King put pen to paper. "The King," Le Tellier noted, "wrote this memorandum . . . at Fontainebleau, where I did not have the honor of being part of His Majesty's suite. I was in Reims. The King came back from Fontainebleau to Versailles on Friday, October 28, 1695. I went there on Saturday the twenty-ninth at noon; His Majesty called me into his cabinet as he rose from table and gave me this memorandum."

As we read it, it is Louis XIV's own voice we hear. "The way your nephew lived in Fontainebleau," Louis XIV wrote in his tall, sloping hand, "is not bearable, it has scandalized the public. He spent his days hunting and his nights in debauchery. He does not work, and that has very serious consequences. His employees, who follow his example, are lazy. The officers can never get in to see him and ruin themselves waiting for him.

"He is a liar, obsessed with women, always about, hardly ever to be found. The world thinks him incapable of application because he is usually seen anywhere but at home.

"He rises too late, spending his nights at late supper parties, often with the princes.

"He is rude in speech and letter.

"If he does not change completely he cannot remain in office . . .

"I will be very sorry to make a change [e.g. dismiss him] but will not be able to avoid doing so; his work cannot be successful when he neglects it so.

"I wish him to amend himself without my being involved.

"It is impossible not to make many mistakes when the work is so neglected; and they must cost me much.

263

"In a word, it is impossible to do worse than he is doing, and it cannot go on.

"[If it did] I would be blamed for allowing this at a time like this when the weightiest and most important business [the war] depends on him.

"I cannot delay reaching a decision for the good of the state, and even to avoid being guilty myself; I warn you [the Archbishop], although perhaps too late, so that you may act in whichever way will seem best to his family. I feel sorry for it, and for him in particular, because of the friendship and esteem I feel for you.

"Do the best you can to show your nephew the abyss where he is about to fall and force him to do what will best suit everyone. I do not want to lose your nephew; I am fond of him, but, for me, the good of the state comes before all else.

"You would not respect me if I did not behave this way.

"This must be settled one way or the other; I would prefer it to be by [Barbezieux]'s doing his duty . . . but he can do that only if he gives up all the amusements which distract him; his office must be his sole amusement."249

All the King's motivations are there: the desire to spare a family that has served him well, his preoccupation with his *gloire,* his devotion to the state. Most interesting, perhaps, is the fact that at no time does he reproach Barbezieux for failing him personally: it is the state that counts, it is the state that must be served.

As it was, Barbezieux improved, if only slightly; the war ended in 1697, thus making his ministry less important; and the King kept him in office until his death in 1701 at the age of thirty-one. More remarkably, all the defects so eloquently denounced by Louis XIV do not seem to have hampered the armies's efficiency. In May 1694, the maréchal de Noailles, having crossed the Pyrenees, took Gerona; he tried to follow this up by besieging Barcelona, but the city was too strongly defended and the siege had to be lifted.

Once again, this was a useless victory: the war continued, but it was becoming increasingly clear that, while neither side could be defeated, neither could win. Still, at the end of the year, what seemed like a great event took place: Mary II of England died, raising hopes in France that her husband might have to leave the throne; in fact, the Queen's death turned out to be no more than a news item. William III went right on ruling and only modified his earlier policy by being more amiable to Princess Anne, his successor designate.

Another death, that of the maréchal de Luxembourg on January 4, 1695, had far more important consequences: he had been the last of the great French generals. His replacement, the maréchal de Villeroy, was an old friend of the King's, a tall, handsome, and seductive aristocrat, famous for his many love affairs and his sense of fashion. His absolute loyalty no doubt seemed a welcome relief to Louis XIV after Luxembourg's indiscipline and intrigues; and with Villeroy, sharing the command, went the duc du Maine. Here was a chance to humble the princes of the blood by raising du Maine still further: a successful campaign and the King and Mme de Maintenon's beloved duc might well be treated as if he were a legitimate son.

Unfortunately, Villeroy, whatever his charms, was an incompetent leader; as for the duc du Maine, he showed himself indecisive, frightened of responsibility—he was given to consulting his Jesuit confessor at key moments—and even cowardly. By September 1695, Namur, whose conquest had been so celebrated, was taken by William III; and with Namur went the Spanish Netherlands: for the first time, the French army found itself defending its own land instead of conquering someone else's. As for the King, he felt the blow keenly.

Du Maine disgraced himself in early July; the news reached Louis XIV on the 14th, and Saint-Simon was there as usual. "It was for M. du Maine that he had taken such care. At that moment he saw that it had all availed nothing, and the pain of it was unbearable to him. He felt, for this beloved son, all the weight of the spectacle given the army, and of the mockery he read in the foreign gazettes, and his disappointment was inconceivable. This King, so even tempered, so much the master of his smallest movements, broke down on this single occasion. Coming out of table at Marly with all the ladies, and before all the Court, he saw a footman who, as he cleared the table of the dessert, put a biscuit in his pocket. At that moment, forgetting his dignity, holding the cane he had just been given together with his hat, he ran to this footman, who no more expected something of the kind than those he pushed away as he went to him, cursed him, and broke his cane over his shoulders. In truth, it was a reed and did not last long. From there, the broken cane still in hand, with the look of a man beside himself, and still cursing the footman who was long gone, he crossed the small salon and an antechamber and went in to

Mme de Maintenon's as he often did at Marly after his dinner. When he left her to return to his own apartment, he came across the Père de La Chaise [his confessor]. As soon as he saw him standing there among the courtiers, 'Father,' he said in a loud voice, 'I have just given a good beating to a rascal and broken my cane across his back; but I do not think I offended God,' and he went on to tell about the so-called crime. All those who were there were still trembling either from what they had seen themselves or from what they had been told. Their fear redoubled upon this speech: those closest to the King started buzzing against the footman."[250]

Louis XIV had never lost his temper before; he never did again; but the duc du Maine's disgrace had obviously touched him in an even more sensitive place than Saint-Simon thought: the duc attributes the King's anger to his disappointment in a beloved son; and, as far as that goes, he is right; but this was also the first time that a deeply thought out policy was wrecked by someone's personal deficiency. There could be no more question of using the duc du Maine to lower the princes of the blood: their respective status remained unchanged and the King's plans were dropped. That may well be why, to the horror of all Europe, Louis XIV ordered that Brussels be bombarded gratuitously. There was no question of taking the city; instead, it was destruction for destruction's sake, something with which we are sadly familiar but which the seventeenth century rightly found unacceptable.

In many ways, in fact, 1695 marks a turning point in Louis XIV's life. Problems—mostly financial—had occurred earlier; but with the loss of Namur, the invincibility of the French army was proved to be an exploded myth after all: fate, which had always been so kind to the King, now seemed to work against him; instead of giving orders, he had to search for compromise. Success, of course, has its own dangers; but it is still better than a succession of reverses. As long as he triumphed, Louis had shown equanimity; the question was now how he would deal with defeat and disappointment.

In fact, once again, his superb common sense took over. Fighting Europe, he decided, was occupation enough: it was time to settle with the Pope; so he accepted a compromise which, a few years earlier, he would have rejected with disdain. This was made possible by the election, on July 12, 1691, of Innocent XII Pignatelli, who was determined not only to reform the administration of the papal states but also to end the estrangement of France and its clergy. In 1693, he ratified the appointment of the bishops nominated since 1682, provided only that they had not participated in the Assembly of that year. On his side Louis XIV revoked the obligation for the clergy to subscribe to the Four Articles. Both parties had apparently retreated; in fact, the Pope lost a good deal more than the King: he accepted the King's view of his regalian rights; and while it was no longer enjoined the clergy to subscribe to the Four Articles, they were not forbidden to do so of their own free choice. Still, for the first time, Louis XIV had publicly acknowledged an error.

The same prudent attitude prevailed when it came to the war. In 1695 and 1696, it spread across the ocean to the French colonies in the Caribbean, while in France itself, Dieppe was bombarded from the sea and largely destroyed; but elsewhere the ineffective fighting of the previous years continued. As a result, and because the Treasury was even emptier than usual, the King began to contemplate a kind of peace in which, for the first time, France would not prevail.

The most obvious way to attain even that sort of arrangement was to split the coalition; and its weakest link was well within reach of the King's blandishments. Vittorio Amedeo II, Duke of Savoy, ruled over Savoy and Piedmont; at the moment, he was generalissimo of the imperial army; but he was always ready to betray an ally if it suited him to do so. "The comte de Tessé", Voltaire wrote, "a clever and amiable man, with a pleasing sort of genius, which is the most essential talent for a negotiator, first acted secretly in Turin. The maréchal de Catinat, as gifted for making peace as for making war, concluded the negotiation. There was no need for two clever men to join in convincing the Duke of Savoy to follow a policy advantageous to him. His country [which was occupied by a French army] was returned to him; he was given money; he was offered the marriage of his daughter with the young duc de Bourgogne, son of Monseigneur and heir to the French Crown: an agreement was quickly reached . . . The Duke of Savoy joined the French army with his troops . . . and . . . in less than a month had gone from being the Emperor's generalissimo to being Louis XIV's generalissimo."[251]

That turnaround, in itself, was enough to shake Leopold I; but, although he might have been ready to make a separate peace, Louis XIV knew very well that his principal enemy was William III, and that no peace would be lasting which did not include him; so, swallowing his pride, he secretly approached the man whose whole life had been spent fighting him. In short order, negotiations began at Ryswick, in Holland. Their exceedingly slow pace was somewhat speeded up when it was learned that, in August 1697, the duc de Vendôme, an illegitimate grandson of Henri IV and a talented general, had just taken Barcelona. Since, at the same time, Parliament had been making it plain to William III that it was tired of the war, and since Louis was prepared to return all his conquests since the Peace of Nijmegen with the single exception of Strasbourg, the conditions for a reasonable peace existed. On September 20, 1697, it was at last concluded.

Louis XIV had given up a good deal: while refusing to expel James II, he promised no longer to work for the restoration of the Stuarts. He returned his duchy to the Duke of Lorraine and gave him Monsieur's daughter as a wife; he abandoned Catalonia, which had just been conquered, along with the cities in the Spanish Netherlands (today's Belgium) which he had seized since Nijmegen; he turned Brisach, Kehl, Freiburg, and Philippsburg over to the Emperor; the Rhine forts were destroyed; and finally William III recovered his principality of Orange, in southern France. In exchange for all this, peace for a generation was, everyone agreed, at last assured.

In France itself, the Peace of Ryswick was greeted with something like sorrow. The very people who were complaining that the endless conflict was ruining the nation now accused the negotiators of having given up far too much. It was, after all, the first peace of the reign in which, far from swallowing new conquests, France had actually given up territory; and yet it was an act of singular wisdom.

By 1697, Europe felt about France much as it would about Germany in 1940. Here was a predatory power, always hungry for new territory, armed with an unequaled army, ruthless in the wars it waged: it had taken no less than this belief to bring together the League of Augsburg. By renouncing all recent conquests, Louis XIV went a long way toward proving that he was far more moderate than his enemies thought; by agreeing no longer to back the Stuarts, he proved that he was not a Catholic fanatic always ready to fight for the extension of his religion. Any less would have made Ryswick a mere truce; and the King was thoroughly convinced that France needed many years of peace. That, barring unforeseen complications, he could now expect. A balance had been reached: it was in no one's interest to disturb it; and no monarch less powerful, less absolute than Louis XIV could have imposed it on his ministers and his people.

That the treaty should have been so badly received pained the King; but he was also beginning to realize that, all politics aside, it had brought him an almost endless source of joy. By 1696, Louis was almost sixty years old, an age considered to be the threshold of extreme old age. No king of France had reached this age since Louis XI in 1483. Partly for that reason, partly because it distracted him from the cares of state, he now began to prize the cheerfulness and exuberance of the young, particularly as his own health was far from good: he was frequently tormented by attacks of gout, and, in the fall of 1696, he developed an abscess on the neck which gave him a high fever and had to be operated on repeatedly. Now, as the result of his accord with Savoy, he had at his Court the most charming, the most lovable of young women.

Marie-Adélaide de Savoie was only twelve when she crossed the border into France as the embodiment of the treaty between her father and Louis XIV: she was chosen because she was available, not because of any personal qualities, and there was every reason to believe she would be yet another of those rather dim princesses whose main achievement was to provide an heir to the throne. Indeed, once the news of the alliance had become public, it was the change at Court people thought about rather than the attributes of the newcomer. "The Court had long been without a queen or a dauphine," Saint-Simon noted. "All the ladies of a certain position and those in favor bustled and plotted, many of them against one another; anonymous letters, denunciations, and calumnies flew about. All the decisions were taken solely by the King and Mme de Maintenon, who never left his bedside while he was ill [with the abscess on his neck], except when he allowed himself to be seen, and who was often alone with him. She had decided to be the real governess of the princess, to bring her up as she thought fit and for her own purposes, and to create strong enough a tie so that she could use her to amuse the King without fearing that, as she grew up, she might become dangerous. She also wanted to have a hold, through her, on the duc de Bourgogne for the future . . . Mme de Maintenon therefore sought out, for the princess's entourage, persons who were either wholly devoted to herself or so stupid that she would have nothing to fear from them."[252]

Saint-Simon loathed Mme de Maintenon, so that he is usually anything but impartial where she is concerned; but in this instance he is clearly right. It had, after all, long been the King's habit to allow the lady in his life a good deal of influence when it came to Court appointments; he had no reason to refuse his wife what he had offered his mistresses, and besides, he was well aware of Mme de Maintenon's gifts as an educator. The duchesse de Bourgogne was a future queen of France; she was still young enough to be molded; it made sense to do so promptly and efficiently.

As a result, the marquis de Dangeau was appointed chevalier d'honneur. An old friend of the King's, and a man with an astonishing ability to win at cards consistently without ever cheating, he was the most zealous of courtiers. The duchesse du Lude, who was appointed dame d'honneur, to her own stupefaction, was virtuous, rich, pleasant, and very, very stupid. The comtesse de Mailly, the dame d'atours, was a friend of Mme de Maintenon's; and the comte de Tessé, First Equerry, was given the place as a reward for the success of his negotiations with the duc de Savoie. There was no one here, or among the ladies-in-waiting, capable of opposing Mme de Maintenon; and it was plain to all that she would be very much in charge.

All these maneuvers were entirely normal and would, with suitable modifications, have taken place at any other European court; what remained to be seen was whether the princess was ready to be molded: the Queen, good and obedient though she had been, had utterly lacked interest; the Dauphine had provoked indifference at best, hostility at worse. There was no guarantee that the duchesse de Bourgogne would be an improvement on these two ladies. It is therefore particularly interesting to read a description of Louis XIV's first reaction on meeting her; and because he sent Mme de Maintenon a letter from Montargis, a little beyond Fontainebleau, where the meeting took place on November 4, 1696, we can do just that.

"I arrived here before five," the King wrote; "the princess only arrived around six. I went to meet her at her carriage. She let me speak first, but then answered me very properly and with a touch of shyness you would have liked. I took her, across the crowd, to her room, showing her off from time to time by bringing the torches closer to her face. She bore this march and these lights with grace and modesty. We finally reached her room, where the crowd and heat were enough to kill you; I showed her from time to time to those who came close . . .

"She is very graceful and has the best shape I have ever seen; beautifully dressed and coiffed; her eyes are very beautiful and lively; admirable dark eyelashes; a fine pink and white complexion which is just such as one can desire; the finest fair hair and in great abundance. She is as thin as she should be at her age; her mouth is very red, big lips, large white and very jumbled teeth, pretty hands but of the color to be expected at her age [e.g., red]. She speaks little, at least in my presence, is not shy about being stared at, and behaves like someone who is accustomed to the great world. Her curtsey is not good, and too Italianate; there is also something Italian about her face, but it is pleasing, I could see that in everyone's eyes. As for me, I am delighted with her . . . I find her just as she should be and would not want her to be more beautiful . . .

"I saw her being undressed; she has a very good body, one might even say a perfect one, and is modest enough to please you . . .

"We took supper together; she did not make a single mistake and is always amazingly polite, but especially in regard to me and my son she did not make a single mistake and behaved as well as you would have done."[253] That was no mean compliment: for a twelve-year-old girl, faced with the Sun King in person, and placed suddenly in the midst of a foreign court, to behave as well as Mme de Maintenon herself showed amazing tact and intelligence.

The next day proved no disappointment. The King and "the princess"* attended mass together and, after dinner, went on to Fontainebleau; at Nemours, the fourteen-year-old duc de Bourgogne came to meet his fiancée; and at Fontainebleau itself, the Court was introduced to its future queen, who was given Anne of Austria's apartment. Because she was still so young—and unmarried—Louis XIV announced that she would see only the ladies of her Household and those specially authorized to visit her; that she would not hold court; and that her fiancé would only attend her every other week. Then, on the return to Versailles, she was given the Queen's apart-

---

* It was very unusual for a foreign princess coming to France not to have been first married by procuration; but Marie Adélaide was still too young to become duchesse de Bourgogne.

ment and introduced to such courtiers as had not been at Fontainebleau.

"The King and Mme de Maintenon made the princess into their
doll," Saint-Simon noted. "Her insinuating, flattering and attentive
spirit pleased them infinitely and, little by little, she took liberties
which the King's grandchildren never dared to attempt, and which
charmed them. It became clear that M. de Savoie knew our court
well, and that he had taught it all to his daughter; but what was truly
astonishing was how thoroughly she used that knowledge, and the
grace with which she did everything: there can be nothing like the
cajoling with which she bewitched Mme de Maintenon, whom she
always called *my aunt,* and respected and obeyed more than if she had
been her mother and a queen; all with a familiarity and apparent
freedom which enchanted her and the King both."[254] It is no wonder, really: the princess had the kind of beguiling charm and lively,
amusing spirit which Louis XIV's grandchildren wholly lacked; she
was at that fascinating time of life when the child turns into a young
woman; and she knew how to blend the deference due the august
couple with an ease they usually never encountered: it cannot sufficiently be said that the royal family was terrified of the King, and that
their relationships with him were accordingly stiff and awkward.

Even better, by showing herself unafraid, by making it plain that
she enjoyed their company, the princess convinced Louis and the
marquise that she liked them for themselves. It is always the ruler's
weakness to want to be loved for himself, not his position; and love
him the princess did.

Just because Louis XIV never hesitated to put the state before his
family does not mean he had no feelings; his tears may sometimes
have been insincere; but he was not proof against finding himself the
grandfather of such a pleasant child. He can have derived few satisfactions from the slow and lumpy Monseigneur besides those connected to having an undisputed heir. Of his grandchildren, the duc
de Bourgogne, the eldest, was an odd mixture of violence and extreme piety, and far too serious to charm the King. The next brother,
Philippe, duc d'Anjou, had deliberately been kept back so he could
never be a threat to the future king; as a result he was slow, indecisive, and gloomy. The youngest, Charles, duc de Berry, was still only
ten years old, a round-cheeked, fair-haired, and noisy little boy far
too obstreperous to appeal to his grandfather. For all his distance

from his legitimate family and his disappointment with the duc du Maine, however, Louis XIV was not proof against normal paternal feelings; and the princess enabled him to indulge them for the first time.

Other changes also took place at about this time. Monseigneur had been left the château of Choisy by a cousin in 1691. "The King, accustomed to dominating his family as much at least as his courtiers and his people, always wanted it gathered around him and had seen without pleasure the gift of Choisy to Monseigneur and the frequent trips he made there with the few people he chose every time as company. That made for a separation from Court which could hardly be avoided at [Monseigneur]'s age [he was thirty-four] as long as the gift of this house made it possible; but he decided at least to bring him closer. Meudon,† much larger and extremely superb because of the millions that M. de Louvois had spent there, seemed to him just right for this." An exchange was therefore arranged with Barbezieux, who was given Choisy and 900,000 livres; of course, Saint-Simon comments, "the King did not do this without having spoken about it to Monseigneur, for whom the slightest indication of a desire was an order."[255]

With Monseigneur just next door, but buried in his own little circle, the King's illegitimate daughters took on more importance. They, however, proved to be a fruitful source of disappointments: the princesse de Conti despised the other two and had an unfortunately well-known taste for low-born officers; the duchesse de Bourbon was given to composing, and repeating, scurrilous songs about her sisters; and the duchesse de Chartres virtually never remained sober to the end of the evening. Of course, whenever one of the three went too far, she earned herself a scolding, from Mme de Maintenon usually, from the King in more severe cases; but they, too, failed to give their father much satisfaction.

Mme de Maintenon's position, on the other hand, was stronger than ever. Her power, at this stage, has been much exaggerated: when it came to politics the King, while frequently asking her opinion, invariably disregarded it; in religious matters, Bossuet and the Père de La Chaise, the King's confessor, outranked her very consistently; only in family matters was she all-powerful; but with all that,

† Meudon is just outside Versailles.

Louis XIV loved and respected her more with every passing year. That became particularly clear when, in April 1697, the Commedia dell'Arte, which had been most popular in Paris and at Court, was suddenly ordered to leave France within a month. Although they were accustomed to mocking politics and religion, they had never before offended the King; but, this time, they put on a play called *The False Prude* which was an obvious satire on Mme de Maintenon, and that was more than the monarch was prepared to tolerate.

Indeed, although the marquise's status remained highly ambiguous —the marriage was never acknowledged—Louis treated her with all the respect due a queen of France. She never appeared at any of the great state functions; but at the daily mass she sat in the Queen's place; she received the princesses sitting in an armchair while they stood; the King, even outdoors, invariably kept his hat off while talking to her, and was often seen, in his gardens, walking next to her sedan chair, bareheaded and bent over. All this, to us, may seem to be no more than common courtesy; in the seventeenth century, it was both startling and shocking.

Indeed, it caused much whispering when, in late August, 1698, war games were held at Compiègne; Saint-Simon, naturally, was there. "The King said he hoped that the troops would be in good condition, and that everyone would do his best: that was enough to give rise to such emulation that all had, later, every reason to regret it. Not only were all the different regiments in perfect shape, and so much so that it was impossible to determine which corps deserved the prize, but also the commanders added [at their own expense] to the majestic and warlike beauty of the men arms, horses, the ornaments, and magnificence of the Court, and the officers strained themselves further by wearing uniforms which would not have been out of place at a ball. The colonels, and even many captains, held open tables that were abundantly served with delicacies."[256] It was a great occasion, and, for the first time, all the ladies were there as well, along with the ambassadors and the Papal Nuncio.

As the climax of these war games, a mock siege of Compiègne was planned; all the maneuvers common to these occasions were carried out in abbreviated form in the plain surrounding the town, and the King, along with his entourage, watched it all from the top of a rampart which also formed a terrace for the château. "I was in the half-circle very near the King, three steps away at most, and with no one before me," Saint-Simon goes on. "It is impossible to imagine a finer sight than this great army and the prodigious number of onlookers of all stations . . . But a spectacle of another sort, and which I could describe forty years from now as precisely as today because I was so struck by it, was the one that the King gave to his whole army and the innumerable crowd in the plain and on the rampart itself. Mme de Maintenon was sitting in her sedan chair in front of the plain and the troops; the glass in her three windows was up, and her porters were gone. On the front left pole sat Mme la duchesse de Bourgogne; on the same side, in the rear, stood Madame la Duchesse, Mme la princesse de Conti, all the ladies, and further still some men. The King stood next to the right window of the sedan chair, with, behind him a half-circle of the most distinguished men there. The King was almost always hatless, and was constantly bending over to the window to speak to Mme de Maintenon, to explain what she saw and the reason for it all. Each time, she was polite enough to let the glass down by four of five fingers's breadth, never even half way, I noticed it especially and must admit I paid more attention to this spectacle than to that of the troops. Sometimes she opened the glass to ask the King a question; but almost always it was he who, without waiting for her to speak to him, would bend over to explain something; and sometimes when she did not notice him, he would knock against the glass. He spoke to her only, except for giving brief and rare orders, and a few answers to Mme la duchesse de Bourgogne . . . to whom Mme de Maintenon now and again spoke in sign language without lowering the front glass through which the young princess would shout a few words. I looked carefully at everyone's face and saw a shy, ashamed, and concealed surprise . . . all with a respect mixed with fear and embarassment."[257] Mme de Maintenon's true position could not have been more eloquently expressed.

By the time the war games at Compiègne took place, there had been one major change at Court: on Saturday, December 7, 1697, the duc de Bourgogne and Marie Adélaide de Savoie were married; the groom was fifteen, the bride thirteen, too young, even by seventeenth-century standards, for consummation to be allowed. The King let it be known he would be pleased to see his court splendidly dressed, and, indeed, the greatest luxury prevailed. Saint-Simon, who naturally conformed, noted ruefully that he had spent 20,000 livres—well over $100,000—on his clothes and his wife's dresses.

There were two balls and an evening of opera; on the day of the wedding itself, attended, among others, by James II and Mary of Modena, the royal family dined and supped in public; there was a display of fireworks, rather marred by the pouring rain, and the young couple were put to bed in presence of the entire Court. There they remained for fifteen minutes, Monseigneur sitting at his son's side; after which Bourgogne left his virgin bride. The next day, the duchesse held court, with far more ease and grace, it was noticed, than the late Dauphine. Although such a marriage could hardly yet be said to be real, a new unit had nonetheless been formed. All those who had no hope of preferment when Monseigneur succeeded to the Crown began to gather around the next heir: the King, after all, could not live forever, and a prudent courtier always thought of the future.

The Court, in fact, now began to split into clans. There were Monseigneur's friends, led by the princesse de Conti; there was an ultrareligious, conservative group which eventually coalesced around the duc de Bourgogne, who, however, loudly proclaimed his absolute loyalty to the King; there was a small circle of free-thinkers, who mocked the King's piety and advocated a more adventurous foreign policy; and it centered around the prince de Conti, the brother-in-law of the widowed princesse. Mme de Maintenon, of course, had her own friends, and they, too, formed a distinct group. All this was very different from the situation in the sixties and seventies; but it never worried the King: all still depended on him; and since the several groups detested each other, they could always be used one against the other.

In the actual exercise of power, though, there were virtually no changes. Even after the war ended Louis XIV continued to govern by himself. The foreign minister, Colbert's brother, died in 1696; but just as Barbezieux had succeeded Louvois, so the marquis de Torcy succeeded his father. At first, he shared the office with Pomponne, whose daughter he married at the King's order; and eventually was given complete charge.

Thus, by 1698, all seemed settled for a long time. The Court was more splendid than ever; France, though it had not won the war of the League of Augsburg, had not really lost it either, and it was still the richest and mightiest European power. The King, more absolute than ever, saw his succession assured for two generations, with every hope of a third in the not distant future. Peace was assured: unlike its predecessors, the Treaty of Ryswick had left no contentious issue unsettled. The only cloud on the horizon was the fate of Spain, where the childless King Charles II was not expected to live much longer; but negotiations between France, England, and the Empire were under way; candidates to the Spanish throne were canvassed; and all were anxious to avoid another conflict. There was no reason why the reign of Louis XIV should not enter a long and golden sunset.

X
The Great Inheritance

*T*HE COURTIERS who gathered around Louis XIV at Versailles, watching, scheming, hoping for advancement, might have been forgiven for thinking that the world as they knew it had become eternal. At an age when most of his predecessors had been dead, the King, who was sixty-one in 1698, seemed as vigorous as ever, and a good deal more majestic. Better still, he had come through the late war almost unscathed; such defeats as the French army had suffered might actually be considered a positive element in that they guaranteed the peace: France, though still distrusted, no longer seemed the enemy of mankind.

It was, in fact, in a successful effort to avoid any future cause for war that Louis, in the deepest secrecy, began a negotiation with the man in Europe who hated him most; and King William III, fully aware that the English had had their fill of war, was equally anxious to reach an agreement. Of course, the subject of these talks was a little awkward since it predicated the death of the King of Spain at a time when Charles II was still quite alive. Indeed, that wretched and childless monarch had been expected to die at any moment ever since his birth, some thirty-seven years before; still, he was growing weaker; and unless an agreed-upon heir was ready to succeed him, a new, and even more terrible war could be expected to break out.

There were, in 1698, three possible successors: one of Louis XIV's grandsons, whose claim came through Queen Marie Thérèse; one of the Emperor's sons, whose claim came through his grandmother; and one of the Elector of Bavaria's sons, whose mother was Queen Marie Thérèse's younger sister. Quite obviously, choosing the Bourbon or the Habsburg would entail far too great an accretion of power to either dynasty; but the Bavarian candidate, a three-year-old child, was the perfect compromise; so Louis and William agreed that he was to inherit Spain and the Indies, while the Spanish possessions in Italy would be split between France and Austria. It was an eminently sensible arrangement, as the Emperor agreed; and thus it was settled.

It remained to inform Charles II of all this; pressed by his ministers, he agreed to do as he was asked and, in November, signed a will leaving his many crowns to Joseph-Ferdinand of Bavaria, upon which, three months later, that richest of legatees predeceased the testator: Spain and the Indies were once again without an heir.

At that point, still as anxious as ever to maintain the peace, Louis XIV came up with a new solution: since there was no longer a compromise heir, let the Spanish possessions be partitioned between France and Austria. A new negotiation was started, Louis and William came to an argreement, only to find that, in the meantime, the Emperor had become greedy and refused his consent; it was mid-August, 1700 before the negotiation failed, and it seemed clearer than ever that Charles II was at death's door. No one could tell what would happen when he actually died; but, clearly, he now had to write a new will: his wife, a German, pressed him to leave everything to the Archduke Charles, the Emperor's younger son; his ministers, who preferred France, urged him to choose, instead, the duc d'Anjou, Monseigneur's second son; and it was perfectly clear to everyone that if either of these two possibilities became fact war would follow.

These grave matters were debated by the four rulers and their ministers in the deepest of secrecy; but at Versailles, another topic seemed far more important: once again, an obscure religious doctrine was arousing violent controversies, and, this time, it looked as if they might involve some of the most powerful people at Court.

The abbé de Fénelon, a churchman highly popular among the more pious ladies of the Court, was not only tall, handsome, intelligent and full of charm, he had also long been a close friend of Mme de Maintenon; and, as if that were not enough, Louis XIV had appointed him Preceptor to the duc de Bourgogne, the next heir to the throne after Monseigneur, a post which gave him virtual control of the young man's education, especially since the governor, the man in ultimate charge of the King's grandchildren, was the duc de Beauvillier, a close friend and fervent admirer of Fénelon's.

That the Abbé was a gifted and effective teacher cannot be doubted. He took a violent and inattentive child, who seemed destined to be the scourge of France if and when he succeeded to the throne and, entirely through persuasion and encouragement turned him into a serious, self-controlled and cultivated adolescent. As a result, of course, Bourgogne became devoted to his Preceptor, a feeling warmly encouraged by the duc de Beauvillier.

Still, for a while, there had been a rather large fly in the ointment: Like many of his fellow aristocrats, Fénelon deeply resented the domestication of his order. From there to saying, sotto voce, that the King was little better than a tyrant was but a short step. That, in turn, led to advocating a radically different system of government, one in which the state would be run by several Councils composed entirely of great nobles, with the sovereign as a sort of chairman of the board. Of course, the Abbé knew better than to propound his theories to Louis XIV's face; but he undoubtedly gave Mme de Maintenon some pretty broad hints, and composed a treatise, *Les Aventures de Télémaque,* in which, under the guise of recounting the story of the Greek hero in the shape of an educational tale, he set forth his views.

As if that were not already dangerous enough, the Abbé, in the nineties, protected an odd religious sect founded by a mystic, Mme Guyon, which relied heavily on ecstasy and messages from above, all bathed in "pure love." Already Bossuet, that strictly orthodox churchman, had fought this rather peculiar doctrine; soon the Bishop of Chartres, Godet des Marais, a man of little merit but much cunning, saw his chance: if Fénelon could be accused of heresy, he, Godet, would become Mme de Maintenon's chief religious adviser, with a number of pleasant consequences for himself. At the same time, the Bishop of Chalons, a member of the powerful Noailles family in which Mme de Maintenon had found a husband for her niece, was pressing her to renounce Mme Guyon's dangerous ideas.

For a woman of Mme de Maintenon's intelligence, the risks of remaining close to Fénelon were all too obvious. When Godet warned her that the school she had founded* and where Mme Guyon's teachings were highly popular, was in danger of heresy, she

---

* Saint-Cyr, founded and run by Mme de Maintenon, was a school for girls from poor but noble families. This gave her a chance to indulge her passion for education

hesitated no longer. The mystic's writings were shown to the King, who thought them pernicious nonsense. Bossuet, helped by two other bishops, spent eight months examining Mme Guyon and her doctrine, upon which he concluded that her peaceful, passive ecstasies led straight to the death of the soul. Docilely, Mme Guyon recognized her error and retired to a convent; and, on his side, Fénelon accepted the verdict. Still, it had been a close thing: Mme de Maintenon, always frightened that the King might turn against her, had seen a precipice gaping at her feet. She hastened to close it by withdrawing her support from Fénelon.

Of course, none of this appeared outwardly: Mme Guyon had been condemned, Fénelon had accepted the verdict, and that was that: his disciples, including first and foremost the duc de Beauvillier, saw it all as a minor and temporary setback. Indeed, Beauvillier, the only great noble ever called to the conseil d'en haut by the King, seemed powerful enough to guarantee the Abbé's position.

As it happened, however, Fénelon had not only give Mme de Maintenon a severe fright, his very position at Court now threatened to undo one of her most cherished schemes: it had long been her ambition to have the determining voice in the distribution of ecclesiastical patronage. Heretofore, Louis XIV had consulted only his confessor, the Père de La Chaise, a man Mme de Maintenon disliked and distrusted, and the saintly Archbishop of Paris, Harlay de Champvallon; then, in 1695, Champvallon died. If the marquise was to succeed in her ambition, it was obviously crucial that one of her closest allies be appointed to his seat; so, to everyone's amazement, that most important See went, not to Fénelon, as everyone thought it must, but to the marquise's trusted friend, Noailles, Bishop of Chalons; and the Abbé's position became clearer still when he was made archbishop of Cambrai.

On the face of it, Cambrai was a dazzling promotion: a title of duc et pair went with the seat, whose income—some 200,000 livres a year—was one of the largest in France; but it was also far away in northern France, and the King promptly announced that he expected the new Archbishop to reside there for nine months out of every year: that came perilously close to permanent exile. Even so, M. de

---

while providing her with a retreat from the Court during her prosperity and an asylum should anything go wrong.

Cambrai, as Fénelon was now known, did not give up: he kept up a busy correspondence with his friends at Court and continued to defend his political ideas.

That was hardly prudent: Louis XIV was still the best informed man in France, and he disliked opposition as much as ever. When, in 1699, the Archbishop published his *Télémaque,* which had originally been written solely for his pupil, the King struck; and so, at his request, did the Pope: on March 12, 1699, Innocent XII published the brief *cum alias* denouncing twenty-three principles from Fénelon's *Explication des maximes des saints.* Without a moment's hesitation the Archbishop submitted to the Holy See, but it was too late. He was forbidden to appear at Court or correspond with his former pupil.

None of this would have mattered much had it not been that religion here was only a cloak for Court intrigues. For a while it looked as if the duc de Beauvillier, too, would be disgraced. "The King, coming back from mass, found M. de Beauvillier waiting in his cabinet for the forthcoming Council. As soon as he saw him, he went to him and said: 'Well, M. de Beauvillier, what do you say now? M. de Cambrai has been well and thoroughly condemned.'

" 'Sire,' the Duke answered respectfully and yet in a firm voice, 'I have been, and will always remain, M. de Cambrai's close friend; but if he does not submit to the Pope I will never again communicate with him.' The King remained speechless, and those present much admired so firm a generosity on the one hand, and so clear a declaration on the other."[258] Only the unexpected support of the new Archbishop of Paris saved Beauvillier; but even so, the balance of power shifted: a potential opposition had just been decapitated while Mme de Maintenon's power grew enormously. Still, with every passing year, it was becoming clearer that the Court was split into several parties, one of which hoped to oppose the Heir Presumptive to his grandfather—the very thing the King wanted to avoid: it is no wonder he struck at Fénelon with such speed and such vigor.

In other respects, however, little changed at Versailles. The légitimés were still being gradually advanced by the King: more and more the duc du Maine and the comte de Toulouse were being treated like real princes of the blood while their sisters were allowed certain privileges—having their ladies-in-waiting ride in the royal carriages, for instance—which had, hitherto, been reserved for

Daughters of France. Politically, too, the changes inevitably wrought by the passage of time made little difference: in 1699, Torcy, who had long had the job without the title, became Foreign Minister; the old Chancelier Boucherat died and was replaced by Pontchartrain, whose job as controller general went to Chamillart, a tall, intelligent, and kindly man with a talent for billiards, somewhat lacking in energy, but certainly adequate in peacetime. With all that, it was as clear as ever that the King was in charge.

In the royal family, at least, 1699 was marked by a major event: on October 22, the duc and duchesse de Bourgogne, married in name only, were allowed to start actually living together; and that rite of passage was accompanied by the duc's entrance into the conseil des dépêches—the least important of the councils, to be sure, but the young man was only seventeen: Monseigneur had had to wait a good deal longer. Of course, the duchesse de Bourgogne remained the King's favorite, a fact which was not lost on her father-in-law. Whether or not he found that a sufficient reason, or whether he simply felt diminished by his son's greater intelligence, it was at this time that Monseigneur began to show a marked distaste for his eldest son: the set around him, led openly by his half-sister the princesse de Conti, and secretly by Mlle Choin, now began attacking the Bourgognes. Within a year or two, it was clear that, whenever the Dauphin became King, his son was likely to have an unpleasant time of it.

With the return of peace, the finances, still disordered, were beginning to improve; and the courtiers noted that, in consequence, the Carnival of 1700 was especially splendid. Ball followed ball, both at Versailles and at Marly; there were costumed mascarades, plays, operas, concerts: once again, the Sun King was setting the standards by which other monarchs lived. It was at this time also that he began giving the duc de Bourgogne large sums of money. Until now, because all their expenses were paid directly by the Treasury, the duc and the duchesse had each received only 36,000 livres a year. At the time of their marriage, "the King had offered [them] a substantial increase. The duc, who thought he needed no more, thanked him and said that, if he found himself short, he would take the liberty of saying so; and, in fact, at this time, he did. The King praised him greatly, both for asking when he felt the need,† and for coming to him directly without the intervention of a third person; he told him always to do the same with entire confidence, to play at cards boldly without fearing any lack of money, for it was of no importance when people like them lost," and Saint-Simon goes on to comment: "The King liked people to feel easy with him, but he also liked to be feared, and when shy people who had to speak to him grew embarrassed and had difficulty with their speech, nothing pleased him or helped them more."[259]

Behind this brilliant façade the King remained as serious as ever. The death of the Bavarian heir had put an end to the earlier arrangement for the Spanish succession, so new negotiations were started. In March, 1700 Louis XIV and William III came to a new agreement: this time the Archduke Charles, Emperor Leopold's second son was to have Spain, the Indies and the Spanish Netherlands while France received a strip of land in the Basque country, the Kingdom of Naples and Sicily and Lorraine, whose Duke would be moved to Milan; and, of course, the Austrian and Spanish crowns were to remain separate.

It was a sensible arrangement, indeed, a generous one inasmuch as the Habsburgs stood to gain far more than the Bourbons, and it says a good deal about Louis XIV's earnest desire for peace; but to everyone's surprise, on August 25, the Emperor turned it down and instead proclaimed his right to the Spanish dominions in toto, something France could obviously never accept. Simultaneously, intrigues raged in Madrid: Charles II was failing visibly; he must make a new will and was known to have been much upset by the earlier partition agreements. He, too, wanted the Spanish Empire to remain intact; but who, then, was to be his heir?

At first, the wretched King plumped for the Archduke; but the departure of the French Ambassador, the marquis d'Harcourt, and the massing of French troops at the border made it clear that Louis XIV would not allow that solution to go unchallenged. Indeed, both Charles and his Council now began to reverse themselves: their first concern was to keep the monarchy intact; it stood in far more obvious danger from its powerful neighbor than from distant Austria: a will in favor of the Archduke would mean the dismemberment of

† Instead of making debts.

Spain's Empire. It was also true that the duc d'Anjou had the better claim as he was descended from Philip IV's eldest daughter, and the Archduke from a younger sister; and so the Council, headed by Cardinal Portocarrero, now urged the King to reverse himself; upon which, in an agony of indecision, he consulted the Pope.

For the newly elected Innocent XII the answer was obvious: Spain, as a weak power, was infinitely preferable to Austria; so he, too, backed the duc d'Anjou. That was enough. On October 2, Charles II signed a Will making "the second son of the Dauphin of France the successor to all his kingdoms without any exception"; after him, if he were unable to assume the crown, came his younger brother, the duc de Berry; then the Archduke; then the Duke of Savoy. With this went a proviso setting up a junta to govern between Charles's death and the arrival of his successor. Thus relieved of his worries, the last of the Spanish Habsburgs declined peacefully. He died on November 1, at the age of thirty-nine, and was buried at the Escorial on the sixth; and on the morning of the ninth, the news reached Fontainebleau.

Louis XIV, who was due to go off hunting, stayed in and announced Charles II's death to the Court, adding that, in consequence, there would be no festivities of any kind that winter; and he put himself and his family in mourning. That afternoon, the Council which met at three and included Monseigneur, continued until seven; after which the King conferred with Torcy and Barbezieux, the Ministers for Foreign Affairs and War, until ten. The next day, November 10, there was the usual morning Council; but it was followed by an evening meeting which lasted from six to ten. Both the special Councils included the King, Monseigneur and the three Ministers of State: Torcy, Chancellor Pontchartrain, and the duc de Beauvillier—all quite in order, except that the meetings, to the Court's stupefaction, took place in Mme de Maintenon's apartment; and that it quickly became known that the King had insisted on hearing her opinion as well.

Obviously, the decision—whether or not to accept the many crowns of the Spanish monarchy for the duc d'Anjou—was a crucial one. For just about two hundred years, Spain had been France's most dangerous enemy: to see it ruled by a French prince might seem, at first glance, like an extraordinarily happy event. Still, the situation was far more complicated than that: as the Council split right down the middle, that became evident.

For Torcy and the duc de Beauvillier, the dangers inherent in an acceptance of the Will far outweighed all possible benefits. They pointed out that, if the partition treaty—which the Emperor had, however, declined to join—was carried out, France would receive either contiguous territories, like Lorraine, or rich Italian possessions, like Naples, Sicily, and Milan, which would be easier to defend and of real advantage; that having a French prince on the throne of Spain was a fugitive gain, since his children, born in Spain, would be wholly Spanish, and therefore conceivably anti-French; that, having just emerged from a long and costly war, France was in no condition to fight the European coalition which would result from acceptance, and that Spain, already in an advanced state of decadence, far from adding to French strength, would merely be an added burden; and, finally, that if France refused the legacy, its very moderation would give it the leadership in Europe.

The Chancellor, on the other hand, argued that refusing the legacy would entail the same union of Spain and the Empire which had proved so dangerous under Charles V at the beginning of the sixteenth century, but with an added degree of closeness which might well be fatal to France; that while Lorraine was indeed a desirable province, the Italian states had twice before been French, and had twice been lost; that Spain being contiguous to France, it would be far easier for France to defend it than for the Emperor to attack it; that, as for the next King being wholly Spanish, it was most unlikely since the ducs d'Anjou and de Bourgogne were not only brothers but friends and would see to it that their children, first cousins after all, were also close; that by the time the next generation succeeded to the Spanish throne, the friendship with France would be of such long standing as to be virtually unchallengeable; that not only had the partition treaty been rejected by the Emperor, but it was also the work of William III, that perennial enemy of France; and finally that while war would indeed ensue upon acceptance, even attempting to carry out the treaty would result in a conflict with the Emperor, so that, war for war, it was better to have Spain and the Indies as the ultimate gain.

There remained Monseigneur, who normally said nothing. Now, to everyone's surprise, he spoke up. First, he agreed at length with

Pontchartrain; then, "turning to the King in a respectful but firm manner, he said that, having opined like the others, he now took the liberty of asking for his inheritance, since he was able to receive it; that the Spanish monarchy was the property of the late Queen his mother, and therefore his but that, to preserve the tranquillity of Europe‡ he wholeheartedly transmitted it to his second son; that he would not cede an inch of ground to anyone else; that his request was just, and at one with the King's honor and the interests and the greatness of his Crown; and that he hoped therefore not to meet with a refusal. All this, said with considerable warmth, caused great surprise. The King listened very carefully, then said to Mme de Maintenon: 'And you, Madame, what do you think of all this?' First, she played at modesty, but then, being pressed and finally ordered to answer . . . she praised Monseigneur, whom she feared and disliked, as he disliked her, and advised acceptance. The King ended the Council without showing where he stood. He said that he had listened carefully and understood the arguments on both sides, that there were weighty reasons on either, and that the affair was well worth sleeping over."[260]

The next day, November 10, several couriers arrived at Fontainebleau bearing assurances that Charles II's Will had the backing of both the aristocracy and the people; another council was held that afternoon, again in Mme de Maintenon's apartment. On the morning of the eleventh, the King saw the Spanish Ambassador and then the duc de Bourgogne; on the fifteenth, he returned to Versailles. "The next day, Tuesday, November 16, the King, after his *lever,* called the Spanish Ambassador into his cabinet, where the duc d'Anjou [was already waiting]. The King, pointing to him, told the Ambassador he could greet [the duc] as his King. Immediately, he knelt in the Spanish fashion [the French bowed, but did not kneel] and made a rather long speech in Spanish. The King said that [the duc] did not yet understand the language, and that he would answer for his grandson. Immediately afterward, and against all precedent, the King had both sides of the door thrown open and ordered all who were there, and they were very numerous, to come in; then, majestically looking over the crowd: 'Messieurs,' he said, 'here is the King of Spain. His birth has called him to that crown, as did the late King in his Will; the

‡ By keeping the crowns of France and Spain separate.

entire nation has wished it and pressed me to allow it: it was the will of Heaven, I grant it with pleasure'; and turning to his grandson: 'Be a good Spaniard, but remember that you were born a Frenchman and keep the two nations united: that is the way to ensure their happiness and peace in Europe.' "[261] Upon this the duc d'Anjou's two brothers, Bourgogne and Berry, came in and embraced him tearfully. In all of Louis XIV's long reign, no moment had been more glorious: here was a triumph so vast that not even the cardinal de Richelieu, in his most ambitious moment, could have imagined it possible.

From that moment on, the sixteen-year-old* duc d'Anjou, having assumed the name of Philip V, was treated like a king. His grandfather insisted that he share all the royal honors; Monseigneur, beside himself with pride, gave Anjou precedence everywhere, and repeated constantly, "The King my father, the King my son," although, as Saint-Simon wryly observes, he might not have been quite so happy had he remembered a well-known prophecy about himself which ran: "Son of a king, father of a king, never a king"; and it was announced that Philip V would set off for his new realm on December 1.

Already on November 12, the King had written almost identical letters to the Queen Dowager and the Spanish Junta.† "The sorrow we feel for the loss of a prince, whose qualities and close kinship made his friendship precious, is greater still because of the touching proof he has given us at his death of his justice and his love for his subjects, and also because of the care He took in maintaining, beyond His own life, the happiness of Europe."[262] And to the Junta, he continued: "All our care will be henceforth, through an inviolable peace, to restablish the Spanish monarchy in its former splendor. We accept, in favor of our grandson the duc d'Anjou, the late Catholic King's Will . . . We will send [Anjou] off instantly so as to give to his subjects, at the earliest opportunity, the consolation of receiving a king whose first duty must be to uphold Justice and our Religion, to work only for the happiness of his realm, to know and reward merit . . . We will urge him to remember his birth . . . but even more whose King he is."[263]

With the possible exception of Mme de Maintenon, who dreaded

---

* He became seventeen on December 3.
† A governing Council set up to oversee the transition period before the new King's arrival.

the prospect of war, the reaction in France was ecstatic. The Court, its breath taken away by such an accretion of greatness, was unanimous in its praise as were the people and Parlements. A verse published in the *Mercure de France* was typical:

"Pour fixer á jamais le repos que tu donnes / A tes rivaux confus tu cèdes des couronnes / Que devaient á tes fils le sang et l'équité. / Mais Dieu pour qui ton coeur fait un tel sacrifice / D'un roi qui va mourir ranimant la justice / Rend ses états entiers á ta postérité . . ." (To establish forever the peace you have given us/ To your surprised rivals you have given crowns/ Owed to your sons by birth and fairness/ But God for whom your heart made this great sacrifice/ Resurrecting the sense of justice of a dying king/ has given your grandson his realm undiminished.)[264]

It was no wonder: Louis XIV and his ministers knew that Spain was really the ghost of its former self, that, in fact, it had virtually ceased being a major power, but for all those who were less well informed—that is, almost everyone—the event was altogether dazzling: France's oldest and—until recently—most powerful enemy had, overnight, become a virtual dependency. As they ascended another throne, the Bourbons were adding not one but many crowns to that of France. The riches of Latin America were still legendary; and it was all done, not as the result of a long and bloody conflict, but through a stroke of the pen.

Of course, Louis XIV himself knew that his grandson's prodigious fortune would have to be bought, and bought dearly; already on November 14, he had sent off a letter to the comte de Briord, his ambassador in Holland; with it went a Memorandum for the States General—an indirect way of approaching William III—in a desperate effort to avoid the unavoidable war.

The first of these is of particular interest because it retraces the King's reasoning. After telling Briord of the Spanish Ambassador's urgent speech in favor of acceptance, he goes on: "I examined, with the greatest attention, all the drawbacks and all the advantages, either of carrying out the [partition] Treaty or of accepting the Will. In the first case, I saw the usefulness of uniting several States to my Crown, of weakening a power that has always been the enemy of mine. I considered the agreements made with the King of England and the [Dutch] States General, and the idea of the general tranquillity that would ensue if I carried out the partition Treaty faithfully.

On the other hand, I had reason to believe that the more my power grew through the accretion of the States which my son had kept for himself, the more I would meet obstacles in having the treaty carried out. The late negotiations, and the present uncertainty, show this all too clearly. The King of Spain's Will added to the difficulties. Since the Archduke was listed after my grandsons, the Emperor would have been even more unwilling to sign the treaty; and even had he done so, it would merely have caused his rights to pass on to the Duke of Savoy, who would have been recognized by the entire Spanish nation as the legitimate heir. Carrying out the treaty would therefore have entailed my conquering all the States dependent on the Spanish Crown in order to distribute them according to the treaty. That decision would have caused a war whose end was not foreseeable: nothing could be more opposed to the spirit of the treaty.

"I see, on the contrary, that, as I accept the Will, no one has any right to complain . . . ; that all pretext for a war is removed; that Europe has no need to fear the union of so many States under a single power; that my own power is not enlarged; that things remain as they have been for so many years; and that it is therefore best for Europe, and more in keeping with the spirit of the treaty, to follow the late King's arrangements"; and after urging M. de Briord to enlist the cooperation of the Spanish Ambassador, he adds: "You will tell him that, at present, my only intention is to keep the [Spanish] monarchy intact."[265]

This letter requires a good deal of analysis. Obviously, it sets out the line the King meant to take toward the two key powers, England and Holland: without their financial and military help, the Emperor could not go to war; and some of it is disingenuous: having a seventeen-year-old, who, furthermore, was neither intelligent nor decisive, on the throne of Spain represented a considerable accretion of power for France: to say that with its own King Spain would be exactly as before was little short of absurd. In fact, Louis XIV, who knew very well that war was virtually unavoidable, was trying to position himself for the future peace negotiations; and by saying that "at present" he intended to keep the monarchy intact, he was signaling his willingness to negotiate its dependencies away at a future date.

At first, it seemed as if, indeed, war could be avoided. In February, both William III and the Dutch Grand Pensionary wrote Philip V recognizing him as King of Spain. The Elector of Bavaria, one of the most important princes in Germany, had also been appointed governor of the Spanish Netherlands by the late King: he promptly signified his readiness to obey the new monarch's orders. As for the Duke of Savoy, his daughter was duchesse de Bourgogne, and Louis XIV immediately asked for her younger sister as the wife of Philip V: under those circumstances, he, too, could be relied on to back the French.

Appearances, however, were deceiving. William III needed time to raise troops and money, as well as to obtain Parliament's consent to a new war. This last was done partly through a process of barter—he signed the Act of Settlement which not only placed the succession to the throne in the House of Hanover should Princess Anne find herself without issue, but also sharply restrained the power of his successors; he pointed out that French troops had quickly occupied the Barrier fortresses in Belgium, the specific purpose of which was precisely to keep France within its borders; and a trading agreement between France and Spain which seemed to threaten the profitable English trade with South America only helped him further. The league between England, Holland, the Emperor, and a number of lesser princes, the Elector of Hanover first and foremost, was only signed in September 1701; but already in the spring, Leopold I, sure that it was on the way, began hostilities in Italy.

*D*ID Louis XIV make the right choice in this, perhaps the most important single decision of his reign? The answer to that question has been argued for almost three hundred years, mostly with the benefit of hindsight. That, of course, is hardly fair: statesmen are restricted to the information they have, so a first appraisal must be made on the basis of the situation as it was in November 1700.

Once that is done, however, the King must also be held accountable for the consequences of his actions in the short term—that is, the dreadful war that ensued; and in the long term—that is, France's relationship to Spain in the decades that followed.

The situation in 1700 was such, if examined carefully, as to leave Louis XIV with very little choice. Whatever the ministers may have said in Council, whatever the claims made by Monseigneur, it is clear that France could not afford a resurrection of Charles V's empire: between the Emperor in Vienna and his son in Madrid, the Habsburgs would have ruled over Austria, Hungary, Bohemia (today's

Czechoslovakia), the Tyrol extending to Trieste, Naples, Sicily, Milan, the Spanish Netherlands (today's Belgium), Spain, and all the Spanish colonies in the Caribbean and Latin America; they would also have encircled France, threatening it on its borders: the one with Italy (the Duke of Savoy being an unreliable ally), the one with the German states, the one with the Spanish Netherlands, the one with Spain.

The King had good reason to remember what had happened in the sixteenth century when that had been the case: from François I's defeat at Pavia to Henri II's weak peace treaties, and through the Wars of Religion which, financed by Spain had racked France into the seventeenth century, the Habsburgs had very nearly added France to their dominions; nor did he forget that in the 1630s, Spanish armies had come within fifty miles of Paris. To leave the throne of Spain to the Archduke, therefore, would have been a plain dereliction of duty.

Of course, it was a proud moment for Louis XIV when he announced to his assembled Court that his grandson had become King of Spain; and many historians have been misled by that legitimate emotion into thinking that it was to raise his *gloire* still further that Louis had accepted the late King's Will; but that is, in fact, putting the cart before the horse. The decision was motivated first by the gravest political considerations; and once he had taken it, Louis derived pride from it.

As for the risks inherent in acceptance, they, too, had been carefully weighed. The King knew, none better, that money was one of the main resources of war, and that the Treasury was still empty. Under those circumstances, a prolonged conflict would prove exceedingly difficult to finance. Then, too, the great generals of the early part of the reign were dead, and the King himself was too old to lead his troops in person. His closest ally, the Duke of Savoy, was notoriously treacherous, so once again France was likely to be fighting the rest of Europe, and there was no guaranty that it would win. Louis, in fact, had been willing to go great lengths to preserve peace as the two treaties, one of succession, the other of partition, had proved: he was under no illusion that the war would be either short or easy.

Still, it was better to fight now, adding the resources of Spain to those of France than to allow the Habsburgs to resurrect their former

European supremacy, since they were then bound to try and crush their old enemy: at least both the Pyrenees and the northern border were safe; and the Spanish possessions could be used to barter for peace.

There can be no doubt, therefore, that with the information at his disposal, Louis XIV made the right choice; and even seen in retrospect, the balance remains in his favor: although the war of the Spanish Succession proved long, very costly, very painful and was, indeed, very nearly lost, the long-term relationship with Spain was everything that could be desired: until the end of the ancien regime, the cousins on both sides of the Pyrenees remained good friends: the power France had fought almost uninterruptedly ever since 1500 remained its ally: given this, clearly, the cost in men and money had not been wasted.

Finally, by his own standards, Louis XIV had behaved like a good king: he had carefully listened to the advice offered him, had considered the possibilities and dangers of his decision, the welfare of his kingdom and the rights of his family, and then, with the help of his common sense, reached what turned out to be the proper decision. The responsibility was his; he had been swayed by neither minister nor favorite.

ON DECEMBER 4, after many tearful scenes, King Philip V left Versailles; his brothers accompanied him to the border, and the three took with them fifteen carriages, fourteen post chaises, and forty-six baggage carts, all pulled by 818 horses; and to that was added the equipage of their numerous suite.

Of course, Louis XIV, as he bid his grandson farewell, had reminded him that he must always remain the friend of France: that was in public; but, before that, and privately, he had also given him a set of instructions; and they ranged from the most fundamental matters of policy to the minutest particulars. Divided into thirty-three articles, they began with "Always do your duty, especially to God" and ended with the following typical admonition: "Do not allow yourself to be ruled. Be the master; never have either a favorite or a prime minister. Consult your Council, listen to it; but decide yourself. God, who has made you king, will give you all the understanding you need as long as your intentions remain good." This, in fact, is exactly the advice he had given the Dauphin over thirty years earlier: in those few words the spirit of the new monarchy is contained.

In between these two admonitions, the advice runs from the bland: "Always declare yourself for virtue and against vice" to the practical: "Love the Spanish and all the subjects attached to your crowns and to your person; do not prefer those who flatter you most; keep your esteem for those who, for your good, will make bold to displease you: they are your true friends.

". . . Only go to war when you are forced to do so."

Naturally, the new King was advised to reorganize his finances, keep up his fleets, watch over the Indies; he was warned never to neglect business for pleasure, but also to keep some time free for relaxation; he was reminded that it was important to get to know his more important subjects so that he might make use of them. Then came the most important parts of the instructions:

"Do not seem shocked by the extraordinary appearance of the people you will see; do not make fun of them; each country has its own manners and you will soon grow accustomed to what seemed to you most shocking.

"Never forget that you are French . . .

"Have complete trust in the duc d'Harcourt‡; he is clever and reliable and will give you advice which will be to your own advantage."[266]

Indeed, this last item was the most important of all. The duc d'Anjou, until his sudden rise, had been no more than a younger brother of the Heir Presumptive, and he had been brought up accordingly—just as Monsieur had been two generations earlier. While the duc de Bourgogne was raised to rule, the duc d'Anjou was trained to obey; he was carefully allowed to remain somewhat backward, since the great object of his education was to ensure he would never lead an opposition against his elder brother. Unfortunately, given the sudden change in his position, his Governor had succeeded perfectly: the young man was dull, lazy, indecisive and very pious. When, in 1701, he discovered sex, it turned into an obsession; and for the rest of the world he cared very little.

Thus, it was perfectly obvious to those who knew him well that he was quite incapable of governing the ramshackle Spanish kingdoms

‡ The French Ambassador in Madrid.

at this moment of crisis: oddly enough,* this Bourbon was remarkably like the last of the Habsburgs. That, of course, left a power vacuum: someone was going to govern through the King. At the start, that someone was to be a combination of the clever and charming duc d'Harcourt and Cardinal Portocarrero, the head of the Junta, and the man most responsible for the late King's Will; but since Philip must marry, it seemed highly likely that his wife would rule him; and, clear-eyed as always, Louis XIV provided for this also.

Whether or not the princess he chose was pretty, agreeable, or bright was not much of a consideration: she might rule her husband, but someone could be provided to rule her in turn; still, in this case, political considerations went hand in hand with a happy selection. It was extremely important to keep the Duke of Savoy from reneging on the French alliance and the best way to do that, it seemed, was by marrying his youngest daughter, Maria Luisa, to Philip V; but, as the sister of the enchanting duchesse de Bourgogne, it also seemed probable that she would be very pleasing.

For the Duke of Savoy to have one daughter married to the Heir Presumptive of France and the other to the King of Spain was obviously a great achievement; but, being both practical and unscrupulous, he preferred enlarging his states to this kind of gloire; and so the negotiations ran into some difficulties. On July 29, 1701, Louis XIV wrote his grandson: "I have thought it best to delay your marriage because I have been advised that the Duke of Savoy was not sincere. You know what he is like. I had written to the marquis de Castel Rodrigo to suspend negotiations but have learned that they are already concluded. Do not be surprised, though, if he [the Duke] creates some difficulties: I hope he will find the means to do so."[267]

In fact, the marriage actually took place by procuration on September 11, and the young King promptly fell in love with Maria Luisa, who turned out to be a good deal brighter than her husband. Still, lively though she undoubtedly was, the Queen was only thirteen— old enough to let her husband discover the joys of sex, but hardly experienced enough to govern the realm.

Louis XIV, however, had provided for that as well. As Maria Luisa's new Camarera Mayor,† he had chosen a lady whose energy,

---

* Or perhaps not so oddly: he was descended from a great many Habsburgs.
† The Camarera Mayor was the chief female Court official. It was her duty to be constantly at the Queen's side; and she also ran her Household.

intelligence and desire to please him were all beyond compare. The princesse des Ursins had led a long—she was fifty-nine—and rather chequered life. Born a La Trémouille, one of the greatest French families, she had married a Talleyrand, the prince de Chalais, who, mistaking Louis XIV for Mazarin, had disobeyed the edict forbidding duels. That, and the princess's sharp tongue had thoroughly annoyed the King, with the result that the Chalaises were forced to leave France in a hurry. Shortly after that, the prince died in Venice of a fever, and his widow found herself penniless and still disgraced; so she installed herself in a Roman convent and looked around.

The result of her contemplation turned out to be a second marriage even more brilliant than the first. Don Flavio Orsini, a man past his youth and racked with gout, was also the foremost nobleman in Rome; his family was traditionally pro-French, so it made sense for him to marry Mme de Chalais; but he also found her captivating, so much so, indeed, that he took her without a dowry. From that moment on, the princesse des Ursins, as she called herself since Orsini sounded far too foreign to a French ear, worked very hard indeed at regaining Louis XIV's favor. In the many disputes which gave life in Rome such interest as it had, she invariably took the French side; and because she was both clever and determined, she proved to be a considerable asset.

That, alone, would not have secured her the post of Camarera Mayor: just as important, in those long ago days when she was still Mme de Chalais, she had been one of Mme Scarron's closest friends. Forty years later, Mme de Maintenon remembered this; and when it was decided to govern Spain through the Queen, and the Queen through the Camarera Mayor, she suggested Mme des Ursins.

It was a brilliant choice. Her years notwithstanding, the princesse was energetic, able to learn and ambitious; she knew that only the closest alliance between Spain and France would keep Philip and Maria Luisa on their throne, and that only the most intimate friendship between herself and Mme de Maintenon would lead to the reward for which she longed—nothing less than an independent principality.

Thus a highly unorthodox, and confidential, chain of command was established. Louis XIV had an official ambassador in Madrid, whose task it was to relay instructions from Versailles and requests from Madrid; but, in no time at all, really weighty matters were settled through the correspondence between Mme de Maintenon and Mme des Ursins: they it was who ran Spain and the war. Of course, it must be added to that that Mme de Maintenon was only Louis XIV's intermediary, and that it was the King's policy she expounded in her letters. Still, as the war progressed, Mme de Maintenon developed a position of her own, and so did Mme des Ursins, the first being markedly defeatist, the second irredentist; and the feelings of these two ladies did not simplify an already very complex situation.

That Mme des Ursins should suddenly have found herself in a position of such power was due, of course, to circumstances rather than outright design; but that she, specifically, should have been chosen reflected Mme de Maintenon's growing power. In 1700, Louis XIV had already been holding meetings of the Council in Mme de Maintenon's apartment for a number of years; but the meeting at which Charles II's will was discussed marked the first time her contribution actually mattered. It was a telling step: henceforth her opinion, usually solicited but sometimes simply proffered, carried a great deal of weight, especially when it came to personnel. On March 19, 1702, William III died and was succeeded by his sister-in-law, Princess, now Queen, Anne; and from then on, the War of the Spanish Succession might well have been renamed the War of the Three Ladies.

One more unforeseen event also went far to bolster Mme de Maintenon's new position: early in 1701, Barbezieux, the War Minister, died suddenly of apoplexy. The King, determined not to have another minister he disliked, promptly appointed Chamillart to his office, while at the same time maintaining him as Contrôleur Général. It was hardly a clever move. Chamillart, who had come to the King's attention because he was a good billiards player, was certainly hardworking, honest and eager to do well. Unfortunately, he was also limited, lacking in energy and short of the most essential knowledge. Already as Contrôleur Général, he was ill suited to manage what was sure to be a severe financial crisis; adding the responsibility of the war department to this was bound to be disastrous, and so Chamillart, who was nothing if not honest, told the King. That, however, was the best way to keep both jobs: Louis XIV was now thoroughly convinced he could do any minister's job better than the holder of the office. Chamillart's open avowal of ignorance therefore turned out, quite unintentionally, to be the cleverest kind of flattery: his very lack of knowledge would underline the fact that it was the King, in person, who was actually governing.

Louis XIV then compounded that very serious error by choosing his generals according to their position at Court instead of their talents: the duc du Maine and the comte de Toulouse were given commands, when one had proved a coward and the other was, as yet, incompetent, but the duc de Chartres, who had shown evidence of real military talent, was kept at Versailles despite Monsieur's unusually determined complaints. As for the prince de Condé and the prince de Conti, a brilliant young man, they too were refused commands. If France had enjoyed overwhelming superiority over her enemies, all that might not have mattered; under the circumstances, this policy, which was certainly neither new nor surprising, might also well prove catastrophic.

To Monsieur, however, what mattered was the insult to his son, and therefore to himself. The King, when he was trying to arrange Mlle de Blois's marriage to Chartres, had promised to look after the young man as if he were his son, instead of his son-in-law on the wrong side of the blanket. True to his word, he had lavished money on the young couple; but when it came to furthering Chartres's career, all promises were forgotten.

The young man reacted to this by plunging into the most spectacular kind of debauchery. On June 8, 1701, Monsieur came from his castle at Saint Cloud, where he was now spending most of his time, to Marly, there to lunch with the King. He had long been angry that his son was refused a command, or, indeed, any place in the army when the war was starting up; and so when Louis XIV angrily criticized Chartres's infidelity to his wife, Monsieur blew up and told the King, according to Saint-Simon, that fathers who had themselves led loose lives were hardly in a position to blame their children (in-law) who did the same.

The King then said that at least his daughter should be spared the knowledge of her husband's misbehavior, upon which Monsieur reminded his brother that he, himself, had so little spared his wife as to have his mistresses travel in her very carriage. At that point the brothers started to shout so loudly at each other that they were clearly heard from the next room; and Monsieur, reiterating the King's unfulfilled promises went on to say that the people who told him that all he would get out of the marriage would be shame were quite right. The King, incensed, answered that, in that case, since the war would force him to retrench, the first pensions he would cut would be those attributed to Monsieur and his family, and upon that, lunch being served, the two men, purple in the face and eyes glittering, emerged from the King's cabinet.

That evening, back at Saint Cloud, and in the middle of supper, Monsieur was felled by a stroke. The King, upon being warned, came to see his brother, but Monsieur had already sunk into a coma. "Around eight in the morning, since there was no hope, Mme de Maintenon and Mme la duchesse de Bourgogne urged him to stay no longer . . . As he was about to leave, and was talking in a friendly way to M. de Chartres, both being awash in tears, that young prince made use of the moment. 'Ah, Sire, what will become of me?' he said, holding the King by the legs,‡ 'I am losing Monsieur and I know you do not like me.' The King, who was surprised and touched, embraced him and said many tender things to him . . .

"The next day M. le duc de Chartres came to see the King, who was still in bed and the King spoke to him in a very friendly manner. He told him that he must henceforth consider him his father, that he would look after his greatness and his interests, that he had forgotten all the little reasons he had had to be annoyed with him, that he hoped that, on his side, he would also forget them, and that he trusted that the friendship he was showing him would attach him anew, and cause him to give his heart as he [the King] was giving his . . .

"After so sad a spectacle, so many tears, so much tenderness, no one doubted that the three days remaining in this stay at Marly would be extremely sad, when, that very day after Monsieur's death, ladies-in-waiting . . . heard . . . Mme la duchesse de Bourgogne singing opera prologues. A little later, the King, seeing [her] looking sad, asked Mme de Maintenon with surprise why she was so melancholy . . .

"After dinner that night, Monseigneur the duc de Bourgogne asked the duc de Montfort whether he wanted to play cards. 'Cards!' said Montfort in extreme surprise, 'You cannot be serious! Monsieur is still warm.'

‡ Chartres was on his knees before the King.

" 'Forgive me,' the prince answered. 'I am perfectly serious. The King, who does not want people to be bored at Marly, ordered me to have everyone play and, for fear no one would dare to start, to begin it myself.' "[268] As for the new duc d'Orléans—Chartres succeeded to his father's title—while he was given all the pensions paid to his late father, he remained without a command.

With Monsieur's death, the last of the generation who had known the King as a young man was gone. Louis XIV was now surrounded by his children, his grandchildren, and courtiers younger than himself. The ministers, too, belonged to the new age; and even if Mme de Maintenon was actually three years older than the King, she, too, was part of the new environment. No one, now, remembered the difficult days of the Fronde, except, of course, the monarch himself. Majestic and imperious, more than ever Louis XIV governed by himself; and in his sixty-fourth year, he prepared, once more, to face a European coalition.

XI
A Fearful War

GOVERNING a great kingdom engaged in a difficult war, overseeing the ministers' work, financing vast new expenditures, and, with it all, continuing to appear in public regularly and often should have been enough for any man; but, without a moment's hesitation, Louis XIV, in 1700, took on the government of Spain as well. On December 15, he wrote the duc d'Harcourt: "I think it necessary to warn you that the King of Spain's intentions are good. He wants to do well and will if he knows how, but he lacks knowledge in many fields. He has learned little, even less than would be normal at his age. It will be easy to rule him if in the beginning you are careful to prevent any prejudice people may try to give him . . . He will trust you and follow your advice."[269]

In short order, the princesse des Ursins took over; but the fact remained that Madrid was governed from Versailles. In any age, that would have been a crushing burden; at the dawn of the eighteenth century, it was made more onerous still by slow, often faulty, communications and by the advanced state of decadence of the Spanish monarchy: as if it were not enough to cope with the war, the government had to be thoroughly reorganized as well. Undaunted, the Sun King set about centralizing and rationalizing the virtually paralyzed administration left behind by the Habsburgs.

He also followed Mme des Ursins's maneuvers with extreme attention. The princesse was to be simply the means of transmitting orders from grandfather to grandson; instead, she quickly developed so strong a loyalty to Philip and Maria Luisa that, in certain cases, she encouraged them to have a policy of their own. Already, on July 13,

1701, Louis XIV wrote Philip V: "I am sending you Marsin who will stay with you . . . I trust him, you may too, and be quite sure that he will never suggest anything that will not be useful to our common interests. I cannot end without assuring Your Majesty of my love and telling you, with all the strength I have, that I wish to see Your Majesty become as great a king as you can be if that is your desire."[270]

This kind of exhortation was repeated again and again. On August 7, for instance, a long letter about the Spanish etiquette and some problems regarding Naples concluded: "How happy I will be when I see you in that high degree of *gloire* to which I hope your courage will raise you! I will love you more; and as my esteem for you grows, so will my tenderness."[271] At the same time, while Philip V was urged to exert himself, he was also given the most detailed guidance: whether it was a reform of the Spanish etiquette or the way to deal with the Cortes of Catalonia, the letters kept coming from Versailles.

Soon, however, a new problem surfaced. Mme des Ursins, who proved invaluable in many ways, was all too clearly in charge: she governed the Queen absolutely, and the Queen, in turn, governed the King. Indeed, any slight resistance on the part of the young man could be overcome by a simple expedient: he was so obsessed with sex that even a single night of chastity was more than he could bear. All the Queen had to do, therefore, was repulse her husband: the next day—if he had held out that long—he caved in.

Of course, everyone knew it; so, on November 13, Louis XIV tackled the problem: "It is essential for your happiness and hers that [the Queen] be disabused of the notions she may have been given according to which she can govern you. Surely Your Majesty would never allow it. You would feel too strongly the dishonor such a weakness would bring you. It is not forgiven in private people. Kings, who are exposed to public observation, are even more contemptible when they are dominated by their wives . . . The Queen is your first subject; as such, and as your wife, she must obey you."[272] That was all very well, but what the King expected to find in his grandson was a younger—and slightly more pliable—version of himself; and in that, he was deceived. As it turned out, Philip V was not without qualities, but a strong will was not one of them.

Annoying though this was, Louis XIV was far too shrewd not to behave accordingly. When, the following year, after many tears, the

Queen reluctantly agreed to stay behind as her husband went off to war, Louis wrote her: "I could not doubt that your strong and tender love for the King of Spain would cause you to feel much pain at being parted from him, but I must admit I did not believe that this separation would cause me to love you still more, and to realize that your intelligence, your reason, and your spirit far exceed what I had seen of them until now. You truly love my grandson in preferring his *gloire* to everything else, and I must give you well-deserved praise rather than the advice for which you ask me . . ."[273] To all his other talents, the Sun King had now added those of a psychologist.

Still, he was not merely flattering: Maria Luisa quickly proved, except for those nightly sessions in the conjugal bed, to be rather more of a man than her husband. It was her indomitable courage that sustained him at the most difficult times; it was her intelligence, assisted by that of Mme des Ursins, which helped him to govern; it was her energy which brought the pair much needed popularity. Alone, Philip would probably have been a liability: together with his wife, he proved an important asset; and when he did not, scolding letters promptly came from Versailles.

It was all the more important for all to go well in Madrid that a European coalition was now backing the Archduke's claim; and as, once again, he faced strong and well-organized enemies, Louis XIV relied on himself most of all. Arrayed against him were the two greatest generals of the time, John Churchill, soon to become Duke of Marlborough, and Prince Eugene of Savoy, the son of the King's erstwhile mistress the comtesse de Soissons, who now served the Emperor. To these men of genius, the King could only oppose the duc de Vendôme, the illegitimate grandson of Henri IV and a talented leader, but not equal to either Marlborough or Prince Eugene; the maréchal de Villars, brave, clever, and, above all, lucky; and the duc de Berwick, James II's illegitimate son by Arabella Churchill, Marlborough's sister, and a highly competent leader, but without his uncle's genius. Far worse, the other French generals lacked even the most elementary competence: Villeroy, the King's friend, knew more about the organization of a ball than about that of an army, and Tallard, Marsin, and La Feuillade, all of whom were eventually created marshals, were courtiers rather than generals.

Nor were the ministers any more distinguished. Chamillart, the most important of them, was way over his head; Torcy, the Foreign

Minister, found himself implementing a policy he had opposed. Of course, he obeyed the King, but with a singular lack of elan. The duc de Beauvillier, straightforward and immensely virtuous, deplored the whole situation; so it was all up to the King himself, who found it rather stimulating.

In fact, for the next twelve years, Louis XIV, besides holding Court as usual, did the work of several ministers while telling his generals what to do, all this at an age when most of his contemporaries were either dead or in retirement; nor did he find reliable support in his most intimate circle. Mme de Maintenon, who remained absolutely obedient, made no secret of her loathing for the war; the légitimés quite failed to distinguish themselves; and the rest of the royal family went on squabbling as ever.

At the very outset, however, the King made a terrible mistake: he issued letters patent to his departing grandson assuring him that his right of succession to the French throne remained unimpaired by his assumption of the crown of Spain. This was not unusual: there was a precedent in the case of Henri III, who became king of Poland, but succeeded as king of France on the death of his brother in 1574. Still, the notion that France and Spain could be united under a single monarch was bound to terrify—and anger—the rest of Europe; and its unlikelihood* changed nothing.

A further irritant to the Coalition came with the death of James II on September 16, 1701. Despite his ministers' advice, Louis promptly recognized James's son as King of England. That, however, was not as ill-advised as has sometimes been supposed: the league against France had been signed a month earlier, and nothing short of war could be expected. By recognizing a Stuart as King of England, Louis XIV, besides giving pleasure to the widowed Mary of Modena, was also providing himself with yet another counter for the future peace negotiations.

The war itself, begun by the Emperor in Italy, started slowly. First, Catinat, a competent but uninspired leader, was beaten by Prince Eugene; then, on February 2, 1702, the Prince surprised Villeroy in Cremona, and took both the town (briefly) and the maréchal (permanently); so Vendôme was sent off to replace him. All through 1702, a

---

* The duc de Bourgogne was after all, likely to have children. In fact, his second son became King Louis XV; but in the very long run, the Coalition was right to worry: today, King Juan Carlos of Spain is Louis XIV's only direct descendant . . .

series of indecisive, but often bloody, battles opposed the two generals; the great change came in 1703 when, little by little, it became clear that the Duke of Savoy, who had been promised money and territory by the Emperor, was about to turn coat once again. Of course, Louis XIV reacted swiftly. In September, he wrote the Duke: "Monsieur, since religion, honor, interest, our alliance, and your very signature mean nothing to you, I am sending my cousin the duc de Vendôme at the head of my armies to explain my intentions to you. He will only give you twenty four hours to make a decision."[274] In fact, the Duke's army was seized by the French while he himself went over to the Coalition.

On the far more crucial northern front, things were not going any better: Neither the maréchal de Boufflers, who was brave but not clever, nor the duc de Bourgogne, were able to stop Marlborough whose steady pressure accompanied by occasional minor victories, caused the French army to fall back quite significantly. The duc de Bourgogne himself was harshly criticized. Louis XIV showed what he thought of it all by bringing his grandson into the Council; and all prepared for the following campaign.

At least, on the Alsatian front, Villars had won a battle at Fridlingen in October 1702. In the spring of 1703, he joined the Elector of Bavaria, France's sole remaining ally; and with Prince Eugene still busy in Italy, it looked as if France could expect major successes: the Imperial army was beaten at Hochstedt in September 1703, Villars took Augsburg while, on his side, Vauban, under the duc de Bourgogne's nominal supervision, took Landau and Alt-Brisach.

Unfortunately, Villars and the Elector had grown to detest each other: Villars thought the Elector hopelessly slow and timorous, the Elector resented Villars's boldness and his overall leadership of the two allied armies; so the maréchal asked to be brought home—he was sent to command the troops fighting a Protestant insurrection in the Cévennes, Marsin replaced him and the successes ended.

Nor where the French armies any luckier in their next campaign on the Northern front: there, Villeroy, released from captivity, led them against Marlborough. The mismatch was grotesque, and catastrophes promptly followed. The Coalition retook the whole of the Lower Rhine and, on July 2, 1704, inflicted a bloody defeat on the French at Donauworth; then, as if that were not bad enough, the maréchal de Tallard, in a rare show of incompetence, partly, it must be said, directed from Versailles, decided to attack the Anglo-Germans. On August 13, just outside the village of Blenheim, Marlborough showed the world that he was a commander of genius; as for the French, they lost twelve thousand men killed, fourteen thousand prisoners, twelve hundred officers taken prisoner and all the materiel: it was a defeat such as France had not experienced in centuries.

The news reached Versailles in the middle of the festivities celebrating the birth of a son† to the Bourgognes; it was Mme de Maintenon who told the King, and he promptly showed the world that no disaster could crush him. A new army was brought forth, Villars recalled from the Cévennes and, because the Coalition often failed to function smoothly, in 1705, the maréchal was at least able to prevent Marlborough from progressing further. Even now, after a catastrophe and four years of war, the French borders remained unbreached: it showed how very far the kingdom had come under Louis XIV's reign.

Unfortunately, the war was also going badly in Spain. On August 4, 1704, the English took Gibraltar,‡ and an attempt by an army under the comte de Tessé and a fleet under the comte de Toulouse failed to retake it; then, in March 1705, an English fleet, while not actually beating the French, forced it to leave Spanish waters. Toulouse had fought bravely, yet prudently; but from then on the British navy was mistress of the sea.

Almost worse, that spring, the English under Lord Peterborough took Barcelona, then the largest city in Spain and the whole kingdom of Valencia. The Archduke followed them and assumed the regnal name of Charles III: Spain now had two kings and no one could tell anymore which of the two would win.

In Madrid, too, Louis XIV was encountering serious problems. Mme des Ursins, who was governing Spain almost singlehanded, had begun to develop her own policies. Worse, she embarked on a long and bitter quarrel with Louis XIV's new envoy, the cardinal d'Estrées. At first, the princess thought to get rid of him by begging Louis XIV for permission to come through Versailles on her way to retirement in Rome; but the King, while urging her to remain in place, did not recall his Ambassador. At the same time, he tried very

† The duc de Bretagne. He died a year later.
‡ Gibralter is still a British colony.

hard to strengthen his grandson. "I would be very pleased to hear that you are behaving like the master," he wrote Philip on May 5, 1703, "and not to have any more reports that you have to be provided with an opinion on the least little things. It would almost be better for you to make small mistakes on occasion because you have followed your own impulses than to avoid them by taking other people's advice."[275]

That was asking too much. Mme des Ursins wanted the cardinal d'Estrées recalled so, naturally, Philip V wrote his grandfather to that effect. On June 24, Louis XIV wrote back, agreeing to the recall—at some future date—and then the Cardinal himself asked to go home, adding: "Were I to do otherwise, it would be thought that I had been fooled by his enemies; you would also be blamed for it . . . it would be said that Court intrigues are no less powerful now than under the late King's reign."[276] Coming from a monarch who loathed intrigue, this evocation of the late Court was a sharp warning to the princess; and when the latter broke open a dispatch from Versailles addressed to the Ambassador, Louis XIV struck: on April 11, 1704, on his order, Mme des Ursins was sent away from Madrid and told to reside in the South of France.

Even that drastic measure failed to reestablish harmony. Philip and Maria Luisa had obeyed—they had no other choice—but, from then on, they begged tirelessly for the princess's return while the lack of a firm guiding hand became more evident every day. On August 20, the King wrote wearily: "You ask me for advice; I wrote you what I think but nothing is any use if you wait until it is too late before you either ask me or act on my advice . . . You cannot succeed while your government is in such disorder."[277] It was not proving easy to govern Spain from Versailles; Philip's incapacity was too great; his subordination to his wife too absolute; her need for Mme des Ursins too complete. So, in an unprecedented reversal, and in order to avoid a complete collapse of the Spanish Government, on November 16, after yet another pleading letter from Maria Luisa, Louis XIV gave the princess permission to come to Versailles: it was obvious that she would be sent back to Madrid from there.

This victory of an elderly lady over the Sun King was all the more remarkable that, in France itself, obedience was absolute. "The old maréchal de Villeroy, who knew the Court well," Saint-Simon noted, "said amusingly that one should hold the chamberpot for the ministers while they are in office, and pour it over their head as soon as one sees that their power is beginning to slip."[278] Indeed, only the King mattered: it was the very reverse of the situation in 1660; and as if to make it all clearer still, defeats or no, Louis XIV saw to it that Versailles remained as splendid as ever. The appointed festivities were held at their unchanging times, the King moved from Versailles to Trianon, Marly, or Fontainebleau as always, work continued on a new chapel for the Palace, and even if money began to be sorely lacking, nothing was allowed to change the routine of the Court.

As for the courtiers, they were more cowed than ever, although even they thought some flattery went too far. The abbé de Polignac, Saint-Simon tells us, "was a guest on every trip to Marly, and all vied for the charms of his company; . . . [but] with all his intelligence, he let go a piece of flattery whose exaggeration was widely noticed . . . He was following the King in the gardens of Marly; it began to rain; the King said something polite about his clothes which would not keep him dry. 'That is nothing, Sire,' he answered. 'The rain at Marly is not wet.' "[279]

It was, in fact, at Marly that Louis XIV received Mme des Ursins on January 10, 1705; but already four days earlier, he had written to his new Ambassador at Madrid, the duc de Grammont: "You know my grandson's weakness . . . The Queen will always control him. We must try and use her power rather than destroy it . . . The King of Spain must not be told what I think of him . . . Try to gain the Queen's confidence, don't let her think you are trying to remove her from the government."[280] As a result, Mme des Ursins's stay with the French Court was triumphant. There were long, private conversations with the King and Mme de Maintenon; special favors were granted her brothers; and when, on June 15, 1705, she left on her way to Spain, it was clear that she would stay there for good.

Never before, in forty-four years of personal reign had Louis XIV allowed a subject thus to defeat his intentions: it is much to his praise that, in this one instance, he was flexible enough to bend: the war could not be won, indeed would certainly be lost, without Mme des Ursins's work in Madrid.

Almost equally surprising is the fact that at this great age the King managed to work harder than ever. After the severe illnesses of earlier years, he seems to have quite regained his health. In the course of the year 1705, for instance, he suffered briefly from gout in mid-

March, had a cold in mid-April accompanied by a severe attack of gout, and except for fairly prolonged diarrhea in late August, and again in October, he remained well until December 23 when he vomited dead worms with, however, no apparent aftereffect.[281] Considering that he was purged at least once a month (with up to ten consequent evacuations) and not infrequently bled, it seems obvious that he had an extraordinarily strong constitution. Still, in April, because of his gout, he discontinued the grand coucher, that ceremony in which he undressed and went to bed before the entire Court: henceforth only a small circle of servants and courtiers remained.

That, however, entailed no diminution in splendor. While the duchesse du Maine, on her side, gave ever grander receptions, the balls at Marly and Versailles in January and February 1706 showed the world that the King of France could fight the rest of Europe and not feel it; but on January 1, 1707, Louis XIV at last found himself forced to retrench sharply in the amount of the customary New Year's presents to the royal family.

There were other changes, too: in 1707, for the first time, the King decided that, much as he disliked giving his relatives any chance to shine, he could no longer afford not to use them: the duc d'Orléans, at long last, was given an effective command,* that of the French army in Spain. It was on that occasion that the King's hatred of religious heterodoxy once again surfaced. Upon Louis XIV's having asked his nephew of whom his staff consisted, "M. le duc d'Orléans named, among others, Fontpertuis. 'What!, nephew,' the King retorted with emotion, 'the son of that madwoman who used to follow M. Arnaud everywhere, a Jansenist? I will not have that sort of person near you.'

" 'Well, Sire,' M. d'Orléans answered, 'I do not know what the mother did, but as for the son, a Jansenist! Why, he does not even believe in God.'

" 'Is that possible?' the King said. 'And are you quite sure? If it is so, all is well and you can take him along.' "[282] It was no wonder that Fénelon's exile was never rescinded.

That Louis should be entrusting his nephew with an army showed how very worried he was: while to the outside world he seemed more self-confident than ever, Blenheim had shown him clearly that

---

* He had campaigned the year before under Marsin in Italy, but in a purely ornamental capacity.

defeat was no longer impossible. Already in 1704, in the deepest secrecy, approaches had been made to Heinsius, the Grand Pensionary of Holland, but to no avail. France would have to fight on; and the war was almost impossibly costly: while, in Colbert's lifetime, the budget tended to run around 100 million livres and to be very close to balance, by 1706, it had gone up to 220 million with a deficit of nearly 170 million; the Debt, obviously, was growing by leaps and bounds; and the State, once again, was dependent on the good will of financiers.

Clearly, however, there was no hope other than to endure. In Italy, at least, the war was going well. On August 16, 1705, Vendôme actually defeated Prince Eugene at Cassano; and on April 19, 1706, he trounced one of the Prince's lieutenants in his absence at the battle of Calcinato; indeed, it looked as if the strongly fortified city of Turin, the Duke of Savoy's capital would soon be taken.

Elsewhere, unfortunately, the French continued to be beaten. Blending the qualities of a statesman with those of a general, the Duke of Marlborough managed to keep the Coalition together, its armies trained and supplied and its finances prosperous; and on May 23, 1706, he trounced the maréchal de Villeroy yet again, this time near the little town of Ramillies. It was another Blenheim, and the appalled Villeroy was so terrified of writing the news to Versailles that he waited five days to do so; but when he reappeared at Court, far from punishing him, Louis XIV simply said: "Monsieur le maréchal, one is no longer lucky at our age."[283]

As if it had not been disastrous enough in itself, Ramillies had yet another consequence. Convinced at last that Villeroy was not the commander to oppose Marlborough, the King called Vendôme back from Italy; and the moment he was gone the French army, poorly led by the duc de la Feuillade, Chamillart's son-in-law, so mismaneuvered as to give the returning Prince Eugene a strong advantage: not only was Turin not taken, but Marsin lost a battle before the city on September 7, 1706, in which virtually all the materiel was taken by the enemy. Marsin himself died soon after of his wounds: that, cruelly enough, was the only silver lining. By the end of the month, France had lost the area around Mantua, Milan and the Piedmont, while, with the help of the British Navy, Austria had taken Naples: no matter where Louis XIV looked, there was only disaster to be seen.

As for Chamillart, who had the jobs once held by Colbert *and* Louvois, he begged the King to let him resign. "He wrote the King," Saint-Simon noted, "a pathetic letter asking for relief: he made plain the sad state of affairs, and added that he could not remedy them due to lack of time and strength . . . and ended by saying frankly that all must perish unless a remedy were found. He always left a wide empty margin where the King wrote his comments in his own hand. Chamillart showed me this one after it had come back to him: I saw with great surprise that the King's short comment ended with: 'Well, we will perish together.' "[284]

Indeed, the fates had clearly turned against France: at least the Emperor Leopold had been slow and inefficient; but in 1705, he died and was succeeded by his son, who took the name of Joseph I. The new Emperor was more energetic and intelligent than his father; he worked hard for the success of his brother's candidacy to the Spanish throne and proved a dangerous enemy.

In Spain, too, there was nothing but disaster. In spite of repeated attempts, the siege of Barcelona failed and Philip V was forced to retreat into Navarre, while Anglo-Portuguese troops under a French Protestant exile, M. de Ruvigny, who had been created Earl of Galloway by William III, advanced deep into Spain, until, on June 26, 1706, he entered Madrid, where the Archduke joined him.

The very extent of this reversal, however, turned out to be helpful: Philip V was popular because he was the late King's chosen heir, Maria Luisa was loved for her energy. In a few weeks, she raised money from the cities as yet not taken by the British; the people and the Grandees alike observed the oath they had sworn to Philip; and, at the head of a reconstituted army, he defeated Galloway and reentered Madrid on September 26.

It was, clearly, a major success, not least because Spain had shown conclusively it would not settle for the Archduke, or, indeed, any other candidate chosen by foreign powers. Of course, it comforted Louis XIV in his determination to save his grandson's crown; but, right near him, someone almost as powerful was ready to end the war on almost any terms.

From the very beginning Mme de Maintenon had opposed the war; indeed, her opinion, as expressed to the Council, owed more to her desire to placate Monseigneur—who would be king when his father died—than to her own conviction. From the very first, she had lamented the strain imposed by the conflict and predicted that things would go from bad to worse; now that they had, her jeremiads were even more constant and more lamentable. In 1706 and 1707, she came to a parting of the ways with her old friend Mme des Ursins who, whether from Navarre or from Madrid, constantly promised ultimate victory while asking for more men and more money. Mme de Maintenon, on the contrary, kept repeating that, for reasons unknown, God had decided to punish France; that it was futile to fight his decrees; and that therefore peace, any peace, must be the sole object, even if it entailed leaving the Spanish inheritance to the Archduke.

The King, of course, was fully aware of the marquise's position; indeed, except for Mme des Ursins, he met with nothing but despair and defeatism wherever he turned; but, for a short while, the wind seemed to turn: on April 25, 1707, the maréchal de Berwick defeated the Anglo-Portuguese at the battle of Almanza; and this great success was followed up by the duc d'Orléans, who had just joined the army: Lerida, along with several less important fortresses was taken; and from then on, in Spain at least, there was a hope of ultimate victory.

Unfortunately, the reverse was true on the other fronts: France itself was now under attack. In August 1707, Toulon was besieged and Provence ravaged by the Duke of Savoy. The city resisted and the siege failed, but troops had to be sent there which were needed elsewhere. In order to strengthen the fighting spirit of the army on the northern front, therefore, the duc de Bourgogne was sent off to command with Vendôme as his second; and it was understood that the prince would heed the maréchal's advice. At this point, the human element came into play. No two men could have been more unlike: Bourgogne was serious, pious, conventional—and legitimate. Vendôme was brilliant, an atheist, a debauchee whose tastes favored young men, a cynic, and the illegitimate grandson of Henri IV. Enmity soon developed between the two commanders; Marlborough took advantage of this; and the loss of Oudenarde on July 11, 1708 was followed by that of Tournai, Gand and Ypres, while, at the same time, an attempt at landing the Pretender in Scotland failed utterly.

Worse was yet to come. Advancing irresistibly, Prince Eugene lay siege to Lille, a city which had been strongly fortified by Vauban and was reputed to be proof against all attack. No one supposed that it could, in fact, be taken; but to the despair of the French, taken it was on October 28; after that, Gand, Bruges and all the remaining French strongholds in Flanders fell as well. And since Joseph I now held sway in Italy, he forced the Pope, who had recognized Philip V as King of Spain in 1701 to switch his endorsement to the Archduke, while, in 1708, the British conquered Sardinia.

All the while, the war continued to be enormously costly; Chamillart relied almost entirely on a small group of financiers to provide him with the necessary funds; up to a point they did, but, not unnaturally, the interest rates rose while the sums loaned shrank; finally, quite overcome by the endless difficulties he faced, Chamillart succeeded in convincing the King he must resign; so he kept the ministry of War while the competent Nicolas Desmarets succeeded him as Contrôleur Général. Under other circumstances, Desmarets might have proved a great minister; as it was, he did his best to keep the government afloat, and no greater praise can be given him than to say that, with the greatest difficulty, he succeeded.

Of course, that entailed subterfuges of every kind. Offices were sold by the dozen; the gold currency was repeatedly debased; a limited paper currency was introduced; taxes were raised; and borrowing went on apace. The King, well aware of the situation, helped when he could: the story of Samuel Bernard's walk in Marly is a case in point. Bernard, the greatest of the French financiers, had already lent vast sums; when, in the spring of 1708, Desmarets approached him yet again, he refused to buy any more government paper. At that, and after consulting with the King, the Contrôleur Général invited him to Marly, where he had followed the Court, for yet another meeting. Bernard came. That day, around five, Louis XIV set out for one of his walks around the gardens. Saint-Simon tells us what happened next. "At the next pavilion, the King stoppped; it was that of Desmarets who came out of it with Samuel Bernard, the famous banker . . . The King told Desmarets that he was pleased to see him with M. Bernard, then, turning to the latter: 'You are just the man never to have seen Marly. Come and walk through it with me, I will return you to Desmarets afterward.' Bernard followed, and, all through the walk, the King talked only to Bergeyck† and to him, taking them everywhere and showing them everything with all the

† One of Philip V's generals.

grace he knew so well how to use when he wanted to reward someone. I admired, and many others with me, this kind of prostitution of
the King's, who spoke so sparsely [to his courtiers] for a man like
Bernard . . .

"Bernard was duped. He came back to Desmarets from his walk
with the King so enchanted that, straightaway, he said he would
rather risk being ruined than deny a prince who had treated him so
well."[285] For a man whose birth precluded his ever being admitted to
the Court, who, indeed, could never expect even a single word from
the King, this was the most dazzling treatment. It is sad to have to
record that Bernard was indeed ruined: within a few years, he had
gone bankrupt.

Around the King, throughout these difficult years, the familiar
faces grew fewer. In 1707, Vauban, the great engineer, died, and so
did Mme de Montespan: Louis deplored the former and ignored the
latter; and in 1708, Mansart, the architect of Versailles, followed
them; but much as he, and some few others, might be missed, nothing apparently made any difference: indefatigable, indomitable, and,
indeed, scarcely human, the King continued on his appointed
rounds.

An incident which occurred in 1708 was further proof of that, if
any was needed. "Mme la duchesse de Bourgogne was pregnant,"
Saint-Simon noted. "She was feeling very unwell. The King wanted
to go to Fontainebleau, against precedent, at the beginning of the
good weather‡ and had said so. In the meantime, he wanted to make
stays at Marly. His granddaughter amused him, he could not do
without her, but so much movement did not suit her condition. Mme
de Maintenon was worried about this, Fagon* kept tactfully mentioning her fragility: this bothered the King, who was accustomed to
having his own way in everything, and had been spoiled by the fact
that his mistresses traveled when pregnant or just after they had
given birth, and wore court dress throughout it all. The remonstrances about the trips to Marly annoyed him but he did not cancel
them . . . The Saturday [following one of these], the King was taking a walk after Mass . . . when we saw the duchesse du Lude coming alone, on foot, at a time when there was no other lady with the
King . . . He understood she had something urgent to tell him: he

‡ Louis XIV usually stayed in Fontainebleau during the month of October.
* The King's First Physician.

went toward her and when he came close to her, we stopped and left them alone. The conversation was short. She left and the King came back to us . . . without saying anything. Everybody had guessed what the matter must be and no one was in a hurry to say anything. In the end, the King . . . looking at the most important people there but without speaking to anyone in particular, said, looking annoyed: 'The duchesse de Bourgogne has miscarried.'

"Immediately, M. de La Rouchefoucauld began to lament, M. de Bouillon, the duc de Tresmes and the maréchal de Boufflers joined him, then M. de La Rouchefoucauld went on to say, louder still, that it was the greatest misfortune in the world, that having had other miscarriages she might not have any more children. 'And even if it were so,' the King, who until now had said nothing, interrupted angrily, "why should I care? Doesn't she already have a son?† And even if he died, is the duc de Berry not able to marry and have children of his own? And why should I care which of them succeeds me! Are they not all equally my [great] grandsons?' And immediately, he went on impetuously: 'Thank God she has miscarried, since she was going to miscarry, and I will no longer be annoyed about my trips by the representations of the doctors and the reasonings of the women. I will come and go as I please and will no longer be bothered.' A silence such that one could have heard an ant walking followed this outburst."[286]

The King's outburst was due, no doubt, to disappointment; but it is true he was often especially intolerant to members of his family. Only a month earlier, a series of incidents in Spain deprived France of one of her best commanders. Louis XIV had never trusted the duc d'Orléans, his nephew (and son-in-law), simply because he was his nephew, and therefore potentially dangerous. Still, he did give him a command in Spain for lack of another competent general; but, once there, the duc behaved in the way best calculated to affront both the King and Mme de Maintenon. Because the war was going so badly, a group of Spanish grandees thought that a way out of it might be to replace Philip V, who was a potential heir to the French throne, by the duc d'Orléans, who was much further down the line of succession. The duc listened without agreeing; Philip V heard about it and, convinced that there was a plot to send him back to France, reported

† The second duc de Bretagne, born in 1705.

all this to his grandfather. Nothing was better calculated to reawaken the King's memories of the Fronde, and he behaved accordingly: in short order the duc d'Orléans was recalled; and although innocent, he never again commanded an army.

As if this were not bad enough there was the story of the insulting toast. Upon arriving in Madrid, Orléans had found neither the supplies, nor the money, he had been led to expect; and since Mme des Ursins was visibly in control, he blamed her for these shortages. In fact, Spain was in such a dreadful state that her lateness did not necessarily imply a dereliction of duty. Still, the duc was infuriated; and at the end of a dinner with his officers, in the course of which the wine had not been spared, he raised his glass. "Messieurs," he said, "here is to the health of Captain Cunt and Lieutenant Cunt."[287] No one there doubted that he meant Mmes de Maintenon and des Ursins, nor did the two ladies when, in very short order, they heard about the toast, and any possibility that Louis XIV might forgive the duc disappeared.

At the same time, a court intrigue very nearly succeeded in ruining the duc de Bourgogne. Monseigneur disliked his eldest son; he was on terms of the closest friendship with Madame la Duchesse who, being illegitimate, hated the real princes and was close to the duc de Vendôme. When the campaigns of 1708 and 1709 went badly, therefore, this cabal saw its chance and openly blamed the duc de Bourgogne for not listening to Vendôme and thus being the cause of the current disasters. The story was plausible, and only partly wrong: it was widely believed, and even the King, it was noticed, spoke little and coldly about his grandson. It was not until the end of the second campaign that, having returned to Versailles, and with his wife's help, the duc was able to convince his grandfather that he had, in fact, done his best. As a result, and to Monseigneur's rage, the cabal failed. Vendôme was greeted more than coldly, the duc de Bourgogne was taken back into the fold; and with that, the split in the Court became deep and permanent.

Dreadful as the situation was in the fall of 1708, the King soon realized that it was rapidly getting worse. One reason for that was the weather: in 1708–9, the cold came early, grew deeper than in living memory and stayed, it seemed endlessly, ruining much of France's agriculture. On January 19, 1709, Madame wrote her cousin: "Nobody can remember its being so cold. For the last two weeks there have been reports every morning of people who have died of the cold; partridges are found frozen in the fields. All the theaters have closed, trials are postponed, neither the présidents nor the conseillers can remain in their courts because it is too cold."[288] On February 2, she went on, to her aunt, the Electress Sophia of Hanover: "The cold is so horrible here that nothing like this, they say, has happened since 1606. In Paris only, 24,000 people have died between January 5 and today."[289]

And still the cold got worse. At Versailles, the ink froze in the King's inkpot; in Paris, and the rest of France, people died of the cold and of starvation: as always in a crisis, the stocks of grain proved insufficient; and it was obvious that the next crop would be substantially smaller than usual. Already on June 8, Madame was writing her cousin: "The famine is so violent now that children have eaten one another. The King is so thoroughly decided to continue fighting the war that this morning he sent his entire gold service to the Mint, plates, platters, salt cellars, in a word all the gold he had, to be coined into louis."[290]

In a preindustrial age, when a country's prosperity depended to a large extent on agriculture, this kind of winter was a severe blow; and while Madame complained of the discomfort at Versailles, people not only starved but were ruined. Of course, the immediate consequence of this situation was to aggravate the financial crisis: with commerce virtually stopped—for months on end it was too cold to move goods—and with money scarce, taxes yielded much less than usual. Given the already critical situation of the Treasury, this seemed like the last blow, and so his ministers told the King. As for Mme de Maintenon, her lamentations reached a new degree of intensity. Here was another proof that God intended to punish France, she said: better yield now before something even worse happened.

In fact, although the marquise was a true representative of that odd strain in the French character which has, on occasion, caused some of its citizens to wallow in defeat, the situation did seem nearly hopeless: not only could the war not be won, but also there seemed to be no reason why the defeats of earlier years would not be repeated; and so, in an act of real courage and utter selflessness, Louis XIV decided to sacrifice his pride, his *gloire,* and the union with Spain.

First there was a Council in which the duc de Beauvillier gave so dire an account of the state of the country that the duc de Bourgogne burst into tears, as did several of the ministers. Chamillart and Desmarets both painted the bleakest of pictures; and Torcy concluded that peace at any price must now be France's new policy. It was then decided that secret approaches would be made to the Coalition; and when these were ignored, Torcy, the Foreign Minister, volunteered to go to the Hague in person to beg for peace. He arrived there, incognito, on May 22, 1709. It was an unheard-of humiliation, but the King had agreed to this as well.

Given this situation, it should have been easy to make peace. In fact, the Allies, drunk with their victories, decided to ask for more than anyone might have thought possible. First, they demanded Strasbourg and Brisach, both still firmly held by France, then Holland was to be given ten fortified cities in Flanders; that might, probably, have been accepted; but then came a demand that Philip V give up the Spanish throne within two months; and, the Allies added, should he refuse to do so, France must then eject him militarily: it was the famous Article IV of these Preliminaries. Finally, in exchange for all this, the Allies would only give France an armistice (as opposed to a peace treaty): there was no guarantee that they would not start the war again.

"If I have to make war," Louis XIV said when these demands were read out to the Council, "then I would rather fight my enemies than my children."[291] That position, however logical, was not shared by many: a majority of the ministers continued to prefer peace at any price, and so did Mme de Maintenon, who not only craved an end of the war, but would also have enjoyed watching the discomfiture of her erstwhile friend, Mme des Ursins; for by now the two ladies, having adopted opposed political positions, had become out and out enemies.

At this point, it would have been easier for the King to give in: that he decided to go on fighting shows the extent of his courage; but he knew so well that the war was unpopular that, for the first time, he decided to justify himself to his subjects. A declaration was sent, on June 12, 1709, to the governors of the various provinces, to be printed and posted everywhere. Not only is it of interest as the first such communication ever made by a French government to its people, it also shows the King at his best.

"The hope of peace has been so widespread in the realm that I feel I owe to the fidelity shown me by my people in the course of my reign the consolation of informing them of the reasons why they do not yet enjoy the rest I had intended to give them. I had accepted, to that effect, conditions thoroughly opposed to the safety of my border provinces: but the easier I showed myself, the more I tried to dissipate the concerns my enemies claim they still feel about my power and my future plans, and the more they multiplied their demands; so that, adding, degree by degree, new demands to those they had made at the beginning . . . they showed that their purpose was to enlarge our neighboring states at our expense, and to open roads on which they could invade my kingdom whenever it suited them to fight a new war." Then the King explained that he would have been forced to carry through all the provisions of the Preliminaries within two months without having a peace treaty in exchange, so that, France having become far more vulnerable, there would have been nothing to stop the Coalition from attacking her anew.

"I do not even mention," the King went on, mentioning them, "the requests they made that I join my troops to theirs so as to force my grandson off his throne, if he refused to leave it voluntarily . . . Such an alliance would have been against all humanity. But even though my love for my people is no less than that I feel for my own children; even though I share all the suffering caused by the war to such faithful subjects and have shown Europe that I sincerely desired peace, I am convinced that they [his subjects] would refuse to seek it under circumstances so contrary to justice and the honor of France."[292]

That being said, there was nothing to do except continue the fighting; and after all those years, and all his attempts at resigning, the King finally decided to replace Chamillart. Daniel Voysin, a hardworking and competent administrator, succeeded him; and like Desmarets he remained in place until the end of the reign. The two ministers discharged their impossible tasks as successfully as possible, making many enemies in the process; and, henceforth the Council included them both, along with Torcy, and the duc de Beauvillier, the duc de Bourgogne, and Monseigneur.

All through 1709, the defeats continued. First Marlborough took Tournai; then he set siege to Mons; and the maréchal de Villars, who had been transferred to the northern army as the last best hope of France, decided to seek a battle. He found it on September 11 near the little town of Malplaquet; and although the French only lost eight thousand to the enemy's twenty-one thousand dead, the victory remained with Marlborough, who had broken the French center: once again, it seemed that the Coalition could not lose. And, of course, Mons was taken.

At least in August the maréchal du Bourg defeated an Imperial army on the Rhine and preserved Alsace from invasion; but since it seemed all too clear that France could never win the war, Louis XIV went on trying to negotiate. It took both courage and endurance to do this: nothing is harder than to go on fighting when you are treating for peace. Early in 1710, the maréchal d'Huxelles and the abbé de Polignac were sent off to the little Dutch town of Gertruydenberg, where they were treated as virtual prisoners; but no matter how much Louis XIV was willing to concede—and at one point, it included paying the Coalition troops that would be fighting in Spain—neither Marlborough nor the imperial Ambassador, Count Zinzendorff would settle for anything less that the expulsion of Philip V by the French army itself. That the Austrians, who wanted Spain for the Archduke, should have been so demanding is not surprising; but it is startling to find Marlborough, that astute negotiator, adopting the same position.

Of course, that, too, can be explained. Back in England, Marlborough's wife, the redoubtable Sarah, once Queen Anne's closest friend, had now lost the royal favor; and in the same way, the Queen, who was tired of the war, was beginning to look with favor on the Tories. Should the war end quickly, therefore, the Marlboroughs had a good deal to lose; but if it went on, the Duke remained the indispensable man. Under these circumstances, it made perfect sense for Marlborough to back the Austrian demands even if they were unreasonable.

As for the war itself, it continued unabated; and 1710 proved disastrous for France; in June, Douai and Béthune were taken while, in August, Prince Starhemberg, who commanded the Coalition troops, inflicted a major defeat on Philip V's army, so it began to look as if that situation might resolve itself by the collapse of the Franco-Spanish forces; but, later that month, the King and Vendôme together triumphed at the battle of Villaviciosa, crushing Starhemberg and ensuring their continued superiority.

At Versailles, where the Treasury was empty, the King insisted on maintaining the splendor of the Court virtually unabated as a way of impressing the Coalition with his ability to fight on; but there were no New Year's presents on January 1, and the guests at Marly were, henceforth, required to provide their own food. And there was at least one happy event: on February 15, the duchesse de Bourgogne gave birth to another son, who was promptly titled duc d'Anjou. Since she already had a five-year-old son, the duc de Bretagne, the succession was doubly assured; and Louis XIV became the only King in the history of France to have two great-grandsons living and in the direct line of succession.

Abroad, too, changes were taking place which clearly favored France: on August 7, Queen Anne dismissed Godolphin, Marlborough's close ally, and promoted two of the leading Tories, Harley and Saint John, with the enthusiastic approval of her new favorite, Abigail Masham. Then, at the end of September, Parliament was dissolved, and the elections brought in a solid Tory majority. Although the government promptly confirmed Marlborough's appointments, it was clear that it would also try to end the war: after a long season of despair, the French had reason to hope again, for, without Great Britain, the Coalition was powerless.

These promising developments might be the subject of much comment at Versailles, but still the war went on; and for five years at least, it seemed as if Louis XIV had borne every one of its burdens. "Our King's face is tremendously changed," Madame noted, "but he still looks strong and awe-inspiring, and when he speaks he is still pleasant."[293] That he should have been was nothing short of miraculous. We know just how difficult his life had become, partly through Mme de Maintenon's letters, partly through Torcy's journal. Scenes like the one which took place on January 27, 1710, were frequent, and greatly added to the King's already unbearable burden.

That evening, Torcy had suggested sending negotiators to The Hague without further delay. "The King said it was fantastic, and almost stupid, for me to think that one day more or less would make a difference in this kind of negotiation. He stormed against those who spoiled everything by this sort of hurry, and by the way in which they let the enemy know they were eager to conclude at any cost. These reproaches were directed principally to M. de Beauvillier, whom His Majesty named, but I was next, for when I pointed out that it was necessary to anticipate the arrival of Prince Eugene and of the Duke of Marlborough . . . the King did me the honor of saying that he was surprised to hear me urge this when I was the slowest of negotiators. I must admit I did not understand the reason for these reproaches or how I had deserved them, since, far from delaying the execution of my orders, I often acted even before receiving them; but as our masters never think they are wrong, I remained silent and tried to profit from this mortification, coming as it did after so many others.

"This happened in Mme de Maintenon's room. From her bed, she urged the King to end so important a piece of business. He resisted, fought back, finally gave in, and told me to bring in the letters the next morning."[294] The next day, in fact, the King delayed sending the negotiators.

From the tone of this entry, Torcy's resentment of the King is clear; he was a minister who carried out a policy he detested on the orders of a king he thought tyrannical and unfair. It is a far cry from the attitude of a Louvois or a Colbert, and cannot have made Louis XIV's life easier; as for Mme de Maintenon's nagging, it never stopped: neither in his moments of relaxation, nor in his Council could the King ever count on any sort of support; his choice was between sullen obedience—Torcy—and bitter reproach from the marquise. The Council itself, in fact, steadfastly opposed the continuation of the war: Beauvillier, Torcy and Desmarets wanted peace at any price; the Chancellor often joined them; the duc de Bourgogne usually agreed with Beauvillier, but did not say so since, after all, it was his brother whose throne was tottering. Only Monseigneur backed continued assistance to Spain; in fact, much to everyone's surprise, he became positively outspoken, once even reminding the ministers that he would be king some day, and that if they had abandoned his son, they would suffer for it. In 1710, Louis XIV was seventy-two: Monseigneur's threat was by no means idle.

Still, the laments continued. Here are Torcy's notes on the Council of February 19. "The state of affairs is deplorable. Money is lacking altogether. There is no credit. The troops cannot be raised again. Officers and soldiers are dying of want: there are no supplies, no means of getting any. No one knows how the army will subsist through the next campaign. It is even doubtful it can fight at all. No generals to lead it. It is not sure whether the maréchal de Villars's wound will allow him to serve, and even if he can, where to find the necessary resources? . . . He speaks only of forcing the enemy to fight at the beginning of the campaign, and when told that the State would perish if he is then beaten, he agrees."[295]

Still, by mid-March, it had become clear that there was no choice but to fight: the Coalition was unwilling to treat seriously, in part, no doubt, because it expected future victories to make the French position more difficult still; so, yet again, Torcy came up with a way to placate the enemy. At the Council of March 26, he suggested giving Naples and Sicily to Philip V in exchange for Spain, and fighting him if he refused; that, of course, supposed Austria would agree since it was in possession of Naples. "M. le duc de Beauvillier was firmly opposed to my proposal," Torcy noted, "and spoke at length and eloquently on the injustice of making war on the King of Spain . . .

"Monseigneur le duc de Bourgogne supported him skillfully, speaking about injust wars as the pious and Catholic prince he is. It is not for me to say whether these maxims applied in this case.

"Monseigneur . . . said that there could never be any reason to fight the King of Spain.

"Everyone having spoken, the King, disturbed by all this, listening with chagrin to the sad discussion caused by this unhappy business, told me that he did not agree with me at all, that he would never promise or even consider fighting the King of Spain."[296] That was all very well, but both Torcy and, more important, Mme de Maintenon thought they knew better, and that, with time and effort, they would wear the King down; on May 9, for instance the marquise told her ally that there was no solution other than declaring war on Philip V, that there was not a moment to be lost; and that she only hoped it was not too late.

In spite of this frenzy of defeatism, the King, aging and sadder than ever before, retained his determination to fight on until he could negotiate a decent peace; and, within a few months, his steadfastness paid off. In January 1711, a secret emissary was sent by Harley, now Earl of Oxford and Saint John, now Viscount Bolingbroke, to France: the abbé Gautier, a priest belonging to the chapel of the Austrian Ambassador in London, was a man of no importance; but he could hardly have been listened to with more attention if he had been Queen Anne herself.

The two English ministers had good reasons, both to want peace and to be so secretive about it: not only were the Queen and the landowners tired of the war, its end would enable them to encompass

Marlborough's fall; but if their approaches became known, there might well be a patriotic reaction against them. Still, the negotiations started in earnest; then, on April 17, an event took place which changed the face of Europe: away in Vienna, the Emperor Joseph I died, and he was succeeded by his brother, the Archduke Charles, the claimant to the Spanish Crown.

All these years, England had been fighting a costly war so as to prevent the accretion of French power consequent on having a Bourbon as King of Spain; and even then, there was every expectation that the French and Spanish branches would remain separate; but now, at one blow, the new Emperor Charles VI would unite Spain and the Austrian possessions, thus creating just the sort of preponderance the English were determined to stop. As a result, peace became possible as long as there was a solemn undertaking on the part of France that the Spanish and French crowns would remain forever distinct.

It began to look, in fact, as if Great Britain was ruining itself for its allies, Austria and Holland, to whom the Flemish cities were to be given and who was, after all, a commercial rival; so the ministers, warmly supported by the Queen, began to negotiate in earnest; but after so long and so bitter a war, nothing was simple; and in the meantime, the fighting continued. Once again, Marlborough pushed the French back. Bouchain was taken in September 1711; there seemed to be virtually no obstacle between the armies of the Coalition and Paris; and these ill-timed victories substantially complicated the peace negotiations.

At that point, political reality took over: backed by a solid majority in the House of Commons, the government dismissed Marlborough from all his offices and tried him for peculation: 1711 had seen the last campaign to be fought by British troops. By 1712, a cease-fire was signed; and on July 19, Louis XIV turned the city of Dunkirk over to the English army under the Duke of Ormonde, Marlborough's replacement, as security for his undertakings in the forthcoming treaty. That, however, left Prince Eugene's army in the field. On July 6, he took Le Quesnoy and went on to besiege Landrecies. In June, the duc de Vendôme had died in Spain: if Prince Eugene reached Paris, if the French army in Spain, deprived of its commander was beaten, the war would be lost after all; and already Louis XIV was considering a move to the Loire in case Paris was taken.

It was at that point that the maréchal de Villars saved his country. He saw that Prince Eugene's lines at Landrecies were overextended and attacked at the nearby village of Denain on July 24; for the first time in many years, the French won a great victory, and they followed it up by taking Marchiennes six days later. In September and October, Douai, Le Quesnoy, and Bouchain were retaken: now it was the French who were going forward, and the enemy back.

These victories carried with them the obvious consequence: the Franco-British negotiations which had been taking place at Utrecht were greatly speeded up. Peace was now in sight. After disappearing behind a cloud of blood and tears, the sun came out again: at Versailles, the seventy-four-year-old King who, almost alone, had resisted the whole of Europe was proved right: never more than in those difficult years had he shown he was fully entitled to be called Louis le Grand.

XII
The Setting Sun

ALL THROUGH the war, as defeat followed defeat and the Treasury grew ever emptier, life at Versailles remained unchanged. The King followed his appointed rounds, surrounded by his vast family and vaster Court; and just as he seemed above the ordinary joys and sorrows of humanity, so it appeared that he would never age. In 1711, he was seventy-three—hardly a youth by our late-twentieth-century standards, extreme old age by those of the time, but he was still as vigorous, energetic, hardworking and imperious as he had been twenty years earlier. Then, in less than a year, between April 1711 and February 1712, everything changed. The King went on governing, it is true; the negotiations at Utrecht were successfully concluded; the war was brought to a not unfavorable end; but the King had begun to grow old.

Louis XIV's relationship to Monseigneur, his only legitimate child, had always been ambiguous: no one could tell whether there was any fondness between the two, but the King liked having his son around, and the Dauphin was nothing if not obedient. Similarly, while the fifty-year-old heir enjoyed no power of his own, he did belong to the Council, and the King probably welcomed the support he invariably gave to Philip V's interests. What is at any rate certain is that Monseigneur, that fat, awkward, and silent figure, was mostly a blank; still, as the heir to a monarch in his seventies, he had gained importance. A whole cabal was centered around him: it was expected that, when he finally succeeded, France would be ruled by a combination of the duc de Vendôme and Madame la Duchesse, and that anyone close to the Bourgognes would suffer in consequence.

Then, on April 9, 1711, the usually healthy Monseigneur fainted dead away as he was getting dressed; and by the next day he was suffering from a high fever which, within another forty-eight hours, turned out to be smallpox. That often deadly disease came, however, in several varieties, and it seemed clear that Monseigneur was suffering from one of its lightest forms. "Up to now," Madame commented on the twelfth, "the illness is going as it should, the fever is abating, the pustules are beginning to whiten, so we hope all will be well."[297] The King, who had had smallpox in his youth, moved to Meudon where the Dauphin had been stricken; the Bourgognes, neither of whom was immune, were ordered to stay at Versailles; and it was noticed that they held court, and were surrounded, much as if they were already the next heirs to the throne.

Until the fourteenth, the disease continued to progress in the most normal way, so much so that a deputation came from Paris to congratulate the Dauphin on his impending recovery; but when it announced that it was ordering a Te Deum, Monseigneur answered: "It is not time yet, wait until I am cured." That day, Madame continues, "I went to Meudon to congratulate the King on M. le Dauphin's being so much better . . . [At six o'clock], I saw the King, who received me very graciously; he told me I should not have complained so much when I had smallpox myself, and said that M. le Dauphin felt no discomfort. I answered that was yet to come, that the pustules would swell up and be painful. As I was about to leave, it was announced that M. le Dauphin was worried, that his head was much swollen; everybody thought that meant the pustules were beginning to suppurate and that it was a good sign . . . At nine, [at Versailles, where Madame had returned] news came again that all was well; but at ten there was a message that M. le Dauphin was beginning to be afraid, that his face was so swollen as to be unrecognizable; it was added that the eyes were especially affected. That was still not alarming; I supped at ten as usual; at eleven, I undressed and spoke for a moment with the maréchale de Clérembault*; I was then going to say my prayers and go to bed but, at midnight, I was very surprised to see the maréchale return in a very upset state; she said that M. le Dauphin was dying . . . A moment

* Madame's chief lady-in-waiting.

later, they came to tell me that it was all over, that M. le Dauphin was no longer alive.''[298]

That turn for the worst, in fact, came so quickly that there was time neither for a confession nor for the last rites before Monseigneur sank into a coma. As for the King, who was there, but not in the same room, he left immediately: the sacrosanct etiquette forbade the presence of the monarch in the same house as a corpse. ''As he came out to get into his carriage,'' Saint-Simon noted, ''he found Monseigneur's berlin before him; he waved it away because he could not bear to see it. He was not so stricken, however, that he did not call Pontchartrain to tell him to warn his father [the Chancellor] and the other ministers to come a little later than usual to Marly for the Council . . . He then had difficulty getting up into the carriage, being supported on both sides; Mme de Maintenon got in immediately after him . . . A crowd of officeholders from Monseigneur's Household was kneeling all along both sides of the courtyard as the King went by, begging him with strange shouts to have pity on them who had lost everything and would be starving.''[299]

That was, perhaps, the truest regret elicited by Monseigneur's death: no one seems to have missed him much; what his cabal regretted bitterly was the sudden loss of their prospects. All those who had counted on being powerful when he succeeded his father were now disappointed; worse, with his death, the duc de Bourgogne had become the next heir, and he was the very man Monseigneur's friends had been slandering so assiduously: their situation when he became king, therefore, was likely to be bleak in the extreme. There is, indeed, something exemplary about it all: those who expected power were cast down, those who expected virtual persecution were raised. Short of the King's own death there could not have been a greater revolution at Court.

As it was, great efforts were made to hide these emotions; but perhaps the most surprising piece of behavior came from the duc d'Orléans. This brave, kind and cultivated prince had been sedulously attacked by Monseigneur and his friends: he had every reason to rejoice, therefore, all the more that he was on good terms with the Bourgognes, and that his eldest daughter had just recently, to the Dauphin's great anger, married the duc de Berry, the youngest of his three sons. Once again, Saint-Simon was there, and we may trust his report all the more that he was on terms of real friendship with Orléans.

"How great was my surprise," the duc wrote, "when I saw the tears falling from his eyes. 'Monsieur!' I exclaimed, standing up suddenly in astonishment. He understood me and answered with difficulty, as he was truly crying: 'You are right to be surprised, and I am too, but the event touches me. He was not a bad man, I have known him all my life; he treated me well and with friendship as long as he was allowed to do so† . . . I realize that my sorrow cannot last; but it will be a few days before I feel all the reasons I have for being consoled considering what they had done to my relationship with him; but right now I feel the blood tie, the closeness, the humanity, all that touches me' "[300] In fact, with the possible exception of the King himself, Orléans was probably the only person at Versailles whose sorrow was so unselfish.

As for Louis XIV, it is not easy to know what he felt. For Madame, there was no doubt: "He is afflicted by such sorrow that it would soften a rock," she wrote her aunt, "and yet he does not give in but speaks to everyone with a settled sadness, but the tears often come to his eyes, and he swallows his sobs. I am deathly worried that he may become ill himself because he looks so terrible."[301] Torcy, who saw him the next day, gives a more complex picture. "We went to the King's *lever* at Marly," he noted. "Once it was over, His Majesty called in M. le Chancelier. He then had the other ministers come in but was hardly able to speak. His sorrow and his tears cut him short every time he tried to explain himself. He even said that, although deeply moved by his loss, he could not understand his condition, that yesterday he had not shed a tear, and that, right then, he could not stop himself from shedding them in abundance."[302]

Madame was, for all her irony, a simple woman; it seemed very natural to her that the King should be devastated by the loss of his son; but Torcy was more subtle; and Louis's own surprise at his sorrow is extremely telling. It is, of course, possible to think that he had not cried the evening before because he was still in shock, and that his tears the next day showed his true feelings; but there is also a case to be made for the fact that he did not, in fact, care much for Monseigneur; that his loss did not affect him deeply; and that it was the

† The cabal around the Dauphin had turned him thoroughly against the duc d'Orléans, but that was merely due to the prince's weakness, not to any real animosity.

shock, the sudden change, and the breaking of so old a relationship (distant though it was) which made him cry so abundantly the next morning.

What is certain, at any rate, is that, on the morning after his son's death, the King was functioning as usual. In the course of the meeting attended by Torcy, it was decided that the appellation of "Monseigneur" would be allowed to lapse and that henceforth the duc de Bourgogne would become known as M. le Dauphin.‡ Dispositions were taken to dispose of the late prince's belongings, a 12,000-livre pension was given to Mlle Choin, his morganatic wife; and that was the end of it: clearly, the King was anxious to put the whole situation behind him. Saint-Simon who, much though he disliked Louis XIV, could on occasion be singularly perceptive, noted: "Never was a man so easily given to shed tears, so inaccessible to real sorrow or so quickly back to his normal condition. He must have been strongly affected by the loss of a son who, although fifty years old, was still six as far as he was concerned . . . On Thursday already, he was amusing himself with the lists for Marly."[303] The duc is probably right; and, after all, the three people for whom the King really cared, Mme de Maintenon and the two Bourgognes were still alive. Finally, we know from Fagon's* journal that for several days after the Dauphin's death, Louis XIV suffered from headaches, exhaustion, and violent constipation.[304]

With Monseigneur's death, the Court took on a whole new complexion. The Bourgognes were eagerly sought, praised, surrounded. Monseigneur's former set, with the single exception of Madame la Duchesse, receded into the outer darkness. People who, like Saint-Simon, were part of the duc's small advisory group, and who had dreaded the accession of the Dauphin, now triumphed; and the King himself, who had already allowed his grandson access to the Council, frequently asked his opinion; more, for certain, less important matters, the ministers were told to work directly with him: clearly he was being prepared to rule.

That, no doubt, helped the King to get over his son's death; so did Mme de Maintenon's company. In September 1711, Madame noted that "Mme de Maintenon does not look her age at all. It is true that she is a little thinner, but she still looks very well."[305] In fact, to the

‡ To avoid confusion, he will still be called duc de Bourgogne here.
* The King's First Physician. A violent purge was administered on May 4.

end of her days, the marquise continued to look ageless; and her intelligence, her quickness of mind, her wit also persisted. More, it is virtually certain that the seventy-three-year-old King and his seventy-five-year-old wife continued to have an active sex life.

Unfortunately, the marquise also nagged—about the war, about the légitimés, about the future. She was, of course, far more secure with Monseigneur gone: the duchesse de Bourgogne, who called her *"ma tante,"* was genuinely fond of her: under the next reign she could look forward to the most favorable treatment. What would happen to the duc du Maine and the comte de Toulouse, however, was another matter: the new Dauphin was known not to approve of their meteoric rise; what one King had done another could undo; and Mme de Maintenon was audibly worried about it.

On the main topic of the day, however, she had increasingly less reason to lament: the war was clearly coming to a conclusion. The negotiations, speeded up by the political situation in London, were also helped by the fact that Philip V gave his grandfather all powers to treat in his name. That included the right of abandoning various component parts of the Spanish Empire in order to satisfy the other side. It was, given the length and bitterness of the war, an enlightened move on Philip's part, and the King took it accordingly.

"I assure you," he wrote his grandson on June 22, 1711, "that I care for your interests as much as for mine, and that it is with infinite chagrin that I must propose to you solutions we always find hard to bear when it is a question of losing a part of the States God has given us. But there are occasions when one must know how to lose, and if it means that you are the recognized ruler of Spain and the Indies, you will have no reason to regret the places you may cede to the English so as to gain the peace. I will use the powers you have given me to that end.

"God grant us success; for I think, by what I see of the state of your affairs, that peace is no less necessary to Your Majesty than it was last year, and that the situation is merely such as to make negotiations easier. Behave accordingly and believe that the only good advice is that which will bring peace while keeping you on your throne."[306]

This sort of cooperation, given earlier refusals to renounce anything at all, greatly eased the King's lot; and so did the undoubted popularity now gained by the Bourgognes. The duc, a serious, highly

pious and hardworking young man had always been a little with-
drawn: now he made himself far more accessible, and was found to
be immensely civil, fair and kind; as for the duchesse, she had always
charmed the Court as well as the King; as she became Dauphine, she
gave up her taste for childish games, which had made her seem
younger than her age, as well as an unfortunate propensity for flirting
which, in fact, may have gone very far indeed; and she applied herself to the duties of her new station with the most marked success. In
August, for instance, the usually critical Madame noted: "People are
quite right to praise M. le Dauphin. He deserves it. Mme la Dauphine is endearing herself to all by her politeness. Last Monday, I
was invited to have dinner with them; no one could have been more
polite than they were: they served me themselves. A whole dozen
duchesses was also there; they spoke to everyone."[307] Most important of all, the duchesse went on bringing youth, gaiety and happiness into Louis XIV's life. Indeed, one may well wonder whether he
would have withstood the disasters of the war so well if it had not
been for her cheerful presence.

Like all her contemporaries, the new Dauphine was subject to a
variety of fevers; and the treatment for these consisted of bleeding
and purging, a therapy which not infrequently inpaired the patient's
recuperative powers. Even without a physician's attendance, life, in
the early eighteenth century, was often short; but doctors were often
more to be feared, and more dangerous, than the multiplicity of
current diseases; thus, royal patients, who naturally were the most
medicated of all, were also the least likely to survive any serious
illness.

Still, no one worried when, in the afternoon of February 5, 1712,
the duchesse de Bourgogne began to shake with fever. She went to
bed, not attending the King after supper as was her invariable habit,
but got up the next morning and seemed quite recovered. That evening, the sixth, the fever returned; by Sunday morning it was much
less intense; and by noon it was assumed that the attack was over.
That evening around six, however, she suddenly felt a headache; it
was so painful that she asked the King, who was at her door, not to
come in, and she suffered greatly all that night. She was bled twice in
the morning, to no avail; then, on Monday afternoon, the eighth, the
pain decreased but the fever returned, stronger than ever. As a result, she became quite weak; that night, and until the tenth, her

condition remained much the same, except that she began showing the spots symptomatic of measles; an epidemic of that disease, conjoined with scarlet fever, was at this time sweeping Paris; it had already caused many deaths.

The treatment for this consisted of violent purgings and bleedings which, to the doctors' surprise, in no way improved the patient's condition; in fact, they must have weakened her considerably. From the very beginning the duc de Bourgogne remained at his wife's side. He was still there on the eleventh, when the fever went so high that it was thought prudent to administer the last rites. At seven o'clock that night, with the King in almost constant attendance, the duchesse was bled and purged yet again. By then, the duc had had to take to his bed with a violent fever. A little after eight the next evening, February twelfth, the young woman breathed her last. "Although you knew how very much I loved her," the desperate King wrote his grandson in Spain, "you still cannot begin to imagine how deeply her loss afflicts me."[308]

"With her," Saint-Simon noted, "vanished joy, pleasure, amusements even, and graces of all sorts. Darkness covered the entire Court. She had animated it all by herself; she was everywhere at once; she fascinated everyone; she understood all its innermost secrets. If the Court survived her, it was only in the most languishing way. Never was a princess so missed, and so deservedly."[309]

The distraught King immediately left with Mme de Maintenon for Marly; and on the thirteenth, the duc de Bourgogne, whose fever continued, joined them, largely so as not to hear the preparations for the funeral; the King, whom he visited, was appalled by the way he looked and called the doctors, who promptly sent him off to bed. Through the fourteenth and fifteenth, the fever grew worse, and the duc himself made it plain he did not expect to survive. On the sixteenth, the signs of measles appeared while the patient weakened. On the eighteenth, at eight-thirty in the morning, the duc de Bourgogne joined the wife he had so recently lost.

For the next eleven days, the King, who had never until now failed to hold Court, retired to his private apartment and saw no one except the ministers and Mme de Maintenon; and he had barely gone through the funeral ceremonies before yet another death was announced, that of the Bourgognes' eldest son, the six-year-old duc de Bretagne, of the same disease as his parents; there now only survived his younger brother, the two-year-old duc d'Anjou; and the doctors would no doubt have killed him as well, had his governess, Mme de Ventadour, not hidden him. Warmth, light food and time did their work: of all the King's direct heirs, only he survived. How long he would continue to do so no one could tell: infant mortality in the early eighteenth century was appallingly high.

"You will understand the excess of my sorrow," the King wrote Philip V, "when I tell you that the Dauphin is dead. In a few days God has demanded of me two terrible proofs of my submission to his commands. I pray that he will keep me Your Majesty and console us of the tragedy I will feel acutely as long as it will please Him to keep me alive."[310] No king of France before Louis XIV had ever lived to see three generations descended directly from him; none had ever lost a son, a grandson, and a great-grandson in less than a year; and with every prospect that the two-year-old Dauphin would follow his parents, it seemed a distinct possibility that the duc de Berry, that nice but stupid and uneducated young man, would one day succeed his grandfather.

Ever since the early Renaissance, sudden and spectacular deaths in royal families had been attributed to poison—a wholly unnecessary explanation given the lack of all hygiene and the ghastly state of medicine. Already, earlier in the reign, poison had been a popular explanation for the first Madame's death. Now, of course, more than ever, the rumors were rife. It seems obvious to us, in the twentieth century, that a severe attack of measles conjoined with scarlet fever represents a danger to life; and that, if the patient is pitilessly and constantly bled and purged, he (or she) is far more unlikely to recover. Indeed, the case of the little duc d'Anjou is exemplary: he alone was not hopelessly weakened by the barbaric treatment inflicted on his parents and elder brother; he alone survived.

In 1712, however, poison was the obvious answer. The rumors, no doubt, would have started without any assistance; but they were helped and encouraged by a dark and disgraceful plot. The duc du Maine was still the apple of Mme de Maintenon's eye, and she longed to have him made a real prince, able to succeed the crown; the duchesse du Maine, a tiny, lively and very bright young woman who was born a Condé was ferociously ambitious; and when suddenly the heirs to the throne consisted of a two-year-old child, whom everyone assumed would soon be dead; the duc de Berry, that mindless and easily managed young man; and the duc d'Orléans, the strategy was obvious—especially since Mme de Maintenon and her whole circle already hated him. If, indeed, people were convinced that he had poisoned the Bourgognes and their children, he would never be able to inherit the crown. It was known that, among his many interests, was chemistry; so rumors started circulating according to which he had distilled a special poison with which he had killed his cousins.

Suddenly, the duc d'Orléans found himself a marked man. At Court, people shunned him; in Paris, the crowds jeered as his carriage drove past; and still the rumors intensified until almost everyone believed them. At that point, and very properly, Orléans went to the King who assured him that he had paid no attention to the rumors, went on to say that he believed in his nephew's innocence and simply suggested he dismiss the chemist, Humbert, whom he kept as part of his household. Immediately, the duc answered that Humbert was as innocent as himself, and, to prove his point, he asked the chemist to enter the Bastille voluntarily so that he could be officially questioned and declared blameless.

Madame tells us what happened next. "My son having sent his Humbert to the Bastille to be examined, the King forbade his being received there; first because His Majesty does not believe what is said about my son, and also because all the doctors who were present at the autopsy of the two bodies say that neither showed any trace of poison, that Mme la Dauphine died of measles, and M. le Dauphin of bad air and sorrow."[311] Slowly, the gossip died down; but, once again, Louis XIV had shown that he was not easily swayed: with that admirable balance which so characterized him, and in spite of his own, bitter sorrow, he had seen through the plot. Besides, although hardly fond of his nephew, he knew him far too well to believe him capable of such horrors.

Of course, we do not know how far Mme de Maintenon may have gone in trying to convince the King that the rumors were true: she was both prudent and subtle; but she must have been as disappointed as the du Maines when the plot failed. What was at any rate clear, in the new state of the Court, was that the duc de Berry did not count for much and that, more than ever, the légitimés were moving forward. As for the King, although he now spent more time than ever with Mme de Maintenon and thus avoided loneliness, there could be no doubt that he was a changed man. He worked as hard as ever; he held court; he walked in his gardens; and he helped bring the war to a close; but that fierce energy, that delight in ruling had gone out of him. He continued being what he had been more from habit than internal necessity. What his seventy-four years had failed to do the loss of the Bourgognes achieved in a moment: in February 1712, the Sun King turned into an old man.

*T*HE successive deaths which had harrowed Louis XIV and appalled his court were much discussed throughout Europe; but they did not slow down the admittedly leisurely pace of the negotiations at Utrecht; what finally speeded them up was the string of victories won by Villars throughout 1712. By the end of the year, the general shape of the new European settlement had been fixed by the negotiators; there remained one most important issue. When, in 1700, Louis XIV had accepted the Spanish Crown for his grandson, he had stipulated, in letters patent, that his elevation did not invalidate his rights of succession to the French throne. This always touchy issue took on still greater importance with the death of the three Dauphins: if the current child-successor died, the duc de Berry would probably succeed although Philip V, as his elder brother had, strictly speaking, the better claim; and, in any event, should he die as well, then the King of Spain was the assured successor, at which, not unlikely point, the French and Spanish crowns would be united. This was the very possibility England had always been determined to prevent. If, on the other hand, Philip V were to die childless, the ducs de Berry and d'Orléans would, one after the other, succeed him, perhaps just as they inherited the French throne.

The English negotiators therefore made it an imperative condition for a peace settlement that Philip V should renounce his rights to the French crown, while the ducs de Berry and d'Orléans did the same for Spain; and that, furthermore, the three renunciations be publicly registered by the Parlement de Paris. Whether, in fact, this was possible under French law as it stood is open to question: since the King did not own the throne, but merely occupied it for life, he could not legislate the succession; nor could inherent rights to it become obsolete. In any event, on March 15, 1713, the two French princes went to the Parlement in state, there to renounce all rights to the Spanish succession, while a message from Philip V abandoning all rights in

France was read out. There was no longer any reason why the fighting should continue; and indeed, peace between France, Holland, and Great Britain was signed on April 11.

The Treaty of Utrecht formally recognized Philip V as King of Spain and the Indies; but the Spanish Netherlands were given to the Emperor while their fortresses were to be garrisoned by the Dutch. Sicily went to the Duke of Savoy, who took the title of King of Sicily; Naples was the Emperor's, who also kept Milan, Sardinia and four ports on the coast of Tuscany.

England kept Gibraltar and the island of Minorca. It received large sections of Canada and Newfoundland, as well as a virtual monopoly of trade with the Spanish colonies in South America; and France recognized the Act of Settlement and the succession of the Elector of Hanover to the English throne. As for Louis XIV, he gave up a strip of land on the Northern border, but was given back Lille and Béthune; and he undertook to destroy Dunkirk.

Given the years of defeats, and the European array it had had to fight, France did very well at Utrecht: it had lost very little of the land conquered under Louis XIV while insuring that Spain would never again be a menace. Even better, because the Emperor refused to ratify the Treaty, Louis XIV kept Strasbourg which he had been ready to give him. As it turned out, Charles VI soon realized that France's exhaustion was more appearance than reality: all through August, September and October, 1713, his armies were consistently beaten by Villars, and the peace which was finally concluded at Rastadt on March 6, 1714, gave the Emperor nothing, while forcing him to return their states to the Electors of Cologne and Bavaria.

Given all this, it must be concluded, on balance, that, in possibly the most fateful decision of his reign after the Revocation of the Edict of Nantes, Louis XIV had been right: France was better off in 1714 than it had been in 1700. As for the often repeated myth according to which the war had ruined France, it is nothing but the grumbling of a few chroniclers endlessly rehashed down the centuries. It is quite true that the Treasury was in a dire state, but the Treasury was not France. In 1714 still, the government's impact on the country and its economy was infinitely smaller than it is today. Thus, even if the King was deeply in debt, France could still prosper; and so it proceeded to do: the great explosion of high living and high spending which followed Louis XIV's death did not appear out of the void. More, the war created a whole new middle class. Men who had made profits in banking, army supplies, or military manufactures now joined other prosperous Parisians in furthering the development of French culture; their children were the enlightened public which helped spread French influence all through the eighteenth century.

There can be no doubt, however, that the Court, or more precisely the circle around the King, never recovered from the gloom following on the Bourgognes's death. "All is dead, here, life is gone,"[312] Mme de Maintenon wrote, and as far as the King was concerned, it was undoubtedly true. There were no more *appartements,* virtually no festivities; and yet, even at Court, splendor was still to be seen. The duchesse de Berry, now the First Lady, was young and thirsty for pleasure. She ate, she drank, she danced, she was unfaithful to her dull husband, and the group of courtiers which surrounded her was quite as animated as ever; the same was true of the Condés and the Contis; but most often, their festivities took place, not at Versailles, but in their own palaces: the Court might be in mourning, the upper classes were not.

Even so, the great events of Court life were celebrated as ever: when, in the summer of 1713, Monsieur le Duc married Mlle de Conti, while the prince de Conti married Mlle de Bourbon, the King spent half a million on presents alone, while the newlyweds and the duchesse de Berry were covered with diamonds. As for the duc and the duchesse du Maine, they were giving splendid parties in their sumptuous castle of Sceaux, and many courtiers prudently accepted their invitations. It might be said, in fact, that while there was darkness at the center, the brightest light shone elsewhere.

The gloom of the Court should not be exaggerated, however: even if the King and his circle were rather mournful, they still lived in the most sumptuous palace in Europe. The Chapel, begun in 1701, to a design by Mansart, was completed in 1710 by Robert de Cotte† and provided a grand and solemn setting for the daily Mass. With its gallery of columns and its royal box on the upper level, its wide windows, its white and gold boiseries and its ceiling frescoed by Coypel, Jouvenel, and Lafosse, it is both grand and light, both impressive and civilized.

† Mansart died in 1708.

The rest of the Palace, too, was incomparably more sumptuous than it is today. In the cour de marbre, for instance, the area just below the King's balcony, there was a white marble fountain with gilt bronze figures, while in each corner shell-shaped fountains with Tritons spouting water were topped by gilded birdcages; these last, however, were taken down in 1703.

In the King's bedroom, the walls, bed and seats were covered with gold-embroidered red velvet in winter, and gold and silver brocade in summer. Everywhere, masterpieces hung on the walls: from Leonardo through Titian and Veronese to Poussin, Reni and Domenichino, the best of Western painting adorned the Palace. Then there were the mirrors, not just in the Grande Galerie, but also, for instance, in the Council Room where they covered the walls and reflected gilt bronze consoles laden with vases of agate, lapis lazuli and other semiprecious stones.

There were doors gilded and carved, fountains everywhere, statues, large silver vases, marbles and tapestries, the magnificent Gobelins which celebrated the great events of the King's reign. The furniture was covered with a brocade of gold and silver flowers; the air of the Hall of Mirrors was sweetened by orange trees in bloom; its walls lined with gilded consoles; and even if the silver furniture was gone, there were still tables of alabaster and porphyry and an infinity of vases and sculptures made of semiprecious stones.

The Throne Room was, of course, especially splendid, with its Egyptian marbles, its pilasters of gold cloth, its walls covered with festoons, vases full of flowers, the King's arms and large nudes, all in high relief gold and silver embroidery, its curtains en suite, and the Guido Renis and Van Dycks hung all around. As for the King's private apartments, the cabinets, Félibien, who tried to describe them, quite ran out of breath: "But how many other masterpieces does one not see there, in the cabinets, the gallery or the salons at either of its ends? It is impossible to describe the sumptuous furniture and the infinite riches to be seen there; for without even mentioning the antique marbles, the bronzes, the gold and silver medals both ancient and modern, it is there that one sees the greatest number of precious vases, made of agate, heliotrope, tourmaline, carnelians, emeralds and other oriental stones."[313]

That magical setting did nothing to soften yet another blow, however. The duc de Berry was no great prize, but at least he was young, strong, and alive. His only child, the duc d'Alençon, had died within a month of birth, but there seemed to be every prospect that the duchesse would be pregnant again: if the little Dauphin died, and the duc de Berry succeeded, he would, no doubt, have children capable of inheriting the crown. Thus, although no eagle, Berry was important. Unfortunately, he lacked both sense and restraint, in particular when hunting; so it was that he rode his horse too hard; the horse slipped, caught itself, straightened up and, in the process, the pommel of Berry's saddle hit him violently in the stomach.

At first, the duc paid it no attention; but the next day, he was seized with a fever and started throwing up dried blood: it soon became clear that a hemorrhage had been caused by the blow; and on May 4, at four in the morning, the young man was dead. For the King, it was another staggering blow, not so much because he loved Berry—although he was fond of him—but because it seemed to him that God was determined to eradicate his descendants from the surface of the earth. Now, only the little Dauphin remained, but not, everyone assumed, for much longer.

Under these dreadful circumstances, and with constant assistance from Mme de Maintenon, the King's fondness for his illegitimate children reasserted itself. The comte de Toulouse was, in fact, discreet, brave, modest and affectionate; the duc du Maine, wholly lacking in these qualities, knew how to pretend fondness even if he did not feel it, and how to court all those who might be helpful, and he had two powerful assistants in Mme de Maintenon and in his wife. As for Louis XIV, who may be excused for not relating much to the four-year-old Dauphin, he could look at two sons capable of comforting his old age.

Nothing, however, not even old age and loneliness, could make him forget his duty: du Maine and Toulouse remained illegitimate. Still, as Mme de Maintenon kept saying, that need not matter anymore; so, for a time, the King hesitated. When, finally, he reached a decision, it was such as gravely to shock the traditionalists; but, looked at carefully, it is, in fact, a careful compromise.

As it was, the King's daughters who had married into the royal family proper had all had children, so that the new generation of princes of the blood royal reflected a mixture of legitimate and illegitimate blood; as for the two surviving sons, they had been raised by degrees to a position immediately below that of the princes of the blood royal and immediately above the dukes; then, they were equated to princes of the blood, but still with the important difference that they could not succeed to the crown. As things stood, therefore, the order of succession was as follows: the little Dauphin; the duc d'Orléans; his son; Monsieur le Duc; his children; the prince de Conti; his son, always keeping in mind the custom according to which, in France, women could neither reign nor transmit rights to the throne.

Had Louis XIV gone as far as the duc du Maine hoped, and Mme de Maintenon hinted, he would have given him the right to succeed as if he were a younger son proper—i.e., after the Dauphin but before the duc d'Orléans. What he did instead was far more moderate: by an edict given out in July 1714, and registered by the Parlement on August 2, the duc du Maine, the comte de Toulouse, and all their heirs male were enabled to succeed to the crown *after* all the other princes of the blood royal, and they were given the same rank and honors as the said princes with precedence immediately following them.

Although this compromise raised the légitimés without in any way detracting from the rights of the princes proper, and although both Court and Parlement were too thoroughly cowed to even hint at resistance, many people found this promotion shocking, in that it equated the King's bastards born of a double adultery with the children of duly sanctified marriages. Still, there was a small difference: du Maine and Toulouse enjoyed the same rights as the princes of the blood without actually *being* princes of the blood: the distinction was subtle but, to eighteenth-century eyes, real. Then, on May 23, 1715, that last difference was dropped: in a registered Declaration, the duc du Maine and the comte de Toulouse officially became princes of the blood royal.

Conjectures are always idle, but it seems probable that this last step in the legitimizing of the bastards would not have occurred had the duc de Bourgogne been alive. As it was, it could be painted as merely a prudent move, given the recent rate of mortality in the royal family; or, by those opposed, as the dreadful result of Mme de Maintenon's influence on an aged and weakened monarch. In fact, it reflects exactly what Louis XIV saw as his position. Just as, earlier in the reign, he had transcended the laws that bind the rest of humanity, so, rather like the Greek gods, he felt that his descendants, albeit illegitimate, somehow partook of his own divinity, that it was more important to be the bastard son of Louis XIV than the great-great-great grandson of his great-grandfather's brother.

Even so, the King clearly had lingering doubts, and resented the pressure to which he had been subjected. Late in July 1714, just before the Edict was published, Saint-Simon tells us, he turned to the duc du Maine in front of several attendants and said to him: "You wanted this; but you had better know that however great I may make you while I live, you will be nothing once I am gone, it will be up to you then to defend what I have done for you if you can."[314]

Just as important, of course, were the provisions to be made for the following reign: in 1714, it was clear to all that the King would not live to see the Dauphin of age. Should the four-year-old child survive therefore, a regent would have to rule in his place until such time as he could assume power. Precedents here were not applicable: the Dauphin was an orphan, so the respective regencies of Marie de Médicis and Anne of Austria meant nothing. The Regent must be the future King's nearest relative, the man who would succeed him should he die childless: the duc d'Orléans.

That might not have worried Louis XIV, whose opinion of his nephew was rapidly rising; but it drove Mme de Maintenon and her coterie to despair. That wily lady therefore started to propound a solution which would obviate the duc's ineradicable right, and nagged the King to enshrine it in his will.

Royal wills were, in fact, a touchy issue: while the King was all-powerful in his own lifetime, he was nothing after death inasmuch as he could not bind his successor: what one monarch did the next could undo. As a result there was a well-established tradition of breaking royal wills: it had been the case at Henri IV's death in 1610, and at Louis XIII's, in 1643. Both times, the Parlement had annulled the regency as set up by the late ruler to defer all power to the Queen Mother. No matter what dispositions Louis XIV took in regard to the regency that was to follow his demise, therefore, there was a substantial possibility that they would be canceled.

Countering this in the King's mind, however, were two anxieties: one, despite his remarks, about the future of his sons, the other, much stronger, about the treatment likely to be meted out to Mme de Maintenon; and there was also his desire to end the marquise's constant pressure. As a result, on August 26, 1714, he solemnly handed his will, sealed with seven seals, to the Premier président of the Parlement, M. de Mesmes. "Messieurs," he said as he gave it to them, "this is my will. I alone know its contents. I entrust it to the Parlement, to whom I cannot give a greater proof of my esteem and my confidence . . . The example of the Kings, my predecessors, and that of the will of my father show me what may become of this; but they wanted it; they tormented me; they would leave me no peace, no matter what I said. Well, then! I have bought my rest. Here it is, take it; happen what may, I will have peace and hear no more on the subject." And the next day, speaking to Mary of Modena, Louis XIV, uniquely repeated himself: "Madame," he said angrily, "I have made my will; they tormented me until I did," and turning to Mme de Maintenon: "I have bought some peace. I know how useless and powerless it is. We can do anything we want while we live; afterwards, we are more limited than private people; one only has to look at what became of my father's will, immediately after his death, and at those of so many other kings. I know it all; but despite all this they wanted it; I was given neither peace nor rest until it was done. Well, then! it is done, Madame; happen what may, I will no longer be tormented about it."[315] We may trust Saint-Simon's report: he heard the words, in both cases, from witnesses to both these scenes.

The will itself was taken to Paris and sealed into the wall of one of the Parlement's towers and it remained there until the day after the King's death; but even so, its contents were no secret: it was assumed, rightly, that a mechanism of some sort had been set up so that while the duc d'Orléans remained Regent in name, France and the little monarch would be ruled by the duc du Maine. The assumption was right: what Louis XIV had done was to set up a Council of Regency, without whom no decision could be taken, or appointment made; the Regent had only his own voice on the Council, whose majority consisted of du Maine and his followers; and finally, the latter became Superintendent of the King's Household, that is to say the man in charge of his safety as well as his education, which, however, was also to be controlled by the Governor, the maréchal de Villeroy. Thus, Orléans, while retaining the title of Regent, became a mere cipher. Further, just before he died, the King added a codicil to his will in which he made du Maine commander of the Royal Guard, thus giving him the armed might he needed to resist any attempt at breaking his power.

It says a good deal for the changes made by Louis XIV since 1661 that not a single voice was heard to criticize these dispositions: in 1714, in 1715, even, when he had begun to weaken and it was clear that he would not live much longer, obedience was as prompt and complete as it had been in the middle of the reign, at least when it came to matters of state. In their private lives, both the princes and the Court, by 1715, were beginning to anticipate the King's death: restraints which had obtained earlier were discarded and the first indications of a new age could already be glimpsed: the regency, that explosion of all the pent-up hungers, was well under way in the King's own time.

Still, the great Court ceremonies continued; but one, at least, took place which would have been unthinkable earlier. In February, a rather dubious character arrived in Paris; posing as the ambassador of the Shah of Persia, he requested an audience at Versailles; in fact, as the ministers quickly discovered, he was nothing more than a merchant, but they thought it would please the King to think that he was admired as far away as Persia, so, keeping the truth quiet, they arranged for a grand reception.

It was the last of the great Court functions which had been dazzling the world for over half a century. A splendid throne was placed at one end of the Hall of Mirrors; the King, surrounded by the royal family, stood before it, while along both sides, splendidly adorned bleachers were set up for the public; and all present were richly dressed, the duc d'Orléans in blue velvet with a mosaic of pearls and diamonds. As for the King, he wore a suit of black velvet and gold cloth almost completely covered with the Crown's finest diamonds; but, Saint-Simon noted, "he was bending under the weight of all this and looked much older, thinner and unhealthy."[316]

In fact, for some time it had been clear that Louis XIV was declining, losing both weight and strength but not his appetite; what his physicians did not know, although it seems clear today, is that he had begun to suffer from diabetes. Not surprisingly, when he left Versailles on June 12 for Marly, he was looking worse still, and people were beginning to speculate openly about the succession, and the respective positions of the duc d'Orléans and the duc du Maine. Always unwilling to take risks, therefore, the court attended both men assiduously.

By now, the King was seen to decline from day to day, and in

London bets were offered that he would not live past September; this rather dreadful piece of sportsmanship was published in the Dutch gazettes, which Torcy ordinarily read to the monarch. One day, when he was doing so, "he suddenly stopped, stuttered, and passed over [these articles]. The King, who noticed it easily, asked him why he was embarrassed, what was happening and why; Torcy blushed deeply, said what he could and finally added that it was an impertinence not worthy of being read. The King insisted; Torcy, more embarrassed than ever, kept refusing; but finally he was not able to resist repeated orders. He read out the story about the bets. The King appeared not to mind, but he did, greatly, so much so, that having sat down for dinner right afterward he was unable to refrain from mentioning it . . . We saw that he was trying to eat but that the food would not go down."[317]

When, on August 10, Louis XIV returned to Versailles, it was clear that he had lost most of his strength, and that, indeed, he would not live much longer, but still the Councils were held as always. On the eleventh, he went to Trianon, but it was his last outing: from that day on, he stayed inside the Palace. Although he still kept his usual schedule, he now began to complain of a pain in his leg; but rather than the sciatica he thought it must be, it was in fact the beginning of gangrene. That day, August thirteenth, he had dinner in public for the last time.

Of course, Fagon quite failed to understand what was happening. For the last two years, he had put his patient on a diet of overripe fruit and sweets of all kinds—more than enough to provoke the onset of diabetes in a man of that age. Now, he assured the King and Mme de Maintenon that there was nothing really wrong.

On August 14, Louis could no longer walk; he was carried to Mass, then, in the evening to a concert in Mme de Maintenon's apartment, after which he had supper in his room, with the Court in attendance; for the next eight days, while spending much time in bed, he continued to hold the Councils, see the ministers and visit Mme de Maintenon, but still he grew weaker. On the twenty-second, he found himself unable to review the gendarmerie, an elite corps and sent the duc du Maine in his place. That was hint enough for the Court: from then on, the duc was worshipped as the rising sun, but many prudent courtiers began to pay attendance on the duc d'Orléans as well. The next day still, however, the King maintained his schedule and although staying in his room, was surrounded by the courtiers who had the privilege of the entrées. He knew he was dying, though, and refused to nominate to several vacant bishoprics in spite of his confessor's urgings.

On the twenty-fourth, for the last time, he tried supping in public, but was unable to eat and asked the Court to leave the room; upon getting back into bed, his leg, which had grown much more painful, was seen to bear the black marks of gangrene. On the twenty-fifth, it became evident to all that death was close; but the King ordered his musicians to play as usual; he met with the Chancellor and added the codicil to his will under which the duc du Maine became commander of the Guard; he then confessed, took communion, and received the last rites, after which he called in all the members of his family, one by one. The duc d'Orléans was first; then came the duc du Maine, followed by the comte de Toulouse, the King's three daughters and the princes of the blood; all through this Mme de Maintenon remained at the King's side.

By the twenty-sixth, the time had come for public farewells. The Court was allowed in again. "At noon," Dangeau noted, "His Majesty had the little Dauphin brought in to his room and, after having kissed him, he said: 'Sweet child, you are about to be a great King, but your whole happiness will depend on your submission to God, and on the care you take to relieve the people of their burden. In order to do this you must, whenever you can, avoid making war: it is the ruin of the people. Do not follow the bad example I have given you on this point. Often, I have started wars without sufficient cause and continued them to satisfy my pride. Do not imitate me, be a peaceful ruler, and let your main object be to look after your subjects. Take advantage of the education Mme la duchesse de Ventadour [the Dauphin's governess] is giving you, obey her and follow the advice of Father Le Tellier when it comes to serving God. I give him to you as your confessor.

" 'As for you, Madame [he said to Mme de Ventadour], I owe you much gratitude for the care with which you are bringing up this child and for the tenderness you show him. I ask that you continue in the same fashion, and I urge him to give you every possible proof of his gratitude.' After this, he still kissed the Dauphin twice and gave him his blessing."[318]

Then, wrote Madame, "he called for us, the duchesse de Berry, myself, all his daughters and grandchildren. He bade me farewell with words so loving that I still cannot understand why I did not faint dead away. He assured me that he had always loved me, and more than I had thought, that he was sorry he had sometimes caused me sorrow."[319]

By now, all the women were crying out loud; but the King remained as composed as he had always been. He called in the duc d'Orléans again and ordered him to have the Dauphin taken to Vincennes as soon as he, the King, was dead; to have Versailles thoroughly cleaned out, and then bring the child-monarch back to the great palace.

It was then that Louis XIV called in all his courtiers. Crowding around the bed, they listened in complete silence to the King who had ruled them so firmly and so long. "Messieurs," he said, "I am pleased with your services; you have served me faithfully and with the desire to please. I am sorry I could not reward you better; these last few years have not allowed me to do so. Serve the Dauphin with the same affection you have shown me; he is only a five-year-old child who may have many setbacks, for I remember having had many myself when I was young. I am going, but the State will remain. Be faithful to it and let your examples inspire all my other subjects. Always remain united and in accord—that is the strength of a state—and always obey the orders my nephew [the duc d'Orléans] will give you; he will govern the kingdom. I hope that you will do your duty and also that you will remember me sometimes." At that, according to Dangeau, "we all burst into tears, and nothing could begin to describe the sobs, sorrow and despair of all those present."[320]

After that, there was nothing more to be said. On the twenty-seventh, only Mme de Maintenon and the King's Confessor were allowed into the room; on the twenty-eighth, he told Mme de Maintenon that, given her age, he hoped they would soon be together again; and seeing two weeping valets reflected in a mirror, he told them: "Why are you crying? Did you think me immortal? As for me, I knew I was not and you must have been prepared to lose me considering my age."[321] Later that day, a charlatan came to the Palace and said he had a cure for gangrene; he was allowed to give it to the King, who briefly regained a little strength, but then started to sink again; and throughout it all he was in great pain. Death, clearly was imminent; and Mme de Maintenon, careful to the last, discreetly went off to Saint Cyr, the school she had founded near Versailles and where she kept an apartment.

Later that night, coming to after a faint, he was asked by Fagon whether he suffered greatly. "No," he answered, "and that annoys me, I would like to suffer more for the expiation of my sins."[322] On the twenty-ninth, there was an improvement. The King ate a few biscuits and drank some wine; and the duc d'Orléans's apartment, which for the past week, had been full of courtiers, was suddenly empty. The improvement did not last, however; and giving orders, he said the King instead of the Dauphin. "He saw a movement in the people near his bed. 'But why?' he said. 'It does not worry me at all.' "[323] At eleven o'clock that night, his leg was examined again; the gangrene now reached all the way up to the thigh, and he fainted several times. Having called for Mme de Maintenon, he was told that she had already left, and he gave orders to have her brought back from Saint Cyr.

All through the thirtieth, he remained half asleep; at five o'clock that afternoon, Mme de Maintenon returned to Saint Cyr. All through the thirty-first, he wove in and out of consciousness; the entire thigh was now gangrened. Early that night, after the prayers for the dying, he said, "O God, come to my help, please relieve me soon."[324] These were his last words. Having sunk into a coma, he died at eight-fifteen on the morning of September 1, 1715.

Afterword

*W*HAT followed surprised few people: within days, the Parlement broke Louis XIV's will, giving the duc d'Orléans an unfettered regency; the duc du Maine also lost the command of the Guard. As for the funeral, it was hasty and simple. The mob that assembled to see the funerary carriages on their way to Saint Denis jeered at the corpse which was driven past them; and everywhere the death of the old King was seen as a huge relief. With him, too, an age had ended: in France, the eighteenth century began on September 1, 1715.

Still, quickly enough, the reign of Louis XIV was seen as a golden era. His great-grandson, who survived against all odds and, as Louis XV, enjoyed one of the longest reigns in French history, greatly admired the Sun King. With the publication of Voltaire's *Le Siècle de Louis XIV* in 1751, that admiration became general. It has endured to this day.

Of course, Louis XIV has been attacked quite as much as he has been praised, often on the wrong grounds: if the King's isolation at Versailles was one of the causes of the Revolution, for instance, that was the fault of Louis XV and Louis XVI: the Sun King himself never thought that his successors would feel bound by his own way of ruling; rather, he expected them to re-create the monarchy in their own images.

He has also been blamed for ruining France: the War of the Spanish Succession, we are told, bled the country white. Yet, we have only to look at France's prosperity in the twenty years after 1715 to see that it was not so. And while it is true that, on his deathbed, the

349

King reproached himself with having made war too often, we may safely take that as the words of a man who had already given up the world for the unreal universe of religion where all men are brothers. The wars of Louis XIV, in fact, left France a larger, richer, and stronger country. In 1643, the Habsburgs still dominated Europe. In 1715, France was incomparably its most important power.

It is also under Louis XIV that France acquired that supremacy in the arts, that refined way of life, that feeling for decor which persisted until the 1850s. If the eighteenth century was also the French century, it was in good part because the Sun King had set the stage for the creators who followed.

In the same way, the form of government he invented survived, virtually unchanged, until the Revolution; and there were good reasons for that. Not only was it far more effective than its predecessors, it was also more fair, more concerned with the prosperity of the state and the happiness of its people. Being human, of course, he made mistakes: the Dutch War and the Revocation of the Edict of Nantes are probably the gravest; but on balance, his was not only the most splendid reign in the history of France, it was also one of the most positive and most successful.

As for the new image of the monarchy he created, it was so powerful that it haunts us still: the crowds which fill Versailles day after day are testimonial to that. It has been given to few men not only to alter the course of history but also to create a myth which endures century after century; and as we look back, even with a critical gaze, we cannot help but be moved by the golden glow which, after so much time, still illuminates the figure of the Sun King.

Notes

1. Motteville, I, 65.
2. Ibid., I, 70.
3. Chevalier, 558.
4. Ibid.
5. Motteville, I, 70.
6. Ibid., I, 90.
7. Dubois de Lestourmières in Michaud et Poujoulat, 1ère série, XI, 157.
8. Motteville, I, 95.
9. Turenne, 382.
10. Lefèvre d'Ormesson, I, 41.
11. Voltaire, I, 55.
12. Motteville, I, 102.
13. Ibid., I, XXVII–XXXV.
14. Ibid.
15. Ibid.
16. La Fare, 162.
17. Motteville, I, 237.
18. La Porte, 412–13.
19. Ibid., 416.
20. Motteville, I, 265.
21. La Porte, 414.
22. Sourches, I, 11.
23. Motteville, I, 295.
24. Ibid., I, 261.
25. Ibid., I, 315.
26. Ibid., II, 385.
27. Ibid., II, 286.
28. Ibid., I, 394ff.
29. Bibliothèque Nationale, Fonds Français, 3858.
30. Motteville, I, 149.
31. Ibid., II, 286.
32. Turenne, 421.
33. Motteville, III, 11.
34. Turenne, 424.
35. Sévigné, letter of July 2, 1650.
36. Turenne, 426.
37. La Porte, 418.
38. Ibid., 421.
39. Erlanger, 90.
40. Motteville, III, 308.
41. Turenne, 433.
42. Motteville, III, 434.
43. Ibid., III, 439.
44. Ibid., III, 443.
45. Bibliothèque Nationale, Fonds Français, 24995 (29).
46. Ibid., 24995 (96).
47. Yorck, 536.
48. Turenne, 445.
49. Ibid., 434.
50. Ibid., 438.
51. La Porte, 428.
52. Voltaire, I, 84.
53. Ibid., I, 85.
54. Lefèvre d'Ormesson, II, 669.
55. Motteville, IV, 35.
56. Colbert, I, 530.
57. Motteville, IV, 51.
58. Ibid., IV, 46.
59. Ibid., IV, 46n.
60. Ibid., IV, 113.
61. Ibid., IV, 51.
62. Ibid., IV, 54.
63. Ibid., IV, 129.
64. Ibid., IV, 127.
65. Ibid., IV, 145.
66. Ibid., IV, 151ff.
67. Colbert, I, 503.
68. Ibid., I, 515.
69. Boislisle, I, 1.
70. Erlanger, 169.

71. Motteville, IV, 203ff.
72. Colbert, I, 535.
73. Louis XIV, *Oeuvres*, II, 122.
74. Colbert, I, 536ff.
75. Boislisle, I, 352.
76. Ibid., I, 1.
77. Ibid., I, 354.
78. Ibid., I, 18.
79. Motteville, IV, 252ff.
80. *Lettres*, 2.
81. Louis XIV, *Oeuvres*, I, 33.
82. Ibid., I, 101ff.
83. Bibliothèque Nationale, Mss. Fr., 22654, fol. 9.
84. Boislisle, I, 364.
85. Sonnino, 5.
86. Louis XIV, *Lettres*, 6.
87. Louis XIV, *Oeuvres*, I, 109.
88. Louis XIV, *Oeuvres*, I, 46.
89. Bibliothèque Nationale, Fonds Français, 6765.
90. Louis XIV, *Oeuvres*, I, 18ff.
91. Louis XIV, *Oeuvres*, I, 117.
92. Sodergard, 8.
93. Louis XIV, *Oeuvres*, I, 12.
94. Louis XIV, *Oeuvres*, I, 9.
95. Molière, *Tartuffe*, V, xx
96. Louis XIV, *Oeuvres*, I, 190ff.
97. Gazette de France, May 23, 1661.
98. Louis XIV, *Oeuvres*, I, 72.
99. Ibid., I, 91.
100. Ibid., IV, 256.
101. Motteville, IV, 258.
102. Ibid., IV, 279.
103. Valogne, 38.
104. Motteville, IV, 301.
105. Louis XIV, *Oeuvres*, I, 5–6.
106. Ibid., I, 18ff.
107. Ibid., I, 84ff.
108. Ibid., I, 36ff.
109. Ibid., I, 23ff.
110. Motteville, IV, 331.
111. Louis XIV, *Oeuvres*, I, 45.
112. Ibid., I, 47ff.
113. Ibid., I, 52ff.
114. Lefèvre d'Ormesson, II, 437.
115. Bibliothèque Nationale, Mss. Fr., 16633.
116. Ibid., 15590, fol. 709.
117. Erlanger, 251.
118. Motteville, IV, 447.
119. Ibid.
120. Louis XIV, II, 49ff.
121. Bibliothèque Nationale, Mss. Fr., 16633.
122. Louis XIV, II, 266.
123. Ibid., II, 56.
124. Ibid., II, 57.
125. Ibid., II, 96.
126. Ibid., II, 65ff.
127. Sodergard, 67.
128. Ibid., 69.
129. Maurepas, II, fol. 453.
130. Sodergard, 24ff.
131. Mademoiselle, p. 37.
132. Louis XIV, V, 402.
133. Ibid., V, 434.
134. Bibliothèque Nationale, Fonds Français, 10261.
135. Ibid.
136. Félibien, *Feste*, 202.
137. Racine, *Britannicus*, IV, 4.
138. Louis XIV, V, 464.
139. Louis XIV, V, 461.
140. Lefèvre d'Ormesson, II, 582.
141. Bibliothèque Nationale, Fonds Français, 10249, fol. 28.
142. Voltaire, II, 61.
143. Gaxotte, *Lettres*, 70.
144. Margry, 40.
145. Truchet, 82.
146. Visconti, 31–37.
147. Ormesson, II, 594.
148. Bossuet, 94ff.
149. Visconti, 10.
150. Ibid., 57.
151. Bibliothèque Nationale, Mss. Fr., 10249, fol. 49.
152. Louis XIV, V, 533–35.
153. Ibid., V, 536.
154. Bibliothèque Nationale, Fonds Français, 10249, fol. 24.
155. Ibid., fol. 28.
156. Ibid.
157. Gaxotte, *Lettres*, 39.
158. Visconti, 113.
159. Ibid., 73.
160. *Mercure galant*, 1672, 174.
161. Ibid., IV, 231.

162. Bibliothèque Nationale, Fonds Français, N.A. 9815.
163. Louis XIV, V, 539.
164. Bibliothèque Nationale, Fonds Français, N.A. 9815.
165. Félibien, *Feste*, 3ff.
166. Ibid., 13.
167. *Mercure galant,* 1672, 252.
168. Voltaire, I, 137.
169. *Mercure galant,* 1672, 101.
170. Voltaire, I, 146.
171. Bibliothèque Nationale, Fonds Français, 6779.
172. Voltaire, I, 149.
173. Ibid., I, 162.
174. *Mercure galant,* 1677, 195.
175. Visconti, 190.
176. Bibliothèque Nationale, Mss. Fonds Français, 6782.
177. Ibid., Mss. Fonds Français, 6781.
178. Gaxotte, *Lettres,* 177.
179. *Mercure galant,* 1674, 135.
180. Ibid., 1677, 169.
181. Ibid., 1677, 95.
182. Ibid., 1677, 189.
183. Ibid., 1677, 214.
184. Choisy, 23.
185. Visconti, 301.
186. Choisy, 114.
187. Visconti, 205.
188. *Mercure galant,* 1677, 236ff.
189. Ibid., 1677, 220ff.
190. Visconti, 181.
191. Ibid., 187.
192. Ibid., 205.
193. Louis XIV, V, 576.
194. Gaxotte, 71.
195. Choisy, 135.
196. Louis XIV, V, 554.
197. Carré, 163.
198. Visconti, 264.
199. Ibid., 266ff.
200. Sourches, I, 11.
201. Bibliothèque Nationale, Fonds Français, 16633.
202. Thuillier, 10.
203. Dangeau, I, 2.
204. Isambert, XIX, 384.
205. Dangeau, I, 87ff.
206. Ibid., I, 37.
207. Sourches, V, 289n.
208. Dangeau, I, 153.
209. Ibid., I, 19.
210. Sourches, I, 201.
211. Choisy, 130.
212. Sourches, I, 220.
213. Dangeau, I, 171.
214. Vertron, 8ff.
215. Choisy, 67.
216. Sourches, I, 437n.
217. Dangeau, I, 266.
218. Ibid., I, 276.
219. Sourches, I, 357.
220. Ibid., I, 361.
221. Choisy, 123ff.
222. Sourches, I, 430.
223. Ibid., I, 457.
224. Dangeau, I, 419.
225. Sourches, I, 463, 463n.
226. Ibid., II, 68.
227. Thuillier, 9.
228. Sourches, I, 229ff.
229. Voltaire, I, 184.
230. Ibid.
231. Erlanger, 434.
232. Choisy, 133.
233. *Mercure galant,* January 1690.
234. Ibid., February 1690.
235. Louis XIV, VI, 14.
236. Bibliothèque Nationale, Mss. Fr., 19601.
237. Ibid., 6679.
238. Erlanger, 438.
239. Louis XIV, VI, 19.
240. Ibid., VI, 20.
241. Ibid., VI, 21.
242. Ibid.
243. Erlanger, 461.
244. Saint-Simon, I, 32.
245. Ibid., I, 35ff.
246. Ibid., 38.
247. Ibid., I, 50.
248. Louis XIV, VI, 24.
249. *Revue encyclopédique,* 4–7.
250. Saint-Simon, I, 245.
251. Voltaire, I, 206.
252. Saint-Simon, I, 307.
253. Gaxotte, *Lettres,* 101.
254. Saint-Simon, I, 341.
255. Ibid., I, 229.

256. Ibid., I, 535.
257. Ibid., I, 542.
258. Ibid., I, 603.
259. Ibid., I, 729.
260. Ibid., I, 779.
261. Ibid., I, 782.
262. Louis XIV, *Lettre á la reine douairière d'Espagne,* B.N.L37b. 4847.
263. Louis XIV, *Oeuvres,* VI, 32.
264. *Mercure de France,* January 1701.
265. Louis XIV, *Oeuvres,* VI, 34ff.
266. Ibid., II, 460ff.
267. Ibid., VI, 69.
268. Saint-Simon, II, 9ff.
269. Archives of the duc d'Harcourt quoted in Erlanger, 521.
270. Louis XIV, *Oeuvres,* VI, 67.
271. Ibid., VI, 70.
272. Louis XIV, *Lettres,* 117.
273. Ibid., 123.
274. Louis XIV, *Oeuvres,* VI, 135.
275. Ibid., VI, 115.
276. Ibid., VI, 129.
277. Ibid., VI, 161.
278. Saint-Simon, II, 461.
279. Ibid., II, 664.
280. Louis XIV, *Oeuvres,* VI, 177.
281. Bibliothèque Nationale, Fonds Français, 6999.
282. Saint-Simon, II, 869.
283. Voltaire, I, 258.
284. Saint-Simon, II, 877.
285. Ibid., III, 133.
286. Ibid., III, 113.
287. Ibid., III, 182.
288. Orléans, 268.
289. Ibid., 269.
290. Ibid., 275.
291. Voltaire, I, 279.
292. Bibliothèque Nationale, Lb 37. 4344.
293. Orléans, 290.
294. Torcy, 125.
295. Ibid., 136.
296. Ibid., 156.
297. Orléans, 301.
298. Ibid., 302.
299. Saint-Simon, IV, 65.
300. Ibid., IV, 69.
301. Orléans, 303.
302. Torcy, 425.
303. Saint-Simon, IV, 98.
304. Bibliothèque Nationale, Fonds Français, 6999.
305. Orléans, 309.
306. Louis XIV, *Oeuvres,* VI, 214.
307. Orléans, 309.
308. Louis XIV, *Lettres,* 158.
309. Saint-Simon, IV, 408.
310. Louis XIV, *Lettres,* 158.
311. Orléans, 316.
312. Erlanger, 647.
313. J. F. Félibien, 67.
314. Saint-Simon, IV, 838.
315. Ibid., IV, 840.
316. Ibid., V, 170.
317. Ibid., V, 208.
318. Dangeau, XVI, 126.
319. Orléans, 351.
320. Dangeau, XVI, 129.
321. Saint-Simon, V, 463.
322. Ibid., V, 464.
323. Ibid., V, 467.
324. Ibid., V, 469.

Bibliography

(printed sources)

The number of books on Louis XIV, his ministers, his mistresses, his Court, and the incidents of his reign is immense; the author has therefore only listed the works quoted directly in the text. The class marks of the unpublished documents are listed in the Notes.

Boislisle, Jean de, ed., *Mémoriaux de Conseil de 1661,* Paris, 1905.

Bossuet, Jacques-Bénigne, *Recueil d'Oraisons Funèbres,* Paris, 1689.

Carré, Lieutenant-Colonel Henri, *Madame de Montespan,* Paris, 1938.

Chevalier, Pierre, *Louis XIII,* Paris, 1979.

Choisy, Abbé de, *Mémoires pour servir à l'histoire de Louis XIV,* Paris, 1966.

Colbert, Jules Armand, marquis d'Ormoy, *Correspondance avec son père,* Paris, 1873.

Colbert, J. B., *Lettres, Instructions, et Mémoires,* Paris 1861–70.

Dangeau, Philippe de Courcillon, marquis de, *Journal,* Paris, 1854.

Dubois de Lestourmières, *Mémoire fidèle des choses qui se sont passés à la mort de Louis XIII,* Michaud et Poujoulat, eds., Paris, 1836–1839.

Erlanger, Philippe, *Louis XIV,* Paris, 1965.

Félibien, André, *Relation de la feste de Versailles du 18 juillet 1668,* Paris, 1696.

————. *Description de la Grotte de Versailles,* Paris, 1672.

Félibien, Jean-François, *Description sommaire de Versailles,* Paris, 1703.

Gazette de France, Paris, 1643–1715.

Isambert, *Recueil des anciennes lois françaises,* Paris, no date.

La Fare, marquis de, *Mémoires,* Paris, 1828.

La Porte, Pierre de, *Mémoires,* Paris, 1819.

Lefèvre d'Ormesson, Olivier, *Journal et Mémoires,* Paris, 1860.

Louis XIV, *Lettres,* P. Gaxotte, ed., Paris, 1957.

Louis XIV, *Mémoires historiques,* in *Oeuvres de Louis XIV,* Paris, 1806.

BIBLIOGRAPHY

Mademoiselle, Anne Marie Louise d'Orléans, called, *Mémoires,* Paris, 1828.

Margry, Pierre, *Un Fils de Colbert,* Paris, 1873.

Marie, Jeanne and Alfred, *Marly,* Paris, 1947.

Maurepas, Recueil, Leyden, 1865.

Mercure de France, Paris, 1643–1715.

Mercure galant, Le, 1672–1715.

Motteville, Mme de, *Mémoires,* Paris, 1886.

Orléans, Elisabeth-Charlotte, duchesse d', *Lettres de la Princesse Palatine,* Paris, 1981.

Racine, Jean, *Britannicus,* Paris, 1967.

Revue Encyclopédique (83ème cahier, tome XXVIII), Septième année, seconde série, Paris, 1825.

Saint-Simon, duc de, *Mémoires,* Bibliothèque de la Pléiade, Paris, 1983.

Sévigné, marquise de, *Lettres,* Paris, 1818.

Sodergard, Osten, *Exercices de Bel Esprit,* Acta Universitatis Ludensis 20, Lund, 1974.

Sonnino, Paul, *Louis XIV's View of the Papacy 1661–1667,* University of California Press, 1966.

Sourches, marquis de, *Mémoires,* Paris, 1882.

Thuillier, Jacques, in *Les Peintres de Louis XIV,* Lille, 1968.

Torcy, J. B. Colbert, marquis de, Journal inédit, Paris, 1884.

Truchet, J., *Politique de Bossuet,* Paris, n.d.

Turenne, maréchal de, *Lettres,* Suzanne d'Huart, ed., Paris, 1971.

Valogne, Catherine, *Louis XIV et Louise de La Vallière,* Lausanne, 1964.

Vertron, M. de, *Parallèle de Louis le Grand avec les Princes qui ont esté surnommés Grands,* Paris, 1685.

Visconti, Primi, *Mémoires sur la Cour de Louis XIV,* Paris, 1908.

Voltaire, Arouet de, *Le Siècle de Louis XIV,* Paris, 1966.

Yorck, duc de, Mémoires du, in Michaud, *Mémoires* . . . , 3ème série, tome III, Paris, 1838.

Index

357

INDEX

INDEX

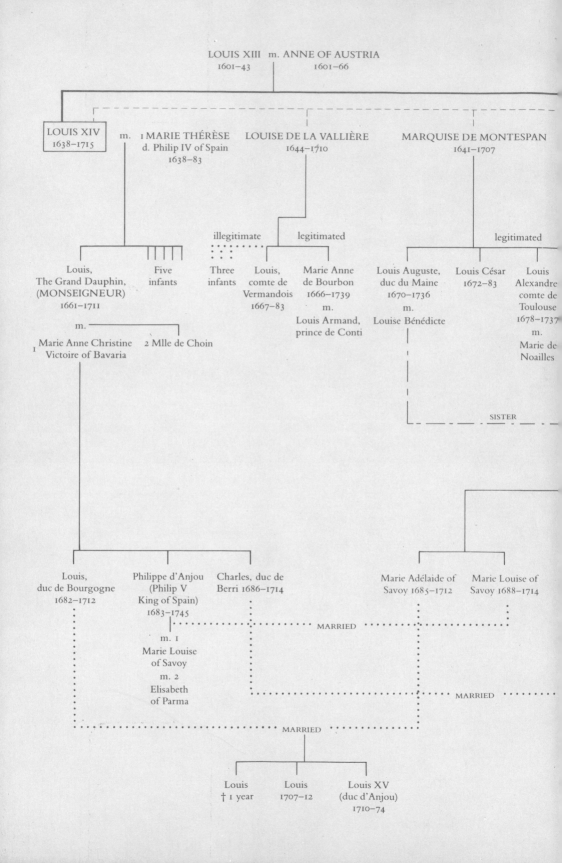

LOUIS XIII m. ANNE OF AUSTRIA
1601–43   1601–66

LOUIS XIV   m. 1 MARIE THÉRÈSE   LOUISE DE LA VALLIÈRE   MARQUISE DE MONTESPAN
1638–1715   d. Philip IV of Spain   1644–1710   1641–1707
                        1638–83

illegitimate   legitimated   legitimated

Louis,   Five   Three   Louis,   Marie Anne   Louis Auguste,   Louis César   Louis
The Grand Dauphin,   infants   infants   comte de   de Bourbon   duc du Maine   1672–83   Alexandre
(MONSEIGNEUR)   Vermandois   1666–1739   1670–1736   comte de
1661–1711   1667–83   m.   m.   Toulouse
                                                Louis Armand,   Louise Bénédicte   1678–1737
m.   prince de Conti   m.
Marie Anne Christine   2 Mlle de Choin   Marie de
Victoire of Bavaria   Noailles

                                                                                    SISTER

Louis,   Philippe d'Anjou   Charles, duc de   Marie Adélaide of   Marie Louise of
duc de Bourgogne   (Philip V   Berri 1686–1714   Savoy 1685–1712   Savoy 1688–1714
1682–1712   King of Spain)
                    1683–1745
                    m. 1
                    Marie Louise
                    of Savoy   MARRIED
                    m. 2
                    Elisabeth   MARRIED
                    of Parma

                                    MARRIED

Louis   Louis   Louis XV
† 1 year   1707–12   (duc d'Anjou)
                              1710–74